The Formation of Peripheral Capital
Value Regimes and the Politics of Labour in Anatolia

This book is a critical engagement with mainstream accounts of thriving regional economies in Turkey commonly encapsulated in the term 'Anatolian Tigers'. Based on twelve months ethnographic fieldwork in Çorum, a city in Central Anatolia that has not attracted much scholarly attention hitherto, Deniz explores the formation, expansion and sustaining of medium-size businesses through political economy and moral economy perspectives. The concept of 'value regimes' runs through the chapters, highlighting the relational mechanisms that turn labour into value in local and global processes of capital accumulation and what local people themselves find worthy. The findings demonstrate the formation of the entrepreneurial stratum as a multifaceted process of economic reconfiguration. They portray how people respond to market- driven changes, experienced sometimes as restrictions but sometimes as opportunities. Entrepreneurs, their workers and their family members are all active agents in shaping their livelihoods in ways that are meaningful to them. Deniz illuminates individual and collective values, sentiments, and the aspirations of non-Islamist actors as well as political Islam. She analyses the role of the state and *longue durée* socio-economic historical changes in explaining business trajectories, which cannot be reduced to the strategies of individuals or to the adoption of 'successful economic models' in the post-1980s era.

In her description of production and social relations at the workplace, Deniz demonstrates the entanglements of market and non-market dynamics, addressing how 'value regimes' create and sustain the core inequalities that are intrinsic to capitalism. Her materials illustrate the importance of kinship, religion and social values in shaping recruitment, working conditions, the organization of work, and negotiations of time, remuneration and incentives. Kinship relations and the practice of Sunni Islam at the workplace are not stable and they too are subject to negotiation. The focus on the everyday politics of labour reveals that central Anatolian workplaces are characterized by complex mutual obligations and expectations, paternalism, domination and autonomy.

This ethnographic study constitutes an original contribution to the field of economic anthropology and anthropology of work and labour. It will also be of interest to wider audiences in sociology, political science, labour economics and Turkish studies.

 **Halle Studies in the Anthropology of Eurasia**

General Editors:

Christoph Brumann, Kirsten W. Endres, Chris Hann, Burkhard Schnepel, Lale Yalçın-Heckmann

Volume 46

LIT

Ceren Deniz

The Formation of Peripheral Capital

Value Regimes and the Politics of Labour in Anatolia

LIT

Cover Photo: Workers exchanging Ramadan feast greetings at a shop-floor in Çorum Industrial Zone (Photo: Ceren Deniz, 2016).

This book is a revised version of a dissertation manuscript, submitted to the Faculty of Philosophy I at Martin Luther University Halle-Wittenberg in 2020.

This book is printed on acid-free paper.

Bibliographic information published by the Deutsche Nationalbibliothek
The Deutsche Nationalbibliothek lists this publication in the Deutsche Nationalbibliografie; detailed bibliographic data are available on the Internet at http://dnb.dnb.de.

ISBN 978-3-643-91407-1 (pb)
ISBN 978-3-643-96407-6 (PDF)

A catalogue record for this book is available from the British Library.

©LIT VERLAG Dr. W. Hopf
Berlin 2021
Fresnostr. 2
D-48159 Münster
Tel. +49 (0) 2 51-62 03 20
Fax +49 (0) 2 51-23 19 72
E-Mail: lit@lit-verlag.de
https://www.lit-verlag.de

LIT VERLAG GmbH & Co. KG Wien,
Zweigniederlassung Zürich 2021
Flössergasse 10
CH-8001 Zürich
Tel. +41 (0) 76-632 84 35
E-Mail: zuerich@lit-verlag.ch
https://www.lit-verlag.ch

Distribution:
In the UK: Global Book Marketing, e-mail: mo@centralbooks.com
In North America: Independent Publishers Group, e-mail: orders@ipgbook.com
In Germany: LIT Verlag Fresnostr. 2, D-48159 Münster
Tel. +49 (0) 2 51-620 32 22, Fax +49 (0) 2 51-922 60 99, e-mail: vertrieb@lit-verlag.de

Contents

	List of Illustrations	ix
	Acknowledgements	xi
	List of Abbreviations	xiii
1	**Introduction**	**1**
	'Hayaller Paris, Gerçekler Çorum': Narratives of Worth, Economy and Development	1
	Resurgence of New Regions and Models in post-1980 Period	10
	'Anatolian Tigers': The Emergent Orthodoxy in Turkish Economy	14
	What Does Anthropology Offer the Study of the Social Reproduction of Capitalism?	21
	Radical Breaks and Miracles, or Historical Processes of Accumulation?	22
	Methodology	29
	Outline of the Chapters	36
PART ONE	**TURKISH ECONOMY AND SOCIETY: STATE OF THE ART**	**41**
2	**Milestones in the Political Economy of Turkey and Path-Dependencies of Anatolian Capital**	**43**
	Introduction	43
	The Economic Legacy of the Late Ottoman Empire (1838-1929)	44
	The Making of a National Bourgeoisie (1930-1980)	48
	The Neoliberal Era (1980 onwards)	59
3	**Shifting Trajectories of Turkish National Identity: A Debate on Turkish Islam, Islamism and *Laiklik***	**71**
	Introduction	71
	The Ottoman Governance System and the Late Ottoman Reforms	72

	The Republican Reforms and Criticisms of Them	75
	Criticisms of Turkish Modernization and Laiklik	77
	Islam, Nationalism, Laiklik and Religiosity in Turkey	83
	The Alevis	95

PART TWO — THE WORLD OF BUSINESS IN ÇORUM: FORMATION, ASPIRATIONS AND MOBILITY   99

4   Formation of Small and Medium-Size Capital in Çorum   101

Introduction	101
Historical Processes of Local Capital Accumulation	103
'Anatolian Tigers are Cats Now'	125
Conclusion	137

5   Narratives of Personhood: Work, Family and Enterprise   139

Introduction	139
The Value of Work in the Narratives of Personhood: An End in Itself or a Means of Social Mobility?	145
Work and Enterprise as a Means to Making a Self	151
The Dark Side of Origin Stories: Suffering, Betrayal and Envy as Forces of Production	154
Enterprise as a Brand, Reputation and the Issue of Public Envy	161
Genealogy of the Enterprise as an Institution and Economic Nationalism	166
Conclusion	169

PART THREE — KINSHIP, RELIGIOSITY AND MANAGEMENT AT ÇORUM WORKPLACES   173

6   Morality and Politics of Kinship in Family-Run Businesses and Workplace Community Identity   175

Introduction	175
Working with Co-Villagers, Relatives and Family Members	179

	Paternalism and Community Identity Beyond Kinship Relations	195
	Conclusion	207
7	**Discipline, Labour Control, Management: Value Realm of Consent and Coercion**	**209**
	Introduction	209
	A Work Day at Çor-Mak	213
	Time in an Industrial Context: Imposition, Discipline, Shirking, Making-Out	219
	The Demise of the Foreman and the Timely-Paid Wage as a Mechanism of Consent	221
	The Rise of the Manager, Employer's Time, Respect and Displays of Loyalty	225
	Wages, Leave and Holidays: Ambiguity and Deservingness	232
	The Gendered Segregation of Spaces, *Namus* and the Sexual Contract	234
	Conclusion	236
8	**Religious Arrangements of Work Hours as an Exception to Time-Discipline**	**239**
	Introduction	239
	Significance of Daily Prayers and Collective Friday Prayers	240
	Establishment of the Duration of a Work Day and Official Holidays	242
	Namaz in the Workplace	243
	Friday Prayers	247
	Slowing Down Work While Fasting: Ramadan Arrangements	251
	Conclusion	256
9	**Conclusion**	**259**
	Findings and Arguments of the Research	259
	Further Implications of the Findings and Arguments	267
	Gaps and Suggestions for Further Research	271

Bibliography 273

Index 297

List of Illustrations

Figures

1	Are business people 'neoliberal'	141
2	How important is … in your life?	145
3	What would you like your children to have?	149
4	Kinship Diagram of Çor Mak	185
5	Kinship Diagram of persons working in Ozan Ticaret	192

Maps

1	Map of Turkey	xv
2	Map of Çorum and its Surroundings	xvi
3	Main Roads and Places in Çorum city	32

Plate

1	'Welcome to the centre of the world Çorum'	3

Tables

1	Amount of SME Incentive per Certificate (million Turkish Liras)	127
2	How often employers of different beliefs attend religious services	248

Source:
Plate 1: https://odatv.com/yalan-olmasina-ragmen-bunu-da-yaptilar-28061 61200.html, accessed on 17 May 2019.

Acknowledgements

This research would not have been possible without the collaboration and generous support of many people. I would like to express my deeepest gratitude to all of my respondants in Çorum who kindly shared their stories with me, some of whom became my friends. I am particularly indebted to the protagonists in this book, who shared their food with me, kindly bore my presence during stressful work hours, patiently answered my questions and invited me to many social occasions. Without their help and trust in me, I would not have been able to carry out this research. As I put the finishing touches on this work, I was very saddened to learn of the passing of an important informant and friend. I cherish the friendship we had during my time in Çorum, share the grief of his loved ones and only hope that he found peace.

I am grateful for funding from the European Research Council REALEURASIA project and the institutional support of the Max Planck Institute for Social Anthropology in Halle (Saale), Germany. I would like to thank the project's leader and the Institute's co-director, Chris Hann, and the project's coordinator and my supervisor, Lale Yalçın-Heckmann. I am particularly appreciative of Lale Yalçın-Heckmann for her meticulous reading of the drafts of my work and for her feedback. I am deeply grateful to Don Kalb for his valuable suggestions to sharpen parts of my argument and for kindly accepting to take part in my defence committee. I would like to extend my sincere thanks to Chris Gregory who has not only been very supportive throughout the process but has also guided me in the preparation of kinship maps. I have benefitted greatly from the constructive comments and warm encouragement of Jenny White, Gül Berna Özcan, Kurtuluş Cengiz and Ayşe Buğra in our various encounters at conferences. I give special thanks to Mehmetcan Akpınar for his valueable comments on the part of this work that discusses Islam. I would also like to thank Berit Eckert, Anke Meyer, Oliver Weihmann, Mattes Angelus, Manuela Pusch, our administrative and library staff and student assistants for their practical support over the last few years. Special thanks go to Jutta Turner for the German classes and for the maps she provided.

I am grateful to all the members of our department for the enlightening discussions held in Wednesday seminars over the last couple of years. I especially thank Dimitra Kofti, Eeva Keskülä, Tomasso Trevisani, Natalia Buier, Charlotte Bruckermann, Samuel Williams and Deborah Jones. If I had not taken Dimitra Kofti's Anthropology of Work and Labour seminar at Martin Luther University, Halle-Wittenberg, some of the themes and arguments in this work would be missing. Our REALEURASIA project group members have also been a great support. I especially thank Matthjis Krul, Daria Tereshina and Lucy Fisher.

This has been a long and difficult journey. Along the way, many friends and colleagues have been with me in times of grief and joy. I would like to thank Hannah Klepeis, Beata Świtek, Kristina Jonutytė, Ivan Rajković, Sabina Cveček, Daniela Ana, Duygu Topçu, Ruben Davtyan, Shilla Lee and Kadir Eryılmaz for their support and friendship. I was lucky to have Laura Hornig and Sudeshna Chaki as my office mates and friends. I wholeheartedly thank Sylvia Terpe for being a source of inspiration, and a personal and an academic guide. Some connections exceed the doctoral process. I would like to take this chance to express my gratitude to my dear friends who have not only shared my enthusiasm for my work and have kept me sane throughout the process but have also contributed their valuable insights and comments: Sinem Kavak, Çiğdem Oğuz, Ülker Sözen, Okan İrketi, Aykut Kılıç, Deniz Şahin, Yasemin Taşkın and Habibe Şentürk; thank you. I am particularly indebted to Sinem, Çiğdem and Ülker for always being there for me. A special thanks go to Karsten Leibrich who has been a close witness to the final stages of this work. I owe much to his heartwarming presence and support.

I am grateful to my family who has given me the strength and the courage to complete this project. My mother Gamze Deniz and my father Mehmet Deniz have supported my goals wholeheartedly throughout my life. I thank my brother Ali Deniz for always being a source of joy and a great friend to me. I am grateful for the ready support of my aunt Gül Deniz and of my grandmothers Gören Önay and Bahire Deniz. Thank you.

This book is a humble attempt to view the province and its history differently from the mainstream accounts; I hope I have done justice to the stories I was told.

List of Abbreviations

AKP	Adalet ve Kalkınma Partisi (Justice and Development Party)
ANAP	Anavatan Partisi (Motherland Party)
CHP	Cumhuriyet Halk Partisi (Republican People's Party)
ÇORUMSİAD	Çorum Sanayicileri ve İşadamları Derneği (Çorum Industrialists' and Businessmen's Association)
ÇOSİAD	Çorum Organize Sanayi Bölgesi Sanayicileri ve İşadamları Derneği (Çorum Industrial Zone Businessmen's Organization)
ÇTSO	Çorum Ticaret ve Sanayi Odası (Çorum Chamber of Trade and Industry)
DP	Demokrat Parti (Democrat Party)
FETÖ/PDY	Fethullah Gülen Terör Örgütü ve Paralel Devlet Yapılanması (Fethullah Gülen Terrorist Organization/ Parallel State Organization)
GDP	Gross Domestic Product
HITITSIAD	Hitit Sanayiciler ve İşadamları Derneği (Hittite Industrialists and Businessmen's Association)
İGİAD	Türkiye İktisadi Girişim ve İş Ahlakı Derneği (Economic Entrepreneurship and Business Ethics Association)
IMF	International Money Fund
ISI	Import Substitution Industrialisation
ITC	İttihat ve Terakki Cemiyeti (Committee of Union and Progress)
KİTs	Kamu İktisadi Teşekkülleri (State Economic Enterprises)
KOSGEB	Küçük ve Orta Ölçekli İşletmeleri Geliştirme ve Destekleme İdaresi Başkanlığı (Small- and Medium-sized Business Development and Support Administration)
MÜSİAD	Müstakil Sanayici ve İşadamları Derneği (Association of Independent Industrialists and Businessmen)
NATO	North Atlantic Treaty Organization
OECD	Organisation for Economic Co-operation and Development
OKASİFED	Orta Karadeniz Sanayicileri ve İşadamları Federasyonu (Central Black Sea Industrialists' and Businessmen's Federation)
SMEs	Small and Medium Size Enterprises

TOB	Türkiye Odalar Birliği (Turkish Union of Chambers)
TURKONFED	Türk Girişim ve İş Dünyası Konfederasyon (Turkish Enterprise and Business Confederation)
TÜSIAD	Türk İşadamları ve Sanayicileri Derneği (Association of Turkish Businessmen and Industrialists)
TUSKON	Türkiye İşadamları ve Sanayiciler Konfederasyonu (Turkish Confederation of Businessmen and Industrialists)
WB	World Bank

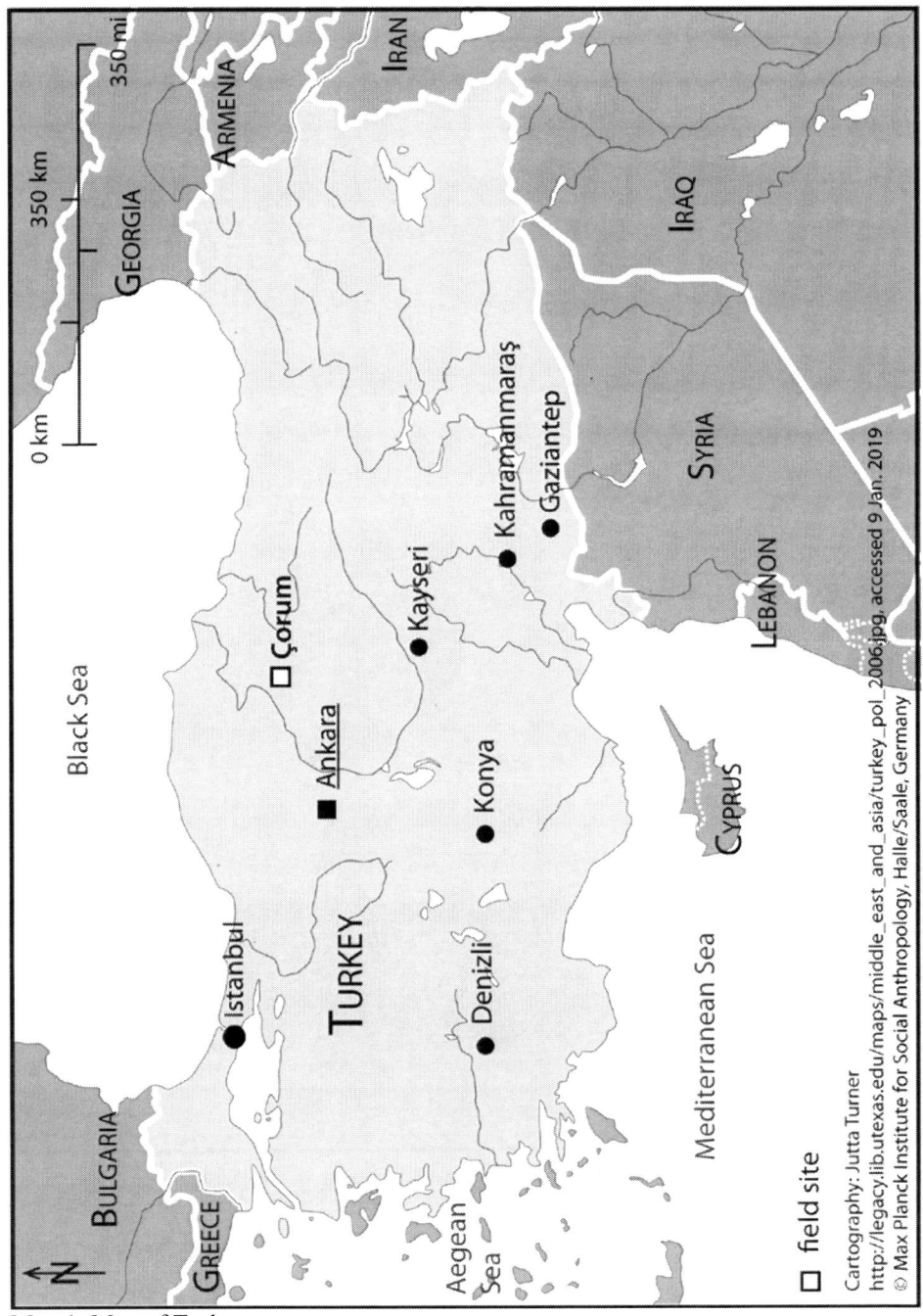

Map 1. Map of Turkey.

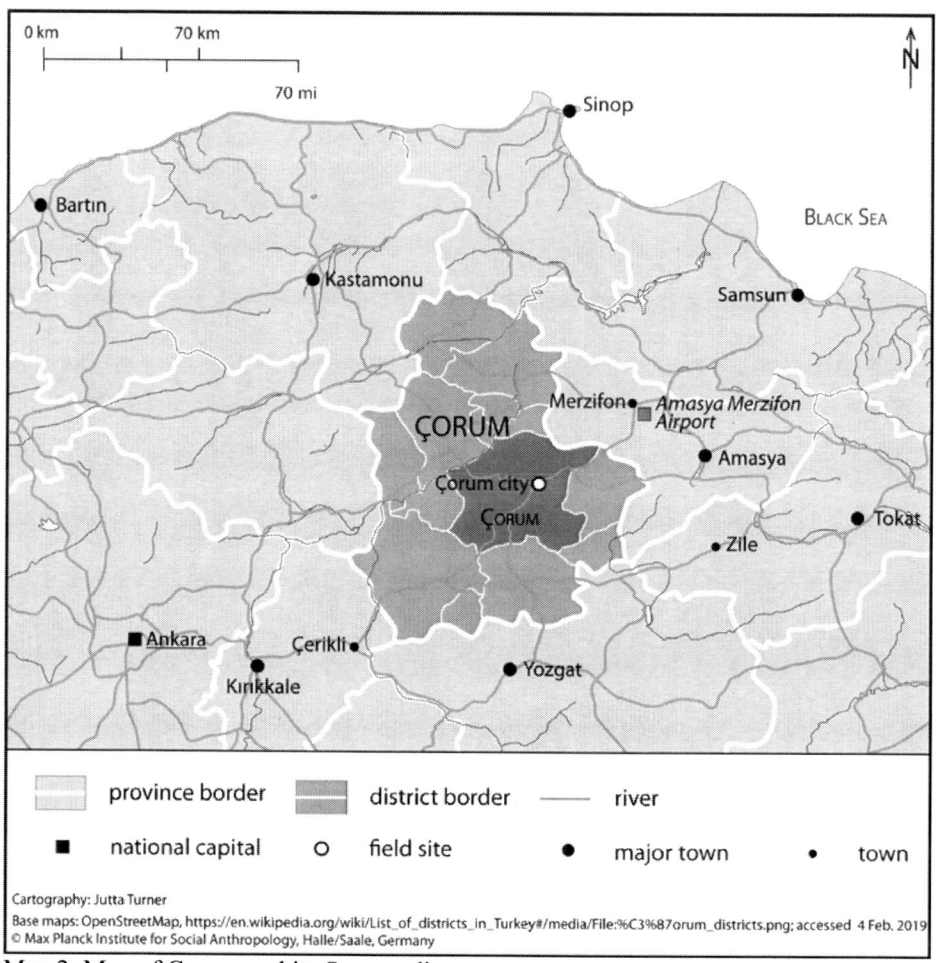

Map 2. Map of Çorum and its Surroundings.

Chapter 1
Introduction

'Hayaller Paris, Gerçekler Çorum': Narratives of Worth, Economy and Development

One of the most hotly debated topics in Çorum public life is the fact that the city lacks its 'own' airport, despite the fact that there is already an airport[1] fifty minutes' drive from Çorum city centre (see Map 2). Declarations of business associations and civil organizations about the need for their 'own' airport, the initiatives of the mayor, the governor and local political party leaders to negotiate its opening, and gossip about whether or not some rich businessmen will take responsibility for this common goal hit the local newspaper headlines at least once every two weeks. Although this specific public debate may at first seem irrelevant, it actually opens up a discussion about the themes of this work, such as ideas of development, value creation, worth and economy. In fact, the absence of its 'own' airport is condemned in the media and by local politicians as a setback to Çorum's economy in that it allegedly keeps away foreign investments and prevents Çorum's business people from making a breakthrough. This perception also has to do with building infrastructure becoming even more closely associated with development and civilization in people's minds during the era of the ruling Justice and Development Party (*Adalet ve Kalkınma Partisi, AKP*), famously known for its big urban infrastructure and construction projects. An article of 12 October 2017 on the local online news portal, *Çorum Times*, wrote at length about the story of the incomplete Çorum airport project that started in 1995 but was put aside in 2000, concluding its thoughts on the problem of

---

[1] Amasya/ Merzifon airport, a military airport that was turned into a civilian airport in 2008, is in the neighbouring city of Amasya. Instead of completing the airport construction in Çorum, this one was opened to public service. Railroad connections to ports and metropolitan cities and a shopping mall were among the absent urban facilities, but they did not dominate the public discourse as much as the lack of an airport. Just after my fieldwork, a new shopping mall was opened in Çorum.

the lack of an airport as follows: 'Although Çorum has kicked off industrialization and added its name to the Anatolian Tigers, because of its unfortunate standstill in the last couple of years it is watching sadly as the gap between Çorum and other industrializing, developing, modernizing and growing cities is increasing and how wide of the mark is its aim of becoming the centre of industry, commerce, culture and art of the region'[2] (see Map 1 for the 'Anatolian Tiger' cities, a term referring to Anatolian provinces that have industrialized since the 1990s).

This quote and the whole discussion around the airport remind me of a popular phrase I also heard in Çorum: '*Hayaller Paris, gerçekler Çorum*' which translates as 'Dreams are Paris, the reality is Çorum'. 'Dreams are Paris, the reality is…' is a slang phrase in Turkish[3] that makes fun of what one perceives is a worse and constrained situation in a certain place, in comparison to the commonly accepted 'ideal' place to be, namely Paris. The humour is derived from the irony that the person's dreams are not in line with reality. The phrase also expresses a degree of self-humiliation and acceptance of one's situation, marking the hierarchy of cities, and generally being used for places one does not want to be in. The discourse around the 'lack' of its own airport claims that, if only Çorum had an airport within its borders with its name on it, it would be able to reach the already listed goals of 'industrializing, developing, modernizing and growing' and become 'the centre of industry, commerce, culture and art of the region' – 'Paris' in this analogy. As the humour also implies, Çorum either becomes the centre of things, or it remains insignificant. Ironically enough, in 2016, the news in the national media claimed that Google had declared Çorum to be the geographical centre of the world, which later turned out to be an unscientific claim, a troll based on a conspiracy theory.[4] A short while after the news had spread, the mayor (*belediye başkanı*) of Çorum made a public declaration by the clock tower in Çorum city centre congratulating the people of Çorum. Later, his administration placed a huge banner by the highway on the city's boundary, saying 'Welcome to the centre of the world Çorum' (see Plate 1). Although the municipality (*belediye*) might have thought this would be a way to advertise the city, ordinary people either jokingly or seriously expressed their pride and happiness in living at the centre of the world and

---

[2] Retrieved from http://www.corumtime.com/iste-yarim-kalan-corum-havaalani/, accessed 2 April 2019.

[3] The earliest I have been able to track this phrase on social media is 2007; it became popular in the 2010s. The phrase has been adapted to refer to *Eminönü* (a chaotic neighbourhood in Istanbul), *Muş* (an Eastern Anatolian city) and probably elsewhere, and became graffiti in inner city streets.

[4] The discussion and refutation of the claim can be found at: https://teyit.org/google-in-corum-u-dunyanin-merkezi-olarak-belirledigi-iddiasi/, accessed 4 April 2019.

being all over the news, even if it was a fabricated account. These two stories express polarized ways of thinking about 'worth' that are frequently echoed in Çorum's local media and that shape how people perceive themselves and the place they live in.

Plate 1. 'Welcome to the centre of the world Çorum, the Mayor'.

In his article 'Regimes of Value and Worthlessness: How Two Subaltern Stories Speak', Don Kalb argues that such local vernacular narratives of worthlessness call on the anthropologist to ask: '[t]he question of what is believed to generate value, the competing folk stories on value, and its opposite (including those usually represented as "expert theories"), the proponents of those theories and the struggle among them' (Kalb 2017: 124). As he suggests, the proponents of the 'lack of an airport' story also debate among themselves what they believe generates value and what kinds of value. While there seems to be a consensus among different segments of the Çorum public in demanding an airport, the way it is expressed as a matter of 'worth' is specific to the townspeople in their comments on social media and in daily life. This perception of 'worth', although not expressed using this exact word in the Turkish vernacular, is constantly kept alive and on the agenda by the local media and local politicians (including business people's associations). However, business people themselves rarely express the lack of an airport by using the vocabulary of 'worth'. Some argue that having one would increase competitiveness, others say that the number of flights and destinations to and from the existing airport can be increased, and yet others think that Çorum's name could be added to Merzifon's. Many found the fifty-minute car ride to Merzifon airport reasonable.

Nonetheless, as the above quotation also suggests, the public view, dominated by the 'lack' of an airport, underlines the perceived 'worthlessness' of Çorum in comparison to larger Anatolian metropolitan centres like Kayseri, Konya and Gaziantep. This 'lack' is also emphasized in comparison to less developed neighbouring cities such as Yozgat, which have not thrived as industrial centres and yet have all these urban facilities. For example, a Facebook group, 'Support for Çorum airport', was started by townspeople to campaign for the cause. They made comparisons with other cities by putting the populations, annual export revenues in dollars and number of tourists received by each neighbouring city and Çorum on a map[5] to make the point that Çorum deserves an airport more than those other cities. The map was captioned with these words: '*Çorum'un üvey evlat muamelesi gördüğünün kanıtıdır*' ('This is proof that Çorum is being treated as a foster child'). The local media and many townspeople also tend to explain the perception of Çorum being a 'foster child' politically: although both Yozgat and Çorum voted nearly 60% for the AKP[6], several Yozgat deputies were appointed as ministers, but none from Çorum. The lack of skills that would allow Çorum's politicians to achieve higher positions within the party and hence be able to bring investors to Çorum are mentioned as reasons for the difference. Furthermore, the deputies are accused of not attending to the needs of the city, the reason often being given that they were born in Çorum but not raised there. The logic behind this is that if some politicians from Çorum had acquired higher bureaucratic positions and had been closer to President Erdoğan, then they would show their loyalty to their hometown by negotiating the necessary budget and bidding for an airport for Çorum. However, in this explanation Çorum MPs are either not sufficiently close to Erdoğan or lack loyalty to Çorum because they were not raised there.[7] As a result, Çorum is treated as a foster child.

---

[5] The numbers on the map are dubious and figures for Çorum are certainly exaggerated. For this reason, I will not put it here but it can be found on this address: https://www.facebook.com/CorumHavalimani/photos/a.1957381991170979/2253801928195649/?type=3&theater

[6] The AKP's votes in Çorum in general elections since 2000s are as follows: 48% in 2002, 57% in 2007, 61.1% in 2011, 54.4% in June 2015, 61.3% in re-elections in November 2015, and 51.09 % in 2018. Yozgat's corresponding figures are 51%, 62%, 66%, 58.31%, 64.8%, and 42.56%.

[7] President Erdoğan's recent local election campaign (2019) in Yozgat gives some reason for thinking this way. At a rally in Yozgat, after listing the investments the government have

Other public narratives reflect a similar sense of 'worth': one narrative bemoans the fact that the founder of the Republic, Mustafa Kemal Atatürk, never visited the city. Another public narrative is that only two state-run factories have been built in Çorum.[8] When local people repeatedly mention these deficiencies, suggesting some neglect on the part of the state, I had the sense that they collectively form and reinforce the idea of Çorum being subject to some sort of exceptionalism, as if there is something special about the city, but only negatively.

While the 'lack' of 'worth' is overemphasized in public discourses, socio-economic indicators tell us that Çorum figures below the national average in many areas, reflecting the urban-rural divide. Çorum has a total population of 532,000 of whom 237,000 live in the city centre, ranking it 40th in size among 81 Turkish provinces (TurkSTAT 2013: 12-13). As opposed to the 91 percent urbanization rate in Turkey overall in 2013, Çorum's rate is 69 percent (ibid.). In Çorum centre, half of the adult population dropped out of school at either 5th or 8th grade, and only one sixth of adults are high-school graduates, showing lower trends than the national figures (ibid.: 88). Labour force participation (52 percent) and the employment rate (49 percent) in Çorum are in line with the overall figures (OKA 2015: 40). Among those who are employed in Çorum, 37 percent work in agriculture, 27 percent in industry and 36 percent in services (ibid.: 41). In overall national figures the ratio is the same for those who work in industry, but lower in agriculture at 23 percent and higher in industry at 50 percent (ibid.). The unemployment rate in Çorum is lower than the national figures (9.7 percent) at 6 percent (ibid.: 46). However, when the number of unemployed who are registered for vocational training and job-seeking is added, the rate increases to 21 percent (ibid.: 47). Among the 26 regions of Turkey grouped together based on socio-economic indicators and the geographical vicinity of their provinces, in 2011 Çorum, together with Samsun, Yozgat, Tokat and Amasya, ranked 15th in its share of gross value

---

made in the city and announcing the opening of Yozgat airport, he slightly resented the crowd for not achieving more while its neighbours were doing better and then boosted their morale by referring to the names of the deputy president, chairman of the parliament, and former and current ministers who are all from Yozgat and saying: '*Böyle bir kadro Yozgat'ı şaha kaldırır ve kaldırıyor*'. ('This is the kind of cadre that is raising up Yozgat'). Erdoğan's rally in Yozgat was reported on Çorum local news the next day together with a lot of disappointment about Çorum's prospects. The rally speech can be found at: https://www.yenisafak.com/gundem/cumhurbaskani-erdogandan-net-mesaj-hemen-kayyumlarimizi-atariz-3448405

[8] Çorum Cement's factory went into operation in 1957 and was privatized in 1992. The factory also served as a recreational facility for city bureaucrats, civil servants, lawyers and engineers, in addition to the factory's workers and personnel. Çorum Sugar Factory has been active since 1991 and was privatized in 2018.

added (6762 USD per person), of the working population (2.29 percent) and of salaries (1.46 percent) (TurkSTAT 2013). Çorum ranks 40th among the 81 Turkish provinces in its import and export revenues. However, when socio-cultural and other economic factors are factored in, as in the socio-economic development index of the Ministry of Development (2013), the city falls to the 50th place.

The purchasing power of people employed in Çorum is lower than in the larger cities. Many go to Ankara or Samsun to shop for both cheaper and higher quality goods, to visit specialized doctors and to obtain better medical treatment. Even though Çorum centre receives migration from its counties, sixteen people from every thousand outmigrated from Çorum to metropolitan cities in 2014, mainly for education or to seek employment (OKA 2015). People who leave for education rarely come back; the well-educated generally prefer to work in jobs in the metropolitan cities, where the salaries are higher, the service sector is better, and the social life is more vibrant and diverse. I have observed that this is changing slowly due to the increasing unemployment, decreasing job security and high living expenses in the metropolitan cities.

Migration is also related to the dark history of Çorum. Forty years ago, just before the 1980 military coup, a massacre took place when numerous nationalist Sunnis[9] were mobilized to attack left-wing Alevis in Çorum; after nearly two months of street clashes 65 people, mostly Alevis, had been killed. During these two months, Alevis' houses and workplaces were burned down, Alevis found themselves trapped in their basements, some were shot on their farms and on the streets, and some were tortured in unimaginable ways.[10] It took years for many people to restart, make new connections and trust one another. Because of the damage caused by the massacre in Çorum, locals often emphasize that the city fell twenty years behind. After the massacre, between 1980 and 1985, 33 people in every

---

[9] Sunni Islam is the Turkish state' officially recognized and culturally and financially supported denomination of Islam, while Alevism, a syncretic minority belief system venerating the Caliphate of Ali, the Prophet Mohammed's nephew and son-in-law, is not. Chapter 3 deals with the institutions of religion-making and the multiplicity of Islamic traditions, including a brief account of Alevism.

[10] A civil-society organization, *Hafıza Kaydı* (The Memory Register), has produced a compilation of newspaper articles and news from the archives and victim and witness testimonies of people who lived in Çorum during the massacre. For a detailed account of how the events unfolded, see: http://www.hafizakaydi.org/29mayis-4temmuz/corum/hikaye/ as well as a short documentary: http://www.hafizakaydi.org/corum-belgesel/ Metin Uçar's (2009) work also offers accounts of the memories of Çorum's people and their perspectives on the massacre, which are discussed through the lenses of citizenship and diversity.

thousand migrated away from Çorum, a trend that continued to increase in the 1990s.[11]

Lower than average development indicators reinforce the public narrative of Çorum's neglect and its connection to 'worth'. This overarching affect has a strong hold over Çorum, which I have observed creating a twofold outcome. First, it makes 'being from Çorum' – because it generates loyalty to one's roots – and 'doing something for Çorum' very valuable for local people because it validates their sense of worth. But 'being neglected' also makes whatever had been done in Çorum 'a miracle' because it happens 'despite' the lack of basically everything. Hence, dialectically the discourse of lack and neglect provides the other side of Çorum's exceptionalism, namely that there is something special about the city, but in a positive way. This became especially apparent when some business people and state officials started talking about the recent leap in the industry in Çorum and the city's increasing share of exports. This interpretation of the 'folk story' was expressed best by Çorum's former governor (*vali*). In 2016, when the governor was newly appointed to Çorum, the journal *Business World*, published by the city's Chamber of Commerce and Industry, quoted his assessment of Çorum's leap in industry: 'There's no air connection, no sea route, no railway ... There's nothing positive, you are not in proximity to raw materials, to marketing routes ... [This all] doesn't make sense'.

What puzzled the governor was how Çorum had managed to make a name for itself in the last forty years, mainly in the flour, tile and machine industries, and had significantly increased its export revenues. But was it a miracle? This work is an attempt to understand how these developments have unfolded by means of an ethnography of small and medium-size enterprises in Çorum, where these developments took place, and it is based on exploring those who have been the very agents of these developments. By paying attention to what Çorum has as much as what it does not have, and to its history and people, I unravel what these polarized discourses of 'worth' might be hiding and/or enabling in an attempt to tell a more balanced and grounded story of economic development in which Çorum is neither insignificant nor exceptional. The economic developments this described in this work are conceptualized within a larger theory and discourse on the post-1980 phenomenon of 'regional economies' emerging on the peripheries of the global capitalist system. In that regard, Çorum people's perceptions of their worthlessness are a reflection and a result of their articulation with capitalism as a periphery. As Kalb has also found, 'stories of

---

[11] Calculated by the author based on the Turkish Statistical Agency's address-based population registration system derived from this link: https://biruni.tuik.gov.tr/ medas/?kn=95&locale=tr

"worthlessness", while affiliated in their deeper existential concerns and in their global placement within a certain industrial value regime linked to the spaces and times of a certain "backwardness", arose from very different local political conjunctures, actual industrial episodes and social relations' (Kalb 2017: 126). Based on my on the ground observations and Kalb's theoretical suggestion, my interlocutors' points of view on their worthlessness is revealed in three main local points of reference for these conjunctures: in comparison to other Anatolian cities in their possession of urban facilities, in relation to the unequal distribution of state resources in respect of processes of industrialization, and in the city's limited ability to create 'value' for and within the global market. The last point of reference is especially important in determining why townspeople perceive the lack of the city's own airport to be an issue of worth but business people do not, despite the fact that it is the latter who will use the airport in the first place to bring in investors and make a breakthrough, as anticipated in the *Çorum Times* commentary mentioned above. This difference signals that perhaps 'having its own airport' might not be vital to business people seeking industrial and other economic developments and hence not vital to the capitalist value creation that has taken place in Çorum in recent decades. Rather, the discourse around it, in Kalb's words, 'serve[s] to both obscure and reveal relational mechanisms of alienation, dispossession and devaluation of labour upon which capitalist valorization is based' (ibid.: 134). These are the exact mechanisms that townspeople have been subjected in order so that the particular economic developments of the last forty years could be realized. On the other hand, the expressed need for an airport and its specific framing as a matter of 'worth' by the townspeople could actually be a demand to be compensated for their devaluation in global value regimes, as voiced by local politicians and media. This brings us to what is being obscured in the whole local narrative of worth or worthlessness and thus to the core of this book, namely the relational mechanisms of capitalist valorization in both regimes of accumulation and value (see further in the Introduction for an unpacking of these concepts). I focus on these mechanisms by paying attention to the time of their emergence and expansion and how they were sustained in the workplace. Only then can we replace the 'miracle' story with a sound analysis of how global value regimes are locally enacted through manifold agents and patterns.

Another reason why I chose to introduce my research with a narrative revolving around the airport folk story is first because it demonstrates the state of mind dominating Çorum's public sphere quite well, a state of mind I was not aware existed as a native of Turkey. Anyone born and raised in Istanbul spends hours in traffic every day and takes it for granted that reaching the airport will take at least an hour or two. Therefore, inhabitants of metropolitan cities would actually find the fuss that Çorum locals make about the absence of an airport when there is actually one only fifty minutes' drive away amusing, to say the least. However, for reasons explained above, I suggest we take them seriously. Secondly, the airport narrative introduces some of the key themes that will come up later in this book, such as the ambition and desire to live a better life, resentments at the lack of certain things, simply being from Çorum or being related to someone who is, loyalties and obligations towards those with the same origin, the state of feeling like a foster child, positioning oneself in comparison to others, trying to reach beyond this and driving your value out of it, and realization of the necessity to overcome the religious divisions if economic development is to be achieved. These convictions and values, along with many others, constitute the 'value regime' through which economic decisions, motivations and ambitions are expressed and enacted regarding how Çorum business people respond to market-driven changes or demands and place themselves in the market in ways that are meaningful to them. As Palomera and Vetta (2016: 423) argue, 'small family firms and farms entering an international division of labour as subcontractors in highly competitive markets is an exemplary case of value enmeshment', as the case of Çorum also demonstrates. It is also important to clarify that in this work 'value' is used in a two-fold sense, first as both bottom-up and institutional meanings of worth and what is worthy in a given society, and second as the relational mechanisms that turn labour into value in local and global processes of capital accumulation. The theme of 'value regimes' runs through all the chapters of this work, offering a contribution to the field of economic anthropology and to the recent discussions of moral economy in the discipline generally and the anthropology of work and labour more specifically.

Certain peripheral economic developments that are at the focus of this book are part of a larger picture of the trajectory of global capitalism after the late 1970s and Turkey's national economy and politics. These developments in Çorum, which occurred after the 1980s, mainly follow the general pattern of small and medium-size manufacturing companies that are clustered in industrial urban districts. They were referred to in various sources (İzmen 2012; Keyman and Lorasdağı 2012; Uzel 2013) and by local representatives of business associations as 'Çorum's model of development', that is, one based on a 'culture of partnership' within a larger rhetoric about the so-called 'Anatolian Tigers', a term that stands for other export-oriented Anatolian provinces that thrived after the 1980s. I will proceed by situating the present case within the emerging economies in the broader context of the

Fordist crisis, the re-territorialization of production systems and new economic models. I will then unpack what is meant by the 'Anatolian Tigers' in the Turkish social sciences literature. After engaging with the problems and gaps in every section, I will discuss how I use anthropological theory and methods to address them. I will then outline the remaining chapters of this work.

Resurgence of New Regions and Models in post-1980 Period

Since the late 1980s and 1990s, a consensus has emerged among scholars from different theoretical backgrounds about the broad contours of the crisis of Fordism, the decline of Keynesianism as its macro-regulatory framework in the post-war period, and the nation state ostensibly losing its importance as the natural economic unit due to globalization (Lipietz 1986; Lash and Urry 1987; Harvey 1989; Scott and Storper 2005). The drastic changes to the global economy increased scholarly interest in understanding the crisis, analysing what is new with capitalism and identifying 'the successor of Fordism' (Tickell and Peck 1992: 190). Scholars attempted to do the latter by referring to different concepts, such as 'post-Fordism' or 'flexible accumulation', and identified new models of the organization of production, such as 'flexible specialization', 'industrial districts' and 'Japanization', all of which scholars have found in small and medium-size firms in the emerging peripheries. These 'models' are considered to be the alternatives to 'Fordist' accumulation regimes. However, some others, including anthropologists, have criticized these 'ready-made' formulas for failing to understand the realities on the ground. Below I shall present those aspects of the wider general theoretical discussion that suit the focus of this work and the 'models' that are also available in Çorum but that are experienced in quite different ways.

Developments since the crisis of Fordism are extensively covered in the literature on 'post-Fordism', which analyses the changes after the 1973 oil crisis as a radical break, a broad range of economic, social and cultural changes being subsumed under this label. 'Post-Fordism' refers to the deeply rooted changes in modern industries, such as the shift to information technologies, the decline of mass production and of the proportion of skilled male breadwinners, the feminization of the work force, the growth of the service sector and the domination of multinationals over the economy (Hall and Jacques 1989). The label 'post-Fordist' also comprises developments associated with postmodernity, such as social fragmentation, the weakening of collective labour movements, the rise of identity politics, pluralism and the maximization of individual choice through consumption (Amin 1994). However, emphasis on the novelties of post-Fordism and its representation as 'a totality' had been criticized by other scholars (Hirst and Zeitlin 1991). In this book, because it fails to encompass different forms of the organization of production and their co-existence, as well as neglecting to distinguish between forms of organization of production and regulatory frameworks, 'post-Fordism' is used only in its loose sense to refer to the post-crisis period.

One of the most widely accepted and cited conceptualizations in critical circles, one that avoids the label 'post-Fordist' as a totality while emphasizing the radical break of the 1973 oil shock and the uneven development that followed, is David Harvey's notion of 'flexible accumulation', which he defines as 'a direct confrontation with the rigidities of Fordism. It rests on flexibility with respect to labour processes, labour markets, products, and patterns of consumption ... It has entrained rapid shifts in the patterning of uneven development, both between sectors and between geographical regions, giving rise, for example, to a vast surge in so-called "service-sector" employment as well as to entirely new industrial ensembles in hitherto underdeveloped regions' (Harvey 1989: 147). On the one hand, spatial clustering of small and medium-size enterprises took place in the 'advanced' capitalist countries such as Britain, Germany, France, Italy the USA and Japan (Piore and Sabel 1984; Scott 1988; Hirst and Zeitlin 1991; Storper 1995; Scott and Storper 2005). On the other hand, it was observed that new regional economies[12] 'appeared to be surging ahead in the race to be leading motors of wealth creation' (MacLeod 2001: 804) due to the re-territorialization of production. These new developments transformed the previously established dichotomy between mass-producing industrial cores and dependent peripheries, leading to new models being devised to identify new forms of the organization of production that can be considered to be alternatives to Fordism.

One of the most frequently discussed models of this sort is flexible specialization, suggested in Piore and Sabel's book *The Second Industrial Divide* (1984) as a remedy for the Fordist crisis that will blaze a new route to prosperity. This notion stands for the new organizational principle that, it is claimed, best fits the growth of flexible markets in mid- or high-tech craft production based on modular, fragmented and specialized production units instead of linear ones. It is also a way of reducing production and management costs through flexible work arrangements in combination with paternalistic and participatory practices. 'Flexible specialization' in small and medium-size enterprises was praised for providing a competitive advantage over larger companies in how to respond to the detailed demands

---

[12] This shift of interest should also be thought of together with the 'spatial turn' in the social sciences in recent decades.

of micro-markets (Lash and Urry 1987: 199). When small and medium enterprises[13] or decentralized branches of large conglomerates are clustered in designated spaces or regions[14], they also resemble the Marshallian industrial district model developed by Beccattini (1990) and named after him based on industrial developments in north and central Italy.[15] In his view, industrial districts offer an integrated and independent network of small companies that can translate the 'cultural potential of a community into goods and services that can be sold in the market' (1990: 212), thus using their spatial proximity as a competitive advantage. Narotzky (1997) adds 'Japanization' as a third model to the list of alternatives to Fordist relations of production. Japanization refers to management techniques that are designed to soften conflicts between labour and capital by giving individual responsibility and independence over labour processes to the workers. It is argued that the Japanization model cultivates trust and cooperation between the workers, who are placed in teams, as well as between workers and management (1997: 208).

There are also a number of scholars, whom Tickell and Peck (1992) call 'agnostics', who argue that there has been a shift in the 'regime of accumulation', but are hesitant to identify a successor to Fordism using a model or a label. The term 'regime of accumulation', theorized by the Regulation School[16], stands for a period of capitalist development that is

---

[13] According to the classification in the European Union's laws (applied in Turkey too), enterprises with fewer than 250 employees are medium enterprises, enterprises with fewer than fifty employees are small enterprises, and enterprises with fewer than ten employees are micro-enterprises. These three categories are unified under the label 'small and medium-size enterprises' or SMEs. For the law see: https://eur-lex.europa.eu/legal-content/EN/TXT/?uri= CELEX:32003H0361, accessed on 26 March 2019. As the social realities, production capacities, organizational forms and governance of these three categories differ greatly, statistical and qualitative generalizations made about SMEs might be misleading for micro- and medium enterprises. Despite this, many scholarly works and policy documents refer to the legally defined category of SMEs as a totality. Hence, it is useful to keep in mind the problems it entails and be sceptical about generalizations made about SMEs.

[14] These are the 'industrial districts of northeast-central Italy; Toyota City; Silicon Valley; Orange County; Route 128; the *cite scientifique*, Toulouse; Baden-Wurttemberg and Bavaria; and even such lesser known and less high-tech cases as the London and New York financial districts; Los Angeles' garment district; Hollywood; Jutland; the metal cutters of the Haute Savoie; Sakaki; and hundreds of others' (Storper 1995: 191). These are where scholars find the flexible accumulation in spatial clusters.

[15] These regions are referred as *Third Italy* in economic geography, political science, urban studies and economic anthropology.

[16] Umbrella term for the research program that theorizes capitalist restructuring within the contemporary Marxist political economy framework. This has been one of the most influential theoretical approaches to the decline of Fordism, post-Fordism, the crisis of capitalism and the restructuring of the state. The research program is informed by a

based on two pillars: the accumulation system, and the Mode of Social Regulation. Tickell and Peck (1992) clarify these two concepts, on which regimes of accumulation are built: '[A]n accumulation system is a production-consumption relationship which ensures that the individual decisions of capitalists to invest are met by demand for "their" products, the value of which is realized in the market.... In order for it to become reality, procedures need to be developed which guarantee its reproduction. These procedures consist of habits, customs, social norms and enforceable laws which create "regulatory systems". These in turn ensure that individual behaviours are integrated within the overall schema of capitalist reproduction, thus mitigating the conflict inherent in capitalist social relations. It is this ensemble of regulatory mechanisms which is captured by the notion of an MSR' (192-3), i.e. the abbreviation for 'Mode of Social Regulation'. While the accumulation system of the previous era was Fordist and its mode of regulation was Keynesian, some of the scholars in this line of thought could not be persuaded to incorporate these models into their analyses of the post-Fordist era. Instead they criticized the focus already mentioned on regions, cities and districts and the associated models because they only offer a 'set of stories about how parts of a regional economy *might* work, placed next to a set of policy ideas which *might* just be useful in *some* cases' (Lovering 1999: 384, emphases in the original) while applying 'ideal-typical theoretical categories to supposedly real-world empirical categories' (ibid.: 385). These criticisms see the intensified scholarly interest in regional models as an 'emerging orthodoxy' and point out that they not only fail to address the specifics of the 'region', but also neglect to place regional changes within the framework of a wider political economy framework (Lovering 1990, 1999; MacLead 2001). Moreover, Lovering (1990) points out that their emphasis on 'culture' totally disregards the power relations that they entail, a point also raised and deliberately elaborated on by economic anthropologists. There are also other voices who question these profoundly different and better alternative models and suggest they could be myths (Amin 1989). In the Turkish case too, the small and medium-size enterprises that flourished in the peripheral regions of Anatolia from the 1990s received considerable attention as new centres of industry and wealth creation. The next section deals with the myths that the literature created regarding the Turkish economy and its political context.

---

combination of scientific realism and Marxism and is particularly interested in the institutions, mechanisms, legal frameworks, norms and customs that inform the reproduction of capital as a social relation. See Jessop (1990) for a detailed account for the variants and common characteristics of this school of thought.

'Anatolian Tigers': The Emergent Orthodoxy in Turkish Economy

In parallel with the resurgence of peripheral regions, which were regarded as the motors of new wealth creation in the wider literature, a significant economic and social transformation has been observed in some of the peripheral provinces of Turkey since the 1990s. Due to the removal of tariffs and quotas during the 1980s, in the following decade economists detected significant increases in exports, from 3 billion dollars in 1980 to 70 billion dollars, or 20 per cent of GDP (Gross Domestic Product), by 2005 (Pamuk 2007, 2008d). The share of manufactured goods in total exports also increased from about 35 per cent to around 95 per cent in 2007 (Pamuk 2007, 2008d). In 2015, small and medium-size enterprises' (SMEs') share of total exports reached 55.1 percent[17], signaling a strong link with the global market (TurkSTAT 2016). The increase in exports of manufactured goods did not take place in older centres of industrialization and trade, such as Istanbul and north-western Anatolia, but in the recently emerging industrial centres in central Anatolia, such as Denizli, Konya, Kayseri, Gaziantep, Kahramanmaraş and Çorum (Pamuk 2007, 2008). The emerging industries mainly specialize in low-technology and labour-intensive industries[18] and rely on cheap labour (Pamuk 2008; Durak 2011). The emergence of Anatolian capital has been prominently and meticulously documented by Eraydın (1999). The popular term 'Anatolian Tiger'[19] was coined to refer to these resurgent cities and their increasing role in the economy. However, the term does not suffice to describe only their increasing role in the economy; it also encompasses the pious Muslim character of the entrepreneurs, organized under the Association of Independent Industrialists and Businessmen (*Müstakil Sanayici ve İşadamları Derneği*, MÜSİAD)[20] and

---

[17] Since SMEs include enterprises from 1 to 250 employees (see Footnote 13), it is important to differentiate between micro- and small-size enterprises' export shares from those of medium enterprises. Small-size firms with one to nine employees had 17.7%, firms with 10-49 employees had 20.3%, and firms with 50-249 employees had 17.1% of total exports. The bulk of export revenues (44.8%) is still produced by enterprises with more than fifty employees (TurkSTAT 2016).

[18] Such as textiles, clothing, food-processing, metal industry, wood products, furniture and chemicals.

[19] The application of the phrase 'Asian tigers' to the Anatolian provinces is no more than a reference to a 'miraculous' economic achievement of a different size and degree in Asia.

[20] The M at the beginning of the abbreviation stands for 'Muslim' in the eyes of the public, partly because they openly distinguish themselves as Muslim and religious, as opposed to the presumed secularism of the Istanbul-based business organization, the Association of Turkish Businessmen and Industrialists (Türk Sanayici ve İşadamları Derneği, TÜSİAD), founded in 1971.

Turkish Confederation of Businessmen and Industrialists (*Türkiye İşadamları ve Sanayiciler Konfederasyonu*, TUSKON).[21] These business owners pursue an Islamic ethic of capitalism, also called 'Islamic capitalists' or 'Islamic Calvinists', as opposed to the Association of Turkish Businessmen and Industrialists (*Türk İşadamları ve Sanayicileri Derneği*, TÜSIAD) representing secular business people mainly from the older centres of industry and trade in the north-west. In the first decade of the 2000s, this line of thought had become the 'emerging orthodoxy' that was dominating the literature to a great extent and providing one of the ideological pillars of the AKP regime's legitimacy.

A considerable number of researchers, saw the rise of the 'Anatolian Tigers' as something distinct from the secular bourgeoisie of the north-west as proof that capitalism and Islam are compatible. They also viewed the freeing of the market from state intervention after the 1980s as a parallel to the freeing of Muslim entrepreneurs from the repression of the Kemalist state (Demir, Acar, and Topral 2004; ESI 2005; Yavuz 2006; Kösebalaban 2007; Demiralp 2009; Özoral 2014), as well as crediting it with the emergence of the 'national' bourgeoisie that the republic had longed for since its formation (Özdemir 2004). Moreover, the term 'Islamic Calvinism' was coined by an NGO called the European Stability Initiative (ESI), a reference to the Protestant ethic thesis of Max Weber (2013) and to Anatolian businessmen being motivated by Islam (ESI 2005), based on the testimonies of businessmen from Kayseri. In this canon, Anatolian entrepreneurs could accumulate wealth without the support of the state[22] (Keyman and Lorasdağı 2010), as Islamic sects, religious community structures and intra-communal solidarity played a role in turning charity into economic value, while the creation of interest-free banking systems had allowed pious Muslims to get a slice of the larger pie (Demir, Acar and Toprak 2004). Some of this research relied too heavily on pious businessmen's normative descriptions of themselves as modest, traditional, and non-elitist[23] (Özoral 2014) and on researchers' own judgments of Muslim entrepreneurial activities as being 'altruistic' or 'hearth-warming'

---

[21] Umbrella organization for local businessmen associations related to Fethullah Gülen movement (also known as *Hizmet*), which had been active since the 1970s in Turkey and became a transnational community in the last two decades inspired by the teachings of the Turkish İslamic preacher Fethullah Gülen.

[22] Like Anatolian Tigers discourse, the role of state intervention in Asian economic achievements is also central to the Asian Tigers phenomenon. See Paldam (2003) for a detailed summary of the different sides in this discussion.

[23] As opposed to secular businessmen who are depicted by Muslim businessmen as Western-oriented, unaware of their own culture and elitist. This kind of research over-interprets a few cases and contributes to the essentialization of the imagined 'Other'.

and motivated by moral energy (Uygur et al. 2017) without providing the reader with evidence of how the researcher arrived at these conclusions. Last but not least, scholars adhering to this canon argued that the development of peripheral economic booms has led to moderation (Demiralp 2009) and pluralism (Yavuz 2003) in Turkish Islam and to liberalization (Özoral 2014) and democratization (Yavuz 2003; Demir, Acar and Toprak 2004) in Turkish political life. All in all, the resurgent Anatolian centres and their successes became one of the important ideological pillars of the AKP regime, which was once praised by both national allies and international media and economic institutions such as the World Bank for its ability to combine Islam and capitalism and serve as a model of democracy for other Islamic countries (Balkan, Balkan and Öncü 2015). Ironically, in 2016 the very same businessmen from Kayseri on whose testimonies the ESI (2005) report relied in labelling pious businessmen 'Islamic Calvinists' were arrested and put in jail (along with many others nationally), and their companies and properties were confiscated by the AKP state, after being charged with membership of a 'terrorist organization', namely the AKP's former political ally, the cleric Fethullah Gülen. It is the followers of this movement who are held responsible for allegedly staging the failed military coup to overthrow the AKP government on 15 July of that year. Since the far-fetched assumptions of the emergence of pluralism and democracy that this literature advocated had vanished into thin air in less than a decade, a number of other researchers have since been offering different assessments of these regional developments and been questioning the thesis of an 'emergent orthodoxy' that was prevalent in the dominant discourse.

One of the main problems of the dominant discourse on the 'Anatolian Tigers' is the underlying assumption that almost all Anatolian entrepreneurs are pious Muslims organized in political Islamist circles and/or associations. Another repercussion of this assumption is the 'misconception', as Hoşgör (2011) puts it, that most Islamic capitalist firms consist of small and medium size enterprises in Anatolia and are rivals of the Istanbul and north-western bourgeoisie. This misconception stems first from the 'centre versus periphery' reading of Turkish historiography (see Chapter 3), and secondly from the story of the emergence Anatolian capital that had generally accounted for what Jenny White (2011) has called the 'vernacular politics'[24] of the Welfare Party[25] (*Refah Partisi*) during its years of success in the

---

[24] Vernacular politics is the underlying dynamic behind political Islamist grassroots mobilization in 1990s and White defines it as 'a value centred political process rooted in local culture, interpersonal relations, and community networks, yet connected through civic organizations to national party politics' (White 2011: 27).

[25] Predecessor of the ruling AKP.

1990s by utilizing politically embedded and multi-layered socio-cultural networks (Karadağ 2010: 9). The literature cited above also emphasized the role of Islamic sects and intra-communal solidarity in its emergence. While these arguments are still relevant, they do not suffice to enable the generalizations and comparisons of regions and capitalist factions that the literature advocates. In fact, other evidence-based research has pointed out the limitations of local industries in comparison to traditional industries (Filiztekin and Tunalı 1999; Pamuk 2008d; Buğra and Savaşkan 2010), especially in their contribution to the share of export revenues in 1990s and 2000s[26] (Bedirhanoğlu and Yalman 2009: 245). Scholars have shown that the export rates and bank deposits of the north-western bourgeoisie could easily swallow those of the newly emerging industrial centres (Buğra and Savaşkan 2010, 2014) and that 'presumed conflict between this fraction and TÜSİAD is an overstatement' (Tanyılmaz 2015: 97). Moreover, they illustrate how MÜSİAD-related enterprises had out-grown SMEs in Anatolia and gravitated to the Istanbul and north-western bourgeoisie. They point out the necessity of differentiating the Islamist capitalists, who are (or were) embodied in the AKP-Gülen coalition comprised of the big businesses as a new capitalist faction (Sönmez 2010) who had an undeniable voice in the political process (Tanyılmaz 2015) and in the formation of a new Islamic bourgeoisie (Yankaya 2014).

Henceforth, therefore, this work will refer to SMEs in Anatolia as 'Anatolian capital'[27] and avoid the other terms used for these phenomena, such as 'Anatolian Tigers', 'Islamic Calvinists' or 'Green capital'.[28] Furthermore, MÜSİAD-related enterprises in Anatolian provinces have a significantly lower export share compared to their counterparts in the northwest, and only a few dozen Anatolian companies figure in the lists of

---

[26] In fact, Bedirhanoğlu and Yalman (2009) argue that it might be wrong to periodize the transition to an export-oriented growth model strictly from the 1980s onwards because the export revenues of north-western capital were quite low in those years, especially for Anatolian SMEs. This trend relates to the 1990s and the beginning of the 2000s with exceptions during the economic crises of 1997 and 2001 that led companies to shift to export strategies as a response. They argue that production for the domestic market always retained its importance and had been a driving force of industrialization.

[27] Cengiz (2013), in his book on the formation of Kayseri capital, also prefers 'Anatolian capital' to refer to a similar phenomenon.

[28] There is a politics of naming behind these terms, as Tanyılmaz (2015) also explains: "'Anatolian Tigers", "entrepreneurial middle class" and "authentic bourgeoisie" vis-à-vis the "Kemalist bourgeoisie" "Istanbul capital" and "Bosphorus bourgeoisie" are generally employed by liberal and left-liberal groups. In contrast, nationalist left-wing groups prefer terms such as "sectarian capital", "green capital" and "partisan capital" versus "secular capital" and "national capital"' (2015: 91). He considers these terms inaccurate, in line with my own argumentation.

the first and second five hundred largest national companies (Buğra and Savaşkan 2010; Tanyılmaz 2015). Significantly no companies from Çorum made it on to those lists, nor did a MÜSİAD branch exist in Çorum until 2013. There used to be a TUSKON local branch in the city, but it has been inactive since 2013 due to a conflict with the AKP government.[29] Given the allegations of terrorism, business people previously associated with TUSKON have basically gone underground. I view Çorum as a perfect example of an Anatolian province in which to study the growth and expansion of small and medium capital because many of the factors that scholars associate with the 'Anatolian Tiger' phenomenon seem to have less relevance in the city, despite which its businesses have still managed to make a significant leap in their own terms. In that sense, studying Çorum businesses provides an opportunity to clear away previous generalizations on the topic. In fact, looking at the everyday workings of economic activities and the social history of the people and place using ethnographic methods is an antidote to the fallacies of the dominant literature. This is what this book aims to offer.

Another main problem with the dominant literature is the fact that its interest is mainly geared towards pious businessmen active in the business associations mentioned earlier, who, as Buğra and Savaşkan (2014) argue, have become political actors. MÜSİAD, TUSKON and the Economic Entrepreneurship and Business Ethic Association (*Türkiye İktisadi Girişim ve İş Ahlakı Derneği*, İGİAD)[30] are business associations with a deliberate emphasis on a morally just capitalism and Islamic work ethic, class projects acknowledging adherence to Islam and capitalism. Therefore research conducted with Islamist businessmen inevitably uncovers the heavily religious interpretations of their identities, politics and capitalism, as exemplified by the works of Adas (2003), Özdemir (2004), Yankaya (2014), Madi-Şişman (2017), and Uygur et al. (2017). While there is already a large amount of literature exploring the 'Islamic spirit' of larger business owners, mainly based on discourse, there are only a few studies that have researched provincial SMEs.

In one of the earliest sociological studies of provincial economies, Ayata (1990) portrays the hardships of small family-run workshops in

---

[29] The roots of the conflict date back to 2013, when Gülen-related law-enforcement officials started a corruption operation against AKP officials and ministers and later on leaked tape recordings of businessmen, AKP ministers and the then Prime Minister Recep Tayyip Erdoğan and his son Bilal Erdoğan talking about money-laundering, asking for favours or giving orders to businessmen.

[30] Founded in 2003 in Istanbul, İGİAD has had a smaller impact area than other associations. It is focused on creating a theory of just capitalism by disseminating its ideas via its own academic journal.

responding to the increasing demands of the market in Denizli. A few years later, Özcan (1995a, 1995b) offered a perspective combining economic geography with anthropology to study provincial economies. She situated peripheral economic developments in Denizli, Kayseri and Gaziantep within the emerging economies in southern Europe's semi-periphery in the post-1980 period and analysed the social relations of small firms and their survival and growth dynamics. Accordingly, she found that networks between small firms, which were often praised for being innovative, were actually governed by traditional values, sectarian affiliations, the family and the social environment, rather than long-term partnerships. As Özcan's work was conducted before the literature was contaminated by the emerging orthodoxy, it serves as an excellent example of an alternative approach to that taken by researchers today. Another important study, conducted by Türkün-Erendil (2000), showed how state policies regarding incentives and industrial district formation became short-cut formulas to integrate the province of Denizli into the global market. However, she also argued that these policies created new dynamics of uneven development that were intrinsic to capitalism. Her conclusion supports the need to be sceptical about the local success stories and that the success was achieved by adopting Western models such as the industrial district model or those I have described above. Özuğurlu (2008) also situated Denizli's industry in the periphery of global capitalism and offered an analysis of an emergent class. Bayırbağ (2007), like Türkün-Erendil (2000), found the discourse on the 'absence of the state' in the economic thriving of the 'Anatolian Tigers' problematic and showed that Gaziantep businessmen received extensive state incentives, utilizing the regional and national policy instruments it offered. A decade after Özcan (1995a, 1995b) argued that local business networks were sectarian, Bayırbağ's (2007) work showed a shift in the businessmen's networking strategies and argued that political activism by the Gaziantep Chamber of Commerce was an important factor in boosting local entrepreneurialism after the 1990s. One of the most comprehensive criticisms of what I called an 'emergent orthodoxy' is Cengiz's (2013) work challenging the prevailing narrative by assessing the industrialization story of Hacılar/Kayseri using origin of capitalism theories and industrial sociology. His work demonstrates the numerous factors that are related to the history, geography and economy of Kayseri and the accumulated experiences of its residents that led to regional development after the 1990s. Durak's study (2011) of worker-employer relations in SMEs in Konya was a timely intervention showing how religious conservatism adapted to market fundamentalism, thus creating a grounding for labour control based on the shared values of workers and employers. Two other studies focus respectively on SME owners in Ankara (Nichols and Sugur 1996) and on the features of the labour force in SMEs in a neighbourhood of Istanbul (Güler-Müftüoğlu 2000). I follow the lead provided by the empirical findings of these scholars to focus on provincial economies in Turkey throughout this work.

The ethnographic methods employed in this research not only enable the researcher to take a deeper look at the social life of work places, they also provide an opportunity to challenge the long-established and well-rooted dichotomy between secular and pious Muslim business people. A considerable amount of research, cited above, tends to describe 'seculars' and 'Muslims' on the basis of biased observations, creating and reproducing the dichotomy based on the normative judgments of researchers and research subjects. However, when 'seculars' and 'pious Muslims' are observed in relation to each other, doing business and forming partnerships with each other and working together, the distinction is no longer that clear. Given the fact that the Sunni interpretation of Islam is promoted in every dominant context in Turkey, in a place like Çorum, where Alevi business people also have a significant role in the economy and politics, business people are less likely to identify themselves openly with Sunni-dominant circles. This is unlike the situation in, for instance, in Konya or Kayseri, which are historically marked by political Islam. Such religious distinctions appear more significant in the organization of daily life depending on the business owners' inclinations and are experienced as power struggles in daily life rather than as identities that draw the lines of business-making, as my ethnography aims to show. Therefore, I prefer to focus on the politics of labour, the ground and limits of community-making, and the practice of religious and non-religious activities in the work place. In so doing, I rely on the anthropology of labour, specifically the works of Burawoy (1982), De Neve (2005) and several contributors to the volume edited by Mollona, De Neve, and Parry (2009). In this regard, this book also aims to contribute to the anthropology of labour. Situating diverse people and their actions and decisions within a moral economy perspective also helps overcome the prescribed differences because it demonstrates the common moral obligations and expectations that transcend the Sunni/Alevi and pious Muslim/secular dichotomies (see Chapters 6 and 7).

Up until now, I have drawn a general picture of regional economies and models, as well as the local regional development phenomenon of the 'Anatolian Tigers', the discourses around it and alternative approaches to it. Now I would like to show how theory and ethnography in economic anthropology can provide a remedy for solving the problems and filling in the gaps that the cited literature poses and that also help us understand and approach the daily organization and social life of work places. To be able to do that, I will go over some of the main currents of theory that inform the present book throughout.

What Does Anthropology Offer the Study of the Social Reproduction of Capitalism?

This book adopts a combination of a political economy approach and a moral economy approach in attempting to understand the social reproduction of capitalism in the industrializing city of Çorum. It critically engages with the separation of models described above and their real-life manifestations, as well as dealing with the complexities of the local specifics that are significant in the articulation of multiple agents and institutions in the global accumulation regime in different regions. The task requires attention be paid to '[s]pecific constellations of social relations and cultural dispositions that make the fabric of everyday life become structurally significant for capitalist accumulation in their relation to each other' (Narotzky and Besnier 2014: S4-S5). Studying the emergence and expansion of small and medium-size capital and its owners inevitably entails studying class. In conceptualizing class, I mainly follow Thompson (1966) in seeing it as a historical and relational phenomenon that does not just exist as a category but happens through inherited or experienced common values such that people identify their interests as different from those of others (Thompson 1966: 9). However, when Thompson talks about 'class', he specifically has the working class in mind. For the purposes of this work, therefore, I expand his relational, historical and 'in-the-making' approach with anthropological definitions that follow a similar path but are more inclusive. Kalb's formulation comes in handy here: he too defines class as historical and relational, but adds that it involves 'never frictionless ties and interdependencies between sets of people arising from their efforts to survive and maintain themselves… work is never just earning a living, but rather the social and cultural crux around which whole ways of life become organized and maintained' (Kalb 1997: 3). This approach stretches the earlier definition to encompass the Çorum local bourgeoisie I deal with here, their class-'making' stories (Chapters 4 and 5) and their relationships to work (Chapter 5) and to their workers (Chapters 6, 7 and 8). I also adopt Carrier's suggestion that capitalist societies vary remarkably and that fluidity in ethnographic research is important in 'describing and understanding classes as they exist in the specific place and time of fieldwork' (Carrier 2015: 33) without losing the sense of their connection to the larger picture. In what follows, I would like to clarify what the political economy and moral economy approaches are and what their combination entails.

Radical Breaks and Miracles, or Historical Processes of Accumulation?

Historical and economic anthropologists who follow a political economy perspective have long been interested in discovering general processes at work in mercantile and capitalist development while at the same time following their effects on micro-populations (Wolf 2010) and revealing which conditions and social relations enable production and capital accumulation (Mintz 1986). Anthropologists following a similar trajectory had directed their efforts at critically engaging with what political scientists, economic geographers and regional studies scholars have described as 'regional resurgence' in the post-1980 period. In fact, economic anthropologists who placed their focus on regional development models, relations of production and the social reproduction of capitalism should be placed among the 'agnostics' of the regulation theory mentioned earlier, not only with regard to the 'successor of Fordism', but also because some question the homogeneity of Fordism with empirical findings. Gavin Smith (1991), in his provocative essay, responds to Marcus's call for a new ethnography capable of dealing with 'disorganized capitalism' by questioning what he calls '"radical break" fictions' (ibid.: 214) using evidence of flexible forms of work in Western Europe prior to the Fordist crisis. For Smith, the term 'radical break' suggests that whatever is to come is completely new, replacing the old situation, whereas he sees these labels and models rather as 'sociological "fictions"' that are the cultural products of a pervasive narrative that describes capitalism without making reference to its lived experiences in the vocabulary it uses. This narrative interprets 'homogenized work experience and workers in large factories [being] concentrated in cities and hence amenable to being encoded in the vocabulary of quantitative methods; and a series of radical breaks, in time and space' (ibid.: 223). Smith points out that factories were not necessarily located in cities, workers were not only occupied with factory work, and that the divisions between rural and urban, agricultural and industrial, factory worker and peasant are also something of a sociological fiction, given that ethnographies have shown the historical blurriness of these categories. While 'flexible' forms of work existed before the Fordist crisis, and while Smith rejects the idea of radical breaks for the sake of defining historical continuities, this does not at all mean denying the crisis of Fordism or the idea that there is nothing new to be identified in the new 'epoch'. The main problem lies in taking 'flexible specialization' as a model that simply works well, as if the facts just speak for themselves. As Smith (1991) himself puts it, 'it would be no exaggeration to say that the role of flexible specialization in the salvation of capitalism and its link to small-scale production units is an issue of major ideological debate which, in the Europe of the 1990s, takes on an especially strong political flavour as central Europe seeks a politically palatable economic fix' (ibid.: 217).

A similar point was made by Michael Blim (1990) in his historical and economic ethnography of the small-scale shoe industry in central north-eastern Italy. His whole project is based on challenging Piore and Sabel's model of flexible specialization as 'spontaneous, small scale, and flexible in production method, export-led and niche-finding in its marketing, familial in its organization and petty entrepreneurial in character' (ibid.: 3), which 'has become darling to neo-liberal development theory' (ibid.). Blim's work[31] shows how the links between share-cropping and merchant capital have paved the way for the spread of capitalism to the towns and rural areas and the development of petty entrepreneurialism over a long period of time. Moreover, he reveals the roles of big capital and of the exploitation of the peripheral proletariat in the emergence of petty entrepreneurialism. Therefore, Blim's work demonstrates that the 'success' of Third Italy cannot be accounted for through technological innovation or fragmented production, any more than it can be seen as just a result of easily applicable formulas but long-term social transformations.

A more comprehensive critique of these regional models or alternatives by economic anthropologists is that by Susana Narotkzy. In her efforts to situate her early study (1997) in Spain within the post-Fordist or in what she sometimes calls the 'neo-Fordist' literature, she identifies some of the problematic aspects of these models. For instance, she regards the industrial district model as 'the creation of cultural isolates developing into economic isolates (the Industrial District) as opposed to global economic processes transforming and being transformed by local and historical situations [and] social and cultural contexts as opposed to economic contexts especially in defining social relations of production and the organisation of production' (ibid.: 207). She refers to the original formulation of Beccattini (1990), cited above, who claimed that peripheral and dispossessed proletariats share common values, suggesting that 'a community can be transformed into economic benefit, from a cultural isolate to an economic one'. However, the model dismisses what works on the ground as this is

---

[31] Blim's perspective also resembles that of Cengiz (2013) in his effort to dissect the discourse of 'Islamic Calvinism', which had also become a darling to the neoliberal theory in the local context of Muslim capitalism.

transformed by global processes of production and vice versa. Also, in Çorum, as elsewhere in Turkey, industrial districts are situated on the outskirts of the provinces and attract young and mostly unskilled people who can no longer live from agriculture alone and who are assumed to have a common value system. These qualities of the new proletariat are decisive in the determination of wages and certain aspects of the politics of labour that are prevalent in local districts. As Narotzky rightly states (1997), the proposed model assumes that these districts operate on the ground of self-evident 'community' and 'identity' but never of conflict – on the ground of 'autonomy' and 'cooperation' but never of monopoly or competition. She contends that the Japanization model, also being promoted as an alternative, has many similarities with the industrial district model: 'Both stress a certain idea of the benefits of "independent" workers' responsibility and individuation. Both give a strong emphasis to cultural contexts as contributing the basic elements in the social relations of production, away from exploitative "economic" relations and power political struggles' (ibid.: 209). Her main criticism is that the culturalization of the economic domain by these models serves as a basis for consensual exploitation by associating it positively with 'community' and 'identity'.

This book follows the lead of 'agnostics' in general and 'agnostic' economic anthropologists in particular in its analysis of economic developments in Çorum after the 1980s that occurred mainly in small and medium-size manufacturing companies. These were clustered in industrial districts and presented to the public as the 'Çorum model of development', which is assumed to be based on a 'culture of partnership' within a larger rhetoric of the 'Anatolian Tigers', which I critically assessed above. I trace the social and occupational histories of the contemporary entrepreneurial stratum in Çorum from the beginning of the twentieth century to be able to describe the various ways of collecting capital, including the dispossession of non-Muslims, the removal of intermediaries, the role of merchant capital, the role of cooperation among Çorum people and transfers of skills, and the role of fragmented ways of labouring and self-exploitation, all constituting the relational mechanisms of capitalist valorisation that are not limited to the political and economic changes since the 1980s but are the result of a longer period of social transformation. By doing so, I also question the notion of 'radical breaks' and instead argue for longer historical processes and continuities of accumulation and their relational aspect. I critically engage with ahistorical typologies of 'models' and the claims of the ideas of an 'entrepreneurial soul' and a 'culture of partnership' in the public rhetoric by actually demonstrating 'what makes them operate in real life and what makes their articulation significant' (Narotzky 2010: 176).

Another point that is at the centre of this discussion is the organization of production and the role of community, cooperation and trust that is thought to create individuation and responsibility, all of which are ascribed to the operation of these models. In Çorum, small and medium enterprises clustered in industrial districts, and therefore falling within the scope of this book, constitute models that have also been adopted to a certain extent to achieve economic efficiency and increase profitability. In fact, ideas of community-making, trust and individuation are very prevalent. What this book aims to show is that ideas of community, cooperation, responsibility, trust and individuation are not prevalent because the prescribed models assume them to be, but because they are pre-existing modes of conduct that enabled economic alignments that led to the emergence of capital accumulation and later produced modes of labour control and discipline, as well as a politics of labour (Burawoy 1985), that sustained the businesses. This is by no means an argument that these processes only led to cooperation and not to a monopoly, or only to consensual exploitation and not to conflict, as Narotzky (1997) critically noted. On the contrary, this book aims to show the discrepancies in daily working lives, the monopolies that undermined cooperation, the betrayals that violated the trust of family members, and the community-making efforts that failed to be entirely inclusive, create dependencies and signal the 'hidden transcripts of resistance' (Scott 1990) to the despotic governance of work places. On the other hand, all of this co-exists within the 'cultural hegemony' (Thompson 1991) that was created at the national level by laws, regulations and customs in aligning religious-conservative ideology with market fundamentalism in the present context of Turkish political economic trajectory, as also illustrated by Durak (2011). Still, this book aims to show that the basis of the 'value regimes' that enable the realization of 'cultural hegemony' is not limited to the current conservatively religious hegemony but has its roots in kinship systems, ideas of loyalty and deference to one's roots and paternalism, which persist despite changing forms of labour and imposed forms of the organization of production. This brings us to the next section, in which I shall discuss the 'moral economy' and value regimes.

Embeddedness: Moral Economy or Value Regimes?

Questioning dominant economic institutions has always been intrinsic to anthropological critiques (Hart and Hann 2009). In fact, its purpose, even 'when still known as "the economics of primitive man" was to test the claim that a world economic order must be founded on capitalist principles' (ibid.: 12). Although the critique of capitalist inequalities comes second in the development of anthropological theory to finding inclusive ways of understanding economic formations, more interest had recently been directed towards the workings of capitalism and its global spread in the period of neoliberal globalization. As Hart and Hann argue, it is no wonder that an interest in Karl Polanyi's *The Great Transformation* has been revived in recent decades as a response to the attacks of market fundamentalism. Its importance and relevance stem from the core thesis of the book, that is, that 'the idea of a self-adjusting market implied a stark utopia' (Polanyi 2001: 3). As famously argued by Polanyi, 'man's economy, as a rule, is submerged in his social relationships' (ibid.: 48), or in other words 'embedded'. For Polanyi, a person acts not only in pursuit of personal interest to secure material goods but also 'to safeguard his social standing, his social claims, his social assets. He values material goods only in so far as they serve this end. Neither the process of production nor that of distribution is linked to specific economic interests attached to the possession of goods; but every single step in that process is geared to a number of social interests which eventually ensure that the required step be taken' (ibid.). In other words, in Polanyi's terms, the economy is an instituted process within which human social interests are inseparable part of economic pursuits.

While Polanyi's overall perspective is also embraced in this book in respect of its exploration of the social reproduction of capitalism, the contradiction arises from the fact that Polanyi's original theory argues that the adoption of market rules has 'disembedded' the economy from the social relationships in which they were once submerged. Hence, I follow Gudeman's formulation of the dialectics of community and market, based on the principle that 'disembedded economies do not exist apart from embedded ones, and the reverse' (Gudeman 2009: 19). In Gudeman's formulation, human economic behaviour, whether in community or market, is not described in terms of opposed endeavours but rather as 'continuously shift[ing] between the contradictory roles of being an "individual" and a "person-in-community"' (ibid.: 24). This is also the case in the context of Çorum's business owners, namely in respect of the social roles they are expected to fulfil and the roles they expect others to fulfil for the mutuality of their interaction. However, Gudeman argues that the continuous shift between these roles would on some occasions enable them to transfer market gains to communal commitments and vice versa, or alternatively might create tensions between these mutually dependent realms and identities. On the other hand, in a newly developing industrial setting such as Çorum, market practices would 'erase their contingency [mutuality] and dialectically undermine their existence by continuously expanding the arena of trade, by cascading, by appropriating materials, labour and discourse and by mystifying and veiling the mutuality on which they are built on' (ibid.: 37).

The ethnography I present here aims to address precisely these kinds of tensions that arise throughout the lives of business people in the ways they build their identities as 'business people' in the community, in their kinship-related obligations and expectations, and in employing family members in their workplaces.

These discussions regarding the social context of market practices and their mutually dependent realms are captured in the recent discussion of the 'moral economy' among anthropologists. The concept of a 'moral economy' was originally coined by Thompson (1971) as a critique of those who explained the eighteenth-century bread riots in England in terms of economic reductionism. For Thompson, the demands of the crowds 'operated within a popular consensus as to what were legitimate and what were illegitimate practices in marketing, milling, baking, etc. This in its turn was grounded upon a consistent traditional view of social norms and obligations, of the proper economic functions of several parties within the community, which, taken together, can be said to constitute the moral economy of the poor' (1971: 79). Another key contributor to the original concept of the 'moral economy' is Scott (1977). In his study of peasant households in twentieth-century Burma and Vietnam, he deployed the term 'moral economy' to refer to the subsistence ethic of the peasants and shifted Thompson's emphasis on 'norms and obligations' to 'moral entitlements and expectations' as the basis of legitimate economic practice for the subaltern. The original formulations of the term by both Thompson and Scott look specifically at the dynamics of mobilization and the resistance of the subaltern. When Thompson revisited his own concept in 1991, he rejected its applicability to all kinds of crowd and insisted that it stood instead for the traditions and expectations of working populations. However, as Hann (2010) rightly pointed out, many have stretched the concept of the 'moral economy' to cover the metaphor of 'embeddedness' in Polanyi's terms. Studies of moral anthropology, on the other hand, have gone further, dropping the 'economy' altogether from their enquiry and focusing on morals and ethics in a general sense, as exemplified in the volume edited by Fassin and Lézé (2014) and Fassin's own work (2014).

Economic anthropologists who had not lost their hopes for the concept and were not willing to drop 'economy' from the formulation suggested new interpretations that aimed to enrich the analytical tool to cover a wider spectrum regarding the relationship between economy and morality than the original formulations. For example, De Sardan (1999) shifted the main focus of the 'moral economy' from the specific social group of 'the poor' or 'the peasants' to 'corruption' as an economic activity. Fassin (2009) was also critical of the vagueness of the term, argued that it can be extended to cover the morals and obligations of different classes, and he suggested referring to 'moral econom*ies*' in the plural. In a similar fashion, Hann (2010) reminded us that, in addition to Thompson's emphasis on the norms and obligations that constitute the basis for the crowd acting as a class-for-itself in Marxist terms, the reactionary right-wing crowds that are not part of the progressive left, like the elites, also have a notion of moral and immoral, legitimate and illegitimate, in their understandings of the workings of the economy. However, in his more recent work, Hann has dropped the concept 'moral economy' as muddled and has adopted instead the notion of a '*moral dimension* in the sense of a collective and systemic basis in long-term shared values' (Hann 2018: 7). Carrier (2018) further extended the term by contending that a 'moral economy' emerges 'when people engage in economic transactions with others and those transactions generate a relationship with those others and an obligation to transact again in the future' (ibid.: 32).

There have been other recent attempts to reconceptualize the notion of a 'moral economy' without watering down its emphasis on social inequalities and class, as Edelman (2005) noted about the moral economy literature in anthropology. Similarly, Kofti suggests studying the moral economy of 'flexible production', which includes the 'moral frameworks of different groups such as workers, managers, clients and shareholders whose decisions affect [the] politics of production' (Kofti 2016: 436) and covers both the work place and the workers' households. She argues that this approach to the moral economy of flexible production captures a wide range of intertwined relations of dependence and inequality manifested under flexible forms of accumulation. Her take on the moral economy aims to overcome the limitations of the original concept by addressing the moral frameworks of multiple social groups, and not only the subaltern, in a similar fashion to Fassin's (2009) moral econom*ies*. She diverges from the original formulations by shifting the focus to compliance rather than resistance, as well as departing from Fassin (2009) and Hann (2020) by keeping the emphasis on inequalities and class. Palomera and Vetta (2016) start from a similar concern to Kofti (2016), but their emphasis is more on 'reclaim[ing] the radical foundations of the term by bringing capital and class back into the equation' (Palomera and Vetta 2016: 414). Their starting point is the idea that 'capital accumulation is structurally inscribed in the everyday dynamics of social reproduction' (ibid.: 423). As Palomera and Vetta emphasize, it is in those everyday dynamics that anthropologists observe the domain of market relations, such as self-interest, competition and commodification, as well as the domain of the non-market, such as obligations, norms, dependencies and incommensurable values that are inseparably entangled with one another. Palomera and Vetta suggest that 'it is this very entanglement that sustains certain patterns of capital accumulation' (ibid.). This realm is what they call 'moral economies' in the plural.

In this book, I follow the reformulations of the notion of 'moral economy' by Kofti (2016) and Palomera and Vetta (2016). I try to uncover the different moral frameworks that people participate in and hold collectively, as well as the compliances that are quintessentially dismissed. I also explore those entanglements of market and non-market relations that enable particular forms of capital accumulation. However, I still feel uneasy about sticking to the 'moral economy' in order to address these various social positions and entanglements for the reasons that critics have raised, discussed above. Rather, I use the concept of 'value regimes' as an analogy and as used in the work of Narotzky (2015) and Kalb (2017) in order to refer to these realms of entanglement in which market and non-market relations, individual and community interests, are moulded in ways that create and sustain the core inequalities that are intrinsic to capitalism. I am also inspired by the work of David Graeber (2001) where he tries to combine the Marxist and anthropological understandings of 'value'. He explains his materialism as 'one that sees society as arising from creative action, but creative action as something that can never be separated from its concrete, material medium' (ibid.: 54). My intention is to study certain economic developments arising out of 'creative action' but to do so without separating these developments from their concrete material medium. Hence, I use 'value' in a two-fold sense, first as both bottom-up and institutional meanings of worth and what is worthy in a given society, and second as the relational mechanisms that turn labour into value in local and global processes of capital accumulation. By doing so, I explore the social reproduction of capitalism in Çorum through the lenses of both moral economy and political economy.

Methodology

The ethnography presented in this book is based on fieldwork conducted from September 2015 to September 2016, comprising a one-month exploratory visit to Konya and a long-term stay of eleven months in Çorum. I spent a month in Konya for purposes of comparison with another industrializing and developing provinces with a history of Islamist political organization and local governance.[32] I visited medium-size factories in

---

[32] In the late 1960s, Necmettin Erbakan (leader of National Outlook, the main Islamist political tradition in Turkey and predecessor of Welfare Party) was elected an independent MP for Konya. In the early 1980s, Konya appeared in the national media with radical Islamist

Konya's industrial district, spent most of my time with a small shoe-manufacturing family, and visited the *Mevlana Celaleddin Rumi*[33] museum and the city's symbolic mosques and museums. Konya is a far more developed urban centre than Çorum, and its industrial share of Turkey's national domestic product is a lot higher. In fact, Konya is one of the exemplars of local Islamist modernization in Turkey, with its fast train connections, inner-city tram line, tea and shisha gardens, and wide urban squares bedecked with Islamic symbolism. One can also feel the dominance of Islam in the public sphere in Konya[34], more so than in Çorum. Still, Konya businessmen were as pragmatic as their Çorum counterparts as far as I could observe in a stay of one month.

After my short stay in Konya, I went directly to Çorum and started flat-hunting. I was lucky to find a place that an elderly couple were renting out just upstairs from their own, a furnished flat where their son and his family used to reside before they left to go to another city in Turkey for other employment options. I have therefore not lived in the same household with the locals, as in traditional ethnographic practice, but I lived close enough to my landlady and landlord to share food and recipes with them, to spend ordinary days in women's gatherings with our neighbours, to spend the evenings together in front of the television, and to celebrate birthdays and special religious and non-religious feasts together. These were times when I gathered general information about Çorum, its customs and its past. My landlord and his wife were both practicing and pious Sunni Muslim Turks, and in fact my landlord was one of the first graduates of the first imam school that opened in Çorum in the 1950s after the Republican reforms; he was a retired schoolteacher, and he had also been performing with the city's

---

protestors. Since then the city's image as highly religious-conservative has shifted to an image associated with radical Islam and bigotry. However, the city was later branded after the message by *Mevlana Celaleddin Rumi* balancing out the radical notions of Islam and associating Konya with tolerance, belief and love for God. See the introduction to Durak (2011) for more detail. Today, many Islamic symbols, including Rumi's image have been commodified. See also Doğan (2007) for an analysis of Islamist local governance in the neoliberal era in Kayseri.

[33] Famous Persian Sufi born in the beginning of the thirteenth century in the Horasan area (today's Afghanistan), who moved to Konya in the early years of his life and lived there until his death. He is famous for his book *Mesnevi*. The museum I visited is the monastery in which he practiced Sufism and lived with his followers. Many precious remnants from Rumi's time are exhibited there. Rumi's tomb is also next to the museum.

[34] There were no women wearing short skirts/shorts or sleeveless tops in more than 25-degree Celsius September days; there was only one affordable restaurant where alcohol was served and women could also go- the rest were either expensive restaurants, hotel roof-tops or restaurants/music halls where women work to accompany and entertain men. Alcohol selling kiosks were rare and only available in the centre and in touristic areas.

classical Turkish music orchestra until recently. In this respect, he represented a blend of Turkish modernization that introduced a secular lifestyle, widespread formal education and the chances of public employment to Muslim Turks. My landlady, his wife, was a housewife who had only started covering her hair in a traditional style and wearing long coats after growing older. Her choice reveals a common trend that comes with age and has parallels with developments in Turkish political life. The religiosity in their family and social circles represented what Lindisfarne (2002) described elsewhere as 'the religiosity of those ordinary people who live in a social world in which Islamic and semi-Islamic values and practices are widespread, and who are at the same time loyal to the republic' (2002: 74). Lindisfarne adds that this type of religiosity is often ignored by sociologists. My landlady and landlord were both supporters of the AKP at the time I arrived in Çorum for the reason that constitutes one of party's ideological pillars: religion had been pushed out of the public sphere, devout Muslims had been suppressed in the Kemalist era, and Recep Tayyip Erdoğan freed Muslims and made Turkey more powerful (see Chapter 3 for a discussion of this 'meta-narrative'). However, a year later, at which time I was about to leave Çorum after the chain of political events that had happened that year and the purges and arrests after the failed 15 July 2016 military coup, my landlord and landlady voted against Erdoğan in the presidential elections that sought to change the regime from a republic to one-man rule. They were conservatives who valued women's education and who believed that Islam, and more importantly morality, 'resided in the heart and not in appearances', a phrase they repeatedly voiced during our TV-watching sessions in the evenings. Moreover, they were Turkish nationalists as they were members of the majority. Our conversations were of great value to me throughout the time I spent in Çorum, and they dwell in the subtext of this book if not openly stated.

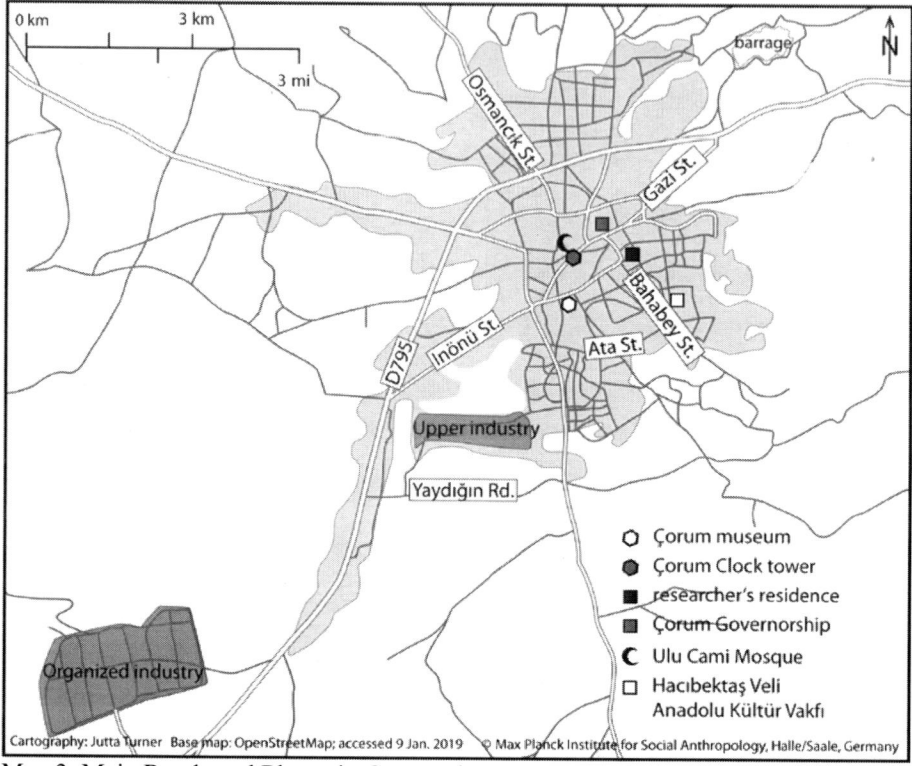

Map 3. Main Roads and Places in Çorum city.

The location where I lived is also of importance because of the segregation of Sunni and Alevi neighbourhoods after the 1980 massacre, after which Alevis and Sunnis who lived in the same neighbourhoods sold their houses and work places at less than their value and moved to separate neighbourhoods, where they lived with people of the same religious beliefs. Locals describe this situation as the red line between Gazi Street to the right above and left below. The area between Gazi Street and Bahabey Street and from Bahabey Street to the Çorum museum are where mostly Alevis live (see Map 3 above). The officially unrecognized and unsubsidised place of worship of Alevis, *Hacıbektaş Veli Anadolu Kültür Vakfı*, is also in this neighbourhood and operates as a *Vakıf* (foundation). Most alcohol-selling kiosks, a few bars, alcohol-selling restaurants and some cafes oriented to youngsters[35] are in this area, where everyone socializes, regardless of being

---

[35] There are also many restaurants and cafes in the city centre on *Gazi* street and in the rear streets of *Gazi* street to the right below *Bahabey* street (see Map 3). The new trend when I was there was the grill restaurants on the highway to Samsun (the continuation of *Gazi* Street) where local meat grilling habit in the countryside was combined with mass meat consumption

Sunni or Alevi. Where I lived is just on the border of this separation (see Map 3), in a neighbourhood that was built in the 1990s during the peak of the construction sector at the time and of Çorum's tile industry. The residents of the building were a mixture of Alevi and Sunni, and most of them were lower middle-class civil servants, mainly teachers. The commonly accepted rule of thumb of conservatism in Turkey entails every single person, especially women, belonging to a family, more specifically to a man, either a father or a husband. As an unmarried woman in my late twenties back then, it was difficult for people to understand that I was doing this research by myself unaccompanied by a father or a husband. Although there were some exceptions, I had to explain this almost every day to somebody new. In that regard, living in a relatively 'liberal' neighbourhood with people who are more sympathetic to women having their own aims apart from being a wife or mother made my research a little easier in comparison to living in a more conservative neighbourhood.

After settling into my new flat, I contacted an industrial engineer and management expert working in Çorum with whom I had already been in touch with the aid of my supervisor, Lale Yalçın-Heckmann. Her help gave me access to a medium-size wheat-related machine-manufacturing factory in Çorum's industrial district (Organized Industry, see Map 3). In this work I will call their factory, which I find emblematic of Çorum's industrialization, Çor-Mak, an abbreviation of *Çorum Makina* (machine). The firm is a partnership between an AKP-voting, pious Sunni man from a nearby village with a background and apprenticeship in machinery, whom I call Cemal Bey[36], and a non-religious Sunni liberal man educated in mechanical engineering in Germany with a state scholarship who came from a civil service and land-owning background whom I call Bülent Bey. The workers in this factory consist mainly of young people from nearby villages in the district and Cemal Bey's co-villagers, as is the case with many other factories in the region. I participated in the full-time working day in this factory for four months and kept visiting regularly afterwards. Another work place with which I became acquainted by chance through a woman employer was a medium-size franchising company belonging to an Alevi couple. Although they are not in the manufacturing business, which is the focus of this book, their business is representative of the service sector that expanded after the 1980s, an example of the flexible work regimes of that period. I call

---

in fancy restaurant chains as in the example of *Nusret*, a global phenomenon of such restaurants.

[36] In Turkish, *Bey* and *Hanım* are the formal ways of addressing males and females respectively, as in Mr and Ms/Mrs in English. Henceforth, I address most of my respondents as such, depending on their seniority in the social context being described.

them *Ozan-Ticaret* (Ozan-Trade) throughout the book, as their job is to supply mainly food products to supermarkets and kiosks, along with cleaning products. I also participated in the full-time working day in this company for some three months and kept visiting them regularly afterwards. My participant observation in these companies included following the daily routine of their work places, spending time with employers and employees outside working hours, attending weekend events like picnics and trips, socializing in and outside their households, and attending special days like weddings and commemorations of dead relatives. The owners and workers of these two companies became the main protagonists of this book.

The rest of my time in Çorum was dedicated to in-depth interviewing a variety of medium and small company owners in the industrial district and the so-called 'upper industry' (see Map 3). Every day, I drove from where I lived to the work places in these two districts; some I visited once to have survey form filled in, and some I visited regularly to catch up with what was going on in their daily working lives, or just to eat lunch or to chat. I spent all of my research time in these districts with people who were either employers or workers there. The survey form mentioned above was a quantitative data-gathering questionnaire based on our collective work at the Max Planck Institute for Social Anthropology with the members of our research group, 'Realizing Eurasia: Civilisation and Moral Economy in the 21st Century', used larger for reasons of comparison. We had selectively combined the questions in the World Value Survey and European Value Study[37] to create a new survey form based on what we thought would be relevant to our own research questions. I conducted snowball sampling from the list of all the registered manufacturing companies I had obtained from the Chamber of Commerce and Industry based on the sectoral and size distribution of those on the list. The sample consisted of thirty people, of whom four were females, nineteen employers, and eight sons or nephews who were working with their fathers or uncles and are their potential successors. Two were not the owners but the managers of their companies, and one was an unpaid family worker.[38] The quantitative data I collected can by no means claim to represent the whole manufacturing sector due to the limitations of the sample size. However, the survey proved helpful in starting

---

[37] Both are cross-national and cross-sectional surveys on different scales that study human values in the areas of family, work, religion and morality, politics and identity. For more details of the World Value Survey, see http://www.worldvaluessurvey.org/WVSContents.jsp; for more details of the European Value Study, see https://europeanvaluesstudy.eu

[38] Except for six of them, all were born in Çorum. Only half had a university degree, and most of them were not the current business owners but their successors. Of the middle-aged business owners, most were primary school graduates or middle school drop-outs. Some had vocational school training or just went to high school.

conversations on not-so-easy topics during the research and provided some general overview of several topics that are central to the research. While this book relies heavily on the ethnographic methods of participant observation and in-depth interviewing, I have benefited from the results of the survey where they were relevant to building the arguments of the chapters.

This research was conducted at a time of political turmoil, when former political alliances were being violently disrupted and the balance of power was being radically altered. The political climate was tense and dominated by the distrust and anger of different political camps towards each other. I had started the fieldwork a year and a half after the 17-25 December 2013 corruption allegations, which brought the quarrel between AKP cadres and the Gülen movement out into the open. It was also a year after the ceasefire and ongoing negotiations between the Turkish state and the PKK (Kurdistan Workers' Party) leader Öcalan, known as the Peace Process, had ended. Just before my fieldwork started, the AKP lost its majority in parliament in the June 2015 general elections and was unwilling to form a coalition government. In the same elections, the pro-Kurdish HDP (Democratic Party of the Peoples) entered parliament by passing the election threshold (10 percent) with 13.1 percent of the votes. In July, the AKP started a war against the PKK and declared a curfew in many southeastern provinces where the HDP has a stronghold. During the curfew, the security forces killed tens of people, including babies and children. Nationalist agitation led to attacks (burning, stoning, looting) in more than two hundred offices of the HDP in western Turkey, including their headquarters. Thousands of HDP supporters and activists were taken into custody, some were arrested, and many HDP mayors were removed from their seats. Within the same timeframe, on 20 July 2015 a group of young socialists on their way to help in the rebuilding of Kobane, freed from ISIS (the Islamic State of Iraq and Syria) by the Kurdish armed forces in Syria, and on 10 October 2015 a peace rally organized in Ankara were attacked by ISIS suicide bombers, killing in 132 people in total. In a repeat election in November 2015, the AKP was re-elected as the majority party by appealing to ultra-nationalist voters in the MHP and some HDP voters, while the HDP itself lost around a million votes but still won enough to enter parliament. During my fieldwork, several other terror attacks happened in Ankara city centre (March 2016, paramilitary Kurdish forces), in İstanbul's touristic centre Sultanahmet (June 2016, ISIS) and at İstanbul's Atatürk Airport (June 2016, ISIS). A scandal that revealed weapon transfers to ISIS by the Turkish intelligence agency and the inadequacies of the state in tracking down ISIS terrorists led to the AKP being blamed for supporting Islamist terrorism. The same year, a group of concerned academics circulated a 'peace petition' calling the government back to the peace process, which received tremendous attention from the state, unlike previous opposition petitions, and many academics were purged from universities and were deprived of their citizenship in the years that followed. Towards the end of my fieldwork on 15 July 2016, Gülen-supporting military officials allegedly staged a military coup to topple the AKP but failed. This was followed by a state of emergency that remained in effect until July 2018. By the end of my fieldwork, hundreds of thousands people allegedly related to Gülen or associated with leftist movements were being investigated, many later being purged and being deprived of some of their citizenship rights. Any remark against the AKP or its war on terror had the potential to spark a conflict in daily encounters, to cause social exclusion of the owner of the comment, or even to put the person concerned in front of a prosecutor. Many opponents were politically targeted by state officials and the AKP's daily newspapers and were lynched on social media; many fled the country in these years.

Inevitably, the political situation affected research like everything else. There is always an element of suspicion regarding who the ethnographer is and what her aims are, but some extra difficulties arose due to the overarching distrust among people generally. Most people did not approve of the research being funded by a European institution, even though many had trade connections with European countries. In almost all my initial encounters, respondent business people and associations hesitated to take part because they mostly felt either that their past was being interrogated or simply felt uncomfortable talking about religious/non-religious values, since these conversations might lead to their disclosing their political opinions. Many people avoided talking about the political developments of the last few years, and I also sometimes avoided them so as not to cause offence or tensions, since disagreement with AKP policies was deemed treasonable on a national level. When political topics came up, many censored themselves or simply shut down by saying they weren't interested unless they were supporters of the AKP. Therefore, during the research most of the political developments that were going on at the time were not brought up as a topic since it was not possible to talk in any detail about them without jeopardizing my research and even my presence in Çorum.

Outline of the Chapters

The book consists of three main parts. Part One is entitled 'Economy and Society in Turkey: State of the Art' and contains two chapters both dedicated to literature reviews. Chapter 2 provides a review of the political economy of Turkey, starting with the late Ottoman period, and emphasizes the state's active involvement in different phases of capitalist formation and restructuring. It also draws general contours around how the relationship between Islam and capitalism has been discussed in recent decades. Chapter 3 challenges the near-hegemonic reading of Turkish history based on the supposed dichotomy between the state and society, to which the 'Anatolian Tigers' narrative belongs. The chapter provides a discussion of the changing role of Turkish Islam, Islamism and *laiklik* in the formation of Turkish national identity, introduces the fundamentals of Islam and institutions of Sunni Islam in the republican era, and finally discusses the formation of Alevi identity from the historical perspective.

Part Two is entitled 'The World of Business in Çorum: Formation, Aspirations and Mobility'. It focuses on the historical and political conditions of capitalist accumulation in the case of the Çorum hinterland and introduces the current business people who come under the scope of this work. Chapter 4 traces the social and occupational histories of the contemporary entrepreneurial stratum in Çorum from the beginning of the twentieth century to demonstrate the various modes of capital accumulation, including the dispossession of non-Muslims, the removal of intermediaries, the role of merchant capital, the role of cooperation among Çorum people, including transfers of skills, and the role of fragmented ways of labouring and self-exploitation. These all constitute relational mechanisms of capitalist valorisation that are not limited to changes to the political economy since the 1980s but are the result of a longer period of social transformation. I critically engage with ahistorical typologies of 'models' and the claims that there is an 'entrepreneurial soul' or a 'culture of partnership' in the public rhetoric by actually demonstrating 'what makes them operate in real life and what makes their articulation significant' (Narotzky 2010: 176). This chapter also draws attention to the importance of treating industrial districts as part of a developmentalist program by the Turkish state which grants immense tax and labour-cost reductions, as well as cheap land and utilities, which are often neglected in business peoples' testimonies. Contrary to the claim that these districts are independent, I show how smaller suppliers and subcontractors in and out of the districts are cyclically connected to those in the industrial district in feeding in the surplus creation in Çorum, as well as skills transfers between the generations. I also demonstrate the role of Islamic business associations in Çorum's industrial development and its limits. Chapter 5 focuses on the motivations and aspirations of current provincial business owners and their changing relationship to 'work' over the course of their life-span through which most of them, from being labourers, became employers. The chapter mainly questions the idea of 'neoliberal subjectivity' that is generally attributed to entrepreneurs in the 21st century, analyses the ways which some have adopted the 'neoliberal' discourse, and illustrates the set of sentiments that have shaped their motivations, as well as their aspirations for themselves, for their successors and for the Turkish nation. I argue that ideas of 'work' and 'enterprise' play a central role in the making of business people's personhood.

Part Three of this book is entitled 'Kinship, Religiosity and Management at The Workplace'. It focuses on the organization of daily life at workplaces and the moral frameworks that shape them. Chapter 6 demonstrates the morality and politics behind recruiting, promoting and laying off co-villagers, kin and family members at work places. I show how different levels of the relatedness of employees to their employers create long- and short-term moral obligations and expectations for both parties. Family workers and employers negotiate different mechanisms of debt, extra benefits and promotion in return for loyalty and self-dedication. This chapter also illustrates how the roles and obligations in a family or a kin group are stretched paternalistically to include non-family employees through various incentives, Islamic and non-Islamic workplace rituals, and outdoor activities. These practices aim to cultivate work-place communities around shared values and to compensate for low wages, flexible working hours and job insecurity in the absence of an organized labour movement. I argue that both Sunni and Alevi employers see themselves as responsible for their workers but that the content of how they fulfill that responsibility depends on their personal perceptions of what is valuable in life and the common good.

Chapter 7 starts with a narrow focus on a regular working day at the factory. It then expands on the different aspects of time, discipline, labour control and management, and analyses how a flexible labour regime operates in a paternalistic factory setting. It explores the consensual and coercive ways in which time-discipline and Japanese management techniques are implemented by employers and managers and how the workers respond to it. I argue that the changes in the organization of production have led to changes in the social structure of the factory which re-established power relations among manager and workers, older and younger workers, skilled and unskilled workers, and men and women. My ethnography demonstrates that coercion and consent are expressed and exercised with reference to values such as respect, loyalty, gratitude, deservingness and honour, oscillating between *domination* and *asymmetrical reciprocity*. The chapter draws on locally specific ways of labour control to reveal the persistence of paternalism, despite changing forms of labour and its organization. Chapter 8 looks at the exceptions to time-discipline in organizing the daily life of work places. The strict rules and measures elaborated in Chapter 7 are breached by the performance of religious practices and rituals during working hours in Çorum. Chapter 8 focuses on these religious practices, namely the daily prayers, Friday prayers and fasting during Ramadan. I demonstrate the multiplicity of time-reckoning systems and their degrees of imposition at different levels of the sector, community and enterprise. My aim is to develop an understanding of how the different value systems of pious and non-pious Sunni and Alevi interact, collide or conflict in the work place. I conclude with Chapter 9, which summarizes my arguments throughout the book, point out the gaps I could not address, and suggests new research agendas for following up the same topic.

PART ONE

TURKISH ECONOMY AND SOCIETY:

STATE OF THE ART

Chapter 2
Milestones in the Political Economy of Turkey and Path-Dependencies of Anatolian Capital

Introduction

In this chapter, I aim to stretch out to focus on the longer history of the political economy of Turkey so as to provide the reader with a background to the economic policies that have been adopted in different periods. By doing so, I intend to emphasize the state's active involvement and class alliances in the creation and maintenance of the both the Muslim bourgeoisie and the market economy, as well as show how the differences between Istanbul and Anatolian capital have evolved down the years. The chapter starts from late nineteenth-century developments illustrating the milestones in the Ottoman Empire's articulation to free-market capitalism and elaborates on its economic legacy for the Turkish nation state. It proceeds by describing the shift to state protectionism in economic policies after the Great Depression of 1929, followed by the gradual transition to a developmental model that prioritized foreign debts and investments after World War II. The next phase, starting in 1960, is characterized by import-substitution, which lasted until 1980, when the liberalization of the market was reversed by the military coup of that year. I then proceed to show the general contours of the economic policies that marked the post-1980s and different phases of the authoritarian neoliberal hegemony and its crises. The final part of the chapter is dedicated to the AKP and the debate it triggered over the relationship between Islam and capitalism. The periodization I follow in this chapter is not based on political changes but on the shifts in major economic policies, parallel with the general argument of the book that questions 'radical breaks' by historically contextualizing the emergence and development of Anatolian capital and showing its path-dependencies. Accordingly, every part scrutinizes the repercussions of the political and economic policies of each era for provincial entrepreneurialism with the aim of shedding light on the ethnographic findings in the following chapters. Finally, the last part is dedicated to a discussion of Islam, capitalism and politics in the AKP era to help explain contemporary debates in Turkey.

The Economic Legacy of the Late Ottoman Empire (1838-1929)

In the nineteenth-century Ottoman economy, the expansion of foreign trade, direct foreign investments and indebtedness shaped the conditions and social structure which the Committee of Union and Progress (*İttihat ve Terakki Cemiyeti*, ITC) and later the republic took over at the beginning of the twentieth century. In these years, the Ottoman economy was based on agriculture and exports of raw materials and became an open market for imports from Britain and later on France and other European countries. Ottoman integration into the global economy had not occurred through merchants' and landowners' alliances with European capital but through negotiations between European states and the Ottoman central bureaucracy (Pamuk 2008b). Emblematic of this sort of negotiation was the *Baltalimanı* Treaty signed with Britain in 1838, which removed all customs protection and gave British investors and their collaborators full access to the Ottoman market, with taxation equal to local traders. The small manufacturing sector, which constituted the majority of industry in the nineteenth century, mainly producing for the domestic market, could not compete with the low prices of imported goods and had to close down, although many resisted and survived to constitute the majority (Kepenek and Yentürk 1994; Tezel 1994; Pamuk 2008a).

Following the Ottoman alliance with Britain and France in the Crimean War, the Ottomans took out their first international loan, which then grew like a snowball in a short time, resulting in the bankruptcy of the Ottoman economy in 1875 and the establishment of the Ottoman Public Debt Administration (*Düyun-u Umumiye*) in 1881. *Düyun-u Umumiye* was composed of representatives of Europeans who owned Ottoman stocks and appropriated one third of the tax revenues like a state institution in exchange for the debt. Furthermore, the privileges for the foreign investors allowed them to open banks and to control and manage the Empire's sea transport. Many of these foreign investments addressed the needs of commercial capital, such as the railways, which connected the coastal cities to the hinterland and linked up the ports for shipping the goods. All these developments are regarded as representing the incorporation of the peripheral Ottoman economy into European capitalism, thus making it dependent and enabling its growth at the same time (Pamuk 2008b), whereas others see it as the semi-colonization of Ottoman society under the control of imperialism (Tezel 1994; Boratav 2006).

Pamuk (2008b) points out that it would be far-fetched to argue that the small and medium-size manufacturing sector that constituted the majority of industry was on the verge of an industrial revolution by the early twentieth century. Nonetheless, open market conditions, local manufacturers' inability to compete with imported goods, heavy debts and hence the dependence that mark that era played a role in hindering the creation of a national capitalism in the early twentieth century (Boratav 2006). The Ottoman bourgeoisie had arisen through trade rather than industry, had comprador features and was composed mainly of non-Muslims, hence it did not and was not expected to play the leading revolutionary role of a national bourgeoisie. On the other hand, the Muslim Turkish bourgeoisie that was active in the domestic trade with small or medium capital was very weak, unorganized and largely dependent on the former. The ethnic and religious composition of the Anatolian population had changed drastically due to the massacres and deportations suffered mainly by Armenians in 1915 and the population exchange between Greece and Turkey in 1923 (Mardin 1980; Keyder 1989; Pamuk 2007). Also, 18 per cent of the Muslim population died in the wars between 1912 and 1922. According to the 1906 census, the population living within today's Turkish borders were 10 percent Greek, 7 percent Armenian and 1 percent Jewish out of a total of fifteen million, though the 1927 census shows only 2.6 percent non-Muslim remaining in a population of 13.6 million (Keyder 1989). Since non-Muslims traditionally conducted trade and business, their departure and mass murder meant that the labour force left in Anatolia consisted primarily of farmers without sufficient capital accumulation or skills. Moreover, the dramatic decline in the non-Muslim population meant that the links of non-Muslim artisans, traders and moneylenders to rural areas, port cities and Europe were lost, as were the commercial, export-oriented farms they had run, which were abandoned (Pamuk 2007). As I will also show in the case of Çorum in Chapter 4, this provided an opportunity to Muslim notables or traders at the time to seize the abandoned land, fill the former business connections and replace the void left by the disappearance of the non-Muslims.

In the meantime, apart from the various obstacles, there were some conditions that would facilitate a national capitalism to flourish. At the ideological level, national protectionist industrialization was quite popular among Young Turk circles, more popular in effect than the liberal doctrine. The doctrine of 'national economy', as we shall see in the following years, treats the inbreeding of the 'local and national' (*yerli ve milli*) bourgeoisies as a prerequisite for modernization and development. The objective factor that accelerated the transformation were the conditions in the First World War, during which, due to scarcities, a considerable amount of primitive accumulation was possible through profiteering on the black market. This was accompanied by the economic nationalism with which the government supported the prosperity of Muslim-Turkish entrepreneurial practices. During the Second Constitutional Era (1908-1920), when the ITC took power, it unilaterally cancelled the capitulations of 1914, which had granted economic and political advantages to European traders in Ottoman lands. The ITC also made some moves in favour of the employers, such as issuing a Strike Law (*Tatil-i Eşgal Kanunu*) in 1909, which can be considered the first modern legal document to mediate the labour and capital relations of the state as a response to the on-going labour strikes. The Promotion of Industry Law (*Teşvik-i Sanayi Kanunu*) was issued in 1913, while custom protections provided local Muslim and Turkish entrepreneurs with incentives to industrialize, though the impact of this was limited for reasons I mentioned above, but mainly due to open-market conditions. The state policy of providing prosperity to Muslim Turks over non-Muslims was also maintained into the republican era (Tezel 1994).

After the war of independence[39] of 1919-1922, in 1923 a republic was declared by a coalition of military and civilian bureaucrats, notables, traders and big landlords, which institutionalized its power in the ITC and later in the Republican People's Party (*Cumhuriyet Halk Partisi*, CHP) as the single party, marking a political break from the Ottoman Empire (Köker 1990; Zürcher 1993). However, its economic policies showed a continuity with the previous era. The creation of a national bourgeoisie constitutes the dominant doctrine, and the founders pursue development and industrialization in an open-market economy. One of the main reasons the early republic continued the open-market economic policy was because the Treaty of Lausanne (1923) obliged it not to implement protectionist customs laws until 1929. These conditions limited the autonomy of the new nation to make its own foreign trade policy (Buğra 1994). At the same time, the treaty required the new republic to pay the debts of the Ottoman period. Nonetheless, in these early years important steps were taken to develop the national economy under open-market conditions. The Izmir Economy Conference (1923) is one of these important steps. All the guilds and associations of all

---

[39] After the Ottoman defeat in World War I, Allied Forces have partitioned the remaining Ottoman land and occupied Istanbul, Thrace, West, East and South Anatolia in 1918. Armed militia forces scattered in these fronts were eventually unified by Mustafa Kemal (Atatürk) under the umbrella of national resistance organisation called 'Kuva-yı Milliye'. The independence war lasted three years and marked the fall of Ottoman Empire in 1922, and resulted with the declaration of the independence of the Turkish Republic in 1923.

occupations, including farmers, traders and workers[40], were present at this conference to discuss and take decisions on economic problems and policies. One of the main aims of the conference was to bring together Turkish Muslim capitalists from İzmir and İstanbul with those from Ankara and the rest who had ceased to be connected with each other during the years of the war of independence. The economic principles adopted by the leadership mainly of traders were developmentalist, encouraging national and foreign investments, moderately protectionist, and facilitating the transfer of domination of the economy from non-Muslims to Muslim Turks. The encouragement of foreign investments occurred not as direct foreign investments but as partnerships with local capitalists (Kepenek and Yentürk 1994). Boratav (2006) shows that among 201 joint stock companies in Turkey in that decade, 66 percent had partnerships with foreign investors. The founders regarded foreign involvement useful for facilitating the growth of Muslim Turkish capitalists as long as their involvement was not a threat to the sovereignty of the new nation state (Köker 1990; Zürcher 1993; Tezel 1994). In line with this principle, the largest direct foreign investment of the late nineteenth century, the Régie Company (*Tütün Rejisi*), which had been formed by the Ottoman Public Debt Administration (*Düyun-u Umumiye*), had certain privileges, was backed by European banks and monopolized the tobacco trade, had been bought by the new Turkish state in this era. At the same time, the railways that were owned by foreigners were nationalized and the coastal privileges of foreign ships were cancelled. National banks such as *İş Bankası* and *Sanayi Maadin Bankası* were also established (Kepenek and Yentürk 1994; Tezel 1994; Boratav 2006).

The developmentalist agenda manifested itself in the implementation of an improved version of the previous Promotion of Industry Law, issued in 1927. However, it was not the industry with the greatest share of the economy, as in fact the agriculture sector grew in these years, especially due to the removal of the *Aşar* tax, which was collected from the farmers and represented ten per cent of their production. By replacing the *Aşar* tax with indirect taxation in 1925, the burden was removed from the farmers and shifted to the urban consumers. Also, plots of land were distributed to the farmers, though the large landowners benefited from this policy more compared to the smaller peasants. Unused parcels were cultivated again by men returning from the war in this period, which also contributed to the increase in agricultural revenues in the country's gross national product. The first years of the republic had been an era in which Muslim traders made

---

[40] Workers' Association (*Amele Birliği*) which represents workers of Istanbul was also present in this platform but was dominated by traders. Workers' demands were discussed in this conference too but were quickly disregarded (Boratav 2006).

significant revenues through their political connections with the founding cadres and mediating foreign investors. Moreover, large numbers of farmers had increased their production and revenues, and their overall income levels also increased, easing somewhat the living conditions of all social strata in the post-war conditions.

The Making of a National Bourgeoisie (1930-1980)

Etatist Industrialization (1930-1946)

The Great Depression of 1929 coincided with the expiry of the customs sanctions imposed by the Lausanne Treaty, leading to a shift to a state-protectionist, closed economic policy. Although state intervention had been a topic of discussion since the early twentieth century within the ITC, the conditions for adopting a systematic étatist[41] and state-protectionist model of industrialization flourished only after the 1930s as a response to the economic crisis. The political elites collaborated with the larger landowners by imposing custom tariffs on imports of agricultural products in order to help them resist the decline in the prices of agricultural products during the economic crisis while building industry where they could sell their products with long-term prospects. This strategy also led to economic growth in the years of economic crisis (Pamuk 2008c).

These early years were formative in the way industrialization unfolded in the following decades. The state's attempts at national industrialization took the form of the first five-year development plan (1934), produced on this occasion with the assistance of Soviet planners (Pamuk 2007; Akgöz 2012). The state reports prepared in the early 1930s specified two areas of investment. One was the large-scale industries that required input into imports, as in mining, the chemical industry and the electricity network, while the other area consisted of industries based on processing certain raw materials which were available in the country, such as sugar, wood and fur. The reports recommended that the state should undertake the former but leave the latter to the private sector. However, the private sector was reluctant (Bayırbağ 2007: 75) or even unwilling to invest in either Anatolia or industry, regarding this as too risky. Moreover, the private sector lacked the capital, technology and know-how and rather preferred to pursue trade,

---

[41] Etatism (*devletçilik*) was established as one of the six principles of the CHP in 1931 and incorporated into the constitution in 1937. The other principles were republicanism (*cumhuriyetçilik*), secularism (*laiklik*), nationalism (*milliyetçilik*), populism (*halkçılık*) and revolutionism (*inkılâpçılık*). The set of six principles are mostly referred as Kemalism, the umbrella term for the founding ideology named after the founder and first president of the republic, Mustafa Kemal Atatürk (1881-1938).

contracting businesses and constructing infrastructure (Sönmez 1987). Therefore, the state undertook the role initially ascribed to the private sector and started building raw material-processing factories, buying off those already available or in the stage of construction. Accordingly, an organization called State Economic Enterprises (*Kamu İktisadi Teşekkülleri*, KİT) was established to act as 'leading producers in a number of key sectors, such as textiles, sugar, iron and steel, glass works, cement and mining' (Pamuk 2007: 277). Emblematical of this development were the largest KİT operating in textiles, called *Sümerbank*[42] and the sugar factories that had been built all around Anatolia (Alexander 2000, 2002).

This state strategy had consequences for small, local manufacturing industries. Bayırbağ (2007) argues that the role given to the private sector mainly concerned Istanbul and Izmir-based capital, which then marked the representatives of the 'national' bourgeoisie and caused a delay in the birth of a local bourgeoisie in Anatolia. Moreover, the government favoured large companies against small ones, thus aggravating the delays to local development and creating differences between the local and national areas of the economy. Moreover, several authors argue that the local actors were politically too weak to influence the national agenda regarding those sectors that were subject to protection and the terms of protection. In fact, local notables had to align themselves with the CHP in order to win advantages in becoming entrepreneurs (Mardin 1980; Güneş-Ayata 1994; Bayırbağ 2007).Writing about Gaziantep, Bayırbağ suggests that 'the state's large-scale industrial investments, made with a territorially sensitive approach, ... contributed to the economic vitality of various Anatolian cities, their spin-off effects [being] initially restricted to [the] creation of employment, as their production did not rely on local inputs' (Bayırbağ 2007: 75-76). While this might be the case for Gaziantep, where the number of total enterprises ranked seventh in the whole country and in regional hierarchies (although not rooted in the republican period but earlier) it cannot be denied that state factories scattered all over Anatolia aimed at much more than creating employment, and their stories tell us much more about what *étatism* stands for.

---

[42] The name 'refers to the ancient Mesopotamian civilization of the Sumerians and endorses the Turkish historical thesis that was first expressed in 1932' (Piart 2018: 126). Between 1934 and 1947, the state opened textile factories in Istanbul (Bakırköy), Kayseri, Ereğli, Nazilli, Gemlik, Bursa and Malatya, all operating under the name *Sümerbank*. Most of these investments were in Anatolia rather than in Istanbul and its vicinity. To give an idea of the economic importance of *Sümerbank*, Akgöz (2012) estimates that 'The bank controlled 47 per cent of all the spindles as well as 47 per cent of the entire workforce in the textile sector and carried out 68 per cent of all the textile production' (Akgöz 2012: 62).

Akgöz (2012) argues that in the Turkish context *étatism* was not simply a response to the conditions of the Great Depression but had several complementary motivations behind it. First of all, *étatism* 'signified an alternative both to liberal capitalism and socialism at the same time. It was a practical solution, not a regime change' (Akgöz 2012: 52). This practical solution did not aim to replace private investments but created an environment that was favourable to both private and public investments. One of the goals of establishing state-owned factories was to create a modern labour force and train competent personnel from which both the private and public sectors would benefit. As Akgöz (2012) notes from the reports and comments of observers at the time, state factories were not established for economic reasons alone but also had political and military motives. For example, observers suggest that they aimed to prevent a repetition of the sufferings of World War I. Moreover, the selection of geographical locations was based not on raw material supplies or energy needs, as it would be in private-sector investments, but on long-term national interests. One observer sees the policy of scattering factories in remote locations in Anatolia as one that 'any sane capitalist would have considered crazy economics' (Akgöz 2012: 71). By penetrating to the periphery, the state used these factories as a tool of social transformation, as well as a way of increasing its hegemonic capacity. The reports of the time observed that the state factories had changed the whole social and cultural atmosphere of the cities and towns where they were had been built. Catherine Alexander (2000) makes a similar point about the state's presence and its goals on the periphery in her ethnography of a sugar factory in Erzurum: 'Sugar factories were touted as being the "Centers of Culture and Civilization" and were seen by the elite as channels of state ideology, symbolizing the state's presence at the periphery, bringing colonies of city people to the rural areas and so setting an example of [a] modern, urban, "Western" way of life' (Alexander 2000: 179).

Turkey did not participate in World War II but suffered nevertheless through the conditions of the war economy. By the end of 1930s, imports had fallen by half, wheat production had significantly declined, and the economic and industrial programme had been deferred because of increasing military expenditure, a precaution in case Turkey also became involved in the war. The war period was one of profiteering by the commercial bourgeoisie and high-ranking bureaucrats, while economic development stagnated. The single-party government of the time had seen the war years as an opportunity to implement long-lasting economic reforms to eliminate unearned incomes, reshuffle income distribution and carry out cultural reforms to mobilize the masses in a Western-oriented, modern fashion. However, the reforms were difficult to implement and were either prevented or taken over by the liberal conservative wing within the single party, representing a deviation from its original aims. In particular, the conflicts over the land reform (1945), education policies and Village Institutes (*Köy Enstitüleri*) (1940) had caused major cracks and structural changes in the single-party regime and paved the way to the transition to a multiparty regime in 1946 (Karaömerlioğlu 1998; Boratav 2006).

The National Security Law (1940) increased state control over both domestic and foreign trade, giving the government unlimited powers to determine prices, seize products and even impose obligatory labour obligations (Pamuk 2008c). This made it possible to ration basic consumption goods, feed the military, and profit from purchasing agricultural products more cheaply and processing them. This, however, took place at the cost of unrest among the big landowners and commercial bourgeoisie. Even these measures could not prevent many incomes being earned on the black market. The land reform, which aimed to solve the problems of landless villagers and increase agricultural productivity[43], and the Soil Products Tax (1943), a one-time return of the direct agricultural taxes of the Ottoman era, contributed to the discomfort stemming from state intervention among the capitalist classes. The Wealth Tax (*Varlık Vergisi*, 1942), on the other hand, again a one-time compulsory tax levied only on traders and shopkeepers that did not distinguish between citizens in theory, was in practice paid mainly by non-Muslims. Indeed, more than half of all taxation was paid by non-Muslims, many of whom had to sell their properties in public auctions, while those who could not pay were sent to labour camps in eastern Anatolia. The Wealth Tax, a racist practice based on ethnic and religious discrimination, contributed to the unjust enrichment of Muslims in Anatolia and Istanbul and constituted 38 per cent of state expenditure in 1942, the year of its implementation (Boratav 2006). However, even though the commercial bourgeoisie gained more economic power in Anatolia through these measures, it still lacked political power and opposed the state control of domestic and foreign trade. In addition, the Village Institutes[44], which had been established for rural development, were where villagers themselves were to participate in building, teaching and learning at village schools, and where topics from agriculture to literature were covered, created further friction between the conservative elements of society and the reformers. The Village Institutes were soon closed down for allegedly posing the threat of communism. All this led to a split in the

---

[43] See Pamuk and Keyder (2008) for an assessment of different explanations regarding the aims and motivations of the land reform.

[44] See Karaömerlioğlu (2006) for a detailed analysis on the history and aims of and political discussion on the Village Institutes.

single-party regime between the communitarian wing (Bayırbağ 2007) or petty bourgeoisie reformists (Boratav 2006) represented by İsmet İnönü, second man of the regime, and the liberal wing represented by Celal Bayar, an economist and the head of *İşbankası*.[45] As a result, Celal Bayar separated from the CHP and, together with Adnan Menderes, ex-CHP deputy and a wealthy landowner from the Aegean region, formed the Democrat Party (*Demokrat Parti*, DP) with a promise of an open-market economic program and less dedication to secularism. As a result, in 1946 Turkey made the transition to a multi-party regime, and in 1950 the Democrat Party came to power with the support of the big landowners and the commercial bourgeoisie in both Anatolia and Istanbul.

Development Based on Foreign Investments and Markets (1946-1960)

The transition to a multi-party regime in 1946 marks both an economic and a political turning point. The takeover of the liberal wing of the CHP, followed by the electoral victories of the DP in 1950, 1954 and 1957, led to an irrevocable change in the class composition of the government: in particular, the weight of the big landowners and the commercial bourgeoisie in economic and political decision-making increased, in place of the top-down reformists of the previous era. Politically, the transition to a multi-party regime also meant that those in power would have to consider the economic and social demands of the wider segments of Turkish society. This consideration, however, frequently came into conflict with the short-term interests of the property-owning classes and brought about what one could call a 'populist' regime. In order to protect the long-term interests of the property-owning classes and to keep the masses under control, this regime sought to counter leftist opposition claiming to represent the interests of working people. This aspect of the DP regime had a parallel with the single-party era given that the republican ideology, which imagined the new nation state as a unified, classless society, had been intolerant of leftist opposition. As for the economy, the Democrat Party attempted a different kind of incorporation to that of the global capitalist system.

After World War II, the global capitalist system entered an expansionist period in which it promoted free-market trade. In line with this principle, in 1944 the Bretton Woods Agreement established a system of monetary management to regulate financial and commercial relations between North America, Western Europe, Australia and Japan. Accordingly,

---

[45] First national bank founded after the declaration of the republic.

all countries had to fix their exchange rates based on their gold reserves, and the US dollar became the only currency that was convertible into gold. The International Monetary Fund (IMF) and the World Bank (WB) were also established to set up the rules, regulations and procedures of the new international monetary system. Moreover, the United States launched the Marshall Plan to help Western Europe recover from the ravages of World War II. In accordance with the global reshuffling of power relations, Turkey allied itself with the capitalist West against the Soviet bloc. In 1947 Turkey became a member of the IMF and the WB and in 1952 joined the North Atlantic Treaty Organization (NATO). The belief that it was not protectionism but incorporation into the capitalist system that was the remedy for payment deficits grew stronger. The policy of neutrality of the single-party government during World War II helped to cultivate foreign trade relations in the post-war period. Hence, the DP government found it had access to sources of credits and aid. Turkey received Marshall Aid from the United States between 1947 and 1951, which it used to cover its payment deficits and modernize agriculture. At the same time, the Industry and Development Bank (*Sanayii ve Kalkınma Bankası*), which provided US-backed credits, was founded.

Integration into the Western bloc meant that Turkey's new economic agenda would be determined according to the division of labour among the capitalist countries. In that regard, Turkey's aim was not to develop through industrialization but as an exporter of agricultural products. This also implied that an anti-statist, anti-communist, liberal programme was to be followed, which was promised and embraced by the DP government (Bayırbağ 2007). The government deregulated imports, causing balance of payment deficits and thus creating an economic structure dependent on foreign credits, aid and investments. In this period, industrialization was no longer based on domestic markets, and development was opened to foreign markets, the agriculture, mining and construction sectors being prioritized. With the help of foreign credits, the DP government invested heavily in infrastructure projects such as road networks, irrigation projects and dams. The modernization and mechanization of agriculture was stimulated by the Marshall Plan. Increases in imports, the opening up of new lands for agriculture, increasing productivity and exports in agricultural products created the conditions to increase real incomes for all social layers. For the masses who still have a clear memory of the World War II period, the early DP years were years of abundance which created the impression with the public, as well as in the political discourse of the years that followed, that it was the *étatist* policies of the early 1930s that were responsible for the economic bottleneck (Boratav 2006).

On the other hand, the anti-statist promises of the DP to transfer KİTs to the private sector were never realized. In fact, in the 1950s, KİTs were expanded further, and the private sector was supported by state enterprises. Çorum's state cement factory was established in 1957 and is still remembered by local people, like the schools, recreation centres and living spaces of that time, in which people from all levels of occupation somehow participated and from which they gained something. As described in Chapter 4, these factories, like those established in the early republican era, had a long-term economic impact[46] on the establishment of today's local industries.

While showing continuity with the *étatist* era, the DP used various strategies to support the private sector. Following Avcıoğlu's findings in his seminal work *Türkiye'nin Düzeni* (1975), Bayırbağ lists them as the 'provision of cheaper credits, using the financial sources received from foreign sources, which were loaned at rates below the interest rates at which this money capital borrowed from international sources; ... the training of engineers and managers and transfer of trained, experienced public servants to the private sector; and the creation of public-private partnerships (over a hundred) in the industrial sector, where the state was either the senior partner or a stakeholder' (Bayırbağ 2007: 85). Especially the last point about public-private partnerships in which the state was a senior partner or stakeholder is documented at length by Sönmez (1987), who shows how different segments of the bourgeoisie (e.g. landowning, commercial, military) were aided through state enterprises until the 1980s. From this perspective, as Yalman has argued, 'the anti-elitist and/or anti-statist discourse of the Democratic Party could be much better understood as being instrumental in the development of a new hegemonic project which attempted to link various particularistic interests under the leadership of an emerging bourgeoisie which had no intention of weakening its ties to the state' (Yalman 2002a: 34, cited in Bayırbağ (2007:85)). It would be useful to note here that this argument concerning the DP and its links to the different wings of the

---

[46] Apart from the long-term economic benefits of these state factories, political motivations behind them sometimes created unintended consequences. Also drawn attention by Alexander (2000, 2002) that many state factories were built at the entrance of the cities as the first things to be noticed when traveling to these places, as monuments that signify the presence of the state and its modern, western, developmentalist ideology. However, these spots could as well be away from water sources as in the example of Uşak sugar factory (established in 1925) or positioned in a wrong direction creating long term pollution as in the case of cement factory of Çorum. The locals of Çorum would complain from the dust coming from the factory chimney that covers the city every winter because the factory built on road from Samsun to Çorum at the northern entrance of the city was in fact positioned without considering the direction of the wind and therefore polluted the city since its establishment.

bourgeoisie and to the state could also be read as foreshadowing an understanding of the ideological foundations of the AKP regime since 2002. The AKP, which defines itself as the successor to the DP, built its political rhetoric on an anti-statist, liberal outlook and similarly positioned itself on the side of 'civil society and the people' as opposed to the state, which is assumed to be represented by the CHP, although it was never elected as the ruling party after 1950, with the exception of Bülent Ecevit's coalition of 1973. However, the AKP also merged the class interests of the rising Islamic bourgeoisie and its already existing segments, made sure of the rise of the Islamic bourgeoisie through various support mechanisms and never intended to weaken its ties with the state. In fact, the AKP became the state itself in the 2018 presidential referendum. The tragic end of the DP, brought about by the military junta, also contributed to the AKP's rhetoric later.

The DP's development strategy started failing in the mid-1950s; payment deficits and inflationist policies caused increases in prices, declines in real wages and unemployment. Despite the insistence of foreign debtors on implementing a standard IMF prescription, the DP government brought back the National Security Law in 1954. Increasing opposition from the CHP and unrest among the masses were suppressed by arrests and limitations on the freedom of expression and protest. In 1958, the Turkish Lira was devalued and other structural adjustments were made, such as liberalizing customs and increasing the prices of state-produced products, in return for a delay in debt payments and more foreign debt. On 27 May 1960, the military overthrew the DP government. Top DP ministers were tried by the military junta, and three deputies, including former Prime Minister Adnan Menderes, were executed. This tragic and inhumane punishment found its place in the Justice Party (1961-1981) of Süleyman Demirel and later even more strongly in the AKP rhetoric as part of their victimhood. Together with the so-called post-modern *coup d'état* of 28 February 1997, this laid the ground of its battle against military tutelage, which constitutes one of the main pillars of its ideological formation and political agenda. It should be noted again here that the rhetoric of victimhood is controversial in the sense that almost all the other ruling parties that took part in coalition governments from the 1950s onwards – e.g. the Justice Party, the successor to the DP, the National Salvation Party that emerged from the ranks of the Justice Party, the predecessor of the Welfare Party, the Motherland Party and the True Path Party – stood at the centre or the centre-right of the political spectrum with a conservative blend and tried to challenge the official secularist principles while following them. Most of these right-wing and/or conservative parties did not openly defend the public display of symbols of Sunni Islam or the agenda of political Islam but remained within the boundaries of the founding principle of secularism while they all recruited political Islamists in state cadres, and overlooked the informal organizations of religious orders and increased the funding of the Directorate of Religious Affairs (Diyanet İşleri Başkanlığı, referred as *Diyanet*), especially after the 1980 *coup d'état* (see Chapter 3).

The Rise of Planning and Industrialization through Import Substitution (1960-1980)

After the 1960 *coup d'état*, its consequences were drawn in the 1961 Constitution, which created a legal basis for broadening and consolidating democracy by ensuring the rule of law and introduced a division of powers by initiating new independent judicial and constitutional bodies to create checks and balances. The constitution guaranteed individual rights and freedoms and also collective rights, such as the right to form labour unions, to strike, to form associations and to protest without prior legal permission. Mention of a 'welfare state' was also added to the Turkish constitution (Akşin 2007). Starting in 1963, five-year development plans were initiated, and a State Development Agency was founded. Unlike the development plans of previous decades, which addressed only economic development, the five-year plans of the 1960s and those that followed them addressed different aspects of economic and social development in a holistic manner, such as the national income, total capital resources, production, job placements and foreign economic affairs (Kepenek and Yentürk 1994). Already in the late 1950s, acting against the debt crisis which the DP government had caused by its aggressive and unplanned investments, Turkey was advised by the OECD (Organisation for Economic Co-operation and Development) and Western countries to follow 'a measured state investment strategy' so that the financial aid could continue (Bayırbağ 2007: 92). In the 1960s, in accordance with the Keynesian economic model of the Cold War period until the oil crisis of 1973, Import Substitution Industrialisation (ISI) was implemented as the new strategy of accumulation. In principle, ISI aims to help underdeveloped countries develop industries and be less dependent on imports from more developed countries in international trade by producing the goods they imported themselves while keeping selective import restrictions in place so that they could start exporting some of these products and diversify their industry.

Due to the industrialization of metropolitan cities, rural to urban migration started gaining pace, leading to rapid urbanization and the creation of masses of the working class in urban areas both as sources of labour and as new urban consumers. At the same time, the urban and provincial professional classes and the bourgeoisie achieved income levels that inevitably demanded durable consumption goods compatible with the new patterns of consumption. These demands were not met through imports but were produced in the domestic market with the help of foreign aid. By following the ISI model, the manufacture of consumer durables started to develop initially as the assembling of parts in local industries before later on creating sub-industries and acquiring the appearance of a modern industry. These consumer durables, such as televisions, radios, refrigerators, automobiles, and office and kitchen equipment, although not comparable with their Western counterparts in quality, became part of urban life in the 1970s.

One of the main goals of ISI was to balance imports and exports and to decrease the country's dependence on debt. However, the planning era did not achieve this goal because exports of agricultural produce remained limited, while the demand for imports of the intermediate goods and technologies necessary for the production of durable consumption goods increased. Since the intermediate goods and technologies could not be produced domestically, the increase in the demand for consumption goods by urban consumers who had more secure and stable jobs in this period brought about an economic crisis and an end to the ISI regime due to the widening balance of deficits by the end of 1970s (Kepenek and Yentürk 1994; Boratav 2006). Another important problem that Bayırbağ draws attention to is the implementation of universal customs protection instead of selective protection on sectors, 'which turned state protection into a considerable source of rent, eventually igniting heated fights inside the bourgeoisie over this source' (Bayırbağ 2007: 94).

This final point brings us to the widening gap between the emerging Anatolian bourgeoisie and large-scale capital mainly in the northwest. The shift in the accumulation regime increased the significance of industrial production and profoundly changed the bourgeoisie's profit-making strategies and organizational structure. Istanbul-based large-scale commercial capital channelled its international trade partnerships into industrial collaborations in Turkey by setting up factories to assemble products that they used to import. They benefited from the protected domestic market and distributed their products without having to go through intermediaries since they had already established domestic trade networks, and their profit rates increased. In addition, large-scale capital financing multiple sectors made them flexible in crisis situations (Buğra 1994). However, even though the profitability of local industries also increased in this period, these industries still faced many challenges, such as their dependence on industrial production as the only source of profit, and the need to deal with intermediaries and to compete with large-scale capital in the absence of international networks and the import protection rents that were mainly dominated by large-scale capital. This example, mentioned by Bayırbağ (2007), explains a great deal about the tensions of this period. The problems of the Anatolian industrialists were voiced by Necmettin Erbakan, leader of the Islamist National Outlook movement and an advocate of development based on heavy industry, who blamed large-scale capital for linking up with Western capital and claimed that the real 'national' capital was Anatolian. Erbakan made his criticisms in the Turkish Union of Chambers (*Türkiye Odalar Birliği*, TOB), the only private-interest association of the time with a semi-public status, and he was elected its general secretary with the support of TOB members. In response, Süleyman Demirel, the prime minister of the time from the Justice Party, the heir to the DP, removed the import quota privileges of the TOB members. This move had repercussions, one being that Erbakan went into parliamentary politics first as an independent candidate, then as the leader of the National Order Party, the first of many in this tradition. The other repercussion was the frustration of Istanbul capitalists with Demirel's intervention, which led them to form the first independent bourgeois-interest organization, the Turkish Industry and Business Association (*Türk Sanayicileri ve İşadamları Derneği*, TÜSİAD), which required a membership that was different from TOB. The strife between Anatolian and Istanbul capital was structurally and geographically rooted in an earlier time but widened in the ISI era, starting a discussion over who were the real 'national' bourgeoisie, and adding a Western/secular versus Muslim flavour to this intra-class conflict, a topic that dominated the literature on Anatolian capital for a very long time, as I have described in the Introduction.

Between 1960 and 1980, the trade unions and leftist movements grew stronger than ever. Given the legal framework of the 1961 constitution, collective bargaining agreements provided for continuous increases in workers' real wages and social rights. Some of the political rights that were secured under the 1961 constitution were trimmed down after the 1971 military *coup d'état*. Nevertheless, the struggles of the working classes and labour militancy succeeded in making gains that went beyond the conventional 'populist' policies that were willing to compromise and started threatening the balance between labour and capital. In the meantime, import revenues continued to fail to cover the export deficits, and monetary adjustments such as devaluation were no longer enough to meet the demand. The economic crisis of the mid-1970s severely affected the working classes, who were worried about losing the benefits they had won for themselves, while the bourgeoisie were scared of losing their profits. The idea that increasing exports while maintaining high wages and social benefits was not possible had become prevalent in business circles and among right-wing politicians. The neoliberal model started to be promoted as the only alternative. In 1979, Turgut Özal, a former bureaucrat of the State Planning Organization in the 1960s and an economist in the World Bank in the early 1970s, who was endorsed by the capitalist class, prepared an economic reform programme called the '24 January measures'. This programme entailed a devaluation, price increases for state-produced products and the removal of price protection in line with standard IMF prescriptions for underdeveloped countries. The military coup that took place on 12 September 1980 solved the political and economic crisis in favour of the bourgeoisie and forcibly launched market liberalization. The new economic programme was implemented in the following three years of military rule.[47]

The Neoliberal Era (1980 onwards)

The 1980 Military Coup and Authoritarian Neoliberalism

The key terms describing the Turkish economy after the 1980s are macro-economic stabilization and structural adjustment with the collaboration of the IMF and the World Bank. There were three aims on the agenda in this era: first, improving the balance of payments; second, reducing the rate of inflation in the short term; and third, creating a market-based export-oriented economy in the longer term. The liberalization of trade, the removal of customs, unfavourable exchange rates, cheap credit and state incentives to export-oriented sectors, along with the removal of subsidies for state-produced products and price controls, drew the general contours of the new export-oriented accumulation regime. The new economic programme was launched during military rule and received enthusiastic support from the representatives of the Turkish bourgeoisie (see Sönmez 1987; Ozan 2011; Yeşilbağ 2015). The 1982 constitution, which brought about the 'technocratization of economic and social issues, centralization for decision-making processes, and domination of executive over legislative and

---

[47] Restoring the political power of the bourgeoisie required disciplining of the left, the labour movement and other forms of democratic opposition. This was done violently, as expressed in the words of Akça (2014: 16): 'Under the military regime, more than 650,000 people were detained; police files were opened on about 1,680,000 people; there were 210,000 political trials, in which 7,000 people faced the death penalty; 50 of 517 death penalties were executed; 300 people died in prisons for allegedly unspecified reasons; 171 people died from torture; 1,680,000 people were classified in police files, 388,000 people were deprived of their right to a passport; 30,000 people were fired from the civil service; 14,000 people lost their citizenship; 39 tonnes of published material were destroyed; and 23,677 associations were closed down'.

judiciary' (Özden, Akça, and Bekmen 2017: 190), drew the institutional contours of the new practices of authoritarian neoliberalism, which established its hegemony under the AKP regime in the following decades up until 2012. The new judicial and political system created with the 1982 constitution limited the political sphere and political participation. This counter-attack by the bourgeoisie, which was backed by the military, was initially put into action by closing down the labour unions and political parties and suppressing the labour movement together with all opposition. Later on, when the labour unions and political parties were allowed to be active again, the former were restricted by new legislation[48], the election threshold was increased to ten per cent, and the ability of political parties to make organic bonds with organized social classes and groups was impaired (Akça 2014). This was made possible by the centralization of executive power and the securitization of politics in general through bodies like the National Security Council (*Milli Güvenlik Kurulu*-MGK), which was directly connected to the prime minister's office. Within this framework, the ideas of the 'sacred state', national security and public order were favoured over the individual and society in legal terms, thus undermining the exercise of political rights and freedoms. Another strategy for establishing the hegemony of the new neoliberal order was the depoliticization of society and the discrediting of the trade union movement, as well as leftist ideology more generally. By doing so, individualism and individual virtues such as being industrious and patriotic were promoted against class-based identities (Yalman 2002; Akça 2014). Real wages declined, and accordingly domestic demand was reduced. Subsidies for agriculture had been cut back, and KİTs could no longer provide high levels of employment. In fact, starting in the 1990s and continuing until the present day (2019), all KİTs had been either privatized or turned into public-private partnerships. The success of the 1980 coup has been described as follows: 'business scepticism was almost totally eradicated, radical aspirations were co-opted or marginalized, and free market society seemed to declare its eventual victory over rival societal visions' (Yeşilbağ 2015: 3). The long-term consequences of neoliberalization for the labour market were further proletarianization and unemployment, increasing job insecurity, declining labour union coverage and density, and falls in wages in general (Çam 2002).

In 1983, the military regime allowed a transition to an electoral system. The Motherland Party (Anavatan Partisi, ANAP), founded by Turgut Özal, came to power in two successive elections in 1983 and 1987 and

---

[48] See more on the topic and on further amendments to this legislation in Chapter 7.

stayed in office until its electoral defeat in 1991.[49] The main pillars of the ANAP regime in this decade could be described as neoliberalism, conservatism and authoritarianism, considered to exemplify the 'New Right' (Özkazanç 1996). This combination allows the free market to be defended by means of an anti-statist, non-interventionist discourse on the one hand, and a strong state with a rhetoric of law and order on the other. This appeals to the wider conservative masses with the promise that gains would come from the modernization project without their having to compromise their identities – the conservative modernization model of the centre-right (Taşkın 2008). Accordingly, individualism, the market, civil society, the family and religious and national bonds were favoured over the provisioning of the welfare state, the market in particular being presented as the miracle solution to all socio-economic problems.

The ANAP government was supported by the different factions of the bourgeoisie, whether secular and religious/conservative or urban middle class. In these years, new professional jobs flourished in newly emerging sectors such as banking, advertising, the media and services, which broadened and diversified the middle class, who became accustomed to the new consumption patterns relatively easily. However, since the country's export-oriented accumulation regime relies on reducing labour costs and disciplining the working population, the living standards and status of the conventional middle classes, such as teachers, deteriorated. This process worsened in the 2010s, resulting in a movement called 'Unappointed Teachers' among whom suicide rates increased significantly, especially given the political pressures and purges of this decade. By the end of the 1980s and early 1990s, wage-labourers were responding to the oppressive market fundamentalism through several major mobilizations. The struggle of civil servants to unionize had led to the spring protests of 1989, and in 1991 the state's pressure on the unions to settle for lower wages in the mining sector led to the one of the largest ever mineworkers' marches, from Zonguldak to Ankara. These events signalled the New Right's failure to establish a neoliberal hegemony. The exclusionary politics directed against Kurds, Alevis, leftists and the impoverishing middle classes also contributed to the failure, since Sunni-Islam-oriented, market-based policies increasingly failed to create consent among these segments (Akça 2014).[50] Although the

---

[49] Turgut Özal remained in office as the president of the country from 1989 until his sudden death in 1993.

[50] Akça (2014) argues that the ANAP attempted to win the consent of the impoverishing middle classes and urban poor by solving the urban housing problem in 1990 through the establishment of the Mass Housing and Public Participation Board (*Toplu Konut İdaresi ve Kamu Ortaklığı Fonu*), into which several state funds were transferred for cheaper housing

mobilization of a Sunni-Islamic identity (see Chapter 3) appealed to the conservative religious social base, the latter was not content with the increasingly consumption-oriented culture that developed in the ANAP period either (Taşkın 2008). On the other hand, both big and medium-size bourgeoisies enjoyed the anti-labour policies of the era. The big bourgeoisie benefitted from export-oriented industrialization, trade liberalization, economic stabilization and financial liberalization after 1989. The ANAP government issued sector- and region-specific incentives, tax reductions, preferential credits and loans to local entrepreneurs on an individual basis to boost industrialization (Bayırbağ 2007). As Chapter 4 will show, these incentives had an important impact on local industries, leading directly and indirectly to the development of the export-oriented manufacture sector, which was often located in the industrial districts. As will also be shown in Chapter 4, the incentives, credits and tax reductions were granted in an informal and clientelistic manner. While the post-1980 regime worked in favour of capital, the financialization of the markets in 1989 created an intra-class cleavage between the big bourgeoisie and the small and medium-size bourgeoisie due to latter's dependence on the former to access finance and loans and to reach and maintain global networks. The ANAP's electoral defeat in 1991 marked the failure of its attempt to restore neoliberal hegemony. It also set the scene for the crisis of hegemony that lasted throughout the 1990s and that could not be resolved by the coalition governments of the period (Özden, Akça, and Bekmen 2017).

The 1990s: The Proliferation of Political Actors and the Crisis of Hegemony

Among the political actors that entered the political scene in the 1990s were the local business associations and chambers. As I have stressed several times, the small and medium-size local bourgeoisies had become more dependent on the big bourgeoisie, especially in the ISI era. The big bourgeoisie, who themselves came from provincial backgrounds such as the Koç, Eczacıbaşı and Sabancı families and holdings, kept up their provincial ties and created more networks of small and medium-size businesses to assemble their products and distribute and franchise them while they held the monopoly of products and international financial connections (Sönmez 2013). These companies had a slim chance of growth without these

---

projects. But according to other research, these only reached the middle classes, not the urban poor. Later on, in 2002, the Housing Development Administration (*Toplu Konut İdaresi-*TOKİ) took over this mission and became an important pillar of consent for the AKP regime at a time when low-interest loans had become available to the masses of urban consumers.

connections, given their limited access to finances. Nevertheless, various authors have emphasized the growing role of small and medium-size enterprises in the economy in provinces such as Konya, Kayseri, Gaziantep, Kahramanmaraş, Denizli and Çorum since the adoption of an export-oriented economic policy model in 1980s (see Chapter 1). Although their political impact outgrew their actual economic success, it is still an open question how they made that leap under circumstances of financial constraints and dependence on the big bourgeoisie. Most of the answers given to this question only attempt to explain what is known as 'Islamic capital' and emphasize the roles of the Welfare Party (Karadağ 2010), of Islamic sects and intra-communal solidarity (Demir, Acar, and Toprak 2004; Yavuz 2006), of the savings of Turkish immigrants abroad (Demir, Acar, and Toprak 2004; Cengiz 2013) and of the promotion of interest-free and hence Islam-friendly banking (Demir, Acar, and Toprak 2004; Demiralp 2009).

Other answers that go beyond the Islamic/secular distinction include the role of accumulated experiences over a longer period of time depending on the socio-economic, geographical and historical circumstances (Cengiz 2013), local entrepreneurs' ability to enter into political negotiations (Bayırbağ 2007) and the establishment and development of industrial districts since the 1990s, when infrastructure and land were provided, and the state reduced taxes and labour costs (Özden, Akça, and Bekmen 2017). However, the limited access to finance remained a problem for small and medium-size local entrepreneurs, whether Islamic or not. Moreover, Demiralp (2009) shows that both Islamic and secular local entrepreneurs were critical of IMF policies because they favour the global financial elite at the cost of the industrial sector. While this criticism is one of the reasons why local Islamic entrepreneurs had supported the Welfare Party for its anti-IMF policies in the 1990s and founded MÜSİAD, findings on MÜSİAD members' attitudes to interest-free banking show that their concerns were not solely based on the Islamic condemnation of interest. Interest-free banking was more appealing because it offered less risky loan options to small and medium-size entrepreneurs than the credits offered by other commercial banks, which come with high interest rates and risk based on the stock exchange (Demiralp 2009). Moreover, Islamic entrepreneurs who did not want to put their money where it could earn interest and preferred to place their money in interest-free banks had provided a safe reserve for loans disbursed to other local companies. Although at first glance it seems as if commercial credits or interest-free bank loans were the only option for those who had shortages of capital and depended on personal savings, more thorough fieldwork showed that for many decades in Çorum many shopkeepers and traders (*esnaf* and *tüccar*) active in the old bazaar areas had operated as interest-free depositories in an unofficial capacity for those wage-labourers, peasants and housewives who did not trust formal banking system to save their money.

In fact, working people's savings have served as rescue capital for local business people (see Chapter 4). Many local entrepreneurs start and expand their businesses by relying on personal loans from their contractors either in kind or in the form of equipment to be paid for later as an in-kind or an end-product, called *vadeli iş*. These types of informal credit relations based on mutual trust are overlooked in many studies. Many of these informal credit mechanisms are not mainly motivated by the Islamic principle that denounces interest as sinful but by a lack of collateral and initial capital, as well as mistrust of formal financial institutions because they are found to be impersonal, risky and unnegotiable. Chapters 4 and 5 describe the variety of ways capital and loans were accessed and contracts were made locally.

By the 1990s, MÜSİAD members had become the vanguards of the Islamist movement represented by the Welfare Party of the time, and they posed a challenge to the secularist principle and the interventions of global actors in the national economy. The Welfare Party advocated the state's withdrawal from heavy industry, an increased share of small and medium-size businesses, and the promotion of an authentic Turkish identity and Muslim ethics in its vision of modernization (White 2012). On the other hand, the Kurdish movement and the associated armed struggle constituted the other pillar of challenge to the militarist Turkish regime throughout the 1990s. In addition to the challenges to secularist and nationalist principles, several failures of coalition governments in the economic, political and social arenas contributed to the crisis of hegemony and led to the sweeping away of all political actors from the parliamentary system in the 2002 elections. The 1990s witnessed three subsequent economic crises: high-interest loans from the banks for public expenditure created deficits and high rates of inflation, causing the bubble to burst in 1994; the Asian financial crisis of 1998, the domestic crises of 2000 and 2001 to which it led. Moreover, the regime's accountability and efficiency had been deeply damaged by the public exposure of the 'deep-state' secrets of mafia leaders within the state body and the armed forces after a car crash in Susurluk in 1996, as well as state's proven incompetence in dealing with the devastating destruction of the aftermath of the Yalova/Gölcük earthquake in 1999. The military intervention pressing for the withdrawal of the Necmettin Erbakan-led coalition government from parliament on 28 February 1997, while succeeding in bringing down the Welfare Party, also contributed to the legitimacy of the political claims of the Islamist movement in the public eye. The political and economic turmoil throughout the 1990s negatively affected local capital accumulation in the provinces, and especially after the so-called 'post-modern coup' of 1997, MÜSİAD-associated local businesses faced some pressure. On the other hand, the pro-business atmosphere brought local business associations forward as legitimate actors in the representation of local concerns. Turkey's agreement with the Customs Union in 1995 was another driving force for local economies to initiate political activism through business associations (Bayırbağ 2007). This includes not only associations like MÜSİAD or others with different political agendas, but Chambers of Industry and Trade that are connected to the TOB and that represent all the businesses that are registered in one city. Hence, as the Çorum case will also show (see Chapter 4), the boosting of local economies cannot be attributed solely to Islamist political connections, although they played an important role in other cities, such as Konya and Kayseri, less so in the cases of Gaziantep and Çorum.

The AKP Era: Capitalism A La Turca?

After the economic crisis of 2001, Kemal Derviş, former head of the United Nations Development Program and a senior World Bank economist, was summoned to Turkey by the then Prime Minister, Bülent Ecevit, and was later appointed the Minister of Economic Affairs with a brief to implement strict IMF prescriptions, produce macro-economic stability and introduce a series of reforms to the banking system.

In the meantime, a group of young reformists within the Welfare Party had detached themselves to form the AKP. Unlike its antecedents in the National Outlook/Welfare Party, which was anti-EU, anti-globalization and openly Islamist, the AKP advocated moderately Islamist, outward-looking, pro-European Union and pro-globalization policies under the leadership of Recep Tayyip Erdoğan, who had been the mayor of Istanbul since 1994. In 2002, the recently founded AKP was elected to a parliamentary majority and since then has ruled Turkey single-handedly. In its founding years, the AKP seemed to offer a synthesis of liberal desire for reform and conservative cultural sensitivities. This helped bring together business, the urban poor and its pious constituents, as well as being granted the overall consent of the non-Islamist sections of the political spectrum to pursue the new economic programme and the negotiation process for entry into the EU, which then seemed to be on track. The AKP responded to national and international pressure by taking certain steps to promote democracy in Turkey. A strong Kemalist state opposed to the excluded religious civil-society argument and the libertarian defence of freedom of expression and of the abolition of military tutelage over civilian affairs constitute the main ideological basis for the AKP's support and its legitimacy. However, the AKP that was celebrated as the democratizing potential of Muslims at the beginning of the 2000s is today regarded as an authoritarian populist party which has established effective one-man rule with the consent of the many behind its back, enabling it to undermine the checks and balances of the political system in several referendums. In this period, many acquired cheap housing in an economy that relies mainly on the construction sector and low-interest consumption loans. Moreover, increasing social spending and expanding the social services have contributed to the consent the AKP has received, a phenomenon some identify with 'social neoliberalism' (Öniş 2012: 5). At the same time, most of the privatizations of public assets, natural resources, and health and education have been achieved in this period, as has the gentrification and urban transformation that uprooted many from their original neighbourhoods and pushed them to the outskirts. The AKP has also been quite destructive of labour rights (see Chapter 7), women's rights, environmental rights and the right to freedom of speech and information, all of which led to the Gezi protests in 2013, one of the largest protests of the republican era. Almost all media channels are now monopolized by the AKP state or its offshoot companies. Many students, political opponents and journalists are behind the bars. Around 125,000 civil servants[51] were dismissed from their positions and stripped off their citizenship rights due to allegations of terrorism after the attempted coup of 15 July 2016. Foreign deficits have reached their highest peak in a long time, as have unemployment rates, interest rates, household debt and the prices of consumption goods. Companies are going bankrupt, and many new construction projects are being left unfinished, with brand-new apartments being left empty. All in all, the AKP has failed those of its allies and supporters who put their hopes in democratization and prosperity under its rule. One important aspect of this hope found its voice in the debate that surfaced simultaneously with the AKP coming to power, namely the debate over the compatibility of Islam and capitalism, which also relates to the emergence of the 'Anatolian Tiger' as an affirmation of prospering 'Muslims'. Even though I problematized this particular assumption as an ideological endeavour and showed how capitalist factions evolved in the 2000s in the Introduction, here I would like to provide an overview of how the relationship between Islam, capitalism and politics in the AKP period has been discussed by different scholars.

---

[51] Information retrieved from the link: https://www.bik.gov.tr/15-temmuzdan-bugune-kamudan-ihrac-edilenlerin-sayisi/ on March 2019.

One of the most best known theses on the relationship of economy and religion is that of Max Weber, who regarded religion as an independent variable and found an affinity between Protestantism and the spirit of capitalism. Based on the doctrine of predestination, Calvinists work hard, methodically and systematically in the hope of being saved (Weber 2001a). However, in his study of world religions, Weber states clearly that the '[Islamic] economic ethic is simply feudal' (Weber 1992: 91), the 'complete opposite of the whole Puritan ethic' (ibid.). He argued that inner-worldliness hardly exists in Islam and that there is no individual search for salvation. It is therefore very interesting to see Islamic entrepreneurs' testimonies appearing in the European Stability Initiative Report in 2005, describing their communities with reference to Calvinism and the Protestant work ethic, and claiming that 'it is good for a religious person to work hard', and that 'to open a factory is a kind of prayer' (ESI 2005: 75). These voices stressed the values of hard-work and self-sufficiency, thrift and investment, to the business and the community. Apart from the ideological rebranding of Muslim democrats that this specific European think-tank was aiming at, the Muslim entrepreneurs' reactions could also be read as a response to Weber's culturally essentialist distinction between modern Western capitalism and 'other' capitalisms (Yanagisako 2002), in which they state that their beliefs are not impediments to their profit-seeking, rational economic behaviour.

In fact, many other scholars have responded to Weber's claims by examining the relationship between Islam and the development of capitalism. Turner argued that Weber, in his analysis of world religions, is 'not narrowly causal' (Turner 2013: 18), and that he studies 'the relations of most important religions to economic life and the social stratification of their environment, to follow out both causal relationships' (Weber 2001b: xl). Rodinson (1973), on the other hand, points to the problem that Muslims and Europeans sympathetic to Islam are concerned to show that Islamic tradition is not a impediment to the adoption of modern economic methods and that it actually promises a basis of social and economic justice, as illustrated in the above example, and that those who are unsympathetic to Islam tend to picture its tradition wrongly as forbidding Muslims any modern economic pursuit. Both perspectives assume that the Muslims of a particular era in a particular region are conditioned by a previous doctrine that was shaped independently of them and that has remained the same despite the immense transformation in the conditions of life, while Muslims go through these changes without adapting to them (Rodinson 1973). Each perspective is doctrine-based, static and essentialist to the extent that it ignores the historical, political and economic circumstances in which Muslims engage in capitalist activities. There are, however, works that show both 'causal' relationships and shed light on the specific constellation of dynamics underpinning the relations between Islam, capitalism and politics, in this case in the AKP era in Turkey.

Cihan Tuğal (2009), for example, based on his ethnographic research on the political organization of Islam in the 2000s, argues that the religious bourgeoisie has established its hegemony over large pious segments of the working classes through Islamist political activity, which, as a result, has absorbed the radicalism; that is, the potential of the pious working classes to challenge Western capitalism is said to have been dismantled. A different perspective on the idea of absorption comes from a radical political Islamist, Kaplan (2002), who argues that the metaphor of Islamic Calvinism is irrelevant because for him the rationalization of Islam indicates that Islam is losing its political claim by being removed from the political sphere altogether. Contrary to Kaplan's perspective, Demirpolat (2002), based on his study of religion and enterprises in Konya, argues against the claim that Islam is being removed from the political sphere through rationalization. Rather, he asserts that the driving force behind the rationalization of Islam is the project of Islamic political elites, intellectuals and Islamist modernists in general. It is not religious beliefs that are intrinsic to Islam, but the will to power of political elites that has motivated the practices that integrated Islamic values and modern capitalism in the example of the 'Anatolian Tigers'. In this line of reasoning, Islam is said to have been instrumentalized for political purposes. A radical and well-known Marxist critique is that of Durak (2011), again based on his short-term ethnographic study of Konya. He opposes the claims about both the rationalization and the instrumentalization of Islam in the last twenty years in Turkey because they imply that Islamic ethics, though in essence very naïve, nonetheless became instrumental in the hands of pious entrepreneurs and politicians. Rather, he argues that attributing meanings to religion has always been an instrument of the bourgeoisie.

Buğra and Savaşkan's analysis offers more on the nature of the relationship between business people and the state, and on how such relationships become meaningful in market situations. As I have previously suggested, the relations of business people to the state have always been particularistic, though they have shifted towards favouritism as the AKP has consolidated its political power in the last two decades (Buğra and Savaşkan 2010, 2014). At the same time, business associations have become political actors themselves (ibid.). The relationship is not limited to favouring one businessman over another or to placing adherents at different levels of governance, but more importantly it involves the governing party's ability to make exceptional amendments to the laws in favour of the business people who support it. These scholars also argue that national and municipal biddings are being manipulated through a number of changes made to the Public Tender Bidding Law, so that the different stages of the construction and provision of both national and municipal public services are subcontracted over and over again to supportive companies or companies that belong to the municipalities. In other words, religion plays the role of a network resource in building trust, while the affirmation of an Islamic religious identity is integral to building solidarity, excluding others who do not share a similar religious identity or political belonging.

Contrary to Buğra and Savaşkan's argument regarding new business people becoming political actors themselves, Düzgün (2012) asserts that the 'rise' of a conservative bourgeoisie was possible because since the mid-1990s the political forms of state support have been eliminated, and therefore 'economic policy-making was ... "depoliticized" – that is, "liberalized" – from popular pressures' (ibid.: 138). Düzgün contends that in the last two decades a separation between the political and the economic has occurred in Turkey in which, '[w]ith private property secured and reproduced competitively, the bourgeoisie has finally become a fully capitalist class' (ibid.: 141). Therefore, the emphasis on the Prophet being a trader or the fact that Quranic verses have been interpreted in a way that justifies economic competition and ensures trust in the fairness of market outcomes (ibid.: 137) 'should be thought of in the context of restructuring of state power, cultural values and human subjectivities in such ways as to guarantee and promote capital accumulation, rather than constituting a buffer against commodification' (ibid.: 142). Once again, we see that Düzgün observes a certain instrumentalization of Islam. On the other hand, as opposed to those who argue for the compatibility of Islam and capitalism as a process of democratization in Turkey, Düzgün underlines the ongoing authoritative nature of the Turkish state and argues that there is an 'inherent incompatibility of democracy with capitalism and human emancipation' (ibid.). In light of his analysis, Düzgün calls developments after the 1990s capitalist modernity *à la Turca*. Karadağ (2013) harshly criticizes Düzgün's arguments by highlighting how political connections still matter in economic success with specific reference to the findings of Buğra and Savaşkan (2014) elaborated above. He also argues that, within the oligarchic nature of capitalism (Karadağ 2010) in post-1980 Turkey, 'both politicians and entrepreneurs are bound to political business making' (Karadağ 2013: 150).

Chapter 3
Shifting Trajectories of Turkish National Identity: A Debate on Turkish Islam, Islamism and *Laiklik*

Introduction

What I called an 'emergent orthodoxy' in the Introduction regarding the scholarly analysis of 'Anatolian Tigers' is part of a larger near-hegemonic 'meta-narrative' (Kandiyoti 2012: 515) that constitutes a particular reading of the republican history of Turkey, or of its modernization starting in the late Ottoman period, based on a dichotomy between state and society. This meta-narrative was originally inspired by Şerif Mardin (1973), who used a different terminology and thought in terms of a centre/periphery dichotomy as the key to understanding Turkish politics, a dichotomy that corresponds to that between the secular Kemalist state and its Muslim constituents. Accordingly, it is possible to narrate the Turkish history as Muslim society's struggle against the secular Kemalist state, which stood for authoritarianism, militarism and unaccountability, and was challenged by Muslims who hold the democratizing potential that is equated with religious expansionism. As I shall show in this chapter, this 'meta-narrative' had also been central to how scholars discuss Islam and secularization, though it also created a divide between secularism and Islam 'of dubious utility from an analytical point of view' (Kandiyoti 2012: 514) that 'distorted our understanding of reality and the actual practices of politics' (Lord 2018: 5).

In this chapter, my aim is to challenge this meta-narrative by reviewing research, mainly in anthropology, sociology, history and political science, that provides the counter evidence and to guide the reader through an alternative way of thinking about secularization, Islam and religiosity in Turkey. To be able to illustrate the reforms that form the basis of the 'centre versus periphery' framework, first I would like to draw a very general picture of the Ottoman governance system before mapping out the changes to the institutions of Islam in the late Ottoman period and further in the early republican era. In what follows, I shall discuss the main criticisms directed at Turkish modernization and Turkish secularism (*laiklik*) that embraced that framework. After setting out the arguments of the 'meta-narrative', I shall point out their analytical problems and actual practices as criticized by other scholars. After providing some general information on the fundamentals and rules of Islam as a religion, I will elaborate on the actual institutions and practices of Islam in Turkey and draw special attention to the historical conjuncture in which Turkish Islamism emerged. I show that whatever constitutes Turkish national identity has always been based on ethnic Turkishness and Sunni majoritarianism, although which comes first in the order has changed throughout the republican era. I proceed with previous ethnographic findings on how secular and Islamic ideas were played out in the public sphere in different periods and how both responded to neoliberalization. My aim is to draw attention to the blurriness of the distinction between secular and Islamic and to show how political identities transcend these binaries. In the final part, I provide a short overview on who the Alevis are and the debate on the origins and content of Alevism, explaining their 'ambivalent' status in relation to Turkish national identity.

The Ottoman Governance System and the Late Ottoman Reforms

The Ottoman Empire was a multinational and multilingual empire governed by a sultanate resembling an absolute monarchy, in which the Sultan had absolute power and from the sixteenth century was the Caliph of the whole Islamic world. The Ottoman governance system is generally described as theocratic because Islam was the state religion and the Sultan was at the same time both the Caliph and an absolute monarch. On the other hand, many historians contest these two definitions. Berkes (2002), for instance, argues that the Ottoman system had features of despotism rather than absolute monarchy. The source of the state's legitimacy derived from the inheritability of the power that had been acquired by the conquest and seizure of both lands and people, such that the state was regarded as a patrimony. This is also how Ibn-i Haldun defined this model, which Berkes (2002) calls *padişahlık rejimi* (sultanate regime). The most important feature of the model is the supreme political power that is based on the support of masses of *kul* (literally slaves, but here meaning subjects) and the *reaya* (the tax-paying lower classes), who are stripped of their political agency and even alienated. The model did come to resemble a theocracy when the caliphate was merged with the sultanate in the sixteenth century, and it acquired even more importance after the eighteenth century. However, there are objections to this interpretation as well. Unlike theocratic regimes, in the Ottoman Empire the state's affairs had supremacy over the affairs of religion. The *Kazasker* (chief military judge) and the *Şeyhülislam* (head of the *Ulema*, the religious elites), who were the leading religious authorities, had to be consulted over judgements in Sharia law concerning certain state affairs, though they did not have the final word (Berkes 2002). Thus, to claim that a certain state issue was solely a religious matter on which the state could not intervene was most unusual. Furthermore, there is a consensus among scholars that the Ottoman state did not impose Islamic state ideology to the conquered lands, namely those marked by the fall of the East Roman Empire after the conquest of Consantinople in the fifteenth century, of Greece and the Balkans in the sixteenth, and further in Balkans and towards the Red Sea of Saudi Arabia and Iran and the North African coast in the second half of the same century.

Although Islam was thus the state religion, other major religious communities living under the Ottoman state were treated as distinct *millets*. The *millet* system regulated non-Muslim ethno-religious communities and also guaranteed each religious group their own representatives and autonomous courts. Accordingly, non-Muslims were tacitly given secondary status requiring them to pay a special tax. The *millet* system was applied to multi-ethnic and multi-religious groups, and as long as they paid their taxes and were obedient subjects, the Ottoman state did not require them to convert to Islam. However, retrospectively claiming that this was a multicultural society would be far-fetched given that interaction between the different *millets* was limited and Ottoman subjects were not equal, nor did they have equal rights to exercise political agency. The duty of the state was to ensure that each ethno-religious group (*millet*) lived in security and order, in other words, in *istikrar* (permanence), which provided the regime with its legitimacy. Since the legitimacy of the political regime relied on *istikrar* in both heaven and earth, as Zürcher (1993) notes the notion of change was received with suspicion. However, this would change in the eighteenth century and even more so in the nineteenth.

Ortaylı's book *The Longest Century of the Empire* starts with a claim that Ottoman modernization cannot be limited to the *Tanzimat* (restoration) period (Ortaylı 2006) that was kicked off in 1839 with the declaration of the Edict of Gülhane. The main principles of the edict were legal equality for all subjects and a guarantee of security of life and property for all, replacing tax-farming with means-based systematic taxing and introducing obligatory military service. Already in the eighteenth century, under the reigns of Selim III and Mahmut II, reforms were carried out regarding the modernization of the military, the centralization of the state, and the introduction of modern finance and of an education system. However, the reforms of the *Tanzimat* period were more radical, shifting the balance of power from the palace to the bureaucracy and established institutions in which a new generation of intellectuals and reformers were trained. As Ortaylı (2006) puts it, the wave of modernization should also not be thought as applying only to Ottoman Anatolia (or Turkey today), but should be understood as a process that was happening simultaneously in other regions of the empire, as well as in non-Muslim communities, and in Russia and among Muslims in India. In his perspective, the desire for modernization was driven by the observations of Ottoman bureaucrats and intellectuals of the changing world around them and their willingness to adapt, independently of the pressures of the Western powers to establish their superiority in relation to the rest of the world.

Contrary to this perspective, Zürcher (1993) draws more attention to the external factors that led to the wave of modernization and to the increasing influence of the West over the Empire in various areas. Accordingly, the Empire's integration into the world capitalist system (see Chapter 2), the increasing political influence of the West over the Empire and the strengthening of ideologies such as nationalism, liberalism, secularism and positivism created a reaction in the Ottoman government which led to attempts to centralize the state, to which different segments of society responded. However, the insistence of the Ottoman government on implementing the *Tanzimat* principles in the face of the popular unrest it had created by granting legal and equal status to non-Muslims indicates that, without the state's willingness, such a reform of the political system would not have been possible if it had merely been a response to the West's political pressure. Still, the *Tanzimat* reformers maintained their traditionalism and caution about the West while trying to respond to the demands of the changing world (Ortaylı 2006). All in all, the nineteenth-century reforms established equal citizenship (1839), constitutionalism (1876), the secularization of the law and education, and the introduction of the first Civil Code (1870-1876), thereby creating a shift away from Islamic law in matters of the family. Moreover, modernization in the military and the efforts to establish a modern state apparatus through the adoption of a central administration based on the French system, the creation of a central taxation system and a mailing service, as well as conducting a census, took place in this era. The transformation that the modernization process created in the institutions, individuals and social and political organization of society and the state reveal the essence of the reforms, which were spread over the 'longest century of the empire'. Hence, when the republic was declared in 1923, the new political regime took over a social and institutional structure and a society that had already been going through these painful processes in the previous century.

The Republican Reforms and Criticisms of Them

The Republican Reforms

The founders of the republic, their background and ideas date back to the reformist period of the late Ottoman Empire, which inevitably shows continuity in terms of political thought and ideologies (Kasaba 1997). However, republican reformists were even more radical than their predecessors: in fact, one of the reasons behind republican radicalism was the idea that late Ottoman reforms were not radical enough (Ortaylı 2006). The founders of the republic were very much influenced by French positivism (Magnarella et al. 1976) and German institutionalism (Aydın 2001). They saw modernization as almost synonymous with Westernization. They anticipated progress by mobilizing the masses through secular education and the institutionalization of education, the sciences and the military, bureaucracy and economy, as well as industrial development and the accumulation of wealth. Parallel to the modernist paradigm of the time, they were dedicated to a linear understanding of history in which all of these would eventually result in secularization, urbanization, democratization and development, and ultimately the nation would reach a higher civilization. In addition, Muslim intellectuals and politicians of the 1930s, not only in Turkey but also in Iran and Egypt, identified Islam as a force that was hindering progress in the Islamic world (Fischer 1982).

Among the principles of the founding ideology, Turkish nationalism and laicism[52] constituted the two main pillars of the republican reforms and signalled the breaks and shifts from the Ottoman Empire. Both of these principles entailed a break with the Islamic past and aimed to create citizens who identify initially with their Turkish roots and practice Sunni Islam as regulated by the state. Implementation of these changes at the legislative and executive levels first involved the abolition of the Sultanate in 1922, thus paving the way to the declaration of the republic in 1923. The republic took the constitutional reforms of the previous century one step further by abolishing the dual system of sultanate and parliament, thereby completely removing the remnants of the previous regime, which rooted its legitimacy

---

[52] Laicism, *laiklik* in Turkish, is from the French *laïcité*, or the principle of separation of the church (religion) and state. It differs from Anglo-Saxon secularism for its insistence on the removal of religious symbols from public institutions (Toprak 2005). I use *laiklik* to refer to a certain interpretation of 'Turkish secularism' because 'laiklik in Turkey is an ambivalent, partial, and inconsistent form of laicism' (Davison 2003: 339). I follow Andrew Davison's view of the concept, which will be elaborated further, this particular choice being explained in more detail, in the upcoming parts. When I write simply 'secularism', it is to avoid repeating the Turkish word.

in the order of Allah, and officially declared the sovereignty of the people. Although this entailed a number of inner conflicts along ethnic and religious lines, with this declaration the subjects of the empire became the citizens of a republic.

The abolition of the sultanate was also a move to delegitimize the Istanbul government, which had already not participated in the war of independence, from representing what was left of the Ottoman state in diplomatic negotiations over the Lausanne Treaty. Ankara became the capital city where the first parliament was installed. In 1924, the caliphate was also abolished; the same year, religious schools (*medrese*s that functioned under *Vakıf*s), the office of *Şeyhülislam*, the Ministry of Religious Affairs and Pious Foundations and the sharia courts were closed down, followed by the outlawing of the religious orders in 1925. The functions of these institutions were replaced by the adoption of the Civil Code (1926), the unification of all schools[53] under the Ministry of Education (1924) to provide a public secular education, and the establishment of *Diyanet*, the Ministry of Religious Affairs (1924). Secularism in the Turkish case, as in its French version, implied the removal of religious symbols from all public institutions. Accordingly, dress codes in public institutions were changed, and wearing a fez (a kind of hat officially worn by bureaucrats and the military) or a *sarık* (a turban worn by religious scholars) in public was banned (1925).[54] The lunar Muslim calendar was changed to the Gregorian

---

[53] Including missionary schools that belonged to non-Muslim minorities.

[54] There was no official ban on women's covering at the time, but women were seen as the carriers of the pro-Western reforms and were encouraged to dress in line with republican ideals, that is, with hair uncovered and in Western style. Only after the 1960s did a few covered women attending universities spark a public discussion. After the 1980 military coup, the National Security Council outlawed women working in public institutions from wearing the *başörtüsü* (head cover), and later the same rule was applied to universities, both students and staff. The ban became stricter after the political intervention of the military against what they saw as the threat of political Islam (*irtica*) in 28 February 1997. The problem manifested itself most vividly in the universities at the end of 1990s, when Istanbul University, one of the oldest universities in Istanbul, with ten thousands of students, issued a by-law banning covered women's entering the university and posting inspectors at its gates. The ban mobilized many young *başörtülü* (head-covered) women students to organize political protests, and some played a crucial role in the rise of AKP. The *başörtüsü* (head-cover) ban was lifted in 2013 by the AKP, eleven years after its coming into force. For further discussion of this topic, see the works of Göle (1996) for the veiling movement and the complexities of the public sphere, religion and sexuality; Saktanber and Çorbacıoğlu (2008) for headscarf-scepticism; and Cindoğlu and Zencirci (2008) for a gender perspective on the topic. A very recent political movement, however, has gone in the opposite direction. An online-based solidarity group, *Yalnız Yürümeyeceksin* ('You shall not walk alone'), started initially by covered young women who told their *açılma* ('uncovering' in a literal sense, but also 'coming-out') stories on Twitter, encourages other young women to question the rules of

calendar, and the weekly holiday was changed from Friday, the rest day for Muslims in the rest of the world, to Sunday.[55] Finally, the clause in the 1924 constitution declaring Islam to be the state religion was removed in 1928.

According to the 1924 constitution[56], the official language of the new state would be Turkish.[57] Unlike Ottoman Turkish, which had been written in the Arabic script, the new official Turkish was to be written in the Latin script and to be purified of its Persian and Arabic elements (1928). Republican reforms entailed a social and cultural transformation that aimed at Turkification in line with the ideology of the new nation state, which promoted social integration and loyalty to the Turkish state above any other loyalties to class or ethnic group. The Turkish Historical Society (1931) and the Turkish Linguistic Society (1932) were given the mission of rewriting the origins and content of Turkish history and language respectively, which were claimed to be rooted in Central Asia.[58] The Quran was translated from Arabic into Turkish in Latin script in 1932, and the call for prayer was made in Turkish until the Democrat Party won its majority in 1950. Executive and legislative reforms, as well as interventions in the institutions of religion and how it is practised in daily life, constituted the main areas of reform along with nationalization in the Empire's transformation into a secular republic.

Criticisms of Turkish Modernization and Laiklik

Turkish modernization has been cited frequently in the literature on modernization[59] as an example of a relatively successful process of secular modernization and state-building in a Muslim majority society which had inspired many independence movements in the Muslim 'Third-World'.

Islam and tradition and supports those who want to uncover, a practice which they argue frees Muslim women from oppression.

[55] See Chapter 8 for a detailed discussion on the establishment of the working days and the rest day(s).

[56] This remained in force until the 1960 *coup d'état*.

[57] Minority languages are still protected by the Lausanne Treaty. This excludes languages such as Kurdish and Assyrian, which were not counted among the minorities subject to the Treaty.

[58] This was followed by opening of departments of Anthropology in Istanbul University in 1925 and Ankara University in 1935. The interest in anthropology was closely related to the need to discover Turkish roots and ancestors whose culture was moulded in the cradle of civilization, even before Islam, which was considered a diversion from the true path of Turkish civilization (Aydın 2001: 345). The institutionalization of sciences was crucial in claiming the Turkishness of the Anatolian population and hence building up the national identity of the citizens of the new Republic. For a more sophisticated and detailed analysis of the role of anthropology in the Republican era, see Toprak (2012).

[59] Well-known examples include Bernard Lewis's *The Emergence of Modern Turkey* (1961) and Daniel Lerner's *The Passing of Traditional Society* (1958).

Western norms, ideals and institutions, along with the longer process of modernization since the nineteenth century, have inspired the development of 'modern' forms of education, law, social life, clothing, music, architecture and the arts at the heart of Anatolia. On the other hand, since the 1970s critical voices grew louder and more comprehensive, especially in the 1990s, influenced by the relativism of the postmodernist critique. Ranging from defenders of the liberal economy to Islamist politicians to feminists, critics publicly denounced Turkish modernization in general for being a patriarchal, undemocratic, authoritarian and top-down project. Some would add that it had alienated its own people from their historical and cultural roots, while others depict it as having been far from a success story and rather as a historical failure instead – more popularly in the discourse of Islamist politicians and the media as 'a ninety-year long commercial break' – that will soon be ended by the AKP, which will return to the original Islamic-Turkish nationalist roots of the people. The latter criticism not only ignores the reforms made after 1923 but also the late-Ottoman reforms, with their uninformed idealization of the imperial order, to an extent that denies modernity altogether.

Nevertheless, historical research has shown that, despite the problematic aspects of the modernization process, the 'institutional, ritual, symbolic, and aesthetic manifestations of modernity have become a constituent element of the Turkish collective consciousness since the 1920s' (Bozdoğan and Kasaba 1997: 5). This leaves us with some questions: How can one and the same historical process be a success story and a historical failure at the same time? Or more importantly, do we, as anthropologists, have to operate with these binaries? If modernity somehow succeeded in constituting the collective consciousness of Turkish citizens, how do we then deal with the wide range of relativist critiques of the country's modernization history or vice versa? Appleby, Hunt and Jacob (2011) offer a perspective that might resolve this problem. They rightly point out that the extreme relativism and cynicism of postmodern thought makes any 'truth' unattainable, whereas *healthy skepticism* encourages social scientists to learn more, discover errors and make connections between events. They argue that the fact that different groups or nations have their own versions of the truth or that there are shifting perspectives in historiography does not mean that certain situations and events cannot be known with certainty. Following Appleby, Hunt and Jacob's criticisms of relativism, against those critics that deem Turkish modernization a 'historical failure', Bozdoğan and Kasaba (2007: 6) suggest that we 'distinguish between modernity as a potentially liberating historical condition and its instrumentalization for a political project of domination... [and] distinguish between the democratic implications of the recent postmodern critique, on the one hand, and its self-closure into a new form of orthodoxy on the other'. My view of Turkish modernization is guided by healthy scepticism that questions new orthodoxies, addresses conflicting claims by utilizing research findings, and distinguishes between the liberating potential of modernity and its instrumentalization for domination, while setting out its failures in the actual processes of its unfolding. This is also how I will approach the debate over secularism, Islam and religiosity in Turkey.

Some critiques of *laiklik* (Turkish secularism) take the form of these new orthodoxies, treated by scholars as a 'meta-narrative'. Similar to critiques of modernization in general, *laiklik* became a particularly contested topic, discussed in mutually exclusive and contradictory terms (Somer 2013). To provide a clearer picture, Somer (2013) nicely summarizes the main trends in the above-mentioned discussion. The first criticism, represented mainly in the works of Hakan Yavuz (2000, 2003) and still a widespread popular view, argues that the Turkish state has been hostile to religion, creating an undemocratic tension between the state elites and the Muslim-conservative majority. According to Yavuz (2000: 21), 'Modern Turkey, like a transgendered body with the soul of one gender in the body of another, is in constant tension.... The soul of white Turkey[60] and its Kemalist identity is in constant pain and conflict with the national body politic of Turkey'. In later writings, Yavuz contends that the Muslim imagination is composed of a set of social, moral and political cognitive maps that are based on Islamic idioms and practices. Therefore, the 'state-centric elite failed effectively to penetrate and transform traditional society, and was similarly unsuccessful in developing an alternative value system and associational life for the rural population of the country' (Yavuz 2003: 4). Thanks to the political and economic liberalization of the 1980s, Yavuz argues that hitherto excluded groups were able to find political

---

[60] Demiröz and Öncü (2005) argue that the term 'white Turk' or 'white Turkey' came into circulation in the media and daily language in mid-1990s as part of a reaction on the part of privileged, educated, urban, middle-class Turks to the increasing presence of rural migrants in the metropolitan cities. The authors point out that the appropriation of the American terminology distinguishing Black and White had to do with freeing the American image and values from the anti-imperialist debates of the previous era and the consequent encouragement of consumerism, thus increasing the value of combining new opportunities with education for success and wealth in the imagery of a new urban Turkish entrepreneur/businessmen. In the counter-hegemonic definition, black Turks signify the poor masses who depend on their labour. However, in both formulations Kurdishness is subsumed into the categories as a sub-category of privileged urban or poor masses. For a detailed assessment of the term's connotations see Öncü (1999), Demiröz and Öncü (2005) and also Ünlü (2018) for a comprehensive reading of Turkish history through the lenses of White/Black studies.

representation, so that Islamists were 'not fuelled by a deep-seated rage and frustration with the authoritarian policies of the secular elites, as is the case in Algeria and Egypt' (ibid.). Rather, in his view, 'Islamic social movements are central agents for promoting a democratic and pluralistic society and that the Turkish example holds long-term promise for the rest of the Muslim world as well' (ibid.), a view shared by a number of scholars listed by Yavuz, such as Nilüfer Göle, İsmail Kara, Şerif Mardin and Mete Tunçay. In this line of thought, most significant religious orders such as the Nakşibendi and Nurcu are considered to be society-centric, oriented from below, 'civil-society' associations that target (private) education, economy and the media in their attempts to achieve integration (ibid.: 32). However, in reality, as Yavuz (2003) himself also points out, the institutions of these 'society-centric' religious orders were funded by the central state, some working with the national intelligence agency, their ideologies having acquired nationalistic elements in the process of their propagation in Turkey (Tuğal 2004; Şen 2010).

The second main criticism distinguishes between assertive and passive secularism and argues that the former, as defended by the Republican People's Party, the military and high court judges, aimed to remove religion from the public sphere and push it into the private sphere. In this view, while assertive secularism wants to neutralize any public role for religion, passive secularists who are moderate Islamists such as the AKP or the Gülen movement promote the state's neutrality towards various religions and its establishment, but are in favour of the public visibility of religion. Based on this distinction, the struggle between 'passive secularists' and 'assertive secularists' has shaped public policies (Kuru 2007: 571). A similar analogy could be found in work by Göle (1997), who uses the terminology of Kemalist elites and counter-elites to refer to the same struggle. In her view, counter-elites are Islamists who aim to redefine the 'authenticity' of Islam by going back to the original references without being apologetic to Western modernity, and they reject both traditionalism and modernity. Paradoxically, they are the products of a modern secular education and of urbanization, just like the Kemalist elites, but they owe their political identity to Islamization since the 1950s. According to her, once Islamists 'acquire a professional identity, as engineers or intellectuals, the more the realms of the sacred and the profane will be separate' (Göle 1997: 58), meaning secularized. While Göle retains the reservation that the Islamist political agenda differs from the other social movements for its lack of pluralism and its claim to exert moral control over the public space, making it a potential threat to secularism, freedom of speech and the press, she also sees the secularization of Islamists as a process that will initiate a public discussion between the two groups of elites over public policies and thereby create an opportunity for democratization and a more passive form of secularism.

In both of these critiques – whether the state was hostile to Islam or wanted to remove it from the public sphere or both – Islamism in general is understood to be a bottom-up reaction by the people to the authoritarian secularism of the Kemalist regime. The argument is generally based on the dichotomy between state and society[61], being associated more particularly with the centre vs. periphery dichotomy that Şerif Mardin, one of the leading figures of Weberian sociology in Turkey, introduced in 1973. According to this, every society has a centre, which refers to the elites who are the carriers of the cultural and institutional power of the institutional structure that is built upon the dominant values and belief systems of that society. Applied to Turkish society, the centre is constituted by the Kemalist bureaucracy, which is the carrier of the modernization project, and the periphery refers very generally to rural populations, who are the subjects of modernization but are at the same time identified with backwardness and traditionalism. Mardin explains the rupture between the centre and the periphery as an outcome of the gradual abandonment of all religious institutions, from the nineteenth-century reforms to the republic, as a result of which society lost its connection to the state. That is why, according to Mardin, with the establishment of the republic, 'an Islamic, unifying dimension had again been added to the peripheral code; what had thus became a characteristic ideology of the periphery' (Mardin 1973: 178).

Accordingly, Muslim 'society' is depicted as an undifferentiated entity in itself associated with a periphery that is inherently Islamic, classless and free of any ethnic or denominational differences. On the other hand, the paradigm also ignores the fact that throughout republican history Muslims in general and Islamists in particular (since 1960s) have acquired the political and economic power to approach the 'centre', while capitalism and modernity have become more localized (Açıkel 2006). However, within this peculiar combination of hegemonic and dichotomized readings of Turkish

---

[61] This represents another hegemonic paradigm regarding the nature of the state in Turkey, generally referred as 'the strong state tradition' (Heper 1985). 'The strong state tradition' is a peculiar reading of Ottoman-Turkish history as an institutional and ideological continuum in which the bourgeoisie is weak against the state and the tension between the bourgeoisie and the civilian and military bureaucracy is the only motor of social change. Accordingly, the state then is depicted as an entity in itself capable of imposing its power on all segments of society even at odds with the dominant classes, while 'the class-based nature of the state and the political sphere is covered up to the extent that the connections between these are ignored' (Akça Bekmen Özden 2014: 3). I try to offer a different reading of this in Chapter 2. For a more detailed analysis and critique of the notion of a 'strong state tradition', see Yalman (2002a; 2002b) and Dinler (2003).

history, Islam is associated with the 'people' of the periphery, whereas secularism is associated with the elites at the centre and is described 'as a non-Muslim way of life' (Göle 1997: 47) that some scholars describe as being at odds with democracy. Over the years, 'Muslims' as political, economic and cultural 'outcasts' have been articulated in the discourses of Islamist politicians, who 'pitted this reified construction of the people (of Islam) against the state, *as if* there has been no historical relations between the two' (Navaro-Yashin 2002: 144, original emphasis).[62] Thus, the victory of the AKP in 2002 has been understood as the 'periphery' approaching to the 'centre' through a process of democratization (Yavuz 2000, 2003; İnsel 2003; Kuru and Stephan 2012). This is the framework which explains why the rise of provincial and/or peripheral economies was understood in a similar manner (see Introduction).

This '*as if*' situation is voiced by those who came up with the third critique of *laiklik*, arguing that Turkish secularism both controls and promotes Islam. I also place myself within this group. This third critique contends that the first and second critiques of *laiklik* are methodologically and theoretically incompatible with their empirical findings, since their claims are testable. Somer writes: 'This can be done for example by counting changes in the number of mosques, identifying state involvement in their construction, and observing other religion-related state practices in public realms such as education, social policy, public security, national defence, and regulation of the public sphere. The first and second criticisms become untenable if it is shown that the Turkish state publicly promotes religion, at least in some important public spheres' (Somer 2013: 587). In fact, all the evidence showing that Turkish national identity is intertwined with Islam (as opposed to the first critique, that the Turkish state was hostile to Islam) and that Islam is a vital part of public life in Turkey (as opposed to the second criticism that the Turkish state wanted to erase Islam from the public sphere) inevitably contribute to this third critique. Contrary to untenable claims, Davison (2003) argues that the republican reforms '"rescued Islam" as a matter of "belief" and "conscience" by institutionally supporting, financing, and promulgating a different version of Islam and its view of its relation to power and social life. .... Islam was not disestablished; it was differently established' (Davison 2003: 341; also Atay 2000). Republican reforms have done this by changing its status from being a political instrument, as it had been for centuries, and reshuffling the political role of Islam in constituting

---

[62] Islamists have also placed themselves discursively within 'civil society', portrayed as a pluralistic and multicultural space exempt from 'the state' especially in the 1990s – a view I illustrated with reference to the work of Yavuz (2003). See further, Navaro-Yashin (2002: 130-7), for a detailed critique of this claim.

the republican national identity. Accordingly, the 'power relations of *laiklik* constituted an alteration in the basic pattern, a shift with ruptures in some regards (legitimation ideology, constitutional, legal, and educational status of Islam), but continuities in others (integrated, established apparatus of religious governance, education, and socialization)' (Davison 2003: 342).

Some of these ruptures, especially those symbolic ones that were designed to be integrated into European social economic life, such as changes to the calendar, script and dress, were perceived by some as assaults on Muslim social and cultural practices and prepared fertile ground for the critique that secularism is 'anti-Islam' or a 'non-Muslim way of life' (ibid.). However, many others have shown that Islam and republicanism are quite well integrated (Tapper and Tapper 1987), especially as Islam has a vital role in religious governance (Lord 2018), education (Copeaux 2000) and social life in republican Turkey (Tapper 1994; Shankland 1999; Atay 2000; Bellér-Hann and Hann 2000). Moreover, a look at its historical trajectory shows that *laiklik* 'has never been a properly defined principle but, on the very contrary, proved to be vulnerable to political developments throughout the entire Republican era' (Şar 2019: 112). These nuances are rarely observed by the 'meta-narrative', which has nevertheless survived until today despite various criticisms of it, including contradictory evidence and methodological inaccuracies, especially in the works of Yavuz (see Tuğal 2004). During the seventeen years of AKP rule, *laiklik* has become more vulnerable than ever, and the political system had lost its already limited pluralist and democratic potential. In a 2019 article, Yavuz and Öztürk define the AKP as an Islamist-populist-authoritarian party, and yet are insistent that it 'is a product of the Kemalist state and its top-down laiklik' (Yavuz and Öztürk 2019: 5), *as if* the AKP has no responsibility for its own policies, and *as if* everything that went awry by 2019 was the fault of first seventeen years of the republic (1923-1940). This is how strong the 'meta-narrative' is; therefore we need to stress over and over again the counter-evidence that reveals the state control and promotion of Islam in its institutionalization, as well as in its daily social life.

Islam, Nationalism, Laiklik and Religiosity in Turkey

The Fundamentals of Islam

Islam, the world's second largest religion, with nearly two billion followers, is a monotheistic, Abrahamic religion based on the belief that *Allah* is the one and only (*bir ve tek*[63]) creator and that Muhammed is His[64] messenger (*onun elçisidir*). Despite the geographical, linguistic, historical, political and traditional diversity among Muslim communities all over the world, some basic fundamentals are shared by all. I will map them out here to give the reader a general idea of them.

The first fundamental principle of Islam, which also gives it its etymological meaning, is submission to *Allah*. It is believed that the Quran is a direct revelation of *Allah*'s word in Arabic to the Prophet Mohammed in seventh-century AD Mecca. The Quran, meaning recitation or reading, is the source of the *ümmet*, the Islamic community. The directness of *Allah*'s message through the Quran gives extraordinary importance to the 'word' (*kelâm*). Muslims recite 'God's word' primarily during their worship and in different parts of their daily lives, as in talismans (*muska*), in the Sufi practice of communal chanting (*zikir*), by referring to God's different names, and formulaic expressions in counting the beads (*tespih çekmek*), to name just a few. Also, the Quranic verses exhibited in individual homes, mosques or public spaces are not meant as simple decorations; they signify the directness of *Allah*'s 'word' (Gilsenan 2000). Moreover, many pious Muslims in Turkey pay great respect to physical copies of the Quran as an object of veneration and keep it in high places in their homes.

An essential belief in Islam is that Muslims consider their religion as God's final, unaltered and universal message. While the Quran confirms the truth of previous revelations sent to Moses, Jesus and other prophets, the original messages are believed to have been distorted by rabbis and priests. Therefore, Muhammed is believed to be the 'seal of Prophets', the last of the series of prophets to transmit the final word of *Allah*. Next to the Prophet Muhammad's distinguished role in delivering the divine message, his family (*Ehl-i Beyt*[65]) also enjoys a venerated status in the eyes of Muslims. Many holy men and rulers in Islamic history claimed to be part of this holy genealogy to substantiate their positions of authority. Yet, as the Prophet Muhammed himself never appointed a successor before his death (632 AD), the question of succession to his prophetic authority remained unresolved for

---

[63] All Quranic concepts are originally in Arabic, but for the purposes of clarity and sticking to local terms only Turkish translations, as they are used in Turkey, are provided, unless otherwise is stated.

[64] In Islam, *Allah* is considered to be omnipresent, omniscient and omnibenevolent and hence does not have human traits. Accordingly, Allah does not have a sex or gender. Also, in Turkish pronouns are not gendered, so Allah is not addressed as a 'he' or a 'she'. However, in the Arabic original *Allah* is referred as *Huwa*, or 'he'. Hence, I also refer to *Allah* using the male pronoun 'he'.

[65] Different Muslim traditions dispute which family members should be considered *Ehl-i Beyt*.

many generations, leading to major conflicts in Islamic history that have caused the main divide between the Sunnis and Shiites until today. The four main legal schools of the Sunni *tradition* are the Hanefi, Maliki, Şafii and Hanbeli schools. The Hanefi school is a branch of the Sunni tradition and is the state-promoted version of Islam in Turkey.

The third fundamental element of Islamic belief after the 'word' and the 'family' is the 'Prophetic tradition' (*Sunna*). This tradition is mainly based on the observations and recordings of the Prophet himself and the original Muslim community in the early Islamic era. The *Sunna* (*Sünnet*) stands for the actions, sayings and approvals that are thought to have been done, said or implied by the Prophet Muhammad. It is understood as the life of the Prophet and serves as the social model and righteous path for all Muslims, apart from the obligatory commands stated in the Quran (*farz*). The *Sunna* is also the second basis of Islamic law (*şeriat*) after the Quran. The reports that record the sayings and actions of the Prophet transmitted via his Companions (*sahabe*) are called *hadith* (*hadis*).[66] These reports were compiled in the centuries following the Prophet's death and formed a unifying framework for the rightly guided community as carefully studied and transmitted for generations. A large corpus of *hadith* texts, together with the Quran, provides Muslims with detailed guidelines for what Gilsenan calls 'the practical readiness of Islam' (2000: 17) from the largest to the smallest issue relevant in their daily lives. Also, *hadith* reports inform Muslims how to practice their ritual obligations, such as performing the five daily prayers (*namaz*), giving alms (*zekât*), fasting in the lunar month of Ramadan (*oruç*) and taking the pilgrimage to Mecca and Medina (*hac*).

Islamic law is based on these three main fundamentals: *Quran*, *Sunna* and *hadith*. Muslims believe in the oneness of *Allah*, the prophethood of Muhammad, His angels, the truthfulness of the message, and also in the day of resurrection (*kıyamet günü*), which provides the essence of most Islamic practice. It is believed that the day of resurrection is predestined by God but unknown to humans and that all humans will be judged on that day based on their good deeds (*sevap*) and bad deeds (*günah*). Accordingly, some will go to heaven (*cennet*), described as a place of blessing and joy, and some will burn in the fires of hell (*cehennem*). The Quran describes many of the sins that will lead to hell, the most important being the denial of God (*kafirlik*). On the other hand, it is also clear in the Quran that, as long as one repents of one's sins, God will offer his forgiveness, if he so wills. The *Sunna* and

---

[66] In Turkey, *hadis* is popularly known as the sayings of the Prophet Mohammed, though some sources have a wider definition of it. Some add his physical appearance and moral behaviour, others his Companions' statements about the definition of *hadis*. Which definition to follow is again a matter of tradition and its sources.

*hadith*s form the basis for good deeds and good behaviour, such as spreading the 'word', being thrifty, being just to others, helping the poor and being honest, while they forbid bad deeds such as drinking alcohol, adultery and taking another's belongings. The idea of being judged based on good and bad deeds on a predestined judgement day brings a 'calculative logic' to Muslim behaviour that is driven by guilt (Kuran 1996): that is, doing good deeds to cancel out the bad deeds and to secure a place in heaven. This is observable in many Islamic daily life practices of Muslim communities as observed by scholars, especially in attitudes towards charity as 'trading with God' (Mittermaier 2013). The beliefs summarized above constitute what most Muslims agree on, despite the vast range of both practice and interpretation (Gölpınarlı 1969).

Since the 'word' of God preserved in the Quran is considered to be unaltered, universal and final, and together with the *Sunna* provides the foundation for the Muslim community, its preservation and institutionalization as a religio-cultural system were of crucial significance. Gilsenan notes ironically that preservation has been a creative process: 'What is regarded as totally orthodox in one age is not so regarded in another; myths appear and disappear or are interpreted in different ways by different groups; genealogies contain strange gaps and often leave out as many people as they include. They must do so in one way or another to stay alive and significant as a society changes or as, say, a religious system becomes part of new economic and political orders' (Gilsenan 2000: 28). And since the identity of the successor of the Prophet was left unclear, the questions of what makes up the 'Muslim community' and who are legitimate persons when it comes to seizing the authority of the office, the institution and action have remained vital questions throughout Islamic history. Hence, what constitutes tradition had to be recreated and rediscovered according to the changing needs of societies while preserving and spreading the Revelation. The descendants of the Prophet or those who were able to claim similar privileged status, the 'men of learning' (*âlim*) that constitute the *ulama* (*ulema*) and who study and interpret the Islamic sources, and holy men associated with the Sufi mystical tradition who claimed a link to the family of the Prophet and to be saints by blessing or through their ability to perform miracles, have been the main actors interpreting and reproducing the answers to these questions. All of this has created a multiplicity of interpretations, practices and everyday manifestations of Islam. Gilsenan (2000), based on decades of ethnographic research in Egypt, Lebanon and Yemen, also adds that anti-imperialism and nationalism have added new contradictions to the struggle over what tradition should consist of or, in other words, what lies at the core of Islam. The abolition of the *ulema* as an elite class of *âlim* by the republican reformists, its replacement with the *Diyanet* and the shifting role of Islam in the constitution of Turkey's new national identity could be read from this perspective as a different interpretation, recreation and institutionalization of tradition while simultaneously demonstrating continuities with the past. *Laiklik* too as the Turkish version of 'secularity, can be regarded as a product of processes of religio-secularization and practices of religion-making' (Dreßler 2019: 1). In the next section, I will elaborate on this particular interpretation and the processes of religion-making in the republican era.

Turkish Islam, Islamism and Laiklik in Practice: Institutions, Politics and Practice

Understanding Turkish Islam goes hand in hand with understanding Turkish nationalism. What dominates Turkish nationalism is nationalism through religion, which is based on the Ottoman *millet* system, which places Turks, Kurds, Bosnians and other Ottoman Muslims, such as Circassians, Albanians, Bulgarian and Greek-speaking Muslims, Tatars and others in the category of the Muslim *millet*, while Greeks and Orthodox Christians form the *Rum millet* and Jews have a separate *millet*. This construction showed continuity in the republican understanding of who is a Turk (Çağaptay 2006). Accordingly, Muslims, regardless of ethnicity, are considered to be members of the Turkish nation, whereas non-Muslims could only be Turkish citizens and are not necessarily considered members of the Turkish nation. White (2012) also points out this distinction between Turks-by-citizenship and Turks-by-nationality. Hence, Turkishness is treated as a derivative of Islam (Çağaptay 2006). The population exchange between Orthodox Greeks living in Anatolia and Greek-speaking Muslims in Greece (1923-7), the embourgeoisement of Muslim Turks by the taking over of non-Muslim property, the Wealth Tax (1942) mostly taken from non-Muslims (see Chapter 2), the mass migration of ethnic Turkish Muslims from Bulgaria to Turkey (Parla 2019) and the relatively smooth assimilation of the other Muslim ethnic groups listed above to Turkish national identity are also evidence of how Turkishness in the republican understanding of citizenship is embedded in Islam. As Bellér-Hann and Hann (2000: 218) write, 'being a Muslim is inseparable from being a Turk'. It is not only the pious Muslim Turks who place Islam at the centre of their national identity; as Özyürek (2012) shows by looking at secular Turkish actors' attitudes to Christian minorities, Islam is also central to the national identity of secular Turks. This logic of Turkish nationalism is one of the reasons for the Kurdish liberation movement being incomprehensible and unacceptable to the state mind and the majority of Turkish people, since Kurds are considered to belong to the Muslim *millet*.

In addition to the centrality of Islam in national identity formation, state policies are implemented to make sure all regard themselves as Turks, embodied in the famous saying of the founder, Atatürk: '*Ne mutlu Türküm diyene*' ('How happy s/he who says "I am Turk"'). In this formulation, Turkishness is the dominant element of the national identity. This entails citizens embracing a 'sense of egalitarianism, becoming modern by embracing the West, emphasis on order, hard work, education, sport and culture' (Shankland 2003: 14), and accept receiving education in Turkish, regardless of what language they speak at home (ibid.). These values that shape Turkishness are compatible with the '[r]epublican version of the faith [that] stressed [the] appropriateness of moral behaviour (*ahlak*) in this world, … while it rejected *Şeriat*, Islamic Law, [and] broadly accepted the legitimacy of five pillars' (ibid.). Earlier ethnographic accounts of daily religious experience in ordinary towns in Turkey reveal that it 'has become less shrine-centred, less ritualistic and more individualistic … [and] narrowed' and that 'normal accepted religious values and activities are seen as those which neither support nor impinge in republicanism' (Tapper and Tapper 1987: 64).

This overlap between republican and religious values is what makes it possible to be a good Muslim and a good Turk at the same time, forming a 'single ideology'. One can, for example, trace a linguistic continuity with the Ottoman heritage in the values that are stressed by local townspeople, such as 'humanity, friendship, generosity, civilisation, sophistication, hospitality and community', to the point that 'any specific republican or Islamic interpretation can be placed on them' (ibid.: 61). Moreover, different value sets are constantly being accommodated to support this single ideology, such as the value of 'hard work' (ibid.). This was evident in my fieldwork, when it surfaced in a discussion between a covered woman worker and two uncovered Alevi women workers who defended the same values of 'rising early' and 'bodily cleanliness', but for different reasons. The former stressed the importance of saying the early morning prayer (one of the pillars of Islam) and of the ablution (*abdest*) required before that, while the latter stressed the dreadful consequences of late rising, such as missing her child's school bus and having to use up one's own petrol to take the child to school by car, while respect for others is a reason for avoiding the bodily scent one might have if one has not showered. Despite the variations behind this reasoning, there is agreement on the essence of values that seem to be rooted in different ideologies. The variation is not only between individual persons, as other studies show that the practice and understanding of Islam varies in regions, and even between villages located next to each other, and that Islam is not only a set of principles but a set of complex practices that shape individual lives locally on a daily basis through rituals of birth, circumcision, marriage, military service and death, as well as individual and collective prayers and Ramadan (Bellér-Hann and Hann 2000; Hart 2013).

Despite the variation and vitality of Islamic and not-so-Islamic practices in Turkey, its redefinition and institutionalization in the republican era to accommodate secular nationalism triggered some tensions, as already emphasized by scholars of the 'meta-narrative'. These tensions are rooted in the secular nationalization process and involve friction between nominal Islam and Islam as a political identity (Çağaptay 2006). The new interpretation and institutional formation of Islam and the new power relationship that comes with it were not carried out to throw Islam into the dustbin of history, but rather to purify Islam from certain forms of Islamic control and expression that are considered superstitious, fanatical, reactionary and obscurantist (Davison 2003). Apart from ethnographic findings on the persistence of the practice of Islam, there is a growing literature focusing on the early years of the republic presenting evidence against arguments that the Turkish state was hostile to Islam and wanted to remove it from the public sphere. For example, Bayar (2012) shows how the founders viewed a nationalized civic Islam as instrumental in providing a moral education and building the nation. Gürbey (2012) argues that, even though the laws are secular, the state relies on religion to discipline individuals to become obedient political subjects, while the military uses religious sentiments to encourage nationalism and self-sacrifice for the homeland. Azak (2012) focuses on the debates over Turkification of the call to prayer (*ezan*) and argues that the aim was to encourage a pure and Turkish Islam rather than suppressing it. Even when the Democrat Party switched back to Arabic for the call to prayer and allowed more religious autonomy after 1950, it did not want to remove the control of the state over religious institutions and education, nor did the AKP.

What do I mean by state control over religious institutions and education? 'Official Islam' is represented by the *Diyanet,* which replaced the elite class of *ulema* and turned 'learning men' into civil servants (*memur*) funded by the citizens' taxes. The *Diyanet* is officially in charge of informing the public on the subject of religion, though its personnel and infrastructure are funded by the state. It performs its role by organizing conferences and publishing on matters of tradition and practice, describing belief and ritual, convening Friday sermons that are distributed nationwide to all mosques, organizing the pilgrimage, collecting donations on religious holidays, offering religious opinions via its hotlines and finally collaborating with other ministries and with religious orders disguised as 'civil-society organizations' to spread its word, mainly in the area of education.[67] The *Diyanet* was given a monopoly on religious life in Turkey after Dervish lodges and religious orders were outlawed in 1925, while in practice Sunni *tarikat*s[68] carried on with their activities, many embedded in the mosques. Although the *ulema* lost financial and political assets, they acquired a centralized budget. Its budget, like the numbers of mosques and personnel, has been increasing throughout the republican era in parallel with the religious expansion of the 1950s and since, especially in the 1980s, with some fluctuations due to the state's fiscal constraints[69] (Lord 2018). Moreover, the *Diyanet*'s share of the total state budget has doubled since the AKP came to power[70], increasing from 0.54 per cent in 2002 to 0.83 per cent in 2006 and to 1.2 per cent in 2012 (Somer 2013: 594), second in size after the Ministry of Defence (Kandiyoti 2012: 516). One might argue that, given the characteristics of the *Diyanet*, its bare existence is an obstacle to secularism (Davison 2003). Quite contrary to notions of the neutrality or separation of the state from religion, by using the *Diyanet* to centralize Islam, the Turkish state promotes and privileges Sunni Islam and rejects Alevism, in doing so reproducing 'religious majoritarianism' since its establishment (Lord 2018: 94), a phenomenon that reached its peak in the

---

[67] Not only in Turkey but also among Turkish diaspora communities abroad.

[68] Turkey's Law 677 legally bans *tarikat*s (Islamic Sufi brotherhoods), though in fact they remain active today. *Naqshbandi tarikat* and its different branches are particularly influential in daily life and politics. The best known *tarikat*s associated with this brotherhood are *Menzil, İsmailağa, Işık, Erenköy, İskenderpaşa* and *Süleymancı* (Lord 2018). *Süleymancı*s currently run an extensive network of Quran courses and dormitories. *Menzil* is known for dominating the Ministry of Health, along with its other preoccupations in Islamic education and publications. The second most active group is the *Nur* community, mostly known for the *Okuyucu* and *Yazıcı* groups, which run similar schools and student homes and are also known for being the basis of *Gülen* movement, a global network of education, a media conglomerate and ally of the AKP government until 2013. For a more detailed account of religious orders and *tarikat*s in Turkey, see the Directorate of Religious Affairs report for 2019: https://mk0medyascopetblqooo.kinstacdn.com/wp-content/uploads/2019/05/diyanet-rapor-1-1.pdf.

[69] See Lord (2018: 93, 94), where she gives figures on the budget, the number of mosques and personnel from the foundation of the republic until today.

[70] Somer (2013: 594) writes: '[A]ccording to official figures, the Diyanet's personnel also increased by about 30 per cent between 2002 and 2011, from 74,374 to 98,555. Government statistics show that there were 82,693 mosques in Turkey in 2011 (up from 75,941 in 2002) and about 10,914 Qur'an courses in 2013, compared with 32,797 schools of primary education. This means that there was approximately one Sunni mosque for every 900 people in Turkey'. *İmam Hatip* (vocational schools training religious personnel), secondary schools and high schools boomed in the 1970s when National Salvation Party shared a coalition government with Republican People's Party. A similar pattern of the increasing number of Quran courses and mosques could be observed for *İmam Hatip* schools in the AKP era.

AKP era. Lord (ibid.) also develops a critical view of the *Diyanet* being mostly a passive agent that 'the state' uses to control Islam. In fact, her research reveals the 'institution's agency in adopting multiple strategies, from cooperation to struggling against other state factions in the pursuit of its own agenda...Diyanet has played a crucial role in providing a more favourable environment for Islamist mobilisation and has delimited the nation's boundaries along religious lines through its engagement with and rejection of Alevism' (ibid.: 32). I will come back to Alevism in the next section.

It could be therefore be argued that, if Turkish national identity was initially engraved in Islam and its practice remained vital, where did Islamism come from? The important point here is that, although Turkish Islam constituted an interpretation of *tradition*, this did not mean that everyone embraced it. There was definitely a demand for a more publicly visible Islam and for social life to have a greater degree of Islamic input. Also, the urban middle classes who represented the republican status quo looked down on the traditional ways of conduct and outfit, which then formed the basis for Muslim resentment or injury. But what is interesting is what Tapper and Tapper wrote about the town of Eğirdir, which they describe as both republican and religious, in 1987, namely that the townspeople were distant from any sort of radicalism. In fact, they talk about the very powerful religious orders at the current day[71] as 'religious fanatics such as members of the two clandestine Islamic sects, the Nurcus and Süleymancıs' (Tapper and Tapper 1987: 61).

So, what are the circumstances that have turned clandestine fanatics turn into powerful networks in the last thirty years? As a general answer to this question, Shankland argues that 'the most cursory exploration of the changing relationship between the state and religion in Turkey will show that in this respect the model of a monolithic secular state is entirely inadequate... it's only through realizing that the state can be open, diffuse and malleable, almost as if it may be drawn in different direction by different groups, that the religious revival can be understood' (Shankland 1999: 3). This remark is important since the rise of Islamism in Turkey is commonly seen as self-evident, a reaction of the periphery to the oppression of the centre. As we have seen, Lord (2018), also very sceptical of the meta-narrative, underlined the historical role of the *Diyanet* in Islamist mobilization. There were also other factors that led to it. Most importantly, developments such as the postmodernist critique of Western universals after 1980s and the Iranian Revolution of 1979 opened up a particular space for

---

[71] See footnote 68.

the Islamist critique and political revival in Turkey. Islamic literature proliferated; works by radical Islamist thinkers from Iran and Egypt were translated into Turkish, such as those of Ali Shari'ati and Sayyid Qutb, while Turkish Islamists' works also started circulating.

Apart from these developments, most important was the military's implementation of a synthesis between Turkishness and Islam in the 1980s. In the 1960s, during the Cold War, Islam was seen as an antidote to the growing influence of socialist and democratic forces, which shaped the ideology of 'Associations to Combat Communism' in which many well-known Islamist politicians of today were involved. Since the 1970s, in institutions such as *Aydınlar Ocağı* (Heart of Intellectuals), right-wing intellectuals produced an anti-communist ideology, which today we call the Turkish-Islam synthesis. Although the military is commonly understood as the sole guarantor of the 'secular' state that has justified its interventions as 'bringing democracy back', it incorporated the Turkish-Islam synthesis into the official ideology. By doing so, it acted to secure the interests of the bourgeoisie and to sweep away rival social and political claims (see Chapter 2).

It is important to note here that the military operated in a double-bind: on the one hand it enforced an authoritarian version of Kemalism, while on the other it implemented what has become known as the Turkish-Islam synthesis after the 1980 *coup d'état*. The basic premise of this ideology is that 'Islam is the precondition to being and to remaining a Turk. Without Islam, Turkish culture would not be able to survive, but without Turks Islam would not be strengthened and disseminated' (Şen 2010: 61). Although at first sight this definition resonates with the idea that Islam in the national identity is a derivative of Turkishness, it actually reverses that proposition by asserting that Turkish culture would not survive without Islam and that Turks should therefore disseminate it. In this formulation, Islam was the dominant element in Turkey before nationalism. Thus, the transformation of 'Turkish' Islamism happened in a three-fold manner: articulation of Turkishness into Islamism through the Turkish-Islamic synthesis, permanent enlargement of the religious field, and articulation between neoliberalism and Turkish Islamism. These processes have 'opened a huge socio-political space for the rise of the AKP to power' (ibid.: 59) and also increased the space, legitimacy and funding for the activities of the religious orders. Unlike the earlier nationalist paradigm, the rise of the AKP and the radical alteration of what constitutes being Turkish and Muslim led to what Jenny White called 'Muslim nationalism', an 'unorthodox view of the nation and its borders' that is 'modelled on a more flexible and inclusive Ottoman past' (White 2012: 50).

The resurgence of Islamism in the 1990s triggered many public discussions over matters such as women's bodies and covering, the gendered segregation of public spaces, religious education, and alcohol consumption and its taxation, which divided the seculars and Islamists politically into two camps. These public discussions occurred concurrently with the neoliberal turn, which Kandiyoti (2002, 2012) describes as having led to a greater fragmentation of identities and the increasing complexity of their public visibility in the 1990s. This is a process that brought about the 'culturalisation of politics and [the] politicization of culture whereby codes of class and status are produced, reproduced and politicized as competing cultural styles, preferences and value orientations' (Kandiyoti 2002: 4-5). How different codes of class and status are played out and politicized by different political camps in everyday life is documented by ethnographies. Esra Özyürek (2006), in her ethnography of everyday politics in Turkey in the late 1990s, shows how, as Islamists stretch the boundaries of the private and spill over into the public sphere, seculars respond by commodifying the symbols of the republic, such as Atatürk pins, tattoos and T-shirts. Privatization of the state ideology appears in the form of private expressions that publicly represent internalized, voluntary and legitimate political positions. Navaro-Yashin's ethnography (2002) looks at the other side of the coin by showing how Islamists have become part and parcel of the same capitalist economy, which they are able to manipulate for the double aim of profit and identity construction. While they allegedly reject secularism and the capitalist economy and aim to replace them, they also rewrite and appropriate the representational mechanisms of a secular and capitalist economy. With reference to the distinction between seculars and Islamists in the meta-narrative, Navaro-Yashin argues that 'secularist and Islamist identities in contemporary Turkey are products of manufacture. They are not original and essential, even though they are experienced as such. In other words, they are not reflections of some primordial Turkishness' (Navaro-Yashin 2002: 79). Özyürek and Navaro-Yashin's ethnographies should rather be understood in the context of how Kemalists and Islamists redefine and renegotiate the boundaries of the public and the private through which they make the 'state', creating and consuming their nostalgias or their imageries of 'the state' in a neoliberal context. White's ethnography (2012) focuses on a later period in the 2000s. Also critical of the binaries separating secular and Islamist, she demonstrates the multiplicity of 'competing and overlapping cultures of Turkishness and other forms of national subjectivity' (White 2012: 18). Moreover, her research has revealed the emergence of a 'cultural aversion to mixing, coupled with anxiety that the boundaries that demarcate the border between "us" and "them"' (ibid.: 102), that is, between secularists and Islamists.

Reading these findings from 2019, I would like to add that the demarcation between 'us' and 'them' that refers to the political camps of secularists and Islamists has shifted to a political polarization between those who vote for the AKP and those who do not. The fragmentation of identities and the complexity of their public visibility are ever more observable and are not dependent on or limited to the secular/Islamic binary. There are uncovered women who piously practise the five pillars of Islam as much as they can in a similar manner to covered women; there are covered women who do not force coverings on their daughters and pious men who question their belief; there are openly feminist women who live a Muslim life but still want to be independent and able to divorce their husbands within the rights given to them by the secular law; there are LGBTI people who vote for the AKP and those who despise its conservatism and promotion of heterosexual normativity; there are provincial and traditional Muslim and secular people who will not support the AKP, although they define themselves as Muslims in their own understandings; and there are young Muslim and secular women and men who have clandestine premarital sex, despite it being strictly banned by traditional conservatism, as well as Islamic rule. As Gülalp (2003) pointed out earlier, Islam as a belief can obtain any characteristic that a Muslim considers worthy and can 'present itself publicly not really as religion as we know it (i.e. with its doctrine, rituals, institutions, clergymen, etc.), but simply as a cultural code for a way of life or a cultural frame of reference for a community of people that think of themselves as sharing a way of life' (Gülalp 2003: 383).

Therefore, the argument of many Orientalists about the centrality of religion in Muslim societies could be a false premise, since it is a marker of social and communal identity as well as class identity (ibid.). Given the variety of interpretations of Islamic *tradition* in the Turkish case, the fragmentation or even the polarization is not merely between secular and Muslim but between the different values (not necessarily stemming from Islamic references) that people refer to in making communities, as will be shown in Chapter 6, as well as different class affiliations. Moreover, lived Islam is not limited to definitions imposed from above, like its entry on the ID cards of all Turkish citizens by nationality. The social group in Turkey which has the biggest problem with state-inscribed Sunni Islam are without a doubt the Alevis.

The Alevis

The Alevis are an ethno-religious minority in Turkey who make up roughly 15-20 per cent of the Turkish population (Shankland 2013; Ertan 2017).[72] They are geographically scattered in Anatolia and consist of Turkish, Kurdish and Arab ethnicities, hence being heterogeneous among themselves. The word *Alevi* means *Ali'ye mensup* (follower of the fourth Caliph Ali, the cousin and son-in-law of the Prophet Mohammed), although Alevi belief is not identical to the Turkish version of the Shi'a tradition, in which the Imam Ali and his lineage (the Twelve Imams) are also central to the belief in Islam's legitimate caliphs. In fact, the issues of the origins and content of Alevism (*Alevilik*) and of its relation to Turkish culture and the Turkish nation state are highly contested. Discussions of it generally revolve around whether or not Alevism can be considered Islamic, a separate belief system or a *tarikat* (*Sufi* religious order), since many follow the Bektashi order.

One of the most common interpretations of the origins of Alevism historicizes its emergence as a result of the conflicts in the early years of Islam in the seventh century over who was the legitimate Caliph after the death of the Prophet Mohammed, implying that Alevism was born out of the Shi'a tradition. This interpretation makes it possible to place Alevism within Islam and is mostly embraced by Sunnis who reject the notion of Alevism being a belief of its own right. Although people and events that belong to the theology of the Shi'a tradition, such as the cult of Ali, the Kerbela Incident[73] or the Twelve Imams, are central to Alevi beliefs today, historians argue that Alevism is a product of a long process that surfaced far later, in the tenth century, when Islam started spreading among the Turks and other nomads. In fact, most important scholars of Alevism argue that many sources of

---

[72] Massicard (2007) writes that it is difficult to make a precise estimate because state policy dictates that in census data collection Muslims are recorded as such without differentiating between denominations or belonging to a sect, while Christian denominations are recognized. This was also visible in European and World Value Surveys administered in Turkey, though the category of *Caferi* (Turkish Shi'a) was counted as an exception to the rule.

[73] According to Islamic history, after the murder of the Third Caliph Osman, the office passed to Imam Ali (656). In the meantime, the Ummayyah leader Muaviye declared himself the Caliph, which led to a divide in Islamic leadership between Ali and Muaviye. After the assassination of Imam Ali (661), his son Hasan made a peace treaty with the Ummayyah Caliph Muaviye. However, when Muaviye's son Yezid succeeded as the Umayyad Caliph after his father's death, Hasan's brother Hüseyin did not accept the authority of Ummayah Caliph Yezid and marched to Kerbela, where he and his small army, including his relatives and companions, were slaughtered by Yezid's army. The incident is central to Shi'a belief, tradition and theology. Hüseyin's suffering is the symbol of sacrifice of the good against the bad, the just against the unjust. The Kerbela incident is regarded as a tragedy by both Sunni and Shi'a, and is commemorated by Shi'a on the tenth day (Ashure Day) of the Islamic month of Muharrem after twelve days of mourning and fasting.

Alevi/Bektashi beliefs, such as *velayetnameler*, *nefes* and *Buyruk*, their traditions such as *Hızır* and *Nevruz* and institutions such as *müsahiplik* and *ikrâr* are rooted in unorthodox religious and mystic cultures in the pre-Islamic period (Melikoff 1994; Ocak 1996).[74] The same sources also point out that Turkish nomads combined their ancient beliefs, such as the cults of Tengri, nature and the ancestors, with the remnants of previous religions, such as shamanism, Buddhism, Zoroastrianism, Manichaeism or Mazdakism, when they incorporated Islamic belief and adapted it to their socio-economic structures. As far as can be understood from its historical development, scholars argue that what we call Alevism today initially had nothing to do with the cult of Ali, nor had any Shi'a elements; it was rather a heterodox interpretation of non-Sunni nomads that flourished from the tenth century onwards. Scholars consider the Babai revolt of the early thirteenth century as an incident in which heterodox Turks encountered Alevi motives and embraced them (Cahen 1970, cited in Ocak 1996: 207; Melikoff 1994). The earliest encounter of Alevis with Shi'a elements is said to have occurred during the late fifteenth and early sixteenth centuries, when Safavid messianic propaganda spread among heterodox groups that were particularly open to such influences at the time. This was due to unrest and resistance fuelled by enforced sedentarization through the centralization policies of the fifteenth century and the brutal suppression of the *Celali* revolts[75], which were mostly led by heterodox groups in the Ottoman state in the sixteenth century. Scholars argue that these revolts have played a central role in the transformation of the heterodoxy into contemporary Alevism (Ocak 1996), which actually arose out of a socio-political dispute (Kehl-Bodrogi 1992, cited in Ertan 2019). Another response of the Ottoman state to the socio-

---

[74] For further information about the content of these beliefs and institutions, see the works of Cahen (1970), Kehl-Bodrogi (1992), Melikoff (1994), Ocak (1996), Massicard (2007), Shankland (2013) and Ertan (2017, 2019), also cited in this subsection.

[75] Some also refer to the *Kızılbaş* rebellion. *Kızılbaş* (red-head) denotes heterodox groups of the period who joined the side of Safavid soldiers, who wore red caps, fighting against the Sunni Ottomans. The revolts had several other reasons, such as increasing taxes, sedentary policies and decreasing recruitment of Turkmens into the Janissary regiments, that contributed to the Alevi supporting the Safavids and falling under the influence of the Shi'a. The brutal suppression of the first Ottoman Caliph Selim I addressed both issues. Local researchers in Çorum also provide accounts regarding the town's involvement in these revolts. For example, Sabuncuoğlu (2015) asserts that Çorum's local governor, who supported the rebels, was changed three times in this era. Another precaution that the Ottoman state took against these revolts was to send the leader of Dulkadiroğlu Beyliği (Chiefdom) to Çorum, where he settled and executed Celal, who had started the revolts. The mansion of this Bey (Chief) has been renovated and is open to visitors without providing any information on the historical background of his presence in Çorum. Aktüre (1986) writes that Çorum was referred as the 'cradle of *Celali*' until the nineteenth century.

political dispute were resettlement policies that resettled loyal Sunni tribes and families in areas in which the Alevi population was concentrated for purposes of assimilation and control.[76]

There are other widespread views about the origins of Alevism, such as describing it as a version of shamanism and claiming that it is the ancient religion of the Turks of Central Asia, who mainly emerge from Turkish nationalist historiography. Given the historical trajectory described above, these views fall short of reflecting the complexity of its history and sources of belief, which, moreover, have been proved to be inaccurate by different scholars. Alevism, as described above, is a syncretic and heterodox belief system that combines Sufi tradition and belief in the Twelve Imams in Shi'a Islam, that venerates the Caliph Ali in an anthropomorphic way, and that retains remnants of other pre-Islamic beliefs and notions in its teachings (Melikoff 1993). Alevis rarely observe the five pillars of Islam. Moreover, Alevism's socio-political references are shaped by disobedience to the establishment, as can be observed from the overlapping of revolts in different periods that led to its emergence (Melikoff 1994; Ocak 1996). However, this does not mean that political opposition is naturally embedded in Alevism (Ertan 2019). In fact, Alevis have been supportive of the republican regime and its secular, western-oriented cultural orientation precisely because it rejects Islamic law. However, as described in earlier sections, the republican regime also entails continuities with the Ottoman past in terms of Sunni traditions and institutions. Accordingly, in his comparison of Sunni and Alevi villages, Shankland (2003) showed that Alevis faced more difficulties and conflicts in becoming a part of the Turkish nation than the Sunnis, since their traditional social structures were dismissed by the modern state apparatus. Alevis, despite their syncretic belief system and internal ethnic heterogeneity, are considered to share a cultural identity on the basis of Turkish nationalism and heterodox Islam which provides the basis of their citizenship status in Turkey. They have been rebranded, so to speak, in the nationalist historiography of the last century in order to fit them into the new Turkish/Sunni nation state (Dreβler 2013). The inability of Turkish nationalism to accommodate ethno-religious pluralism as an inclusive basis for national identity led to Alevis being defined as 'ambivalent citizens' (Açıkel and Ateş 2011). On the one hand,

---

[76] The revolts resulted in the massacre of many Turkmen and Kurdish nomads in central Anatolia and the initiation of new settlement policies by the Ottoman state. In this era, after annihilation of the rebel groups, in seventeenth century Cerit, Mamali, Dedeslu, Selmanlu, Karakecili, Alamaşlı, Cihanbeyli, Kangal, Alembeyli Bozdoğan tribes (Aktüre 1986: 128; Sabuncuoğlu 2015: 313) and in the eighteenth century the Kınık tribe were brought to Çorum (Sabuncuoğlu 2015: 313). These might be assumed to be Sunni families loyal to the state.

they embrace republican ideals and regard themselves as 'secular' and 'modern' as a response to Sunni majoritarianism and Islamization. On the other hand, they resent the fact that the same state ignores their rights and their demand to be treated like equal citizens, such as official recognition of their places of worship (*cemevi*) and the banning of compulsory Sunni religious education at schools.

By the 1990s, Alevism had started organizing itself as an identity-based movement in parallel with the global trend of the period following the collapse of the Soviet Union, which had questioned the legitimacy of nation states and the increasing emphasis on cultural diversity. However, the Alevi identity movement followed a different path than the political Islamist movement, which demanded organization of the public sphere based on Sunni belief, or than the Kurdish movement, whose demands range from autonomous governance to education in the Kurdish language, a movement built on Kurdish identity. Instead of emphasizing the particularism of Alevi identity and cultural differences, the Alevi political movement frames its demands on the basis of the equal participation of Alevis in social and political life, as with non-Alevis (Ertan 2017). The reasons behind this difference could be observed in the 'ambivalence' of Alevism, meaning that its syncretism and heterodox character does not allow it to build a systematized aggregate, nor a set of rules to be followed by all; Alevi cosmology is constantly evolving and pluralistic (ibid.). Moreover, Alevis are ethnically diverse and are a minority in every Turkish province, including Çorum, except for Tunceli province. By the same token, Massicard defines the Alevi movement as an 'identity movement without an identity' (Massicard 2007). Nevertheless, one very important aspect of Alevi identity that transcends its diversity in belief and ethnic belonging is the successive massacres of Alevis in Dersim (1937-1938), Ortaca-Muğla (1966), Malatya (1978), Kahramanmaraş (1978), Çorum (1980), Sivas (1993) and the Gazi neighbourhood of Istanbul (1995), either performed directly by the state or by state-backed Sunni groups. These outbreaks of violence have played a fundamental role in the formation and articulation of Alevi identity and have deeply marked their collective memory.

PART TWO

THE WORLD OF BUSINESS IN ÇORUM:

FORMATION, ASPIRATIONS AND MOBILITY

Chapter 4
Formation of Small and Medium-Size Capital in Çorum

Introduction

Çorum is known for its success in the last forty years in developing mainly flour, tile and machine industries, resulting in increases in the city's export revenues from 24 million US dollars in 2003 to 149 million US dollars in 2012 (Güven and Kaygın 2013: 73). These economic developments follow the general pattern of small and medium-size manufacturing companies clustered in industrial districts. They are referred to in various sources (Keyman and Lorasdağı 2010; İzmen 2012; Uzel 2013) and by local representatives of business associations as 'Çorum's model of development', which is based on a 'culture of partnership' within a larger rhetoric of the 'Anatolian Tigers', or other export-oriented Anatolian provinces that started thriving after the 1980s. The features of the 'Çorum model of development' are described with emphasis on the following phrases: 'even though there is almost no public investment', 'without the assistance of the state', 'with their own means' and 'a city with an entrepreneur's soul' (Keyman and Lorasdağı 2010: 202-218). Similar descriptions are prevalent, for example, in the European Stability Initiative Report (2005) for Kayseri and in the testimonies of a Gaziantep entrepreneur who depicted their model using 'phrases like "entrepreneurialism", "competitive, hard-working people" and "successful without direct help of the state"' (Bayırbağ 2007: 126).

As I showed in the Introduction, Çorum's locals and politicians frequently complain that they are not getting their share of the pie and that they are facing setbacks because of the state's negligence and unfair treatment of the city by denying it its 'own' airport, and hence the global connections they consider necessary for foreign trade. At the same time, it is difficult to place Çorum's economic development within the 'Anatolian Tiger' canon for several reasons. First, Çorum did not have a MÜSİAD branch until the end of 2013. Second, unlike Kayseri and Konya, Çorum is not a historical stronghold of political Islam due to its mixed population. Third, even though the Gülen community has had a significant presence in

Çorum through its TUSKON branch, it is not possible to trace those links anymore since those in this community had gone underground during the period of my research due to the allegations of terrorism against them. Still, it is possible to find a similar regional development discourse in conversations with Çorum's locals that is as prevalent as it is in other contexts.

The aim of this chapter is to shed light on the historical process that evolved into what is currently defined as the 'Çorum model of development' and to reveal the real-life manifestations of what is meant by a 'culture of partnership' and success 'without the help of the state'.

The chapter is divided into two main parts. The first main part, 'Historical Processes of Local Capital Accumulation', is dedicated to the local factors that became significant in the historical process of Çorum's articulation to capitalist accumulation in the Turkish and global economy. Each sub-section in this part will present stories of different business people in each era, their socio-economic backgrounds and material resources, and the social relationships they accommodated to form their businesses. To be able to help the reader place each story in its own context, sub-sections will follow the periodization used in Chapter 2, where I describe in detail the political and economic shifts in the Turkish economy. The aim is not only to point out the local factors but also to show how the potential came to surface as a result of historically shaped social and economic conditions. These efforts have created powerful actors and new inequalities that fed into the next phases in different ways, depending on changing circumstances. Accordingly, the sub-sections of the first part focus respectively on the creation of a Muslim Turkish bourgeoisie in the early republican era, the collective industrialization efforts, the spread of the big bourgeoisie in the local market from the 1960s, the role of state incentives, the establishment of industrial zones from the 1980s, and finally the new generation of entrepreneurs that emerged in 1990s. There is also a special section dedicated to the circumstances of Alevi business people who arrived and navigated their economic interests after the 1980 massacre, despite the economic losses and physical segregation of urban areas that took place as a result.

The second main part of the chapter, entitled 'Anatolian Tigers are Cats Now', aims to address how the whole discourse and attributes related to the 'Anatolian Tiger' notion have resonated in Çorum. In this part, I try to explore the role of religious community structures in Çorum's capital formation, as this is one of the main foci in the literature. However, as the main religious community active in business organizations, the Fethullah Gülen movement, was under investigation during my fieldwork and was then accused of plotting the failed military coup attempt on 15 July 2016, I compare and contrast my limited findings before and after July 15 and uncover the meanings attached to 'culture of partnership' in this context.

Historical Processes of Local Capital Accumulation

The Merger of the Hasırcı and Buğdaycı Families[77]

For centuries, Çorum was a 'low-grade administrative centre and local bazaar town' (Faroqhi 1986: 107) not connected to either sea or land routes. Until the end of nineteenth century, it was on only second- or third-degree trade routes. As Aktüre (1986) reports, Çorum, whether rural or urban, was a small settlement that provided the link between big city consumers and rural areas by collecting and distributing the surplus product in its role as a market. Its economy was based on agriculture (mainly grain), husbandry and husbandry-related crafts[78] supplying the local market.[79] On the whole, the town's economic activities have been shaped by its mutual dependence with its hinterland, as well as by the needs of larger trading centres. The intermediaries who exchanged villagers' products with local traders for money controlled the circulation of cash in Çorum (Faroqhi 1986).

By the end of the nineteenth century, fresh and dry fruits, grain and *cehri*[80] started being exported to foreign markets from Samsun, due to the reconfiguration of trade flows and demand changes by foreign markets as a result of industrialization in Europe (Aktüre 1986; Tekeli 1986a: 197). Yet, a city with the size and position of Çorum could only integrate itself into the global economy through its connections with regional centres (Tekeli 1986a: 197). In this context, the ways in which people, animals and goods travel from Çorum to Samsun determine the scope of the trade. In those years, there were hardly any animal carriages in Çorum, and even with them, Tekeli estimates the journey from Çorum to Samsun as taking 32 hours, which could extend to four days in summer and nine days in winter (Tekeli 1986a: 201).[81] When Ankara (southwest of Çorum) became the capital of the

---

[77] All names of people and workplaces have been anonymized except for the few who hold a bureaucratic position that matters to the argument.

[78] That is, mainly tannery, weaving, *çirişcilik* (herbal glue produced from a fruit that grows in the area), and shoe and sack making. Almost all these crafts have disappeared or remain as low-income activities in central Çorum bazaar.

[79] Istanbul's need for grain was supplied mainly from Rumelia. Çorum and inner Anatolian producers sent grain only when ordered by the central government.

[80] A kind of herbal cloth dye obtained from the fruit of the jujube trees found in Çorum area and also in Amasya, Tokat and Zile. However, its production ceased because of technological advances.

[81] With the highway connection, it takes three hours by car.

republic, Çorum gained a new trade connection. Yet until the 1950s the closest train station was at Çerikli on the way to Yozgat, which that connected Çorum to the west or southwest provinces but was nevertheless 150 kilometres away (see Map 2). Only in 1937 was a road link created from Çorum to this station (from the memoir, see footnote 85), followed in the 1950s by a direct road connection from Çorum to Ankara via Kırıkkale.

Buğdaycızade Kemal Efendi[82] (1857-1948) and Nuri (Hasırcı) Agha[83] (1850-1949) were born in mid-nineteenth-century Çorum, in the conditions described above. The two men are respectively the maternal and paternal grandfathers of Hikmet Hasırcı, the heir to one of the four flour factories[84] in Çorum in the late nineteenth and early twentieth centuries. This factory, which I will call Çorum-Flour, was founded in the late 1920s and modernized in the 1960s. The following life and occupational histories are based on Hikmet Hasırcı's personal memoir[85], which provides important anecdotes on the economic, social and cultural history of Çorum in the early twentieth century. I have combined the data in the memoir with the in-depth interview I conducted with the current manager of Çorum-Flour, Nuri Bey, and have cross-checked it with the available scholarly works.

The story goes as follows. Kemal Efendi was around ten years old when he and his friends first saw a four-wheeled horse carriage in Çorum city centre in 1867. Kemal Efendi's father was a farm owner who was known for cultivating tobacco; he sold his products and bolts of fabrics he had bought from nearby merchants in Çorum. When Kemal Efendi was in his mid-thirties, he would regularly ride to Amasya (between Çorum and Samsun) on his horse to buy the fabrics from an Armenian merchant and would ride back again. One day, as he later told his grandson, he again went

---

[82] *-zade* is a suffix from Persian meaning either 'son of' or 'a noble person'. The affix *Efendi*, used in Turkish, Arabic and Persian, and deriving from Ancient Greek, means master or lord. It was also used as a title of respect or as an indication of a (religious) education. Its use as a title was abolished by the Surname Law of 1934, which required every citizen to take a Turkish surname.

[83] *Agha* means landlord or more generally a provider. Its use as a title was also abolished by the Surname Law, but it continued to be used in the daily language.

[84] The first flour factory (Unat) in Çorum was established in 1898, followed by Kadıtarla and Ocakbahçe respectively in 1914 and 1924. When Çorum-Flour was established at the end of 1920s, there were four factories in Çorum. I have also changed the names of these factories. The original names mentioned in the memoir (see next footnote) match those in the publication by Yılmaz (2004) in the development of Çorum's industry. Thus, it verifies the information in the memoir.

[85] Hikmet Hasırcı wrote his memoir in 2015. It was handed to me during my fieldwork by the current manager of Çorum-Flour and Hikmet Hasırcı's nephew on his mother's side, Nuri Bey. The leaflet contains 24 anecdotes in 33 pages. The quotations I present here from the leaflet are my translations to English from Turkish.

to Amasya, but instead of going straight back to Çorum he 'rebelled against his father' and took the road to Ankara, where he took the train to Istanbul. There he realized that the prices of products in Istanbul are one tenth of the prices he had been paying the Armenian merchant in Amasya. After this discovery, they started buying their fabrics from Istanbul. From then on, Kemal Efendi established close connections in Istanbul, and opened a store first in Çorum and then in Istanbul. By removing the intermediaries and directly buying from Istanbul, as his grandson puts it in his memoir, 'the family got very rich in those years'.

The connections Kemal Efendi made in Istanbul were not limited to his first discoveries there. One of his four daughters married Celil Ondur, a businessman who made money in the 1920s. Hikmet Hasırcı explains the source of Celil Ondur's wealth as follows: 'the 1920s and 1930 are the years when non-Muslims were being liquidated (*tasfiye olup*), while Turkish and Muslim people were getting active in industry and trades, while ... When the Greeks and Armenians left, there was a huge void. In those days, a few Turks who started trading had a chance. Those who used the opportunities wisely found themselves, out of the blue, with a fortune (*Bu şansı iyi kullananlar birden kendini servetin içinde buldular*) ... Celil Ondur was one of those'. Hikmet Hasırcı goes on to explain that his grandfather Kemal Efendi's business contacts improved as a result of his son-in-law taking over the non-Muslim business network (probably property too). He says this was not the only 'fortune' the family acquired. Kemal Efendi took over a grain mill from the villagers whom he controlled on his farm.[86] He adds that, although he did not need it money-wise, he decided to modernize the mill and run it.

Celil Ondur, the son-in-law of Kemal Efendi, owned houses both in Çorum and Istanbul and two phaetons. He and his wife had maids and a cook from Istanbul and a piano in their house in Çorum. Compared to living standards and conditions at the end of the nineteenth century and the beginning of the twentieth in Çorum, described above, this was a huge leap up the socio-economic ladder. Kemal Efendi also adopted 'modern' ways of dressing and dining in his household, bringing imported goods, such as a gramophone, a radio and later a refrigerator, from Istanbul to his house in Çorum. After the establishment of the republic, he was one of the few figures to wear a felt hat and a suit, in line with the change in dress codes with the republican reforms. Contrary to the *laiklik* criticism (see Chapter 2)

---

[86] How Kemal Bey took over the mill from the villagers, who these villagers were and where they went are not clear. It is tempting to see these villagers as deported Armenians, but without any other historical or archival investigation or knowledge of local history and dynamics, this would be pure speculation.

that the republican reforms encouraged a non-Muslim way of life, doing the daily prayers five times a day was one of Kemal Efendi's most important habits. Hikmet Hasırcı recalls as a child his amazement at how his grandfather's suit would never get wrinkles in it despite him regularly doing his prayers. Kemal Efendi, then, appears to have been an Anatolian merchant who was supportive of modernization in general, and of the new republican regime and its reforms in particular.

Nuri (Hasırcı) Agha, on the other hand, came from a family that had migrated from the Caucasus and settled in Amasya. He and his brother and their sons kept a farm there, where Nuri was the head of the household and the Agha of the villagers working on his land.[87] Nuri Agha had three sons: Alim, Salim and Halim. For each of his sons, Nuri Bey selected daughters of factory owners in Çorum (see footnote 84) as their wives. Alim was married to the daughter of the owner of the Ocakbahçe factory, Salim to the second daughter of Kemal Efendi (owner of Çorum-Un, introduced above)[88], and Halim to the daughter of a factory owner who took over the Kadıtarla Factory from two Armenians named Sarkis and Agop in 1916, just after 1915. Here Hikmet Hasırcı mentions that there were rumours that taking over the factory from the Armenians was unlawful. The factory was burned down in a mysterious fire around the same years, the date not being specified in the memoir.

The point at which of Kemal Efendi decided to modernize the grain mill coincided with the time the brothers Salim (Kemal Efendi's son-in-law) and Halim (apart from running their farm) were submitting public bids to obtain contracts for road construction, which the area needed most to be able to transport goods to Samsun and Ankara. Hikmet Hasırcı writes that they were not very successful at this, so in the late 1920s Kemal Efendi, together with his sons-in-law Salim Hasırcı and Celil Ondur, turned the grain mill into a factory. According to the current manager, they bought the modern wooden mills second-hand from a German flour factory in the Merzifon area, and the Armenian technicians and artisans who were still there in the area converted the factory in Çorum. The first thing the Hasırcı family

---

[87] Many of the Circassians who fled from war and ethnic cleansing in Russia after 1864 settled all over Anatolia, including the Çorum area. However, not all Caucasians who settled were given large plots of land together with the villagers living on it to cultivate. This and later connections signal that Nuri Hasırcı Agha and his family might have been considered Muslims loyal to the state and were settled in Amasya, where the Alevi population was high as a continuation of settlement policies aimed at their assimilation and control since the sixteenth century. See the subsection on Alevis in Chapter 3 for more historical background. This is only a possible interpretation, given that in the wars of the late nineteenth century and the early twentieth century millions of people migrated and settled elsewhere.

[88] Hikmet Hasırcı, the writer of this memoir, is their son.

invested in after opening the factory in 1934 was a Ford truck they bought from Samsun, probably one of the first in Çorum. After the factory started operating and after Kemal Buğdaycı died in 1948, Salim Buğdaycı and his son Hikmet Buğdaycı inherited the factory and ran it. Later on, in the 1960s, they consulted an Armenian middleman in İstanbul, as the current manager recalls, who helped them make a deal with a British company to renovate the factory. To do so, they took out bank loans with the Industry and Development Bank. The factory became one of the largest enterprises in Çorum, provided jobs for many people, and trained many factory workers, artisans, technicians, engineers and managers, some of whom opened their own factories later on. Their stories have shaped the trajectory of Çorum industry, as I will describe in the following sections.

The story of the Hasırcı and Buğdaycı families is a snapshot of how some Turkish Muslim landlords of the previous century became capitalists under the republic. Kemal Efendi's discovery of the Istanbul textile market had a significant impact on their trade, but more significant still was the transfer of business contacts to Turkish Muslims as a result of the population policies of the early twentieth century. Through these contacts, they accumulated mercantile capital and later invested in buying second-hand mills from a German factory and their installation. However, the resources of the two families were not limited to this mercantile capital. The Buğdaycı and Hasırcı families married their daughters and sons to people who owned factories and/or took over Armenian property. By doing so, they merged these contacts and capital in order to finance their future industrial complex. There are also a few points in the memoir that at first glance seem like details. Hikmet Hasırcı talks about how Celil Ondur filled the void left from the departure of the Armenians, an example of 'those who use the chance wisely'; he also mentions that, when Halim's father-in-law took over the Armenian factory in 1916, there were rumours that it was unlawful, as we have seen. It is difficult to read between the lines without further investigation of this topic, but there is still a quantity of literature on late Ottoman history focusing on the impacts of the Armenian Massacre and how properties and contacts changed hands in those years, indicating what might have happened.

The Armenian Massacre (1915), also called the Armenian Genocide or Deportation depending on the source, has been discussed in the framework of nation-state building, Turkish nationalism and human rights (Akçam 2004, 2012), but a handful of scholars have also pointed out its economic consequences (Kıray and Hinderink 1970; Keyder 1987; Boratav 2010; Önal 2012). Yet only a few historians have documented the seizures of abandoned Armenian properties and their distribution by the ITC (*İttihat ve*

Terakki Cemiyeti / Committee of Union and Progress; see Chapter 2) in order to reshuffle the socio-economic structure and boost a national economy led by ethnic Turks in Adana, Diyarbakır and Kayseri (Polatel 2009; Üngör and Polatel 2011; Gözel Durmaz 2015). This literature argues that the abandoned Armenian properties became a significant link between the local elites and the central government. Those with a connection to local ITC cadres created a wide network of local notables who acquired these abandoned properties in exchange for their loyalty to the state and support of the deportations. In other words, 'The regime bought the loyalty of the old urban aristocracy by appealing to their sense of economic self-interest and thereby created a new bourgeoisie' (Üngör and Polatel 2011: 167).

The direct involvement of those mentioned in the memoir with the ITC cadres is not clear, nor is the extent of their support, if any, of the deportations in exchange for loyalty to the ITC. Yet, when considered together with the historical context and the available literature on the topic, hints in the memoir suggest that some involvement in a wider local ITC network is plausible. In the case of Celil Ondur, 'using the chance wisely' might also mean making business contacts with people who had the political affiliations or involvement in this network, which linked him and his family with the central government. Hikmet Buğdaycı's remark about rumours of the illegality in Halim Hasırcı's father-in-law taking over the former Armenian factory in 1916 hints that when the Armenian owners were forced to leave, they either had to give the factory away for free or sell it at a lower price, the local authorities possibly overlooking these transactions. Two decades later, in the 1930s, the Hasırcı family invested in a Ford truck, as already mentioned. At the time, Vehbi Koç who would later become the wealthiest man in the country, became the only Ford dealer in Turkey by a parliamentary decision of 1928. This suggests that Hasırcıs' investment must have been made through Koç's contacts in Samsun, which strengthens the possibility that the family entered into business contacts through those who had political affiliations, if not directly themselves.

Michael Meeker's (2002) meticulous study, which covers a longer time-span from the eighteenth to twentieth centuries, offers insights into the continuity and transformation of the relationship of the local elites to the central government, which is not limited to the events of 1915. His main argument is that local elites (such as local notables and *agha*s, and their male descendants) of Of (a county of Trabzon on the Black Sea) formed a social oligarchy that was recognized as the imperial agents in the periphery and that shared the social, political and military authority of the central government following the decentralization of the Ottoman administration in the late eighteenth and early nineteenth centuries. Meeker (2002) finds that this trend showed continuity during the twentieth century into the republican era, even though republican accounts dismiss the role of *agha*s and *hodja*s, especially in the nationalist framework of the republic's social and political life. Accordingly, the events told in Hikmet Hasırcı's memoir must be put into context without dismissing the possible connections of Çorum's *efendi*s and *agha*s with the central government.

However, the content of these relations must remain open-ended until archival research can be conducted on Çorum's political and social history that sheds light on them. Nevertheless, the tentative conclusion to derive from the memoir is to acknowledge that in the Çorum area too, the deportation of Armenians from Anatolia played a role in the 'original sin', as Karl Marx called it, and resulted in 'primitive accumulation' on the part of the new Turkish Muslim businessmen. That is to say, with the forceful expropriation and distribution of Armenian land and property by the Turkish state, the use of existing means of production for the formerly farming Turkish Muslims was gradually transferred to industry (Fine and Saad-Filho 2004: 75-76).

The 1960s Onwards: Multiple Partnerships and Transfers of Technology and Know-How from Abroad

From the 1950s in Turkey, development, especially of the infrastructure for the new social, administrative and industrial facilities, speeded up, and rural migrants to metropoles became workers in the new industries. In this context, a cement factory was established in Çorum, the first state investment of 1957. The 'upper industry' (*yukarı sanayi*; see Figure 4), as it is called today, started to flourish in these years as a side effect of the establishment of the cement factory providing the equipment to fix and repair machines in small workshops. Apart from small-size manufacturers and repairmen, many businessmen carried out large investments in this sector. Çorum's wealthy families wanted to use the city's advantages in raw materials to meet the market demand for building infrastructure. These families cooperated with workers who had a knowledge of the local trade routes and had experience working with the raw materials. Mehmet Korkmaz, a rich businessman who owned the franchising rights to many garment companies and real-estate firms in Çorum in the 2000s, tells how his father and partners started a tile factory. Mehmet Bey's father Şahin Bey was an 'ambitious' and 'hardworking' construction worker who wanted to open such a factory but lacked the capital to do so. At this time, better-off local families in Çorum, who were in the clay-pot manufacturing business and had experience of working with the raw materials, were also in search of a partner. Somehow their paths crossed, so they suggested to Şahin Bey that they do business together. After long negotiations, Şahin Bey became a partner in this new venture on the condition that he would himself find the machines with which to build the tile factory, while his partners provided the capital. He used his previous contacts in the construction business and learned that the Spanish had the best automated press machines he needed, then he headed to Eskişehir (240 km west of Ankara), where the artisans could mock up a replica of the required technology. Şahin Bey brought the automated press machines to Çorum, and that is how they started two tile factories in the 1960s.

In those days a tile factory was a cheap investment, in the sense that one needed a worksite, clay and a machine to press the clay into tiles and bricks. The rest of the work was done by the sun, which dried the product. The backbone of this business was the cheap and unskilled labour available. As their rural economy no longer allowed them to be self-sufficient, and as they were gradually becoming dependent on the market, especially for basic consumer goods, in-migrating villagers worked in these tile and brick factories, where child labour was also very widespread. In fact, every man above the age of fifty in Çorum can remember carrying piles of bricks from one place to another as a child or knowing someone in his circle who had done so. Apart from the fact that the working conditions were merciless, the job was mostly seasonal and insecure, and the pay was very low, without any social security coverage. Another reason for investing in brick- and tile-manufacturing was that it was a lucrative business back then because of the advances provided by the state. As Mehmet Bey put it, 'In those years, Turkey was going through a developmental phase, and the state was building schools and public buildings, lining up for bricks. They would pay in advance, wait for six months, then get the product. Not like today's system, where they would pay a year later in instalments'. There were eight tile and brick factories in Çorum in 1967, increasing to twenty in 1972 and forty in 1980 (Tekeli 1986b: 249). Additionally, as described in Chapter 2, the 1970s were years of planned development, and Çorum was listed among the priority regions for development in 1972. The fact that the state was the sole buyer of these products and that it had paid advances without auditing the working conditions in these factories clearly shows its support of these activities, at variance with how Çorum's economic development is usually described. Many established businessmen like Mehmet Bey tend to overemphasize the role of their fathers' ambition and hard work, placing the persona of the male character at the centre of their narratives of 'success'. Yet, this leaves the story incomplete and downplays the important role of the high demand for the product, the cheap and insecure labour of uprooted villagers and children, and state incentives in the economic success of these enterprises.

This does not mean that people's efforts to create new economic opportunities were unimportant or trivial. Multiple partnerships were in fact common in those decades. Many traders and small manufacturers who were not necessarily in the same sector but were individually short of capital would pool their money to invest in big business ideas. One of the best known examples of this in Çorum is the paper factory. Cengiz Bey, now in his sixties, is a timber manufacturer and merchant like his father, who was involved in the initial stages of the establishment of the paper factory. His story about his father's 'adventure' is as follows. In 1977-78 there was a drought in Çorum, and people had to carry water in plastic cans from the public fountains to their homes. At the same time, demand for the plastic cans increased because of the need to keep oil, pickles and diesel fuel in something. So, some merchants from other cities would come to the local bazaar and sell the cans for unreasonable prices. Nesim Bey therefore formed a group of eleven people, including Cengiz Bey's father and his uncles, his original idea being to build a plastic can factory in Çorum. They consulted a senior engineer who was himself from Çorum but who lived and worked in Germany. His advice was to drop the plastic can idea but to go into the paper business because that market was more promising. This senior engineer came back to Çorum later on and led the next steps in the investment. After contacting some agents in Istanbul, they found out that an abandoned Italian paper factory had machines, which were being sold below price due to new environment regulations there. Finally, in 1981 the partners were able to buy the machines, transport them and install them in Çorum. As Cengiz Bey and later other middle-aged men whose fathers witnessed this adventure in Çorum industry explained to me, when the factory was opened, the partners had almost no clue about how to run the machines, how to keep the books or how to manage such a large enterprise. So they invited consultants from abroad to teach their technicians the know-how and the managers the production process, while the workers learned how to use the machines through practice and repair. In the meantime, they constantly acquired new partners, ranging from teachers to farmers, to finance the factory's needs. Cengiz Bey claims that the factory became one of the important 'A league' firms in its sector, but it was severely affected by the 1994 economic crisis and was sold out to a multinational company. When it was sold, the factory had 96 partners. Not only the economic crisis but also the imbalances between the partners' shares and their sons becoming involved complicated the situation. The next generation preferred to withdraw their shares from the paper factory to reinvest and deploy the skills and techniques they had acquired in different businesses.

The experience of the paper factory could be seen as an example of a 'culture of partnership'. Small manufacturers and traders formed an alliance, explored new investment ideas and transferred knowledge from abroad to overcome their shortages of capital, technology and know-how. Multiple partnerships were also common in the case of the numerous flour factories that opened in Çorum after the 1960s. The relative stability and increasing welfare in the post-war period, as well as the spread of mechanization in agriculture, had a positive impact on the growth of population in Çorum city centre, which hit a peak of 6.6 percent between 1955 and 1960 (Çoban 2016: 419). However, it dramatically fell to 2.4 percent in the next five years, due partly to continually increasing outmigration from Çorum to other major cities[89], as urban employment opportunities in state factories attracted many, and the increased demand for durable products led to a decrease in the demand for local crafts. The main employment options were limited to state jobs for the educated or to technical and manual jobs in the 'upper industry' or the cement factory. Those who did not join the waves of rural-urban migration in the 1960s and 1970s had to create something to make a life for themselves and for others who had stayed. Therefore, even though we might talk about a 'culture' of partnership, we have to acknowledge that it was driven out of necessity. The contributions of townspeople to such an enterprise could be understood as an act of solidarity with the initial group of partners, who, by their efforts, had created new jobs. Yet, in different conversations with people whose families invested cash in the paper factory, some claimed that their families did not receive anything back when the factory was sold. Moreover, in numerous multiple partnerships formed to overcome the shortages of capital, when companies achieved higher rates of turnover and thus the economic power to invest in more profitable, high-tech, export-oriented sectors, the second- and third-generation partners were not willing to remain in these multiple partnerships. It would therefore be more accurate to say that there was a collective effort to boost Çorum's economy, though it would be far-fetched to label these efforts a 'culture of partnership', as is common in academic works also (see Chapter 1). Nonetheless, the establishment of factories with multiple partners has enabled four simultaneous processes: local notables' savings were converted into capital that created a profit; former peasants gradually became wage-labourers; some professionalization was achieved; and skills and know-how

---

[89] According to Çoban (2016), the net migration rate for 1975-1980 was 46‰. This is the earliest accessible date for these statistics. Although not demonstrable with numbers, many Çorumlu emigrated to Germany as *Gastarbeiter* (guest worker) in the 1960s.

were transferred from abroad and passed on through imitation and the repair of machines.

Özal Incentives: A Push Forward from the State

Although the tile and brick industry seems to have been thriving already by the end of the 1970s, after the 1980s developments in both the tile and other sectors accelerated in an unprecedented way. The ANAP government issued sector- and region-specific incentives, tax reductions, preferential credits and loans to local entrepreneurs on an individual basis to boost industrialization and exports. Those who had become a part of already established domestic trade networks dominated by the large bourgeoisie in north-west Turkey had more opportunities to obtain franchises for imported or import-substituted goods and hence dominate local markets. The accounts of two businessmen illustrate such cases and reveal further details about the mutual relations between the state, the large bourgeoisie and politics.

Memduh Bey was one of the industrialists in Çorum whose father had already entered into a few partnerships involving tile factories by the end of the 1970s. His grandfather settled in Çorum from Malatya, a province in eastern Anatolia, and was involved in *çirişçilik* (see footnote 78) and tannery. When chemical dyes replaced *çiriş*, his father did not pursue tannery anymore but instead opened a small grocery store, where he first started selling retail, then went into the wholesale trade. This was in the decades following the Second World War, when the number of motor vehicles had increased in Çorum. Local bus companies started to operate from Çorum and its surrounding towns to Izmir, Ankara, Samsun and Istanbul (Tekeli 1986b: 238). That is how Memduh Bey's father would go to Ankara to buy the wholesale goods directly from the centre. Later, he invested in a truck himself. As in this example and in others, those who had some savings if they invested in motor vehicles gained an absolute advantage in accumulating further capital because they could act as a link between Çorum and the central markets. By removing the intermediaries in his trade, as Memduh Bey puts it, his father's business expanded exponentially. Memduh Bey's father kept running his wholesale business from Ankara and in addition started transporting cement from the Çorum state factory to construct the Middle East Technical University in Ankara in the late 1950s.

In the meanwhile, Memduh Bey's cousin (his father's brother's son) was manufacturing clay pots and bricks. Encouraged by the boom in the tile and brick industry, and given Memduh Bey's father's lucrative business transporting cement, in 1966 they too decided to open a cement factory by pursuing partners like Şahin Bey. As a result, by the end of the 1970s

Memduh Bey's father, brother and cousin became partners in several tile and flour factories (owned by non-relatives), and in 1978 the former purchased the franchising rights to Ford trucks in Çorum and dropped his wholesale business. By that time, the Ford company in the U.S. had expanded its production to Europe, and in the late 1950s Koç Holdings initiated a joint-venture to produce and sell Ford vehicles locally. Memduh Bey's purchase of a Ford franchise indicates that he had become part of a local domestic network of Istanbul bourgeoisie that enabled it to dominate domestic markets and at the same time increase the rent capital Memduh Bey acquired and hence his capacity to invest further in Çorum's industry.

Memduh Bey did not say much about those partners who were not relatives, but he explained that his father and others had commercial debt accounts with the banks, that they had credit limits based on their assets and good relations with the bank manager, and that they could take a certain amount of money in exchange for a note (*senet*). The note, whether covering the whole loan or divided into instalments, had to be signed by a non-relative of the debtor to provide a payment guarantee to the bank. Memduh Bey said that the guarantor could be a friend or a next-door neighbour, and that people would help each other on the basis of '*bugün sana, yarın bana*', a Turkish saying meaning 'today for me, tomorrow for you' and expressing a kind of reciprocity. On the other hand, it is not hard to envisage these non-relatives signing notes for each other. It is also possible, although not mentioned in the interview, that Memduh Bey's partner Şahin Bey or his other partners (who started the tile and brick factories) might have used a similar credit mechanism. For Memduh Bey, however, after some point it was not even necessary to show a guarantee to the bank in exchange for his loans. As he puts it, 'The bank had extensive authorization. The bank branch manager has issued very significant amounts of loans. Plus, because we are these local businessmen generally, we would have the chance to object to bank decisions. One of the most important things was investigation by the Central Bank: they would check if your bills had been "protested", or if you had any distraining orders and so on. Not having these was a condition. They would come from the regional office, ask around about you [to the bank managers] and give their opinion. I remember very well, I still have credit in Xbank through my father. Without guarantees or collateral, just with my signature I can use it'. These credits he is talking about are huge amounts that he and his father apparently took out. Given that local businessman can object to a local bank's decision and can acquire limitless amounts of credit through generations of the Central Bank personnel's opinions suggests that these might be politically influenced, individual-based decisions. One can also assume that from the 1960s onwards other local businessmen might have gone down the same paths, if not before, then since. This was especially after the 1980s (see Chapter 2), when financial liberalization was introduced, loan and deposit rate controls were cancelled, and most of the credit requirements were eliminated to increase competition and efficiency in the banking sector (Akın, Aysan and Yıldıran 2008). In a short time, the need for regulatory measures was recognized, and in agreement with the IMF and World Bank, in 1985 a new banking law was passed that gave the treasury the responsibility for regulating and supervising the banks. However, 'the regulatory institution was not independent of pressures from politicians and influential banking lobbies ... [and] tended to overlook the unacceptable credit, interest rate and exchange rate risks of banks' (ibid.: 8-9). It was in these circumstances that Memduh Bey could obtain limitless credit just by providing his signature.

The 'Özal incentives', named after Prime Minister Turgut Özal, who implemented them in the 1980s, are region-specific incentives and tax reductions provided by the treasury in many new sectors, but mainly in industry. Although it is tempting to think they were as individual-based as in the bank credits given in the above example, my findings suggest that they were part of a regional development plan. Moreover, the findings also negate the dominant discourse on emerging economies being achieved 'without the support of the state' (ESI 2005; Keyman and Lorasdağı 2010: 202-218). Memduh Bey was in his twenties when he finished his undergraduate degree in Ankara in the 1980s and came back to Çorum, just when his family was planning to start a flour factory, which also coincided with the Özal incentives. During our interview, on the one hand he explained in detail what these incentives were all about, while on the other hand, by going back and forth in the story and repeating complicated details of calculations, he tried to blur the content of the incentives. According to his detailed account of the percentages of the cost covered by the incentives and tax reductions when the flour factory started in 1987, the value added tax, which was 12% percent at the time, was indefinitely delayed. 70% of the remainder would be provided as an incentive at very low interest directly by the treasury, and 30% would be taken out as a loan with a bank. At the same time, 40% of the costs of all machines and construction would be covered by the contribution of the incentive. The back-payments of these credits and incentives are unclear, especially the 70% provided by the Treasury, because it was common practice in the 1980s to issue amendments for incentive back-payments. Thus, what is left for the factory owner to pay back is only 60% of the bank loan, or 18% of the whole investment, excluding the tax. When I asked rhetorically whether this was more like a state investment, Memduh Bey said 'Yes'. By the end of our conversation I was also interested in knowing who used these incentives, so I could interview them too. He replied that almost all flour, tile and brick factories and over two hundred chicken farms established in and after the 1980s were involved, and he named many of the factories that are sectoral leaders even today. As Özuğurlu (2008) has argued for the case of Denizli, the economic development of the provinces after the 1980s was made possible not because the state retreated – on the contrary, the state transferred capital through its laws and incentives. This was also the case in Çorum.

Although mentioning the Özal incentives as a reason for the industrialization and the growth of the economy in the 1980s and 1990s is common, its content is rarely spelled out in the way that Memduh Bey did in our conversation. Also, their impact has been under-estimated, as we have seen in the discourse about the rise of emerging provinces. With these incentives, by the end of the 1990s, 40% of the tiles and 10% of the bricks used in Turkey were being produced in Çorum (Güven and Kaygın 2013: 94). Onur Bey was also one of the industrialists who owned a medium-size factory in Çorum and who openly spoke about the relationship between the state, the big companies and provincial developments. He recalled that the 'state made us [meaning the provincial entrepreneurs] rich' through these incentives, and also mentioned the role of conglomerates in developments in the Anatolian provinces. According to Onur Bey, the Turkish state gave the Koç Group, Sabancı and Eczacıbaşı[90] the mission of creating the capitalists of Anatolia (cf. Hikmet Buğdaycı's memoir). This was done mainly by handing out franchises of the products they supply to the country, just as in the case of Memduh Bey's father, who bought the Ford tractor franchise. Another mode of capital transfer was to offer provincial businessmen shares in his companies, as Onur Bey himself was offered by Vehbi Koç[91] in the 1990s solely on the basis of trust, so that he could use them later on to invest in his own business. Memduh Bey's and Onur Bey's accounts document the direct and indirect ways the state intervened, incentivized and contributed to the development of Anatolian capital. Moreover, the information they provided and their assessments are valuable in understanding how they both served as bureaucrats, the former at the local, the latter at the national level, until recently. Because they no longer bear the responsibilities of their positions, I assumed they could talk openly about the past. Secondly, they are both typical examples of how provincial capitalists have been created in Turkey.

---

[90] Three of the largest conglomerates, all having started as family firms in Turkey.
[91] The founder of Koç Group, who died in 1996.

The Çorum Massacre's Impacts on Alevi Businessmen

Alongside these economic developments, the 1980s were traumatizing years for many people in Çorum, especially the Alevis. Eren Bey's father is one of the Alevi businessmen whose workplace and house were burned down during the massacre in Çorum. Before the 1980s, he used to live from the trade in animals and owned his own trucks. He made a large profit and had a range of contacts from this trade. Alongside this business, he also started another business as a food wholesaler. Eren Bey's father's conditions were no different from those of Memduh Bey's father, and a similar path was also open to their family. However, after the massacre they had to move to a new neighbourhood and start all over again. The strategic move Eren Bey's father made at that time was to open his new workplace not in the Alevi neighbourhood, but in the central Sunni neighbourhood, and restart his wholesale food trade there with his savings from the trade in animals. Eren Bey described this era as follows: 'Many of the workplaces left [the neighbourhood]. Only a few people, who did not differentiate between Alevi and Sunni and considered themselves their brothers, even after those events, stayed in the city centre and pursued trade. The customers we called Sunni kept shopping with us; only a few did not come. However, those customers we called Alevi couldn't come to us, so they shopped in their own neighbourhoods'. He would not even refer to them as 'Alevi or Sunni customers' in short, but preferred to say 'customers we call Alevi/Sunni'. He says he is using this specific phrasing to avoid discrimination. By doing so, he distinguishes between the customers and their religious beliefs, saying not that the customer is Alevi/Sunni but that we call them Alevi/Sunni, and thus not identifying the customer in terms of his/her religious belief. This logic suggests that what matters in business is the fact that they are customers, not the latter's religious beliefs, as we may choose to call them one or the other or neither. This becomes even clearer in Onur Bey's account of two other Alevi wholesalers who kept their workplaces in the Alevi neighbourhood, but could not survive because of their narrow customer base. He then compared their choices to his own: 'but we did, we traded with everyone, [but] they got stuck and disappeared'. If Eren Bey's father had been someone with a grudge and had stayed in the close community, he would either have had to migrate to another city at some point, as many Alevis did after the 'incidents' (as the massacre is commonly called), or he would have to settle for a smaller business with less chance of expanding.

Apart from his savings from the animal trade, when Eren Bey took over his father's business in 1986, he did not have the capital to move forward. The wholesale business was not very profitable unless one could buy directly from the factory. He then started searching for a franchise in the food sector and managed to make some connections in 1994, purchasing the franchising rights to several brands and later a distributorship of national and international brands at the end of the 1990s. Unlike Onur Bey's situation, he was not offered a share by the Istanbul bourgeoisie, but he did use bank credits when creating a fleet of transport vehicles for the distribution. I was not really convinced that his business managed to survive without any additional capital investment and only using the profits of his trading in animals, so I kept asking him further how he had accumulated his capital. He explained why he did not have much financial trouble as follows: 'We had such an advantage that villagers were reluctant to put their money in the banks, so they would come to us – back then people did not know about interest rates – and would leave their cash in our safe, so we had so many people's money in our office. They thought this was more solid than putting it in the bank. I find it funny myself now, but really when I think about it, we would never make the customers sign notes. Instead we had a notebook where we recorded them, and there would not be any delays. Hence, we were able to do our finances without needing any finance [meaning bank loans]'. I interpret this to mean that the firm used the money the villagers had left with them as a capital investment, but at the same time they lent money to them without interest. When I asked who exactly these villagers were and why they did this, he replied that 'they are customers who are co-villagers or acquaintances who are not customers. It was just after the 1980s: they had the idea that, if things get out of order, the state would confiscate the banks and would not give them their money back'.[92] It is much more likely that 'acquaintances who are not customers' were mainly Alevis who lost trust in the state following the 1980 massacre and therefore provided a source of capital to Eren Bey.[93]

The second capital investment, at the end of 1990s, came from his paternal uncle, who had migrated to Germany in the early 1960s as a guest worker. With his savings as a factory worker with BMW in Germany, he bought 49% percent of Eren Bey's company and became a shareholder without interfering in how the company was run. As the stories of different businessmen reveal, there were different sources of capital and different social relations they drew on to expand their businesses. In the earlier

---

[92] This fear was a realistic one, since in those years many private banks embezzled people's money, creating what was known as the Bankers' Crisis in 1982.

[93] However, one should not jump into the conclusion that the exploitation of ethnic ties and trust through informal saving and lending mechanisms is specific to Alevis as a closed community. Many people recalled these sorts of transaction from the past, yet it is certainly not something that ceased to exist. Many people save their money in the jewellery or currency exchange shops in central Çorum in the form of gold or the more valuable currencies such as the Euro or US Dollar.

examples, this was a matter of signing notes for each other to obtain bank loans and working in exchange for a share in a company; in the last example villagers' savings and lending, and together with capital brought back by workers form Germany, became further sources of capital.

Çorum's Supply Chain of Machinery and Realization of Accumulated Experiences

From the 1990s onwards, the direct contributions to the development of local industry, like Özal's incentives, were no longer available. Instead, regions were classified according to their development indicators, and a certain budget was transferred to them, either annually, based on local governments' demands, or based on project applications through the local branches of central institutions such as the Small- and Medium-sized Business Development and Support Administration (*Küçük ve Orta Ölçekli İşletmeleri Geliştirme ve Destekleme İdaresi Başkanlığı*, KOSGEB), the development agencies that were set up in every region. Moreover, industrial zones were established in many provinces at the beginning of 1980s within the framework of a state development programme. This was established initially in Çorum in 1978 and started developing in the late 1990s. The initial infrastructure was financed by the provincial administration, the municipality, the Çorum Chamber of Trade and Industry (*Çorum Ticaret ve Sanayi Odası*, ÇTSO) and the Çorum Industrial Zone Businessmen's Organization (*Çorum Organize Sanayi Bölgesi Sanayicileri ve İşadamları Derneği*, ÇOSİAD), the latter having almost half of the shares and seats in the governing structure. Later, in 2013 and 2015, the plots of land and infrastructure were expanded with three large-scale loans from the Ministry of Industry, Science and Technology.[94] Based on regional classifications, those who invested in Çorum's industrial zone could benefit from exemptions from value added tax and customs tariffs, reductions of taxes and interest rates in investment, allocations of space in the zone, and reductions in employers' contributions to workers' social insurance with varying percentages and durations.[95] By the late 1990s, there were already several big companies specializing in flour and tile-machine production in Çorum's industrial zone. As mentioned earlier in the case of the Çorum-

---

[94] Data from a booklet provided by the Directorate of Çorum Organized Industry during fieldwork.
[95] Many details regarding the eligibility conditions for these incentives in different regions, and the duration and percentages of the incentives offered by the state, are set out in the latest incentive legislation published in the official gazette in 19.06.2012, issue 28328. Although the legislation has been amended, the 2012 legislation remains its basis.

Flour factory, once the factories had been installed from the 1960s onwards, the workers in them learned how flour machines operated, how to fix and repair them, and even how to produce them by imitation. In fact, many manufacturers in today's Çorum would say that imitation was the most important source of knowledge for them. As one third-generation factory owner explained:

> This Çorum-Flour that we worked for bought up a complete factory from a British company. Carpenters, blacksmiths, those foremen who have seen a bit of industry, welding, hammer, wrench such as the *muhacir*[96] came and looked at the machines in Çorum-Flour to see which of them they could make themselves. And they tried to copy the machines exactly, then started their own workshops. These workshops were born out of these people striving to build these machines, like we did. Later, when the businesses developed a little bit, foremen emerged who could build them. One knew how to make a sifter, another a purifier, a third part of a mill. They also taught their apprentices. If I were a big company and had money, I would find the foreman who can make a sifter, the one who can make a purifier, find them all and tell them to do this and that, and outsource the raw materials needed to make these according to the lists these foremen made for me.

In many interviews, similar trajectories of imitation and the transfer of skills were mentioned, referring to the fact that the second generation of factories were opened by these foremen and/or larger companies who pooled foremen who specialized in manufacturing parts of different machines used in flour and tile and brick production in the 1990s. From the memoirs of Ümit Uzel, the head of the Chamber of Industry and Commerce of the time, we learn that a couple of large enterprises that grew out of Çorum-Flour had already been thriving in the export market by the beginning of the 2000s. These large, export-oriented factories with more than a thousand workers, situated in the segment with the highest turnover in Çorum, led to two developments in the 1990s. First, they functioned like Çorum-Flour and created a new generation of foremen specializing in certain parts of the machines. Second, this new generation of foremen created a supply chain to meet the market demand and/or to outsource these demands by manufacturing machine parts or sometimes the machines themselves. In today's Çorum, hundreds of workshops of this kind are active in the 'upper industry', supplying around fifty flour and tile-machine factories in the industrial zone (see Figure 4).

---

[96] Term used to refer mainly to Ottoman Muslims in the Balkans and also Muslims in Russia and the Caucasus who migrated to Thrace and Anatolia between the late nineteenth and late twentieth century.

Some of the factories in the industrial zone started in the upper industry and later enlarged their businesses. The kinds of project-based support offered by KOSGEB and the development agency are mainly oriented towards the second and third generations of manufacturers in these two zones.[97] In the following section, I present the origin story of the main protagonists in this book, namely the factory I will henceforth call Çor-Mak, a third-generation factory specializing in machine manufacture, which emerged out of the processes described above.

Cemal Bey, in his early fifties, comes from a village of Çorum, where his family did small subsistence farming. At the age of thirteen he dropped out of school, and his father took him to the upper industry to become an apprentice and learn a manual skill. He had to earn his own pocket money when his father left the family to work as a guest-worker in Switzerland. During his apprenticeship, he says that he learned all about metals and counters, how to bend sheet metal, assemble it according to the measurements, and read and do the calculations. As he acquired more and more skills, his master took him with him to set up the new flour factories that were being built in Anatolia in 1980s. After Cemal Bey completed his military service, he became a master himself and started working at Çorum-Flour as a foreman. Years later, Çorum-Flour bought a new machine with a pneumatic[98] system from Germany which Cemal Bey had to install as the factory foreman, while Bülent Bey was hired as a German-speaking mechanical engineer to work with him.

Bülent Bey's story was quite different from Cemal Bey's. He grew up in a better-off family, his father being a civil servant. After finishing high school in Çorum, he won a state scholarship to study engineering in Germany. Later he worked in Germany, in Africa, for a few years in Istanbul and in another central Anatolian city, mainly in the automotive sector. However, in the 1980s his brother became unemployed, which influenced Bülent Bey's decision to return to Çorum. Together with his brother, he started a poultry farm which benefited from the Özal incentives of the time. Bülent Bey never saw the farm as something he would pursue all his life, so he tried to find an engineering job in Çorum, the sort of job that was very scarce. He also tried different sectors like assembling elevators, but that also

---

[97] KOSGEB and the development agency support projects in all sectors, not only manufacturers. On the other hand, the KOSGEB office in Çorum is located in the Organized Industrial Zone, twenty kilometres from the city centre, indicating that it is actually oriented towards the needs of the manufacturers.

[98] A branch of engineering that uses pressurized gas or air. In the case of flour-producing and processing machines, it is used to replace human power with pipes to move the products from point A to point B.

did not work out well. Finally he found the job at Çorum-Flour, where he met Cemal Bey. They were both looking forward to a new stage in their professional lives, and both thought this new pneumatic system could be a profitable business, with a potential market in the Çorum flour industry.

Cemal Bey and Bülent Bey laid the foundations for their partnership in the mid-1990s. However, they only had limited capital. Bülent Bey had seventeen thousand Deutsche Marks, and Cemal Bey had received compensation from Çorum-Flour, making ten thousand Turkish Liras in all. Hikmet Buğdaycı, who was still running the factory himself, lent them some money, and Cemal Bey's father also gave them some of his savings from having worked in Switzerland, so they rented a small workshop in the upper industry and bought some counters and equipment. However, the machine was difficult to imitate, as it required a lot of engineering, skills and studying from books, all of which took time. At times, Bülent Bey had to use loans backed by his brother's poultry farm to pay the workers in his workshop. In the meantime, they produced simpler machine parts and discovered new needs in the flour sector, such as a regulator. Once they had managed to produce the pneumatic machines, they made a deal with larger second-generation factory in Çorum which outsourced their manufacture to smaller companies like Çor-Mak and sold it to a flour factory in Tekirdağ in north-west Turkey. However, a problem occurred with the machine in that the original producers had not been consulted directly. When Bülent Bey and Cemal Bey heard about this, they went to Tekirdağ themselves and stayed there for a while to properly install their product. They also sat together with the managers and bosses there, explained the kinds of machines they could produce, calculated the costs and finally made a deal, thus removing the intermediary company from the transaction. The owners of the Tekirdağ factory paid them 300,000 Deutsche Mark, with cheques in advance. This kind of capital investment turned out to be very profitable because during the 2001 economic crisis the Turkish Lira was devalued against other currencies. This meant that Bülent Bey and Cemal Bey had double the amount of money in their hands, while the Tekirdağ factory owners also cashed the cheques in advance to avoid the crisis breaking their deal.

In local reports, experts estimate that in Çorum half of all factories were closed after the 2001 economic crisis (İzmen 2012), mostly factories producing for the domestic market, as was the general trend in industrialization in Turkey. On the other hand, those business people who had savings in Dollars or Euros and large Çorum companies who were already exporting machine parts from raw materials they had acquired on the domestic market were relatively less affected by the crisis. Even though the transition to an export-oriented economic model started in the 1980s, in practice, as Bedirhanoğlu and Yalman (2009) also pointed out, companies shifted to an export strategy as a response to the crises in 1997 and 2001. This trend was accelerated in Çorum, as people accumulated more sophisticated skills that they could channel into machine production, and consequently companies found new customers abroad through their own efforts or via business associations.

After securing their first big business deal and surviving the 2001 crisis, Bülent Bey and Cemal Bey's business got on track. They started receiving orders from different flour factories in Turkey. The reason their products appealed to so many new customers was that the pneumatic system they had initially imitated and later developed further was able to store and weigh the ground wheat and then pack and load the sacks to be transported in a shorter time and with fewer workers. Cemal Bey explained that in normal circumstances in a factory where two hundred tons of wheat is ground in 24 hours, sixteen to twenty workers are needed in the packing and loading section. If their system is installed, however, the number of workers needed in the process decreases to seven or eight, and manufacturing defects in the automated weighing and packaging system also fall. The increasing demand for Çor-Mak products in the initial phases with the aid of self-exploitation and the cheap labour of workers who were relatives (see Chapter 6) meant increasing turnover. Up until that point, using a loan from KOSGEB was something they avoided because of the complicated bureaucratic procedure and paperwork involved. However, by now they could spare the time to apply to purchase the mechanical counters used to cut the metal sheets themselves, which reduced the costs of outsourcing it. A KOSGEB loan covered one third of this investment. However, all this new equipment required more working space, and increasing numbers of orders required more workers, more raw materials and more equipment. In other words, market demand forced the expansion of the company. After a few years trying to maintain a balance, they moved their workplace to the industrial zone. Now they are themselves outsourcing some of the machine parts from the smaller workplaces in the upper industry, and some of their foremen have started their own businesses there. For a decade now, they have been exporting their products mainly to post-Soviet and Middle Eastern countries.

When telling the story of their start-up, they would always underline three factors that had enabled this process: that they were lucky to enter this sector at a time when the flour-machine industry was developing, that the engineering and the book study gave them an advantage over others in the sector, and that cheap labour is what they relied on. Cemal Bey and Bülent Bey's partnership also shows that people had to put aside their prescribed differences of class and culture and prioritize their concerns to earn a livelihood in a context and at a stage in industrial development with only a few engineers and only a handful of skilled manual workers and craftsmen.

In this section of the chapter, I have tried to show that Çorum's economic development was not a 'miracle' but a historical process which unfolded by bringing together specific constellations of social relations and cultural dispositions that enabled capitalist accumulation in Çorum and articulated the city to global capitalism as a periphery. I also revealed the real-life manifestations of abstract notions such as the 'entrepreneurial soul', the 'Çorum model of development' and the 'culture of partnership', as well as the emphasis on 'without the help of the state', often underlined in reports and the media. For each era, I described the socio-economic background of the actors involved, the material resources they brought together and the social relationships they entered into to create their businesses. We have seen the landlords of the previous system becoming the capitalists of the republican regime, first by removing the intermediaries and accessing cheaper markets, but mainly through primitive accumulation. Some who were involved in traditional trades in the nineteenth century, such as trading in animals or clay pots, have been able to access motor vehicles before others, which enabled them to expand the scope of their trades, giving them an absolute advantage in accessing central markets. Those who did not have capital found better-off partners and made deals in exchange for searching for technologies, or else had each other sign notes to obtain bank loans. Those involved in the tile and brick industry used the advantage of the raw materials and previous experiences at a time when there was a demand for infrastructure. On the other hand, through the influence of the big capitalists, the state has directly and indirectly incentivized and supported the boom in flour producers, tile manufacturers and poultry farms, or channelled provincial investors into becoming distributors of their own regions. The Alevis, who had had their workplaces and homes destroyed, had to leave their identity issues aside, at least when doing business, while their ethnic ties and relations of trust provided them with the finance to keep going. The factories that were built in the early years of the republic and later on became schools for others who worked there, and two more generations of manufacturers and their suppliers were born, who created a supply chain. All these developments have followed one another, not so much in a linear way, but as a circuit feeding back into the Çorum economy and its people's experiences in acquiring skills, collecting capital and doing business. Finally, contrary to theories of flexible specialization, these developments occurred in low-tech and labour-intensive economic sectors, such as Çor-Mak.

'Anatolian Tigers are Cats Now'

In my initial conversations and encounters in Çorum, when I raised the question of what they thought about Çorum being one of the 'Anatolian Tigers', people laughed at me, saying the 'Anatolian Tiger has become a cat now'. They said that the city had been advertised in such manner by Ümit Uzel, the Head of the Chamber of Industry and Commerce (*Çorum Ticaret ve Sanayii Odası*-ÇTSO) between 1985 and 1997. In many people's opinion this slogan exaggerated the reality. In fact, Uzel himself talks about his efforts to advertise Çorum and other people's criticisms of him in this respect in his autobiography, *Korumasız Başkan* (2013: 71-88). In Uzel's opinion, his lobbying efforts to promote Çorum's industry had contributed immensely to bringing branches of KOSGEB and other commerce-related institutions to Çorum. Interestingly, Uzel was a retired teacher and a bureaucrat who was a dedicated Kemalist, a hint that leads to questioning of the assumptions that the rise of Çorum capital is related to the rise of political Islam. Later on, I discovered that there was no branch of MÜSİAD in Çorum in those years, one being created only at the end of 2013. In my understanding this was a way to separate themselves from the Hittite Industrialists' and Businessmen's Association (*Hitit Sanayiciler ve İşadamları Derneği*, HITITSIAD), which existed under the auspices of TUSKON, linked to the Gülen movement, after the corruption allegations of that year. There were two other businessmen's associations in the city. One was the Çorum Industrialists' and Businessmen's Association (*Çorum Sanayicileri ve İşadamları Derneği,* ÇORUMSIAD), where Erdem Çenesiz, the CEO of one of the largest companies in Çorum, Ece Banyo, was very active and in 2004 united the associations in the Central Black Sea Region under the Central Black Sea Industrialists' and Businessmen's Federation (*Orta Karadeniz Sanayicileri ve İşadamları Federasyonu*, OKASİFED). In 2006 OKASIFED joined the nation-wide Turkish Enterprise and Business Confederation (*Türk Girişim ve İş Dünyası Konfederasyon*, TURKONFED), which is known to be the Anatolian branch of TÜSAD. Later, Erdem Çenesiz was elected President of TURKONFED, but resigned from his position in 2012 due to his unhappiness at not being able to act independently, as he declared in his own resignation speech[99], reflecting the conflict between Anatolian and north-western capital elaborated in Chapter 2. The second of these business associations is ÇOSİAD, which includes all business people with a factory in the industrial district, but elects an executive board to decide on issues related to the zone. None of these

---

[99] See the news about his resignation, retrieved in March 2020 from: https://www.hurriyet.com.tr/ekonomi/turkonfed-baskani-cenesiz-istifa-etti-21359780

associations were particularly active during my presence in Çorum, although the recently formed MÜSİAD and ÇOSİAD had occasional meetings.

At the end of the 1990s, Ümit Uzel was replaced by Kenan Malatyalı, a local industrialist from a notable Çorum family, as the head of ÇTSO. Coming from a liberal economic political tradition, he had a close attachment to - if not only sympathy for the AKP in the initial years of its rule and consequently served as a high-level bureaucrat in Ankara as head of the Turkish Standards Institute in the early 2000s, but was later dismissed due to corruption allegations. In 2009, Malatyalı was replaced by Çetin Başaranhıncal, a local industrialist, as the head of ÇTSO, who is still in office. These changes recall certain changes in the politics of the AKP, which started drifting away from its initial liberal coalition in 2002 after the 2007 election. Interestingly, the Özal incentives of the 1980s, issued directly by the treasury, and the KOSGEB incentives for SMEs of the 1990s coincided with the Kemalist schoolteacher Ümit Uzel's era, which continued increasingly in the 2000s after his replacement (see Table 1). As Table 1 below demonstrates, Çorum has the highest SME incentive per certificate on average of all provinces. However, during my presence there, two of the largest industrial complexes in Çorum were going through troublesome times; one was about to go bankrupt, and the other, inherited from the founding father, had been split in two because of a quarrel between two brothers. Also, there were rumours about some factories going bankrupt because of debt, and many flour and tile factories built in the 1970s and 1980s were closing down due to the lack of technological investment and increasing labour costs. Even though the construction sector constituted the backbone of the economy in the 2000s, the types of tile and brick produced in Çorum had become outdated by that time because of the introduction of security measures after the 1999 Istanbul (or Düzce, to be exact) earthquake and the proliferation of construction materials with which Çorum's factories could not keep up. Moreover, in 2004 Çorum tile- and brick-factory workers organized a rally, followed by a strike demanding shorter working hours, the payment of social insurance and the right to unionize.[100] The protests were relatively successful: avoiding paying social insurance is no longer as widespread as it used to be in this sector, but this has increased the labour costs from the employers' perspective. In addition, after 2016 Gülen-related

---

[100] This was one of the best attended labour strikes in Çorum's history, other than the paper factory workers' strike against subcontract work in 2016 and the barefoot march of municipality workers from Çorum to Ankara in 1966. Çetin Başaranhıncal, the head of the ÇTSO and himself the owner of a tile factory, talks about how the labour costs are a burden to the employers and should be subsidized by the state: see http://www.yildizhaber.com/ayrinti.php?katid=5&id=12214

businessmen went underground. These developments were probably the reasons why business people laughed at me and joked about Anatolia's tigers being cats now.

Table 1. SME Incentive per Certificate (million Turkish Liras) (Source: Bayırbağ 2007: 147).[101]

	1997	1998	1999	2000	2001	2002	Average
ÇORUM	15,674.03	18,953.75	26,204.06	27,729.31	44,462.50	89,908.06	21,555.26
GAZİANTEP	13,959.67	11,932.45	18,005.23	31,958.62	46,455.00	102,498.00	21,029.53
İSTANBUL	14,180.18	14,731.15	22,968.83	31,169.09	42,070.00	60,260.95	18,191.64
BURSA	13,639.76	12,812.94	24,050.00	26,337.14	20,750.00	61,964.29	16,793.66
KAYSERİ	11,913.11	15,305.43	20,368.52	25,946.88	13,800.00	77,507.14	14,994.25
İZMİR	13,575.10	14,235.40	19,047.37	20,815.00	16,233.33	93,723.07	14,418.21
ADANA	12,842.86	29,955.56	23,550.00	22,564.29	32,000.00	30,009.09	14,245.93
DENİZLİ	13,285.91	12,045.00	29,600.00	27,625.00	0	92,870.00	12,802.06

Source: adapted from

http://www.kosgeb.gov.tr/Ekler/Dosyalar/BilgiBankası/13/Tesvik%20istatistikleri.xls

Since Gülen-related businessmen had been on the state's radar since 2013 due to their clash with the AKP after they released audio recordings of AKP politicians implicating them in fraud, I could not reach HITITSIAD during my presence in Çorum. They had no address or phone number one could use, only a website which disappeared a few months after my arrival. I did not pursue this matter in order not to jeopardize the rest of my research. I merely downloaded an issue of their journal, in which many well-known local industrialists had full-page advertisements, a sign that could be read as one's endorsement of the specific organization. One salient aspect of the issue was the emphasis on HITITSIAD's aid in Sudan. A second salient aspect was its coverage of two 'cultures', respectively the 'culture of partnership' (*ortaklık kültürü*) on the cover page and in several interviews and short opinion pieces in several pages of the journal, and the 'culture of living together' (*birlikte yaşama kültürü*) disseminated in a panel organized by the association. On

---

[101] My initial aim was to make a more recent and comparative table of SME incentives received by 'Anatolian Tiger' cities myself. However, all my efforts to bring together this data were inconclusive both in the Kosgeb website online and in my contact with the local representative of Kosgeb in Çorum. Hence, I used Bayırbağ's (2007) table to demonstrate my point.

the pages where the 'culture of partnership' is mentioned, this phrase is used interchangeably with the 'culture of togetherness' (*birliktelik kültürü*). The main idea is to advise entrepreneurs with less capital to pool their resources so as to be able to make larger investments because, as also stressed on page 36 by the head of HITITSIAD, one can no longer do business with small amounts of capital. They give the recent investments by their members in building factories in Sudan as an example of the 'culture of partnership', appropriating the earlier historical connotation of the concept that referred to the multiple partnerships of the 1960s and 1970s.

As already noted, the second main theme of the journal was the 'culture of living together', a reference to one of the pillars of Fethullah Gülen's ideology of intercultural dialogue that can easily be found in his writings and talks. In the local context, however, it refers to the attempts of civil-society organizations to 'face' the traumatic effects of Çorum's incidents and reconcile Alevi and Sunni. The timing also coincides with the Alevi opening of the ruling party AKP in 2009, which initiated a dialogue with Alevis to re-configure the relationship between them and the state. According to the news in the HITITSIAD journal, in 2013 state bureaucrats, NGO activists and theologians gathered in a panel organized to promote the 'culture of living together'. The journal's argument was that those who provoked the attacks in the 1980s were 'outsiders' unknown to people in Çorum at the time. Hence, if only these people could be found and prosecuted, then there would be a remedy for these crimes. Secondly, they argued that Alevism belongs to Islam and that only if the two sides can come together by getting to know each other and showing tolerance of each other can the past be mended. Moreover, the panelists argue that there are 'some others' who are trying to eject Alevism from Islam (i.e. demands for *Cemevi*s to be given official status as sanctuaries as an alternative to mosques), namely those who were responsible for the ongoing tensions and the reason why Çorum has not yet been able to recover from the 1980 'incidents'. As elaborated in Chapter 3, this particular interpretation of Alevism is embraced by Sunnis in general and by some Islamists in particular who deny that Alevism is a belief in its own right. It was also the dominant state view during the Alevi opening that Alevism should be defined on the basis of Islam. Yet, these views are not limited to HITITSIAD panelists or state officials, nor was referring to the Çorum massacres as 'incidents'. Many Sunnis in Çorum use a similar vocabulary, preferring to explain the events of 1980 as a clash between the Alevi and Sunni, instead of Alevis being attacked by right-wing Sunnis. Also, many Sunnis would emphasize that Sunnis also lost their lives and workplaces during these events. There was a constant effort to depict Alevi and Sunni as having participated and suffered equally through these horrific attacks. As demonstrated above, these efforts extend to calling on Sunni and Alevi to take joint responsibility for recovering from the past. Moreover, othering Alevis who demand equal citizenship clearly echoes the assimilationist tendencies of the hegemonic construction of national identity, which prioritizes being Sunni to being a Turk in the 'new Turkey' (see Chapter 3). The question is then why was the 'culture of partnership' and the 'culture of living together' so central in the agenda of a business association, and why was it understood through this particular interpretation?

Findings before the 15 July Military Coup Attempt

Some businessmen who had appeared in the pages of the HITITSIAD journal published in 2013 were arrested in 2016 during my fieldwork and sentenced to long years of imprisonment in the Fethullah Gülen Terorrist Organization/Parallel State Organization[102] (FETÖ/PDY) trials of 2017 and 2018. During my research, but before the coup attempt of July 15, I had asked questions about membership of business associations in in-depth interviews. Even at that stage, businessmen were reluctant to talk about the matter. Not many were members of a specific association, but all those located in the industrial zone were members of ÇOSİAD, as this is the administrative body that regulates and organizes the costs and shares of the zone. Impartial though this organization sounds, in the 2000s it was run by leading figures in HITITSIAD. This means that Gülen-supporting businessmen were active in decision-making on issues regarding the industrial zone. However, ÇOSİAD was inactive in its lobbying and gathering activities and in making business contacts at that time. For this reason, a few businessmen who owned medium-size factories in the industrial zone and were supporters of the AKP, such as Şükrü Bey and Cemal Bey, were eager to organize regular events in which they could meet local pioneers in the sector. They considered this an honour because some of them had worked in those early generations in factories as foremen before starting their own workshops.

In one of our conversations, Şükrü Bey recollected some of his memories from the past when he was contacted by Gülen-supporting industrialists inviting him and others to dinner. Back then, he recalls that he was happy to join and re-engage with the pioneers of the sector. At this point, Şükrü Bey named some of those industrialists who were engaged in the activities of the Gülen movement (the same names that appear in the

---

[102] The trials took place after the 15 July 2016 military coup attempt allegedly organized by Fethullah Gülen community, which was deemed to be a terrorist organization.

journal) and stated that bringing industrialists together was one of the good things in which this community succeeded. They had a few gatherings where Gülen's life story and sayings were told and quoted, among other conversations, following a session of prayer (*namaz*). Then Şükrü Bey was asked to pay for one of these dinners, which he considered fair, since he had eaten at their table before. But then, after a few meetings, he and others were asked to donate to the Gülen community. Şükrü Bey hesitated to do so, since he did not know where the money would go, and also he found that he could not decide himself how much he wanted to donate, but was arbitrarily told to pay a certain amount. In his own words, 'They held many fellow tradesmen ransom. They [donation collectors] were coming! I wrote you six billion! You have to give that, you are obliged to. No chance of not giving', Also, when he raised concerns about the way the money would be spent, he was silenced and criticized. After this encounter, he sometimes avoided giving donations and later stopped attending these gatherings, using his Alevi partner as an excuse: 'I told them my partner was Alevi. When they asked for donations, I said that my partner is against those donations, OK? I said I cannot make the donations without his permission, so I sometimes got away with it'. When I asked about the relevance of this excuse, his partner Ali Bey, who was present in the room during this conversation, replied: 'Ceren *Hanım*, I have already told you that Sunni and Alevi shed blood!'

It was not uncommon for Alevi and Sunni or people of different political party affiliations to form business partnerships in Çorum both before and after the 1980 massacre. Partnerships created after the 1980s in particular show that people do not always perform a certain identity in the way it is attached to them but act pragmatically in their business-making behaviour. Bülent Bey and Cemal Bey's partnership is typical of this kind of partnership. Even though they both have Sunni origins, Bülent Bey is a secular and culturally liberal man from a civil servant's family, while Cemal Bey is a pious conservative and a Turkish nationalist from a village background, as already described in detail. Their differences did not stand out as much at the time they formed their partnership in the 1990s, when Bülent Bey traditionally supported the CHP and Cemal Bey the centre-right parties that came from the DP tradition. They both leaned towards the liberal understanding of the economy and still have this as their common ground. However, their differences became more acute in parallel with the increasing political polarization of Turkey between the AKP and non-AKP. Bülent Bey, who used to read *Sözcü*, a Turkish nationalist and secularist newspaper, dropped the nationalist edge in his views and started supporting the democratization reforms in 2000s and remained supportive of democratization measures thereafter, while Cemal Bey incorporated the

Islamists' critique into his centrist views and developed a distaste for the republican reformism associated with Atatürk. Cemal Bey, as a devoted AKP voter ever since 2002, also supported the democratic changes made in the early 2000s, such as the Kurdish and Alevi openings as long as they were on AKP's agenda, yet gave his full support to the 'war on terror' and the religious-nationalist coalition of the AKP and MHP in 2017.

While their political positions are therefore at polar opposites of the spectrum[103], I never heard them talk about any political issue in the year I spent with them, nor when I visited them later. The key to avoiding their political polarization from spoiling their personal and business relationship was to disregard these topics completely. When I hesitantly asked them about this, Cemal Bey would say he has great respect for Bülent Bey as his senior and an engineer, as well as a friend, while Bülent Bey would say he is not interested in political discussions: what mattered to him was their achievements together as partners and friends and the goal in keeping this place running. Cemal Bey, like Şükrü Bey, had cut all ties with Gülen-supporting tradesmen after a few meetings. He and Bülent Bey occasionally make donations to those religious orders and associations that came to their doors, but they both disapproved of being racketeered by Gülen supporters. Cemal Bey was not a member of Çorum-MÜSİAD either, even though he thought MÜSİAD's late formation in Çorum was a result of the political oppression of the 1990s. Still, he would say these businessmen's associations required high membership fees but did not offer much in return. Perhaps if Cemal Bey did not have a partner he would have become a member of MÜSİAD, but this was not something he could do individually but only as a company, and that was not possible since MÜSİAD is exclusively pro-AKP. Çor-Mak was only a member of the impartial ÇOSİAD, like all companies in the industrial zone, and the only regular donation made as a company was the scholarships provided to those of its workers whose children were attending university.

As I have shown in the earlier sections, the Çorum massacre has had an impact on the economic development of the city, and when the Alevi isolated themselves, it reduced their chances of doing or succeeding in business. This made them put aside their differences in doing business. Another repercussion was that many Sunnis in Çorum are ashamed of being remembered for such horrific assaults – another reason to refer to the 1980 events as 'incidents' – and hence want to distance themselves from bigotry and discrimination against Alevis, which actually opens up a window for

---

[103] The oppositional parties, *İyi Parti* (Good Party), *Demokrasi ve Atılım Partisi* (Democracy and Progress Party) and *Gelecek Partisi* (Future Party), had not been founded back at the time I was doing my fieldwork.

dialogue between people of different beliefs. Ali Bey's firm reaction to my question above and Cemal Bey's eschewing MÜSİAD membership indicate that in such partnerships, in which business partners have a common budget, supporting the causes of political Islam and Sunni indoctrination would not be approved by their Alevi or secular partners. Given the Alevi and secular business people and bureaucrats who are active and influential in business associations and local politics, their existence might also have hindered the spreading of political Islam's business networks. Therefore, the emphasis on a 'culture of living together' in the HİTİSİAD journal, though influenced by the national agenda of the time, could be seen as a rhetorical tool for breaking Alevi resistance to donating by incorporating them into Islam.

There were other industrialists who said that they had avoided such donations, not only to the Gülen organization but also to others, giving similar excuses such as their partner being Alevi or saying that they themselves are not interested. But as stated above, it is not easy to avoid giving a donation to a religious order and explicitly taking responsibility for it, so many made the donations asked of them. There are of course others who gave donations willingly to the Gülen movement and the Süleymancı or Menzil orders, which are said to be very active in Çorum. However, in making business contacts, businessmen were not as selective in where to get support. I have noted that businessmen of different religious denominations, life-styles or party affiliations have attended local events or fairs abroad in the past, regardless of which association is organizing it. They were looking for new clients for exports, and some of these attempts were successful and some not. Another way of finding clients abroad was through internet searches or Çorum industrialists being directly contacted by the company abroad. This kind of business activity is more prevalent in the small and medium-size factories that were founded in the late 1990s. Although not voiced by many, finding clients and making business arrangements through politicians and their connections with the state was an important aspect of this. As one discredited former AKP bureaucrat and industrialist put it: 'You know what all the industrialists do here? Get into a plane with politicians to go where? To Sudan. The Turkish Republic makes a 500,000-dollar donation, following which he [the politician] says that he will have a flour factory built in Sudan. Then he [the politician] bestows the job on one of the industrialists here – that's what a donation is!'

Findings After the 15 July Military Coup Attempt

These bits of information I collected during fieldwork made more sense when I read the testimony of a Çorum businessman, Memduh Çıkmaz[104], in the FETÖ/PDY trial in 2018. He recalled that he and seven other people had been partners in building a brick factory in Sudan[105], and in another trial he admitted that Bank Asya personnel had helped him when he needed cash for his business and had provided him with credits at low interest.[106] However, we cannot know whether or not Çıkmaz's (or others') partnerships and investments happened as a result of donations made by the 'Turkish Republic', as the businessman cited above claimed. We also cannot know which politicians were involved in these transactions because it all comes down to AKP politicians who avoided taking responsibility for the rise and takeover of state cadres by the Gülen movement by simply stating that they had been 'deceived' (*aldatıldık*), as President Recep Tayyip Erdoğan claims.[107] The aim of my research is not to investigate people and their now criminalized political links but to shed some light on the possible role of religious communities in doing business in Çorum and developing a local industry. Still, there are a few things we can derive from this information.

Given the hints and testimonies in the media in the aftermath of July 15, it is safe to say that many businessmen related to HITITSIAD had been favoured over others in obtaining bank loans, making domestic and international business contacts, and probably winning public and private bids. These favours were not exclusive to Gülen members, as AKP members and voters most probably benefited from them too, since the distinction was vague until 2013, and in my opinion still is. In fact, these business relationships could also be read as Islamic factionalism aiding political affiliates in Anatolia and offering them a share of the pie through their connections to the AKP. This pattern resembles the kind of indirect incentives provided to the businessmen of earlier periods through the large bourgeoisie's connections with state power. However, it is also very different due to the fact that the Gülen movement was a transnational conglomerate and a powerful political network that used its political and

---

[104] This person was not a part of my research. I am using his real name as it appears in the newspapers, since it is publicly available information. All other persons' names, except for those who can be identified because of the positions they held, have been anonymized here.
[105] See http://www.milliyet.com.tr/feto-nun-para-kasasi-mahkemede-gundem-2615027/ accessed in June 2017.
[106] See http://www.milliyet.com.tr/feto-nun-para-kasasi-na-10-yil-hapis-corum-yerelhaber-2824727/ accessed in June 2017.
[107] See http://www.gazetevatan.com/-tum-ulke-aldatildi-yanlis-yonlendirildi--751734-gundem/ accessed in June 2017.

economic power to exclusively benefit its supporters (e.g. stealing central university entrance and state-job exam papers to place its adherents in schools or state jobs) or destroying its opponents (e.g. fabricating false evidence to accuse and imprison high generals, the so-called *Ergenekon* trials). Given all this information and previous findings, it appears that the 'culture of partnership' strongly encouraged by the HITITSIAD journal is first of all a call to participate in the network, and secondly a way of disguising favouritism under the power of the word 'culture', an appropriation of a term that is frequently used to refer to the multiple partnerships of previous decades.

The enlargement of the religious field in general and the increase in the space and funding for religious orders and communities specifically has also increased the legitimacy of their activities, as shown by the way Gülen members could insist on donations being made by pressuring those attending their activities. Similarly, donating to a religious order (not necessarily to Gülen), going to Friday prayers, fasting, or organizing *iftar* (a fast-breaking meal during Ramadan) for workers and other businessmen have on the one hand gained more social and political value and were therefore done more demonstratively by some, while on the other hand creating more pressure on those who practice none or some of these Islamic practices or rituals, especially when performing them in public. Even though expressions of the religiosity and practice of Islam are diverse and cross-cut class and party affiliations, during its one-party rule the AKP has promoted and monopolized certain expressions of religiosity in ways that have polarized society. Nationwide quantitative research conducted in 2010 shows that political polarization in Turkey does not vary according to age or gender but based on educational levels and political party affiliations. In fact, AKP and CHP voters often respond with the exact opposite attitudes and opinions when it comes to the issue of *laiklik* (Konda 2010).

This trend has increased in the last decade and has had repercussions for how and with whom people conduct their daily lives in the economic sphere. For instance, when belonging to a political group is spatially and temporally linked to the practices of a certain kind of religiosity, it is inevitable that those who do not practice religion similarly are excluded from the social circles in which these activities are carried out. In order not to be excluded, others might start practising as well. Generally, business people with opposition views tend to seem impartial, prefer not to talk explicitly about politics and/or religion, and maintain a low profile so as to be able to sustain their business relations with people of opposite opinions. Still, what kind of news one shares on one's Facebook pages and which newspaper one reads very easily reveals which political camp one belongs to. Openly leaving an opposition newspaper on the desk for others to see was, as far as I could observe, a bold move. Therefore, many business people, tradesmen or industrialists try to seem impartial and avoid introducing symbols of political affiliation in their offices. Yet there are exceptions to impartiality. For instance, business people associated with Çorum-MÜSİAD, which is like a party social club rather than a business association, openly support the AKP by declaring their public support of it on every possible occasion. Their offices are often decorated in a neo-Ottomanist style, they often publicize their meetings with AKP politicians on social media, and they and organize social activities such as prayer events for school kids. Another exception are well-known Alevi businessmen who definitely have a picture of Atatürk on their office walls and hang enormous Turkish flags outside their workplaces on national days such as 19 May or 23 April.

Although most business people try to appear impartial, I was told many times that 'everybody knows who is who in Çorum'. People of different religious beliefs or political orientations inevitably do business with each other, have subcontracting relations and receive marketing support from the ÇTSO, which all business people have to be a member of. Again, many business people stated that they would invest in higher quality products and services at reasonable prices, thus giving themselves a competitive advantage. This rationale has little to do with who the producer is or which political or religious group s/he belongs to. Therefore, I would argue that some privileges might have been exclusive to those who are and were active in political circles, whether in obtaining low interest loans from Bank Asya or other banks, or in making business contacts through politicians. However, given the findings of the first part of this chapter, namely that the manufacturing industry of today is an outcome of decades of collective and individual efforts by people to acquire skills, collect capital and learn to do business, it is misleading to overemphasize the role of the rise of political Islam and its networks in the boom in Çorum's economy. One could actually argue that Çorum business people have not been able to undertake political activism as a collective body – unlike Gaziantep, for example (Bayırbağ 2007) – whether in HITITSIAD, ÇOSIAD, ÇORUMSIAD or ÇTSO, nor have they been able to utilize the networks of political Islam as efficiently as in other cities such as Kayseri (Cengiz 2013).

Following the attempted coup on 15 July 2016, investigations started immediately nationally, including in Çorum, to eliminate alleged Gülen supporters from the political, social and economic spheres and to prosecute them. The gathering of AKP and other party supporters in the city centre continued every evening for almost a month to protest against military coups and to make a display of '*milli irade*' (national will) in favour of democracy.

During these protests, which later became social events where tea and fast food were distributed and concerts were performed, the Turkish flag was appropriated as the symbol of solidarity with the AKP regime and the protests against undemocratic interventions. The flags were everywhere and in all sizes: in peoples' hands as tiny flags on sticks, on their cars or backs as cloaks, and gigantic one's hanging on buildings. In the meantime, local newspapers and social media outlets started publishing 'FETÖ lists', probably already obtained from police sources in August. There was a deep silence about the matter among business people until rumours spread about one businessman fleeing the country and another being arrested, both having been well-known figures in HITITSIAD and ÇOSIAD circles. Interestingly, on the same days huge Turkish flags appeared on the outer walls of the factories belonging to the two businessmen, as well as of others as a display of their adherence and loyalty to the AKP regime. This was then ridiculed by some other businessmen, and also in the social media, saying that whoever were hanging up Turkish flags in the industrial zone were '*Fetöcü*' (Gülen sympathizers and terrorists) themselves, and if the government was looking for them, they should arrest those who were frequenting the protests and other events going on in the city centre because they are actually hiding behind the flag. While only those well-known figures who were already subjected to police raids were being fingered, I encountered smaller business-owners who were former sympathizers of Gülen but were going in and out of factories and doing their business as usual.

In the last months of my research, after the coup attempt in July, the topic of the 'culture of partnership' came up once more while the investigations were still ongoing. During this period many high-ranking bureaucrats were asked by the central government to name those whom they thought were associated with Gülen. In an encounter with one of these locally influential bureaucrats, who was not willing to contribute to the research, he said that if I wanted to understand Çorum's economy I should pay attention to the 'culture of partnership'. This overarching concept appearing to be an explanatory tool making sense of different eras of economic development in Çorum, but this time with a different meaning than previous explanations, given the extraordinary circumstances of his being forced to report business people as criminals. Given the long-history of multiple partnerships in Çorum since the 1960s, this bureaucrat's use of the phrase 'culture of partnership' while the investigation was still going on could therefore be interpreted as an attempt to protect business people who had been involved in these circles in one way or another from being criminalized by framing the economic activities of those from different social backgrounds or political orientations as a 'culture' that enabled Çorum to thrive as a 'Anatolian Tiger'.

Conclusion

This chapter has addressed two arguments about the impact of the emergent orthodoxy on regional economies. One argument claimed that new development models emerged after the 1980s and thrived in the absence of the state because of the existence of an 'entrepreneurial soul' based on a culture of partnership. The second argument overemphasized the role of political Islam in the emergence of Anatolian capital whereas the actual focus was on Islamic capital. In the first part of the chapter, I have demonstrated various ways of gathering capital that were shaped by the economic, political, historical and circumstantial conditions of each era and that gave substance to the entrepreneurialism involved. Thus, I approach the 'break' in the post-1980 period critically, as I argue all these developments were the result of the accumulation of experience. I showed that the state was always present in the process directly or indirectly, but not in order to build a state industry, except for the cement factory erected in 1957, which the townspeople remember as having had an important effect on transfers of skills and know-how. The large bourgeoisie of Istanbul, as it is often called, incorporated Çorum into its domestic trade network, which gave a competitive advantage to those Çorum who used these networks to make larger investments. In this era factories acted as schools for training foreman and masters, some of whom became the next generation of industrialists. The Islamic bourgeoisie, as it had emerged by the 1990s, offered its export connections to local industrialists directly through political connections. All these connections created a supply chain in Çorum that allowed smaller enterprises to emerge as subsidiaries and subcontractors to larger exporting companies, all of which would have been almost impossible without external influence. I agree that local economies became dependent on the large bourgeoisie, whether Islamic or secular, as I argued in Chapter 2, but without a consistent state investment programme (or one might say, state capitalism), which was absent not only from Çorum but also most of Turkey's provinces. Accordingly I argue that the economic developments under question here would not have been possible without the connections Çorum businessmen made with the large bourgeoisie and global trade chains, nor without the cheap and insecure labour of uprooted villagers and their children.

In respect of the second part of the argument, which emphasized the role of political Islam, I have demonstrated that Alevi and Sunni, as well as those of different political views, did business together and made partnerships that thrived in the 2000s. Gülen-supporting business people appropriated the term 'culture of partnership', frequently used to refer to the multiple partnerships of previous decades, first as a call to participate in their network, secondly to disguise favouritism under the screen of the word 'culture', and thirdly as a rhetorical tool to break the Alevi's resistance to donating to Gülen and serving their organizations by incorporating them into Sunni Islam. However, given the findings of the first part of this chapter, that the manufacturing industry of today is an outcome of decades of collective and individual efforts by people to acquire skills, collect capital and learn to do business, it is misleading to overemphasize the role of the rise of political Islam and its networks in the boom years of the Çorum economy. One could actually argue that Çorum business people have not been able to develop political activism as a collective body in order to use these networks for their own advantage.

Chapter 5
Narratives of Personhood: Work, Family and Enterprise

Introduction

The business people who are included in this research comprise roughly four categories and three generations: those who started their businesses before the 1980s, those who took them over in the 1990s and 2000s, those who started their own businesses in the 1990s and 2000s, and sons, nephews and daughters working with their fathers or uncles. Many of those in the first and second generations, some of whose origin stories I recounted in the previous chapter, started in self-employment in different crafts or trades, then became petty bourgeois and later local bourgeoisie in Çorum. Some in the second generation were manual or non-manual wage-labourers before they became engaged with entrepreneurial activities. Whether one's place in the class structure has shifted through one's own lifetime or through generational transmission, I have observed that the way these business people relate to work, how they see the individual and society and their position in it, as well as the work ethic they followed and transmitted to the following generations, have undergone a change. The transition is not only limited to what they personally achieved or inherited but is also largely affected by shifts in political and economic trajectories. The spread of global capitalism from metropoles to provincial towns and its people brought about new resources, technologies and goods, and also put a new vocabulary into circulation. Hence, many business people simultaneously responded to the transition by reconfiguring inherited values to create new ones in accordance with their new class positions as local bourgeoisie or the new middle classes. In the process of Turkey's integration into global capitalism, Çorum's local bourgeoisie created new subjectivities and made new persons out of themselves over a century. This chapter will attempt to unravel the changing and/or persisting values and meanings attached to work, enterprise and 'personhood' that business people of different generations formed through their narratives of their lived experiences of 'becoming'.

'Neoliberal' is the most widely used term to describe the late capitalist era that we live in, yet there are competing theoretical frameworks for interpreting what it stands for. According to scholars who are broadly influenced by the Foucauldian perspective, concepts such as personhood and subjectivity resonate mostly with the 'self-enterprising' subject who has 'a new ethic of the active, choosing, responsible, autonomous individual obliged to be free, and to live life as if it were an outcome of choice' (Miller and Rose 2008: 18). This subject is created by the 'the deployment of new technologies of governing from a centre through powerful means of governing at a distance: these appeared to enhance the autonomy of zones, persons, entities, but enwrapped them in new forms of regulation' (ibid.). It is these new forms of regulation, or better governance, that denote the concept of neoliberalism in Rose's account, that is, 'a political rationality that seeks to govern not through command and control operations but through calculative choice of formally free actors. It operates, in other words, according to a rationality of a market type' (cited in Collier and Ong 2005: 13). Ong (2006: 14) takes Rose and Miller's concept of the 'self-enterprising subject' even further by saying that 'the neoliberal subject is therefore is not a citizen with claims on the state but a self-enterprising citizen subject who is obliged to become an entrepreneur of himself or herself'. Martin (2009: 41-42) agrees with Ong in stating that 'individuals become like a node in a network... and as the nation state yields its prominence in the world affairs to the multinational corporation, individuals more from being citizens, oriented to the interest of the nation, to being mini-corporations, oriented primarily to their own interests in the global flows of capital'. This approach frames neoliberalism as the desire to encourage individuals to assume responsibility and be enterprising by engineering their souls and building them as calculable, governable, industrious and responsible self-disciplined subjects. Some of my respondents' narratives of personhood and enterprise, as I will try to show in this chapter, echo the discursive elements of self-responsibility, hard work, individuality and autonomy 'as if they were an outcome of choice'. Also, at first glance, my survey findings suggest that the 'neoliberal subject' as defined by the scholars mentioned above is prevalent in my field site. Indeed, the ethnographic evidence will reveal that these qualities predate late capitalism and are motivated by multiple desires and sentiments related to one's self and self-image, family, enterprise and nation.

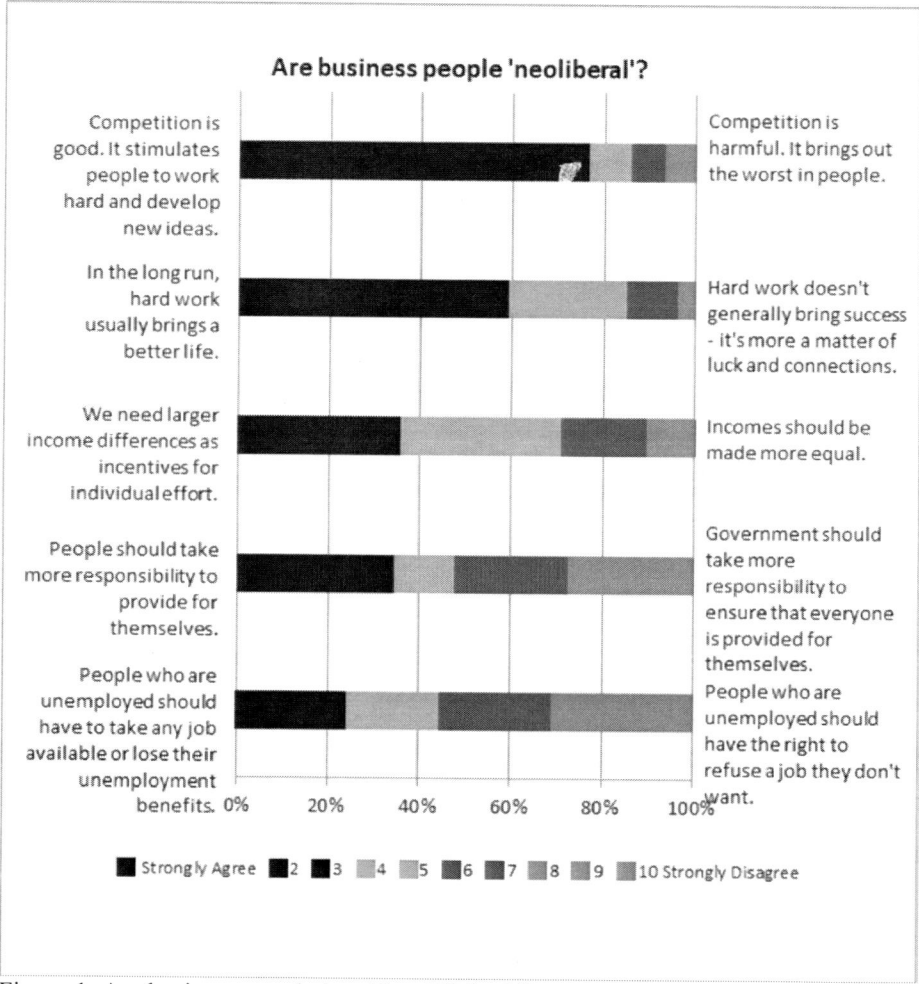

Figure 1. Are business people 'neoliberal'? (n=30)

In the survey I conducted with business people, some statements were placed in opposition to one another to assess the respondent's attitudes towards self-responsibility, hard work, individualism and free choice, in contrast to state regulation of income levels and economic equality, or the roles of competition, luck and connections in success (see Figure 1). Respondents were asked to rank how much they agreed with the statement on a Likert 10-scale, 1 and 10 corresponding opposing statements. Thinking about how to make sense of the survey results, I have compiled five of these opposing statements, as they resonate closely with the description of the 'neoliberal' above, to see whether or not there might be a pattern.[108] The findings show that almost 80 percent of respondents agreed that competition motivates people to work hard and develop new ideas. The figure goes up to almost 90 percent if those who ticked 4 and 5 are considered to be more or less in agreement. Sixty percent of respondents strongly agreed that hard work will bring a better life. Those who ticked 5 and below total more than 80 percent, in a similar ratio to the affirmative answers given to the previous question. These two together might at first glance imply that my respondents tend to think of the individual as a free agent outside his or her socio-economic context and agree that individual responsibility, effort and competition-driven hard work by themselves are enough to have a better life.

However, when it comes to the question of whether or not differences in income should be increased to boost individual effort, those who ticked 5 and below drop to 70 percent, and more differentiation among answers can be observed. Those who strongly agree decrease by half in comparison to the same answers given to the first two questions, and around 10 percent strongly agree that incomes should be made equal. Moreover, in the fourth statement, when respondents are asked directly whether people should assume responsibility as individuals to provide for themselves, the ratio of those who strongly disagree increases to 30 percent, while those who strongly agree and agree (marked 1 to 5) decrease to 50 percent in total, 20 percent less than the approval given to the previous statement. A similar trend can be observed in the responses given to the last statement, when more than 30 percent strongly disagreed that people should take any job, whereas those who strongly agree had the lowest percentage among all other statements. The last three findings suggest that my initial supposition about the first two statements, that respondents tend to think individual responsibility, effort and competition-driven hard work as the basis of the self-enterprising subject, might be wrong. Rather, the findings of the last three statements suggest that such notions as hard work, individual responsibility and effort are rooted in different moral frameworks and value regimes (see Chapter 1) while still being in agreement with the neoliberal vocabulary. In fact, a significant fraction of the respondents did not necessarily think that it is only the person's individual responsibility to provide for themselves, nor did they think that the unemployed should take just any job. The response to the last statement also hints that freedom to choose how you provide for yourself is important and that work might mean much more to people than just providing for one's self.

---

[108] This was originally Sylvia Terpe's idea.

These results, then, should rather be seen as a reminder that we should take a breath before labelling all ideas about hard work, responsibility, competition and individualism as referring to the enterprising self or in fact being neoliberal. In a similar fashion, Don Kalb (2014) warns us to be careful about such labels and 'wonder[s] whether those epithets were not in fact the timeless properties with which the West as a whole has always tried to distinguish itself from the properties of the East (and the rest) since the rise of Athens. We could even add "rational" to that list, or "manly" and of course democratic.... These are typically classical liberal notions, rather than necessarily neoliberal ones' (2014: 199). Kipnis (2008) also criticizes the governmentality approach because it tends to imply 'that neoliberalism is more of an all-encompassing and distinct "regime of truth" than it is' (2008: 280). Both authors point out how ahistorical the Foucauldian approach is in, for example, deciding how audit cultures are handled, as if there were no monitoring or subjectifying in bureaucracies or there had been no calculating or numeracy during the past century. Kalb expresses his frustration in saying: 'we almost seem at the point where we would begin to equate the sheer human capacity to count with neoliberalism as such' (Kalb, ibid.). Kipnis expands further on this point by stating that 'over the past century, this centrality [of calculability] correlates with industrialization, the increasing universality of numeracy in addition to literacy, and the ongoing growth in the volume and distance of trade' (2008: 283).

In a similar vein, the kind of industrialization process and personhood under investigation here are not the products of a 'political rationality' of neoliberalism but, as already shown in Chapter 4, a product of a longer period of cooperation among entrepreneurs and lay people, involving partnerships, imitation, transfers of skills, state policy and political negotiations. Therefore, the kind of subjectivity or personhood I will be talking about in this chapter will not necessarily be that of the 'neoliberal subject' as discussed by some of the authors cited above, like Ong (2006), Miller and Rose (2008) and Martin (2009). If hard work, individualism, responsibility and similar notions do not stand for the 'neoliberal subject' alone, then the question to be answered in this chapter is what they stand for from the perspective of my interlocutors in Çorum.

That said, I would also like to stress that I do not mean to downplay the issue of neoliberalism; rather, I employ a different theoretical framework to define what neoliberalism stands for. Although 'neoliberalism' may have become a 'planetary vulgate' (Bourdieu and Wacquant 2001) that says everything and nothing at the same time (Kalb 2014). Its explanatory power as an analytical category having been weakened (Ferguson 2010), it still needs to be taken seriously, as suggested in the edited volume on personhood and neoliberalism by Makovicky (2014b). Among the various takes on neoliberalism[109], this chapter builds on the rich multidisciplinary trend one finds in the works of scholars such as Harvey (2005), Narotzky and Smith (2006), Brenner, Peck and Theodore (2010), Kalb (2012) and Wacquant (2012), who frame it 'as a historically specific, spatially uneven and hegemonic project of capitalist social transformation' (Mikuš 2016: 214). The anthropologists who approach neoliberalism as a hegemonic project point out that it 'is not a cultural consensus but a structured field of social relations of dominance' (Kalb 2014: 198) within which not all social relations can be dominated – therefore it is always incomplete. Kalb (ibid.) also points out that neoliberalism imposes certain pressures and limits on personal becoming. What this kind of approach allows us to do is to disentangle the particular from the universal by studying its relational mechanisms at the multiple levels involved in local, national and global processes (Mikuš 2016: 214). For example, the work of Dunn (2004) on an American baby food manufacturer in Poland provides an account of personhood that is not completely taken over by the neoliberal measures that impose flexibility on the company's Polish women workers. Although the workers inevitably become market players, they still construct their personhood around notions of motherhood.

This chapter follows the lead of the scholars cited above and tries to decipher the narratives of personhood, enterprise and the work ethic of my informants. Given that my universe of research does not consist of baby-food factory workers or the like but medium-size work-place owners, two studies which specifically focus on enterprises and their owners will be my guide. First is the edited volume by Makovicky (2014b), already mentioned, in which the authors question what Makovicky calls 'the proselytizing of a rhetoric of responsibility, self-help, flexibility, and choice' (2014a: 2). In doing so, they identify three main types of 'enterprising' selves: 'the enterprising character (as in the classic, charismatic "self-made" man), those able and willing to adapt to the changing socio-economic circumstances of the globalized economy (the "flexible" citizen), and those who live at the margins and enterprise to survive' (ibid.: 12). As I will show, my respondents mostly started from the margins, became self-made men (mostly) and then adapted to the changing circumstances of the globalized economy. Going through all these phases places them in a similar context to Yanagisako's (2002) self-made men in industry in Como, Italy. Her work will therefore be my second guide, as I adopt her generational approach and

---

[109] For a discussion of the anthropology of neoliberalism, see the debate in the 2012 and 2013 volumes of the journal *Social Anthropology*, also Makovicky (2014a) and Mikuš (2016).

discuss her notion of a 'patriarchal desire' with a view to developing it further.

The Value of Work in the Narratives of Personhood: An End in Itself or a Means of Social Mobility?

One does not need to be a researcher to be aware of the dominance of the discourse and presence of the family in Turkey. From soap operas to reality TV shows, from cooking shows to commercials, somewhere behind them is an echo of the truism that 'family is everything'. In the survey conducted in the fieldsite, respondents were asked to mark the importance of six different 'spheres of life' (Terpe 2016) on a scale from 1 to 4. Unsurprisingly, all marked 'family' as 'very important', and with one exception all marked 'work' also as 'very important'. When we rank the means of the given replies, family is 'the most important', and work comes just after, followed by 'friends'. 'Religion' appears to have an almost equivalent importance as 'leisure time', while 'politics' ranks at the bottom of the list as 'not very important' (see Figure 2).

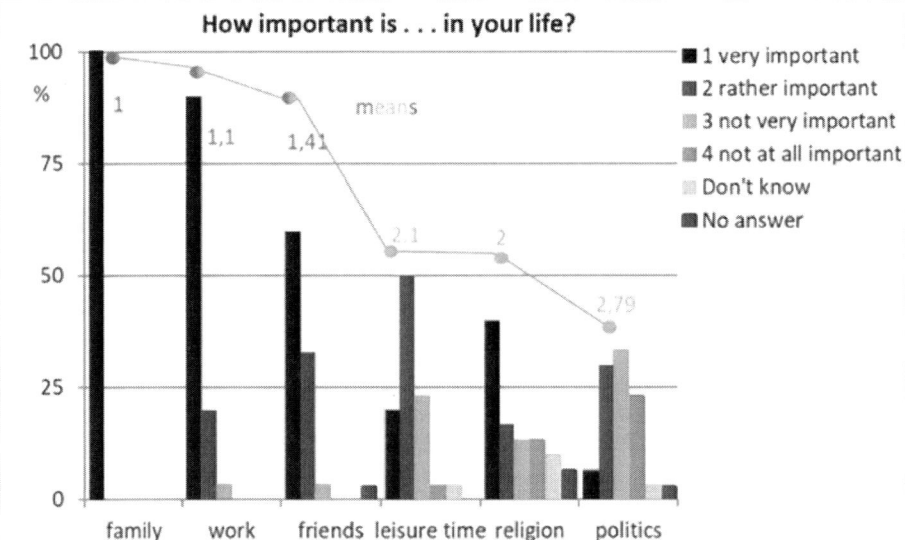

Figure 2. How important is … in your life? (n=30)

Although it may be an over-simplification to ask business people to rank the importance of 'spheres of life', there are clearly areas where people agree and disagree. Despite the variety of answers given to religion and politics, the business people who filled in the survey (and on the basis of my ethnography, I can say this of others as well) agreed that work and family are the most important things in life. As also appears in the survey results, one quarter of the respondents thought leisure was not very important. Already in the first months of my research, I had discovered that business people prefer not to spend time in the city centre, tend to drive cars worth less than they can afford, and would rather not be seen in public very often to protect themselves from gossip. Leisure was not only 'not important' but was also confined mostly to private spaces out of town where not everyone can go or spend money. For instance, the main leisure activities were eating out at a hotel restaurant (with or without alcohol) or a steakhouse, going to *bağevi*[110] at the weekends, driving to Samsun and Ankara to shop for domestic wares and clothes, or to Antalya and the like for summer vacations, and to thermal hotels (spas) for winter vacations. In one such conversation I had with Cemal Bey (co-owner of Çor-Mak; see Chapters 1 and 4) and another industrialist in which I asked about leisure activities, it all came down to them explaining why they do not enjoy holidays much and their emphasizing the place of work in their lives:

> This is how industry is: for instance, I try to go to *Ayvalık* in the Aegean [they have a summer house there] for a week every year because the kids insist so much, but even on the way I start counting the remaining days to our return. ... I mean, there is a routine here, we only sleep and work. The thing is this, the essence of this. I was just telling XX [the other industrialist in the conversation] the other day, there was a documentary on state TV, they were doing an interview with a leather craftsman, probably at the age of 75-80. He was saying, if I die, I will die in [one of] three places: either on my shop floor, or at home in my bed, or third on the way in between my home and work.

With reference to the previous discussion of 'neoliberalism' in quotation marks, neither the leather craftsman's nor Cemal Bey's dedication to work can be considered neoliberal. Secondly, the essence mentioned here and the kind of sense of duty towards work described in these lines might resemble what Weber (2001a) framed as the ethos: 'all the idea of a duty of the individual toward the increase of his capital, which is assumed as an end in itself. Truly what is here preached is not simply a means of making one's way in the world, but a peculiar ethic. The infraction of its rules is treated not as foolishness but as forgetfulness of duty. That is the essence of the matter. It is not mere business astuteness, that sort of thing is common enough, it is an ethos' (ibid.: 17). However, other evidence more usually

---

[110] Country cottage.

elicited from my respondents suggests that we should think twice before arriving at the conclusion that work has become 'an end in itself'. For example, the same businessman who uttered the lines above recalls the time he was a manual labourer and explains his relationship to his labouring as such:

> It makes me happy... Back then, I was making a lot less money, as much as an apprentice can make. In the later periods, when I started making money, you also become happier, you produce and even make money out of it. We hardly used to get by back then, when I was living with my father, so when you put money in the family budget, it makes me happy. Also, for me it is an amazing thing for a person to make money from his skill. This made me really happy; if I learned more, if I worked more, if I did more, then I would make more money, I thought. I mean, I didn't have the thing like to marry, to buy a car, to buy a bicycle, to hang out, have a girlfriend. We opened our eyes, and since then [we have been working].

As is evident in this quote, work for this person is not an 'end in itself' but actually a means of making a livelihood that comes through developing skills and applying them, which in turn provides personal happiness and a sense of pride. The narrative also hints that work is thought of as a form of social mobility and also contains the underlying belief that if the individual works hard enough, then one can lift oneself and one's family out of poverty and have better lives. This opinion is also reflected in my survey results, since many of the business people included in the survey come from a working-class background: 21 of the 27 business people who responded to the survey question 'In the long run, hard work brings a better life' ticked between 1-4 in a spectrum of 1 to 10 (1 being affirmative, 10 being negative). Work as a means to a livelihood and the provision of the family was mentioned in a conversation in which Cemal Bey defined what 'a good life' is, namely one in which one can provide for one's family. The logic in this was that, if you are a wage-earner, then you will remain in the same socio-economic status, since these workplaces are considered schools where young men can upgrade their skills from being apprentices to being foremen. Hence, Cemal Bey and many others thought that it was possible to take another step forward and start their own businesses. Then other opportunities for social mobility open up for the start-up owner's family. This, of course, should be evaluated as a retrospective narration of the 'possibility', mainly because those who talk about it are also those who made that 'possibility' a reality, meaning that they circumvented some of the limits and obstacles within the structured field of social relations of dominance. Birelma's (2019) literature review of working-class entrepreneurship around the globe shows that, although wage-labourers aspire greatly to become entrepreneurs, only a minority ever do so full-time, if at all. This is no different in Turkey: Birelma (2019) found that only a few of his interlocutors could start a company, and even fewer could manage to maintain these businesses for a long time. Failed attempts to become an entrepreneur in Çorum did not feature in my sample due to the research design, but I have observed that they were not at all uncommon. There was no 'cultural consensus' around the idea that 'hard work will bring a better life/wealth'. It resonated very differently for other people, such as the retired civil servant whom I met on the 1st May (Labour Day) march, who said: 'If there were such a thing as working hard bringing wealth, then the donkey in the village that carries the bundles of wood up and down the hill would already be the richest'. Accordingly, whether hard work brings wealth and a good life depends on the life experience and class of the person who is saying it. However, because the political language of class had been silenced and delegitimized in the neoliberal era and replaced with a story of overall embourgeoisement (Kalb and Halmai 2011), we hear about the merits of hard work more often than the story about the donkey. Nevertheless, there is more to Cemal Bey's and others' love of work than their embourgeoisement, as I will explore below.

Even more encompassing than the value attached to work, illustrated in Cemal Bey's account and in those of many others, was its ability to feed the family. Graeber (2001) makes a similar argument about Baining society, pointing out that the value of productive labour is merely potential, though 'value is only "realized" when one gives some of that food to someone else. Hence the most truly prestigious act is being a good provider to children, thereby turning them into social beings' (2001: 70-71). Yanagisako (2002) also found, based on her research among industrial-capitalists in Como, Italy, that: '[t]o head a family is to provide for it, including to provide the productive means of the independence of the family and the means to reproduce that independence in the next generation' (ibid.: 86). In my cases too, the value of work derives from its realization through providing for the family and using the profits of the firm to educate one's children. Ozan Bey (see Chapter 4 for his origin story), who loves his trading job, as he puts it (see below), did not expect his children to run his firm after him. His daughter, now in her twenties, studied medicine and became a doctor; his younger son goes to maths camps during the semester breaks and aims to become an engineer. His wife, while working as the accountant in Ozan Bey's company and later becoming a partner in it, obtained her university degree in her thirties, years after giving birth to the two children. Cemal Bey's youngest daughter (of three) was one of the first to obtain a university degree in his family, and although Cemal Bey thought she would come to work with him, she had other plans, such as freelancing in Ankara and later starting her own firm there.

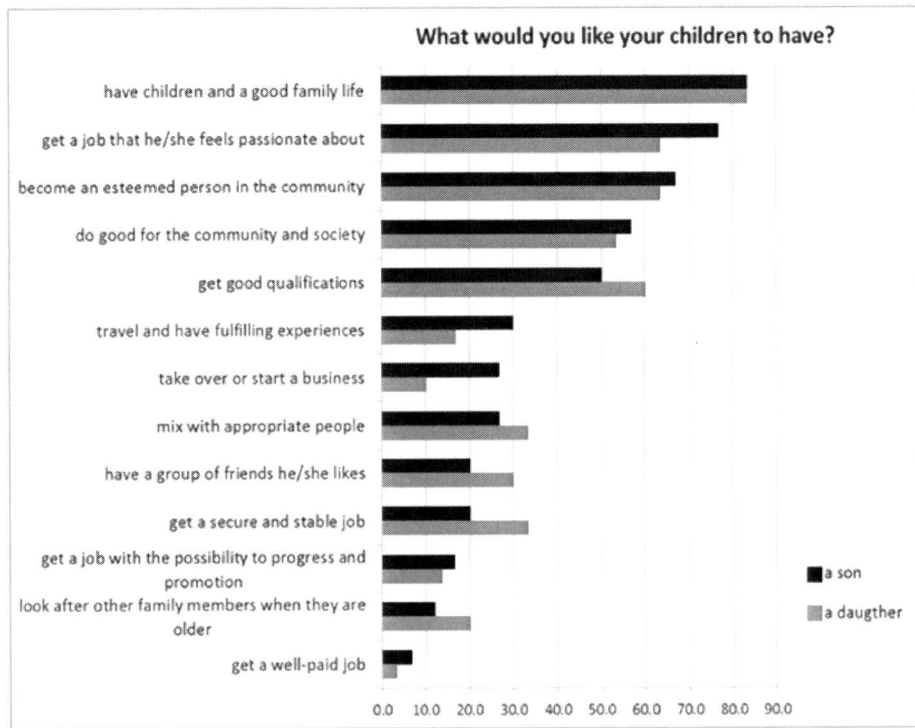

Figure 3. What would you like your children to have? (n=30)

When asked what they would they want their sons and daughters to have in their lives, in the survey (see Figure 3) those who wanted their children to take over the business were fewer than 30 percent for sons and only 10 percent for daughters. They overwhelmingly ticked 'having a good family life and children' equally for both sons and daughters, while 'getting a job they feel passionate about' ranked second in their preferences, although slightly less for daughters. While the results consistently signal the centrality of the family, they also show that the business people in my sample prefer their children to have a job they are passionate about, rather than expecting them to take over the business. On the continuity and unity of the family and the firm, Yanagisako (2002) writes: 'All men who head family firms and who have sons want to be succeeded by them. Indeed, many men say that the only reason they have worked so hard to build a successful firm is so that they can hand it on to their son or sons' (ibid.: 86). Her argument would not apply to business people in Çorum for several reasons, apart from the other possibly relevant differences, such as the productivity, profitability, prestige and location of this particular industry. First, my sample not only consists of 'family firms' in the formal definition of their being started and managed exclusively by family members. Second, my sample includes both father-employers and son-employees. Third, two thirds of my sample had fewer than fifty employees, contrary to Yanagisako's sample, in which the majority of firms had more than fifty. Nonetheless, these details do not change the fact that all (male) employers are fathers, so why do they not always expect their children to take over the firm? The most obvious and in fact simplest answer can be found in the actual motivation behind founding the firm in the first place, namely provisioning for the family, the education of the children, and attaining better standards of living than most of their fathers had as wage labourers or petty bourgeoisie. Once this aim has been fulfilled, the fathers desire their children to use the resources they have earned to go through higher education, acquire language skills, go abroad, widen their world views and then do things they feel passionate about, because their fathers did not have a chance to live such a life in Çorum. At least, that is my understanding of the survey results, given its limited coverage and other cases I have observed. Nonetheless, many sons and nephews did take over the family firm from their fathers or came back from their studies to work with them in both the 1980s and 1990s, some willingly, some out of necessity, and some despite their fathers pushing them to discover the outside world. I shall explore their reasons below, and also partially in the following chapters.

For now, I would like to point out that there was more pressure on sons than daughters to come back and take over, as I show below in the case of Çiğdem Hanım. The fathers' desire for their daughters, as Figure 3 shows, highlights earning good qualifications and having a secure job. The reason for this, which emerged during my fieldwork, was that fathers want their daughters not to be financially dependent on their husbands and to be able to end a marriage if they want to. Low expectations from the daughters that they would take over the businesses allowed many of them to seek out their own futures and discover their possibilities without having to worry about the unity of the firm or the family. The third most important quality that respondents wanted for their daughters to be ticked in the survey was 'becoming an esteemed person in the community', followed by 'doing good for the community'. The ethnography also shows that the issue of reputation requires more attention. I will therefore return to this theme and its relation to the family name and enterprise in the following sections. It suffices to say here that the fact that my survey findings are at variance with Yanagisako's arguments about succession in family firms do not mean that Çorum businessmen lack patriarchal desire. What she writes here applied to Çorum too: '[f]athering a family and fathering a business are interdependent projects of creation in the cosmology of kinship and business, family and capitalism, which are conveyed in firm origin stories' (2002: 86). In the next section, I will expand on the origin stories of the second and third generations in Çorum, who hold patriarchal desires along with other desires and sentiments. Kinship and family in the business, on the other hand, are the topics of Chapter 6.

Work and Enterprise as a Means to Making a Self

Harris (2007) asks a very central anthropological question, which is 'What makes people work?', and like my respondents she gives the 'straightforward answer [that it] is in order to live' (2007: 137). She then goes on to tell how, in the Western perception, work has primarily been associated with pain, coercion, exploitation and alienation, suggesting that the 'obligation to work should not be equated with a notion of coercion' and that 'value lies not in the product of work but in its very performance' (ibid.: 159) as she observed in Andean peasant society. In my cases, too, alongside the provisioning aspect of work, the performance of it also has a central role in the kind of happiness it generates in respect of self-realization and satisfaction. This was expressed by many respondents. For example, Ozan Bey expresses his love of work as follows: 'I love this job (trading). I have come here since I was nine [years old], but still, you know, some people would become weary when they do a certain job constantly, [but] for me it is the opposite. I come to work every morning with great joy, because it is important also to give workers that motivation. My energy hasn't finished yet, so I can still do this job because I love it. I mean, although I am fifty, the thing that gives me the ambition and energy is the fact that I love this job. I like the dynamism. I cannot do, let's say, car-selling: you'll [only] sell two cars a day, [and] I can't do that even if I make a lot of money'. Work, then, is also a medium for making a self and is an inseparable part of one's personhood. This was the case for others too.

    Çiğdem Hanım is one of the few women industrialists in Çorum who works in her own business, unlike many women in industry, who work alongside their husbands. She is the daughter of a renowned tradesman in Çorum who transferred his enterprise to his sons, which allowed Çiğdem Hanım to go and study engineering in one of the best universities in Turkey. Later, she worked on a plantation in Sivas and in many other engineering projects, then, after marrying a doctor who was posted to Çorum, she settled back in her home town. In the meantime, she kept working in a senior position at a factory in the area. In her own words:

> I worked for seven years. Then, of course, the first few years of these seven years were very exciting. But then later it is always the same things done in the factory... The same drill every year, certainly that bothered me. I mean, I couldn't develop myself anymore, no need to say anything to the foreman anyway, I mean, in the facilities there was nothing new, or only if something went wrong, I mean, there was nothing that excited me. So, I decided to quit, I told my husband. He didn't object, I thought I'd draw projects myself, I'm an engineer, I will rent an office. It was 1994. In the meantime [in this business], I go to the fairs about my job. I come across something, or I just take a bus and explore the fair and just come back in the evening, so I am away only for one day [from my child].

Then I asked if this was all out of curiosity, and she said: 'Yes, only that'. In our previous conversations she would always underline her sceptical approach to projects that come to her desk, her 'key to success' being never to put them into action before questioning them and herself being convinced first. The concern here is not whether the type of personality is a 'key to success'; rather, we observe that the curiosity and perfectionism at work are an important part of her personhood, so much so that she quit her job because she could not develop herself anymore. Her narrative also provides a sense of the 'enterprising self'. This becomes even more pronounced in the narratives of younger businessmen.

Emir Bey runs a programming company and gives lectures on 'entrepreneurialism' to workshops organized by the local university. He started his business in his twenties and is now in his thirties. We are sitting in his office; he was sitting behind his desk wearing a suit and a tie, which is quite unusual for the older generation of businessmen I had met, while he was telling me about his earlier years starting the business:

> My first internship (*staj*) was in a TV repair shop, and then in a computer shop and in a radio repair shop. By internship I mean working in the summer holidays. ... Later on with our savings from here and there, let's say a hundred euros or maybe two hundred in today's conditions, I mean we made a start and then made an effort to expand the business. I had been doing this job since I know myself, we did investments in other areas as well, but on our way from the beginning to today, if appropriate [I was] an apprentice, a journeyman, a master. I mean, we have haven't been a master yet, but we will put effort in it ... I like doing research. I mean, especially

earlier, we attended very serious trainings. Maybe in a year, let's say, in those conditions if I made 10,000 dollars I spent 15,000 on training, I mean, I took bank loan for that. ... It could be for a week or a day trip. And then I got certificates, very difficult examinations. We are one of the few who got [name of the programme] certificates in the region, but then we profited from its advantages ... After this point we started reaping the fruits.

The first thing that grabbed my attention was his use of certain words. For example, it is very common to work in a shop as a teenager in the summer breaks, but he frames it as an 'internship'. The term is crucial here, since it makes an ordinary summer job the start of his professional career. It also serves him in representing his whole career as a continuum, starting from his 'internship' in a computer-radio repair job to running a business in programming as if they are the result of the conscious choices he made. I am not denying the person's agency here, but would rather highlight the formulation, word selection and narration, which suggest that Emir Bey is using a 'neoliberal' discourse that diverges from the accounts of earlier generations, who would have placed greater emphasis on provisioning the family and personal satisfaction. However, in line with an earlier suggestion of Martin (2009), Emir Bey talks about himself in terms of 'mini-corporations, collections of assets that must be continually invested in, nurtured, managed, and developed' (ibid.: 42). This kind of self-representation was also present in Çiğdem Hanım's account, although it was less prevalent. Emir Bey's case might also be related to the fact that he teaches 'entrepreneurialism' courses at the local university as an exemplar of an 'entrepreneur', hence he is accustomed to using the vocabulary of the hegemonic 'neoliberal' political rationality. Still, underneath that discourse are the summer job, the apprenticeship and all the other, more locally embedded versions of personhood. On the other hand, it should not be forgotten that for Emir Bey and others, 'success' depends on how much they can adapt and respond to the demands of the market with new assets and abilities that allow them to 'expand'.

The story of Osman, which I will take further in Chapter 6, represents a counter example of someone who could not equip himself with 'certificates' in the same sector and therefore went bankrupt and started working with his uncle. What also stands out in Emir Bey's narrative is how he refers to himself using the first person plural pronoun 'we', by which he does not mean the total number of people who work there or other people who did all this together with him. Rather, he is referring to the 'enterprise' while talking about himself, a clear indication that he as a person is identified with the enterprise. Then again, Martin's (2009) argument is personified in Emir Bey as himself being a 'mini-corporation'. As I will show in the following sections, this sort of identification with the enterprise goes even further than Emir Bey's account in certain other narratives. The meaning of work not only entails self-realization and provisioning, but also links to personhood and, through that, to the enterprise as a whole.

The Dark Side of Origin Stories: Suffering, Betrayal and Envy as Forces of Production

Harris (2007) and Graeber (2001) offered frameworks to explain the value of work in respect of its performance and provisioning aspect while breaking the link between the obligation to work and coercion. However, my ethnography offers other evidence from the narratives of my respondents suggesting that we cannot simply dismiss coercion as an aspect of work. Business people who started from scratch and did not complete a formal education often refer to the days of poverty and hardship when narrating what Yanagisako calls the 'origin story', one of the important features of which is the fact that 'the founder's decision to start a firm is commonly associated with a break with his past' (2002: 43). In the origin stories that I came across, 'suffering' had a central role in the decisive break, in which starting a firm is framed as ending the suffering.

For example, Esat Bey is in his forties and employs around 25 women workers in his dumpling factory. In the last ten years, his business has thrived through the contracts he has made with supermarket chains. At our first meeting, I explained my research as we were entering his office. One of my initial questions was how Çorum's business people started their businesses and why they chose to do so. He immediately replied: 'To get rich'. As I was baffled by his direct reply and said: 'Excuse me?', he continued: 'For two years, there had been days when I couldn't buy food for my kids. You see, we suffered. Then at last I started with the *gözleme* (filled and folded phyllo dough cooked in a pan) shop, taking so many risks'. The link Esat Bey makes between taking risks in order to end suffering caused by poverty and 'getting rich' is a very strong and direct one, and the way it is immediately brought up again shows the intensity of his desire to 'get rich', which stands for having a better life through social mobility and thus being able to take care of his family's needs, as in my previous examples. However, in Esat Bey's account the decisive break is the one that ends the suffering. His memory of the time he worked at a furniture shop before starting his own business is as follows: 'We transported four lorry-loads of furniture that day. We had not eaten anything, no dinner. I told my boss's son: "Man, just have somebody make some sandwiches". The boy came back then. Let me say, if I were eighteen or nineteen years old, then he would have been a junior in middle school. How old does it make him, you calculate? [I reply, not even fifteen.] Then the guy (*herif*) said, "You will go home, go and eat your dinner at home". Then I said "I am not coming to work tomorrow". Then I quit. I said then "I will not work in *el işi* (working under a stranger in wage-labour) anymore"'. As the narrative demonstrates, the suffering that Esat Bey wants to end is not only related to poverty and not being able to feed his child, but to his suffering in *el işi*. This colloquial term for wage labour also comes up in Birelma's recently published article, where he shows that '*el işi* entails a kind of popular resentment toward and non-identification with wage labour' (2019: 61). One can sense a similar resentment and non-identification with wage labour in Esat Bey's words, yet his narrative illustrates more about the content of such resentment. In his case it stemmed from his demeaning experience in *el işi*, in which his basic human need (hunger) was dismissed and his masculine pride and generational status was subverted. Hence, his experience is narrated as the decisive break. Yanagisako suggests that the male desire for independence from the authority of other men constitutes a symbolic and crucial part of the masculine ideology (2002: 86), as is also evident in Esat Bey's narrative of his decisive break. Reading into his account, one can argue that he wished to reverse his lower socio-economic position and himself be a man with economic and social power and therefore independent of the authority of other men.

I am not making this last point solely on the basis of the above quotation, but also of my own observations and further conversations with him. Esat Bey really liked to brag about himself generally, but mostly about his honesty. He would talk almost without restraint about issues that many people would withhold so as not to give a negative impression to the other person. For instance, he told me extensively about how he adjusts the dumpling machines himself to produce more in a shorter time and showed me his room for equipment, although he said it was against the work-safety rules to have such a room. He also told me about his indecisiveness over what kind of birthday present it would be appropriate to buy for a local AKP politician. The most interesting things he talked about were how he deals with his workers. For example, he particularly prefers to employ women in their forties or fifties, whom he thinks mostly have *işe yaramaz* (useless) husbands. These husbands are useless from his point of view because they are unemployed, either because they have lost their jobs, are lazy or cannot work because of a physical injury. As a result, their wives are the primary bread-winners of their households and have no choice but to work uninterrupted until the day of retirement. He also views these women as more docile in comparison to younger women workers in their twenties or thirties, who, he says, constantly message their boyfriends or ask for time off because their children often get sick. He avoids these 'problems' by choosing older women workers. Moreover, he prepared an application form for people to fill in when applying to work in his company, in which he asks the applicant how much salary s/he expects, immediately eliminating those applicants who actually fill in their expected salary on the form. His reasoning behind this is that a worker shouldn't expect something for nothing: he himself didn't ask what his salary would be when he was working earlier as wage labourer. From his perspective, workers will always find a way to cheat or shirk, but even then he would not fire them; instead he would assign them tasks that they are not physically capable of, such as carrying heavy boxes for transport, and then watch them struggle from his office window. In one of our last conversations, he complained about women workers asking to be picked up by the personnel shuttle in the morning not from one central spot but from several spots, thus allowing them to walk shorter distances from their homes at 6 am. For Esat Bey, however, this demand only meant postponing the start of the working day. He would talk about his past as a wage-labourer himself, saying that he would leave home before sunrise to go to work and would smoke cigarette butts from the waste bins to make the point that his workers actually don't want to work and are lazy. In this logic, if they really wanted to work (or needed to), they would not complain about where the personnel shuttle picks them up.

Esat Bey is one of the respondents with whom I had regular meetings and who also filled in the survey. When I cross-checked his responses with statements I sceptically framed as 'Are business people neoliberal?' in the introduction to this chapter, I discovered that he strongly agreed with all of those statements: competition stimulates hard work, hard work eventually brings one a good life, greater differences of income motivate individual efforts, and individuals should take more responsibility to provide themselves and should take any job if they are unemployed. His responses to these statements seem to cohere with his desire to be autonomous by starting his own business, his calculating, market-driven behaviour in adjusting his machines, his taking responsibility for himself and his family's provision, and the way he expects his workers to be self-responsible, hard-working and industrious. As Kipnis (2008) and Kalb (2014) pointed out (see above), these notions are not necessarily neoliberal but typically classical liberal. Even when the ethnographic details are evaluated from a Foucauldian perspective, Esat Bey does not act with a political rationality stressing governance through the calculating choices of formally free individuals in the way Rose (2008) defined 'neoliberalism'. First of all, the individuals he is dealing with are not 'free' to calculate their choices, nor do they have any illusion that they are free. Secondly, he acts with pragmatism and cunning, exerting direct control and using punishment when he thinks it necessary, as can be understood from how he recruits and treats his workers. Esat Bey and his women workers are rather in a structured field of social relations of dominance, in which on the one hand applicants and working women are confined by their conditions, yet, by continually voicing their expectations and demands, cannot be considered completely dominated. On the other hand, Esat Bey is constantly making the effort to increase his turnover by tricking the machines and to dominate his workers and keep their demands under control by his own direct control and punishment, yet he cannot fully achieve this, so he keeps coming up with new strategies. Throughout my fieldwork I came across some employers who had come from a working-class background like Esat Bey but who would rather say that they make use of their prior experience as a resource in order to build a better working environment for their workers because they could empathize with them (see Chapter 6). Whether or not they could achieve this is a different topic, yet in the case of Esat Bey the shift in his class position from being a wage-worker to a member of the local bourgeoisie also reflects his proudly voiced shift from being the 'oppressed' to being the 'oppressor', I argue that only then does his narrative of 'suffering', which keeps coming up, fit into the puzzle of his subjective justification and moral grounding of his exercise of power over his workers.

I have analysed this specific case at length because this particular kind of personhood is both highly typical and familiar to most Turkish people from the earlier popular Turkish movies (called *Yeşilçam*), where a mean, crafty, interest-driven factory owner or tradesmen, who had often migrated to Istanbul from the Black Sea region and was referred as a *taşra kurnazı* ('a cunning guy from the provinces'), is depicted in opposition to the good-hearted, '*fakir ama gururlu*'[111], the poor but proud and ethical urban worker. Before the 1980s, class vocabulary was a lot more dominant in the cultural scene and in politics, and therefore the depictions were exaggerated and sentimentalized caricatures of class antagonism. However, as the issue of class became depoliticized and delegitimized in the following decades, the 'mean provincial employer' of the *Yeşilçam* movies disappeared from popular culture and was replaced with modern, urban, yet traditional, ethical and rich businessmen in TV soap operas. Although disappearing from the TV screens, the typical pragmatic, interest-driven, crafty employer still

---

[111] In this emic phrase, the poor are proud because, unlike the rich, it is assumed that they did not behave in immoral ways, such as doing injustice to others, or being mean and solely interest-driven.

exists with further legitimacy. Moreover, the narrative of suffering as a justification and moralization of inequality and oppression ceased to be specific to the 'employer', provincial or otherwise, but spread to the society at large. In today's (new) Turkey, it is common to hear people of any social class explain their preferences, whether political or economic, by referring to their previous sufferings. Throughout the 'transition', saving oneself from economic hardships became more individualized or familiarized, and being an oppressor rather than the oppressed, although not always voiced openly, has gained recognition in the wider society. This ideological shift, I believe, could partially be interpreted as a long-term effect of the New Right policies implemented in the 1980s that favoured individualism, individual virtues and familial, national and religious bonds against class-based identities, and represented the market as the miracle solution to all socio-economic problems (see Chapter 2).

Another striking aspect of Esat Bey's story was his relationship to his family, which brings us to the centrality of 'the patriarch' in one's life trajectory, especially when it comes to founding and maintaining a business. Cengiz (2013), in his analysis of Kayseri-Hacılar businessmen, points to the role of patriarchal structures in how their businesses are managed. Although, he writes, all families have their unique histories, socio-economic status and conditions, he writes, the commonality amongst successful businesses was the centrality of the patriarch as the founding and unquestionably legitimate power around whom everybody else is positioned. He adds that the path to collective success in a provincial context, where brotherly envy is very common, requires collective compliance with patriarchy (2013: 305-6). In the absence of a powerful, resourceful and charismatic patriarch who manages the conflicts among members in favour of the long-term interests of the family and the firm, the members of the family can easily fall into conflict and come apart. Yanagisako expands on Blim's (1990) remarks on how brotherly betrayal can 'occasionally' result in casualties and argues that 'betrayal and estrangement are as much a regular part of the organizational dynamics of the Como family capitalism as trust and kinship solidarity… they are among the forces of production that incite, enable, constrain and shape production' (Yanagisako 2002: 114). In my cases, too, I have observed brotherly envy, betrayal and the absence of the father due to an early or sudden death, all which have fuelled sentiments that have destroyed families and firms or facilitated the emergence of new ones. The sentiment of suffering, as I have discussed it above, usually goes along with the previous loss of a father and brotherly betrayal, as in Esat Bey's story and others.

Esat Bey, born in a county in Çorum, is the youngest son of his father, who had five other children from his previous marriage. He says that he grew up without knowing about the distinction between biological and step-siblings until his father died: '*Babam ölene kadar öz-üveylik bilmezdik*'. A year before his death, his father had a stroke which signalled his coming demise, so his children wanted to complete the construction of their father's flour factory for him to see it before he did so. Esat Bey and his mother borrowed money from their acquaintances to contribute to the construction. However, when the father died Esat Bey's step-brothers took over their father's factory and left Esat Bey and his sister and mother out, refusing to help them pay off their debts. Later on, Esat Bey said that they also forced him to take far less than his share of their father's inheritance and never asked how he was doing or whether he and his mother needed anything after they moved to Çorum centre and when Esat Bey started working in the furniture shop, as mentioned above. After he quit his job at the furniture store and started the *gözleme* shop, within two years he expanded the business due to a good subcontract he made with a wholesale trader in Ankara. At this time, he was employing sixty women. While listening to the story, I pointed out how quickly the business expanded, and he replied: '*Ya* there was *hırs* (ambition with negative connotation)! I mean, I had this *hırs* to ace my brothers. And now they have gone bankrupt in the last two years, they are not in the market anymore, and I am still trying to buy that place [his father's factory and some real estate he couldn't inherit]. I want to buy it! But not to run it, I will just fix the backyard wall and will furnish a flat there. I will leave [Çorum] on Friday evening with my kids [to my flat in my origin of place] and come back on Sunday. Only once a month or every three months. For what? So that others [in the origin of place] can [see me and] say: "Look, the guy was sacked but has done well (*helal olsun*)! He got back the place he got sacked from"'.

As is self-evident in the narrative, the loss of his father and his betrayal by his step-brothers fuelled a feeling of *hırs* that could be translated as 'ambition'. However, 'ambition' does not do justice to the local term, as *hırs* should be understood rather as a mixture of the desire to achieve, anger against unjust treatment and a bit of vengefulness, all of which had played the role of forces of production in his attempts to start and expand the business. Esat Bey says that he resented but never got cross with his brothers because 'they were my [his] seniors and he [I] was brought up with discipline'. Discipline stands here for his upbringing, which requires him to be respectful and not to question or revolt against 'the patriarch' (see Chapter 6 on paternalism and Chapter 7 on the role of respect in discipline). On the other hand, he was glad now to be in a superior position to his step-brothers, since they had gone bankrupt, whereas he owned a factory, as well as the two white and black Mercedes parked in front of it, which he pointed out with his finger later when we were standing by the window, while the step-brothers ended up having none. Also evident is how *hırs* is related to saving his reputation, as he wants others who remained in the county to know that he had taken back what had been unjustly taken away from him. Esat Bey named both his company and his son after his father's first name to commemorate him, but avoided naming his factory after his family name since that would inevitably have included his step-brothers in his legacy. As in many cases of inheriting sons, he has portraits of his father in his office, but he also has his mother's and wife and children's portraits too, which is quite unusual. By doing this, however, he gives credit to those who had stood by him in his own struggle, like his mother and also his wife, who worked in the *gözleme* shop in the first years as a part of the family strategy; moreover, it also demonstrates his break with his step-brothers.

In cases where the father is still alive but there is a conflict between brothers, even when the latter go off in different directions and start their own businesses, they tend to stick to the family name by adding a different suffix. This was what the two brothers in the Kaya family did after years of conflict and cycles of starting the business and going bankrupt. The conflict stemmed from the fact that the older brother lacked skills in book-keeping, negotiating prices and customer relations, which reduced the business's profitability. However, because of the 'discipline' that requires respect to be paid to the senior by the younger brother, who claims to have better skills, the latter always had to sort out the 'mess' the older brother had caused. The older brother stole money, went to jail, caused bankruptcy and still came back and sat in the patriarch's chair until the day his younger brother wanted to take control once and for all, after which they later split the business and its assets. In fact, few men live up to the standards of the powerful, resourceful, charismatic patriarch, and even when they do, it is very challenging for the next generation to keep up the legacy and reputation of the name.

'Aslan' is the family and company name of a well-known industrialist, who, like Cemal Bey, started from scratch and became an exporter and subcontractor of machine parts. However, a few years ago, father Aslan unexpectedly died in a car accident. After his sudden death, his three sons, who had all studied in areas related to their father's business, took over the firm. In our conversation, which took place under the 'gaze of father Aslan' looking down at us from the portrait hanging on the wall of the office, the three sons were telling me about their father's hard work and success and how difficult it had been to adapt to their new situation. Although more than a few years had passed since they had lost their father, it felt to me that what they had gone through was more than the loss of a father and more the loss of a guide, a compass. In the father's absence, things got out of control. Since they had taken over the firm, their chief engineer and foreman had left to start their own business. The brothers nearly went bankrupt and took out loans from a usurer, then got into trouble with a mafia-like gang. Later on, in a conversation with a former employee of this firm at his home, I learned that the Aslan family was no longer seen as trustworthy in the sector as it had been in their father's time, and it had accordingly lost its reputation. As the above cases show, the absence of the father or brotherly betrayal can create sentiments like ambition, anger and envy that play the role of forces of production in establishing a new family and company. On the other hand, the absence of the patriarch or betrayal by other relatives can also lead to brothers becoming estranged, or to downsizing and despair, possibly leading, if not to the demise of the firm and the family, then at least the loss of its reputation. At the core of these different narratives, in which the patriarch has died and/or brothers have betrayed each other, lies the fact that all other men position themselves in relation to the patriarch for better or worse and either become patriarchs themselves and form a new family and firm, or symbolically disappear with the family name.

Enterprise as a Brand, Reputation and the Issue of Public Envy

'Yiğit bu dünyada nam için yaşar'.
(The brave man in this world lives for reputation)
Kemal Tahir[112]
Rahmet Yolları Kesti
(1957)

In my fieldwork, reputation was frequently mentioned as a key concept that connects the narratives of hard work, suffering, the enterprise and the family name. In a way, the company's name and the value attached to it are

---

[112] Prominent Turkish novelist and intellectual who lived between 1910 and 1973. He was accused of spreading Marxist ideas in the army and sentenced to 15 years of prison in 1938. He spent 12 years in prisons of Çankırı, Malatya, Çorum, Nevşehir and Kırşehir. His ideology could be described as vernacularizing Marxist terminology and re-evaluating historical materialism with realities of Anatolian people and history. Çorum trilogy that comprises of the books *Yediçınar Yaylası*, *Köyün Kamburu* and *Büyük Mal* are inspired by his observations of Çorum, its surrounding area, and its people during the time he spent in Çorum semi-open prison. The Trilogy tells about the changing property regime, agha system, banditry in the area from the start of modernization in the Ottoman Empire in 1839 (*Tanzimat*) until the death of Mustafa Kemal Atatürk in 1938. The novel I am referring to here is a more popular novel of Kemal Tahir, focusing on banditry and agha system.

determined by the hard work and suffering of the owner, as well as his work ethic. This concern with reputation also leads business owners to identify with the enterprise more and more strongly. Ahmet Keskin, a man in his fifties, owns a window-pane design factory employing around thirty workers. He started working as self-employed in the beginning of the 1990s after ending his partnership with his brother-in-law, who told everyone Ahmet Bey was his apprentice and his driver, whereas in fact he was his equal partner. Ahmet Bey found this belittling and, after a while, went his separate way, even though his brother-in-law was older than him and had taken Ahmet Bey into his own household after his father's early death and his mother's remarriage. In a way, Ahmet Bey has violated the discipline he learned in his upbringing and betrayed his brother-in-law in order to recover from the resentment resulting from his being belittled and to declare his autonomy as an independent man. However, those years had been very difficult for him, and he expressed his memory in these words: 'I earned by putting labour into it, I earned by putting *alın teri* (literally "sweat of the forehead", but meaning great effort). I installed window panes while crying. I fell off the roof, got up and then again installed window panes. I worked while my hands were bleeding; I have scratches all over my body. I was crying when I was operating the machines. Because I am obliged. Because I had to earn to pay my debts'. As previously pointed out, the amount of suffering one undergoes is a trigger for the decisive break; in this narrative, the suffering gives value to the work and to the enterprise. Ahmet Bey, like many others, had not previously accumulated any capital, nor even tools; all his assignments were done using borrowed money and tools, which were then paid back to the lender. If one cannot meet the deal's deadline and make the repayment as promised, the possibility to borrow money in the future might be lost. That is why Ahmet Bey continued working even when his hands were bleeding, so that he would not lose the moneylenders' trust: as a self-employed man he was dependent on his dealers, as also pointed out by Birelma (2019). As the next quotation will show, this indicates that timely payment and delivery in trading are at the core of emic understandings of the 'work ethic' and provide the person with a *temiz* ('clean'), that is, 'untainted' name.

Ahmet Bey, in his vivid, dramatic and emotional description, also wanted to teach a lesson to his children who were present in the office, namely that the value of the company comes from suffering and hard work. As I sensed the increase in the tone and strength of his voice and of his selection of words, I wondered if any other emotion was lying beneath this, so I asked if he had any other motivation than paying his debts. He replied: '*Hırs* and coming from destitution, from poverty. Not to fall again into destitution, I must maintain this *hırs*. If I don't, then I'm done, psychologically done'. Ahmet Bey described his hardships as so unbearable that even today *hırs* from his prior period of poverty is still playing a role in his life after more than twenty years. His life story involves all the elements I have examined one by one in this chapter: suffering, the loss of a father, the demeaning of one's masculinity, resentment at wage-work, the desire for autonomy and hard work. Only one sentiment is missing: 'love of work', which appeared in the form of 'pride in the enterprise and its name' when we were talking about public envy, the company name and its reputation:

> Ahmet Bey: This means that [the one who] finishes the job on time, he is clean and honest. That's it, I mean, I have made a *nam* (reputation). So, when I go somewhere and knock on the door, I get the job. I mean, Keskin has a clean slate. That's what I am trying to say. And then you have a next-door neighbour, *hesabını yapar* (looks into my finances). He keeps an eye on how many customers come and go, he looks into your finances.
> Ceren: Why is there so much *çekememezlik* (envy)?
> A: This is how it is in Turkey; the society is like that.
> C: What do you mean?
> A: There is *çekememezlik*, in fact people with this mentality cannot *kalkınamazlar* (develop). That's why, when I was building this factory like this, I thought nobody should see [the front elevation]. Nobody sees my front elevation, so nobody can look into my finances.
> C: Yes, I realized when coming here, I wondered why the front elevation is reversed.
> A: That's how I am, I don't want people to see me. Nobody can look into my finances. They did a lot of that. I mean, making money, establishing a firm in a real sense, founding it is really very difficult. Otherwise, you would go and start a firm, that means nothing to me. The name Keskin has value. It has thirty years of value.
> C: What does Keskin mean to you?
> A: It means my life, my everything, my pride, my honour, my dignity, my everything. I am proud of Keskin. It connects me to life. This is my factory; I come here at 6 in the morning. This place connects me to life. I can't sleep in comfort in my home. I must be in my factory, [it] gives me the joy of living. I get pleasure from hearing machine sounds here. When the machine sound stops, I am devastated. I can't sit here… that's why I am saying making money from scratch is not everyone's cup of tea (*Her baba yiğidin harcı değil*). These [pointing to his children] came to it, when it was ready,

so they should appreciate the value of it. I always say, in businesses, earning with honour (*namusuyla para kazanmak*) is really difficult, but only if you lay a foundation, then you are solid.

This conversation demonstrates some of the core issues about how the enterprise generates value, how that is attached to one's reputation, and how this reputation is at the heart of one's honour. As I have already suggested, the emic understanding of the work ethic involves the constant cultivation of trust between producer/seller and buyer, money-lender and borrower, which keeps one's name untainted and reproduces one's reputation. Ahmet Bey makes these links at the beginning of the conversation while bringing the issue of how reputation is under constant attack from the gaze of other men. That is when he repeatedly says he doesn't want anyone to 'do his finances', that is, to let others see how many customers visit, how many lorries arrive and depart from his factory. This is the reasoning behind building the factory facing in the opposite direction to those along the same aisle. In our conversation, I mentioned certain feelings as '*çekememezlik*' (envy) because I had heard that term several times before, when business people were talking about how their neighbours would keep a constant eye on their customers, workers, the car they own, how often and when they come to work in a similar manner to which Ahmet Bey was referring. A similar feeling is addressed by Cengiz (2013) in his study of industrialization in Hacılar/Kayseri, where industrialists talked about a '*günücülük*', which has a dictionary meaning of *kıskançlık* and *haset* (respectively, softer and bolder versions of jealousy/envy). However, Hacılar businessmen explain this as the kind of *azim* (ambition seen positively) that urges one to put a constant effort into achieving a better deal, a better product, a better life, all inspired by and in comparison to a previous example established by other men in the community. As opposed to solidarity among businessmen, Hacılar industrialists talk rather about how *kin* (grudge)-driven competition has been the motor of industrial development and how many imitate others' models for products and steal their customers once they get the chance (Cengiz 2013: 280-289). The set of sentiments that played a motivating role in establishing and maintaining businesses and industry in Kayseri is expressed in Çorum with the slightly different vocabulary of *hırs* (ambition seen negatively) and *çekememezlik* (envy), which were so prominent in Esat Bey and Ahmet Bey's narratives.

Interestingly, Ahmet Bey positions *çekememezlik* (envy) in opposition to 'development'. This, I believe, has to do with the fact that *çekememezlik* operates paradoxically in two different directions that nonetheless feed into the same system of honour and hence reputation. On the one hand, I have shown in other cases that the kind of ambition that is either negatively connoted by *hırs* or positively connoted by *azim* stems from one's positioning to his father, brother, former employer and other males. The desire to declare autonomy from one's relatives is also fuelled by the have-not feeling that generates the envy that is inherent in the word *çekememezlik*. This was also voiced by Cemal Bey, as well as by others, that is, that these feelings have their origins in thoughts such as 'Why has the neighbour's kid got a bike and I don't?' 'He made that deal, has that car; why don't I?' 'He succeeded; why can't I?' This led to their 'decisive break' to establish an enterprise through years of work and the cultivation of trust that gave their names their value, and themselves their reputations. Therefore, in this case *çekememezlik* is a sentiment that played the role of 'a force of production' that actually led to industrial developments in Çorum, like *günücülük* in Kayseri.

The paradox here in why Ahmet Bey places this type of envy in opposition to development lies in the necessity to protect one's reputation in the community and in the understanding that one's success creates anxiety in the successful and envy in others. In this logic, envy produces gossip about the successful, which then actually taints their reputations, ruins their success and hinders development. Another industrialist confirmed this finding in his reply to my question about solidarity among Çorum businessmen: 'When a company expands, jealousy starts. If one becomes a leader, those who cannot catch up, who remain behind, become jealous of you. It's natural, and not only in Çorum, it exists in every city'. In so far as I could be a part of Çorum's business life during my fieldwork and participant observation, I heard a lot of gossip about some firms, such as they were not able to pay their debts, had lost money in a deal, were members of the Fethullah Gülen movement, etc. Once the company's name is tainted by such gossip, the trustworthiness that has been attached to the family or company name also becomes damaged, so you hear people talking: 'Oh, you shouldn't do business with such and such anymore, they have debts, they lost money, they are unreliable'. This explains why some businessmen avoid being seen in the public, as I mentioned in the beginning of this chapter; some of them also underdress and drive cheaper cars than they could afford. As is evident from the above conversation with Ahmet Bey, gossip about his enterprise is far from being only a matter of business, it is a threat to 'his life, his everything, his pride, his honour, his dignity, his everything'. His personhood has become merged with his enterprise through his reputation, which has become, as it were, a brand in its own right, as is apparent from how he talks about Keskin as a separate entity.

Genealogy of the Enterprise as an Institution and Economic Nationalism

When such enterprises are passed down to the following generations, both their owners and the enterprise itself gain other features than being only a brand. Mehmet Korkmaz is a second-generation businessman in his fifties. His father, Şahin Korkmaz, was one of the first tile-plant owners at the time the tile industry was flourishing in the 1970s, and later one of the first contractors in Çorum (see Chapter 4 for their origin story). Mehmet Bey, a middle-school drop-out, worked with his father in the construction business and in the 1990s invested in a textile plant which went bankrupt in the 2001 crisis. Afterwards, he sold the plant and invested in franchising many well-known garment brands and later on café chains in Çorum and all over Turkey. Mehmet Bey describes his current franchising business as *'Elimiz cebimize girmeden etrafı harekete geçirerek para kazanmanın yolları'* ('ways to make money by creating a stimulus without putting our hands in our pockets'). The family is also known to be rich through the real estate it owns, and they use the rentier capital for their construction business, mainly in Çorum, in building condominiums for the new middle classes. Mehmet Bey's son is in charge of the contracting business, as well as the cafés, and of a new investment in electronics in the United States. Mehmet Bey talks about his father using phrases such as 'the most hardworking man of Çorum', 'an investor', and 'smart man' who 'was the first to do things', Then he goes on to describe himself: 'I'm a master, that is how I was brought up. I was brought up in the industry. Plus, I'm an industrialist, a contractor, a marketer, a textile supplier, I was brought up in a wide range of things; my father raised me in a special way'. After stressing that his children ought to take him as an example and take his legacy further, he says that being hardworking is in their genes and roots going back to the Hittites (1600-1179 BC), who had their capital at Hattuşa in the Çorum area, adding that they were the same people who invented the wheel and the horse carriage[113] and who fought the Egyptians at the Battle of Kadesh (1274 BC). Throughout the conversation he uses 'we' to refer to himself and the company at the same time, just as Emir Bey identified himself with his company. Here, identification and reputation transcend these individual self-made men to cover three generations of male owners, the first starting the business on the margins the later ones gradually adapting the business to the global economy:

---

[113] Evidence of wheels and wheeled vehicles appeared more or less simultaneously in several regions of Eurasia and dates back to the fourth millennium BC (Bondár 2018).

I have seven other *usta* (master/teacher), other than my father. I did my master's degree with my father. Ours is Korkmaz University. I go to give lectures at the university, at the college. I am a drop-out from middle school. I have two sons, both are university graduates, also my two daughter-in-laws, one is even an associate professor. When the four of us sit together, you know, there are these quiz shows, me alone and those four together, I never get defeated. Because I am very inquisitive, I have knowledge about everything, whatever you ask. I never wasted even two minutes of my life. I travelled the world and four continents.

Very similar themes to the earlier cases also appear in Mehmet Bey's narrative and life story, though there are several points that stand out in the latter. First, it shows the social mobility that has been achieved in the last three generations. Their grandfather, Şahin, is the classic 'self-made' man who transferred his skills and knowledge, as well as his capital and assets, to his son Mehmet. Mehmet then went into the textile sector, a more regulated sector that requires more expensive technical equipment and raw materials, as well as more sophisticated organization in comparison to the tile and brick sector. He had the time and money to travel around the world and discover new places, a luxury the previous generation did not have. Even though the textile factory went bankrupt, the family still had the capital resources to invest in a rentier business by trading in the franchise rights to café chains. Unlike Mehmet Bey, his sons were born into wealth but were not trained next to their father; instead they went through formal education and married highly educated non-local women. On the one hand, the sons invested their rentier capital in the construction business, which was the backbone of the economy until recently. On the other hand, with the skills they had acquired through formal education, they have been developing business relations in the U.S. in electronics. All in all, in three generations the Korkmazs have shifted their status from working-class to rentier bourgeoisie by fully adapting to the changing socio-economic circumstances of the global economy, as is evident from their turning their leisure-time activities into new business strategies.

Secondly, unlike the previous cases, in this case the family and company name were promoted from being a 'brand' to become an 'institution' due to its longevity, durability and success. Korkmaz University is described as an institution that goes beyond the time span of three generations, and in the narrative the hard work as its source is linked to a genealogy that goes back centuries to an ancient empire and to one of the first inventions in the history of humanity, hence increasing the emphasis on the rootedness of innovation and hard work in the family's self-image.

Moreover, the narrative suggests that the kind of knowledge and training provided at Korkmaz University is superior to the training and education of the formal education system. This resonates with the distinction that emerged in the nineteenth century with the opening of modern military schools between army officers and bureaucrats being *mektepli* (formally educated) and *alaylı* (learned by practice). It is still used in daily life to refer to these two different types of training and learning, as well as the contrast between modern and traditional. By pointing out the superiority of his practical life experience, Mehmet Bey attempts to align different forms of social capital, achieved by the traditional and the modern, for himself and his sons, and hence to strengthen the genealogy of hardworking 'genes' while polishing his own self-image.

When the enterprise is described as an entity that still has the qualities of the self-made man at its core but that eventually outgrew him, his heirs or the actual business itself, this is often accompanied by a retrospective narrative of the businessman's selflessness and higher purpose. This clearly came out when I asked Mehmet Bey why he started the textile factory. He replied:

> A feeling of nationalism, of loving your homeland. ... I built that [textile] factory all by myself. If my father did the tile and brick, why wouldn't I do this? If your father or an elderly member of your family is an industrialist, then the child also becomes one. You can't make the child of a civil servant an industrialist: he works on minutes and hours and quits his job at 5 pm. We don't have work hours in our job, we don't have holidays. My worker is more comfortable than I am. But I cannot feel comfortable as they do, I think of my workers' *rızık* (livelihood). S/he only thinks of what goes into his/her stomach. But I have to think about his/her children too. This is how I worked for years. Otherwise, I could have put my money in a bank and become a billionaire if I'd put my money in the bank at a high interest. If you do that, you don't love your country, you're a false nationalist.
>
> Ceren: So you mean creating employment is nationalism?
>
> Yes. Look, we are in the construction sector now, we completed 48 flats, are building one more building.

In Martin's (2009) interpretation of neoliberalism, individuals will lose their status as citizens as the nation loses its prominence and become self-interest-driven nodes, mini-corporations, in the global economic network. Contrary to that presumption, in Mehmet Bey's narration, nationalism still seems to be an important motive for starting and maintaining his own economic enterprise. Nonetheless the notion of a 'mini-corporation' is relevant to his story, being described not as motivated purely by self-interest but as the institution that runs through the family's genealogy as hardworking industrialists. If we disassociate the heroism and exaggeration of personal traits from the discursive tone that is often emphasized by the entrepreneurs themselves, being an entrepreneur means undertaking the risks of the whole economic process in order to make a profit from it. Petty entrepreneurs and employers mostly give voice to worries about not being able to meet their workers' pay cheques because they lack accumulated capital and depend on customers' monthly payments. Although this is unlikely, assuming this was the case, at least when he first started his textile factory in 1990s, the crucial twist in Mehmet Bey's narrative is how he over-emphasizes the risks and heroism, while completely dismissing the profits the family makes from his entrepreneurial activities. By portraying himself as the selfless true nationalist who thinks of his workers' livelihoods and children but views the workers themselves as selfish people who do not think about their own children but are only interested in feeding themselves while comfortably having work-hours and holidays, he reverses the antagonism between labour and capital ideologically and builds his personhood upon his self-proclaimed moral superiority and nationalism.

Conclusion

This chapter has focused on the changing and/or persisting values and meanings business people of different generations attach to work, to the enterprise and to 'personhood' by examining the narratives of their lived experiences. In the neoliberal era, the notions of personhood and enterprise are often understood as the locus of calculable, governable, industrious and responsible self-disciplined subjects operating as nodes in a global economic network. Conversely, my own ethnographic evidence revealed that attributing these qualities to the neoliberal subject predates late capitalism and is motivated by multiple desires and sentiments related to the self and the self-image, the family, the enterprise and the nation.

Accordingly, the chapter has shown that earlier generations of business people, especially in the initial years of their enterprises, see work as a means to make a livelihood that comes from developing skills and applying them, which in turn creates personal happiness and a sense of pride. What gives the work its value is that it makes it possible to provide for the family and educate one's children through the firm's profits. When this value is realized, business people do not necessarily expect their children to take over the business but rather prefer them to find a career they are passionate about. Alongside the provisioning aspect of work, its performance also plays a central role in the kind of happiness it generates from self-realization and satisfaction. Work, then, for many business people becomes a medium for making a self. Through work, these business people perceive the enterprise as an inseparable part of their own personhood. Younger generations tend to be more accustomed to using the vocabulary of neoliberalism, describing themselves as collections of certificates and trainings, and emphasizing the importance of the constant cultivation of the self and professional skills. Still, beneath this discourse is a more locally embedded trajectory of the working life.

This chapter has also explored the dark side of origin stories and revealed 'suffering' as having a central role in the decisive break, while starting a firm is framed as ending the suffering. This certain feeling is mostly expressed as resentment of wage-labour and poverty, and it fuels envy and ambition in starting ones' own business. Yet, repeated vocalization of the suffering in one's narrative might suggest identification with the role of an oppressor, as well as subjective justification and moral grounding of his exercise of power and direct control over the workers. Apart from 'suffering', the chapter also showed that sentiments such as envy, anger and ambition mainly emerge in the absence of a father, in the betrayals of brothers or under the gaze of other men. Based on my interlocutors' lived experiences, I have shown that these sentiments play the role of forces of production in establishing a new family and company, but they can also lead to estrangement between brothers, downsizing and despair, which can cause, if not the demise of the firm and the family, at least the loss of its reputation.

Indeed, it is reputation that stands out as the central notion in business people's lives because it connects the enterprise, the family name, the businessman himself and his honour. The individual's untainted reputation depends on years spent cultivating trust among business partners, which constitutes the emic understanding of the phrase 'work ethic' and must be sustained. However, the sentiment of envy which initially fuelled the urge to start a business for these individual men is a collective state of mind often referred as *çekememezlik*. My ethnography has shown that this negative connotation of collective envy (*çekememezlik*) can produce gossip, ruin hardly won reputations and damage businesses. Hence, successful businessmen with reputations tend to be emotionally attached to their company and family names, referring to them almost as a separate entity, a brand. This is even more the case for companies that were passed down to more than two generations: then the brand is declared to be almost an institution with heroic qualities centred around the founding father and with centuries of roots in the family genealogy. My final case shows that, once the businessman himself is no longer personally engaged in the operations of the business or has a decision-making role while having a constant turnover from rentier capital, he becomes more likely to portray himself as not being self-interest-driven but motivated instead by higher purposes, such as being a true nationalist in comparison to earlier generations.

PART THREE

KINSHIP, RELIGIOSITY AND MANAGEMENT AT ÇORUM WORKPLACES

Chapter 6
Morality and Politics of Kinship in Family-Run Businesses and Workplace Community Identity

Introduction

Theories of modernity often treat the involvement of relatives and the family in business as an anomaly in modern capitalism (Yanagisako 2002). This idea mainly rests on Max Weber's ideal-typical distinction (1978) between economic action and other types of action that correspond to the fundamental distinction between 'modern' Western capitalism and other forms of capitalism. For Weber (1978), economic action 'is concerned with the satisfaction of a desire for "utilities" ... which is in its main impulse oriented toward economic ends' (1978: 63), whereas all other action is oriented towards the satisfaction of other desires. Accordingly, economic action in modern capitalism is motivated by the calculated and rational pursuit of profit accumulation. On the other hand, in Weber's view, households are committed to 'direct feelings of mutual solidarity rather than on a consideration of means for obtaining an optimum of provisions' (ibid.: 156). Thus, in the Weberian understanding, the involvement of family and relatives in business that brings community commitments and obligations into the equation does not belong to modern capitalism and rather qualifies as an 'oxymoron' (Yanagisako 2002: 21). Based on this fundamental divide, many studies have discussed the 'persistence' of family relations in business as a notion that will perish since their involvement goes against the primary logic of the accumulation of profit.

On the other hand, in the Marxist understanding, social relationships are understood with reference to the antagonism between labour and capital, whereby the main feature of a capitalist economy and its logic becomes its extraction of surplus labour. In *Capital* (1978), Marx describes at length how the production of surplus labour, either by decreasing costs or improving technology, is necessary to create surplus value and hence make a profit. By this token, the idea of the 'family worker' blurs the antagonism between labour and capital. A family worker can obtain extra benefits or a share of profits without having any claim on the means of production in exchange for his or her assumed loyalty to the employer. Analysing local communities only on the basis of the antagonism between labour and capital leads to cultural processes being envisaged merely as a dependent variable and their capacity to shape capitalism being overlooked (Yanagisako 2002). While the necessity of extracting surplus value and its production is evident, 'the same cannot be said for the mechanism involved in the production of surplus labour and its extraction' (Smart and Smart 1993: 10). That is to say, it falls short in explaining how workers are made to work more but are paid less. It is often the case that the reallocation of production to less developed countries and resurgent regional economies is explained by their advantage in having cheaper labour costs: this is also the case for local industrial provinces such as Çorum (Demir, Acar, and Toprak 2004; Pamuk 2007). On the other hand, Smart and Smart (1993) rightly argue that 'it would be overly simplistic to assume that the lower wages automatically generate greater surplus value' (ibid.: 10).

A similar argument could be made about the involvement of family and kin in business. Often, those who challenge the idea that working with relatives is an anomaly tend to stress its function and advantages in the formation and development of the business (Khalaf and Shwayri 1966; Capello 2015). This argument is also shared by anthropologists to some extent, but the problem lies in the treatment of family workers' utility as a natural outcome. For instance, Piore and Sabel (1984), who heralded 'flexible specialization' as the new organizational principle in mid- or high-tech craft production in innovative small firms, also recognize that firms' owners draw on 'traditional familialism' as a part of the model they declared to be the alternative to mass production. Yet, these approaches simplistically assume that hiring relatives automatically ensures greater surplus value or enables development and economic growth by treating the family, community and kin as 'a stable cultural resource rather than a historically situated, negotiated process that is itself continually being produced' (Yanagisako 2002: 3).

Alternatively, anthropologists who offer detailed ethnographic analysis of how family and kinship (and its discourses) work in forming and organizing modern capitalist businesses in western or other contexts view these enterprises within a broader nexus of social action that is shaped by the interests as well as the sentiments and commitments of individuals who are connected with enduring bonds of relatedness. Studies focusing on formal settings of family-owned enterprises inherited down the generations have revealed issues concerning origin stories and myths in relation to gender, legal regulations and maintenance of the family together with the business in relation to motivations, sentiments, cultural symbols, family genealogies and the role of knowledge transfer in the success or failure of succession by sons or others (Marcus and Hall 1992; de Lima 2000; Yanagisako 2002). More relevant for this chapter are ethnographic studies that reveal how the politics of kinship is interplayed at the workplace (De Neve 2005); the constitution, deployment or denial of discourses on kinship among workers and employers (Dubetsky 1976; Smart and Smart 1993; Haynes 1999; De Neve 2005); 'fictive' kinship that makes relations of power and domination appear natural in the context of mutual obligations (White 2000, 2004); and ideas of 'collectivism' that obfuscate gender, ethnic and other inequalities that enable flexible forms of capitalist accumulation (Greenhalgh 1994).

In very general terms, as a discourse, kinship morality is invoked by employers to create a more loyal and reliable labour force. However, when it actually comes to recruiting, promoting or laying off kin, there appears to be a limit to their benefits and incorporation for both workers and employers (De Neve 2005). Bloch suggested differentiating between the moral and tactical meanings of kinship terms, which, when they are used strategically, 'may have little to do with kinship in any strict sense of the word' (1971: 80). On the other hand, in his later writings he clarifies further the morality of kinship and argues that its limits can be estimated 'by observing the degree of tolerance of imbalance in reciprocal aspects of the relationship. The greater degree of tolerance, the more morality' (Bloch 1973: 77). Accordingly, relationships between distant kin, friends and neighbours fall into the category of 'short-term morality' because there is less willingness to accept imbalances and it is therefore easier to discard it when it becomes too costly in the short run, whereas kinship is subject to 'long-term morality' because it tolerates the imbalances of delays and renumerations in reciprocity. Moreover, Bloch argues that 'the long term effect is achieved because it is not reciprocity which is the motive but morality' (ibid.: 76).

This last point resembles James Carrier's recent interpretation of 'moral economy', where he reformulates the content of the 'moral' in economic relationships. According to him, 'the content of these relationships accumulates over the course of time… Each interaction is shaped by those that preceded it and is part of the foundation of those that follow. In this sense, those interactions are not only the content of the relationship. They also are the basis of the expectations that each party to the relationship has about the other party, about the obligations each has toward the other and about the relationship itself' (Carrier 2018: 23). In both arguments, the 'moral' is achieved in the long run through recurring interaction and/or tolerance regardless of the content of the reciprocity. One could argue that, when working with kin, the moral content of these enduring bonds is actually what enables the mutuality of the often contradictory roles of being both an 'individual' and a 'person-in-community', as is also prevalent in the context of Çorum's business owners. Gudeman (2009) argues that the continuous shift between these roles would in some cases enable them to transfer market gains to communal commitments and vice versa or lead to tensions between these mutually dependent realms and identities. As my own ethnography also shows, employers and related-employees constantly shift between their roles in pursuing both market gains and the goals of kinship. However, regardless of how long-established or morally motivated the interactions are, tensions among kin who work together can also reach breaking point. This is not because they are immoral, but because market practices have the capacity to 'erase their contingency [mutuality] and dialectically undermine their existence by continuously expanding the arena of trade, by cascading, by appropriating materials, labour and discourse and by mystifying and veiling the mutuality on which they are built' (Gudeman 2009: 37). This is why Bloch's and Carrier's interpretations, while having great explanatory power, are limited, given that the content of reciprocity, even in long-term kinship morality, matters.

In this chapter, I focus on the workplaces of the protagonists in this research, whom I introduced in the first chapter, and whose origin stories I presented in the fourth. The first is a medium-size factory, Çor-Mak, where the two owners of the company are unrelated, though they mainly employ the close family members, relatives and co-villagers of one partner, and did so especially in the first decade of the company's existence. Over the years, the ratio of related workers to non-related workers has decreased, yet the major positions in the management and on the shop floor are given mainly to relatives. My second case is a second-generation, family-owned, medium-size distribution company, Ozan Ticaret. This firm employs some family members and close relatives in the offices and some distant relatives and co-villagers as manual workers in the transport section. Given the theoretical background, and based on my ethnographic research in these two workplaces, in the first main part of this chapter I will tackle questions such as: How do employers and workers use the discourse of kinship? What does it mean to be related to an employer as a co-villager or a nephew? What kinds of obligations arise from the meanings and expectations attached to these modes of relatedness? Are social obligations necessarily oppressive, or could they provide some sort of autonomy as well? How and when do different social roles and interests collide or conflict? What happens when personal interest trumps social obligations, and how does this apply to people of different degrees of closeness? What constitutes the limits to these roles and interests? To be able to address these questions, I introduce the work-place settings, map out the kinship diagrams of Çor-Mak and Ozan Ticaret, and elaborate on selected members' life and work stories to bring out the disputes, negotiations and agreements that occur as people continuously shift between their roles in the community as senior and established males and females in their places of origin and their place in relations of employment as employers. In doing so, I use the concepts of the strategic, long- and short-term morality of kinship (Bloch 1971, 1973) to analyse and differentiate between the moralities that far and close kin and family members respectively are subject to.

As I have discussed above, long-term kinship morality or the moral economy as redefined by Carrier (2018) emphasizes that the long-term affect is achieved by the moral content of a relationship that is itself based on obligation. However, the ethnography shows that, even if long-term commitments can be discarded, the content of the reciprocity also matters, and interrelations of dependence and inequality have an impact on whether or not long-term obligations persist. Hence, to understand how long-term commitments are established or discarded, how fictive kin ties are created, and on which sets of values workplace communities are built, I follow Kofti (2016) and Palomera and Veta (2016) in their contributions to the discussion over moral economy to examine 'the moral economy of flexible production'. As also noted in the Introduction to this work, I aim to capture a wide range of the moral frameworks of employers, related and unrelated workers and managers, whose decisions shape the context of capital accumulation on a daily basis. Accordingly, in the second main part of this chapter, I explore how the roles and obligations of a family or a kin group are stretched to include non-family employees through various incentives, Islamic and non-Islamic workplace rituals, and outdoor activities in a paternalistic manner in order to widen workplace communities. The two cases under scrutiny in this chapter depart from different 'moral frameworks' in their pursuit of creating workplace communities, as their rituals and activities do not necessarily reflect or guarantee workers' consent or participation from the perspective of their moral framework.

Working with Co-Villagers, Relatives and Family Members

The Puzzle of Recruitment of Far relatives and Co-villagers in Çor-Mak

By 2016, Çor-Mak was employing some sixty to seventy manual workers and around ten office workers to provide Çorum's supply chain in the flour-machine sector through subcontracting relations both locally and abroad. The owners of the factory are Cemal Bey, an ex-factory worker and foreman from a peasant family in a village in Çorum, and Bülent Bey, an engineer from a civil-service family with roots in Çorum notables and an education in Germany. Discrepancies in their socio-cultural backgrounds were manifested in the division of labour of their responsibilities. Cemal Bey dealt with production and controlling the workforce, Bülent Bey with the engineering and finance. They both knew most of their workers by name and were familiar with the calculations and technical drawings of the machines, but Bülent Bey seemed not to know much about matters related to the recruitment, promotion and control of the workers, nor did Cemal Bey know the details in pages and pages of advanced calculations that Bülent Bey kept in thick files in his office. The factory's social organization was therefore based on these fundamental premises.

When Cemal Bey filled in the quantitative survey for my research, he initially indicated that no family members worked in the factory. It was the first weeks of my presence in the factory, so I raised this topic in our conversations with women office-workers. Sevim, an unrelated worker, laughed out loud when I said that I thought relatives didn't work here. She said: 'Inside (meaning the shop-floor) is full of Cemal Bey's *akraba* (relatives) and *köylü* (co-villagers). He filled the whole place with them. Ayfer here (pointing to the tea-lady Sevda who was present) is also a relative of Cemal Bey's.' Ayfer later explained that her paternal grandmother was Cemal Bey's paternal aunt. She also explained her *akrabalık* (relatedness or kinship) to other workers (such as her maternal uncle's son) and others who were related to Cemal Bey and his wife. However, her explanations were too complicated for me to follow, especially when she introduced the different branches of a lineage, which were not necessarily from the same descent line.[114] When Sevim referred to Cemal Bey's relatives working in the factory, she used the term in a general, conventional sense, not meaning that she knew who is related to whom. In fact, most of them would be either distant relatives or co-villagers rather than close relatives. Something similar happened when I spoke to the shop-floor workers in their tea break. They said that at least eighty percent of the workers were Cemal Bey's co-villagers, but over the years this figure has fallen to a half. Still, it was difficult for me to differentiate who among these people were close or distant relatives or just co-villagers. The ambiguity in the use of kin terms resonates with Bloch's (1971) distinction between the moral and tactical

---

[114] When Çorum people use the term *akraba*, they either refer to all related people through blood or marriage in general, or to those who are *yakın akraba* (close relatives), which includes spouse's relatives. Others, such as the relatives of grandparents, would be *uzaktan akraba* or *hısım* (distant relatives), a distinction made by Delaney (1991: 154) in her study of Turkish village society.

meanings of kin terms. When it is put into circulation in a tactical sense, in words already quoted, it 'may have little to do with kinship in any strict sense of the word' (Bloch 1971: 80). In the case of Çor-Mak, the tactical use of kinship terminology shows that there is a value attached to being related to the employer (not really in kinship terms, but simply having a relationship or link through having been born in the same village), which apparently leads non-related workers to distinguish themselves from their co-villagers or related employees for a reason. I will elaborate on that reason below.

Later, on going over the survey questions with Cemal Bey, I brought up the topic again. This time he started by explaining that Çor-Mak was not a family firm; after all, he was not related to Bülent Bey. Then he kept telling me about the problems of working with relatives, that they would always expect privileges and sentiments to become involved. As I insisted, he half-heartedly mentioned that Bülent Bey's son Ulaş had joined them that year after finishing his undergraduate studies, and added that Yavuz, the foreman, was his brother-in-law, but he was going to retire this year. He was reluctant to talk about the matter further, as was, Fatih, the manager and paternal second cousin of Cemal Bey, who said that they do not like to hire relatives – not even his brother – because people would rely on their good relations and become lazy, asking for more wages. While it was a bit ironic to hear a relative of Cemal Bey saying this, apparently neither man wanted to present the company as one that hires relatives and co-villagers. Although Cemal Bey, Bülent Bey and Fatih would all say that they are 'like a family' here, they would deny this when I asked about the existence of kin ties in the factory. This puzzled me, since non-related workers would point out the co-villager or kin ties of workers to employers, which the employers themselves would deny. This denial reveals a puzzle: hiring relatives and co-villagers seems unprofessional, especially at a time when they had recently hired a management expert to modernize working practices. This management expert brought in the Weberian idea that, since the family resonates with 'mutual solidarity', to work with family members is at odds with company interests, a line also repeated by Cemal Bey. Yet, it was also evident that they had hired relatives and co-villagers at first, only changing their policy subsequently. The question is then a double one: why did Cemal Bey and Bülent Bey hire relatives and co-villagers to begin with, and why did they change their policy and now deny the existence of kin ties?

In an old study, Paul Stirling (1965) pointed out that Turkish villagers were uncomfortable relating to others outside their geographical vicinity. Mübeccel Kıray (1984) showed that one third of the townsmen and two thirds of the villagers she interviewed would consider anyone born outside their settlement as a *yabancı* (stranger). Even in the middle-class urban context, it is common for one to prefer to approach a *tanıdık* (acquaintance) to get things done or ask for advice or aid. Similarly, Carol Delaney (1991) linked her villagers' self-identification with their roots in terms both of their relations and their relatedness to one another, and their sense of ethnic superiority to 'their desire to remain one inside, closed group, untainted and unpolluted by a mixture of outsiders' (Delaney 1991: 149). When one projects these attitudes on to the recruitment of workers in small and medium-size workplaces like Çor-Mak, it is very likely that co-villagers and relatives turned to Cemal Bey when they needed their sons to generate a new source of income at a time when subsistence farming was no longer able to meet the household expenses.

The many villagers arriving in Çorum city centre (assuming they have not migrated to other cities) have followed a similar pattern since 1960s. Many of the young men who live in Çorum's villages with their extended families migrated to the city gradually, initially leaving their wives and children in the village, perhaps commuting at the beginning, but bringing in their families once they could afford a proper flat to rent or purchase. Similarly, when young men and boys dropped out of school[115] they were handed over to industry[116] (*sanayiye verilmek*) to work with someone their father knows and trusts, or were placed on Quranic courses or sent to vocational imam schools for a while before finding industrial jobs as apprentices. Kadir (35) and Hasan (43), both currently welders in Çor-Mak, are examples of this for their respective generations. They were both advised and encouraged by people from the village (*köyden kişiler*) that it is good if one learns one's religion, so Kadir attended Quran courses and Hasan went to imam schools after primary school. Hasan dropped out after a short time and found a job in industry through his acquaintance with Cemal Bey. Kadir, on the other hand, thought he would pursue the imam school further, and make a career out of it, but he found the courses boring and too restrictive, so he too went into industry. Both migrated to the city, bought flats with bank loans and brought their families there.

As the life stories of Kadir and Hasan show, young men who dropped out of school or were simply not interested in studying found themselves in

---

[115] The young male workers I met in Çorum who have not dropped out of school were more likely to skip the apprenticeship stage and work as operators in factories or find white-collar service-sector jobs. My second ethnographic example represents such a group.

[116] The verb is used here in the passive. The child or teenager is not the active agent in making the choice: the family patriarchs make the decision. They see industry as being like school or the military, where a boy is disciplined, prepared for life, acquires merit and then becomes a man. Maybe not surprisingly, in many male workers' testimonies they described resemblances between the school, the military and industry with reference to bells, rules, authority and discipline.

industry either by their own or their fathers' choices. This is thought to be the way to acquire manual skills and be trained as an apprentice in order to become a foreman someday. Therefore, Cemal Bey is very likely to have employed his co-villagers and relatives, especially in the first years of their start-up, when he needed to build a loyal workforce that would stand the long hours of work, low pay and self-exploitation. Today, Cemal Bey describes half his workers as coming to him from apprenticeships and constituting the backbone of the factory. This form of recruitment, as in Cemal Bey's case, is quite different from what Alan Dubetsky (1976) found in relation to migrants from Anatolia to Istanbul. In comparison, in Çorum, Cemal Bey recruited almost solely from among his co-villagers, who had hardly any skills, nor were there many other job opportunities for them. However, he and his co-villagers had a sense of familiarity with one another, as they shared primordial ties based on common geographical origins and had trust and loyalty in each other because of these demarcated and personalized relationships, similar to Dubetsky's Anatolian migrants. At the same time, being one of Cemal Bey's co-villagers would still help distinguish one worker from the others, as in the logic of the strategic usage of kinship terms by unrelated workers. Only co-villagers and distant or close relatives of Cemal Bey were not truly *yabancı* (stranger) in the sense that Stirling and Kıray indicated in their studies.

On the other hand, bounded and personalized relations between them required more than just recruiting. As Haynes (1999) states of employers' understandings of the relationship: 'Rarely did these characterizations refer to the fairness of salary or legal benefits; instead they concerned a wide range of social considerations beyond the wage relationship' (Haynes 1999: 149). It was a common practice in Çorum (and probably elsewhere) for employers to provide for their workers, for example, by lending them money. Later in my fieldwork, I came to realize that one of the reasons for changing the policy of recruitment was in order to avoid being expected to lend money. Cemal Bey, months later, told me how widespread money-lending was in the factory and that almost all workers would borrow money, for instance, a sum of 5000 TRY[117] all at once, which would be paid back in instalments of 100 TRY through deductions from the employee's monthly wages. However, the workers' debt increased incrementally over the years in such amounts that they started having difficulties in paying them back. As a result, Cemal Bey and Bülent Bey wanted to put an end to the practice, shifting from their roles as 'person-in-community' to 'individuals' thinking what was best for their business. They did this by legally laying off workers

---

[117] As of January 2016, one Lira was worth 3.21 Euros according to the Turkish Central Bank.

and giving them their legal redundancy money, which the workers would use to pay off their debts to Çor-Mak. Then some would be employed again, while others at the age of retirement were forced to retire. Non-refunded debt determined the limits to short-term morality between Cemal Bey and his co-villagers and his distant relatives because, as opposed to the long-term morality of kinship, the short term is less moral, shows less willingness to accept imbalances and delays, and is easier to discard (Bloch 1973). Many of Cemal Bey's co-villagers developed the manual skills they later used to find more senior jobs; some bought flats in the city, and a few started their own businesses. Cemal Bey resented those who started their own businesses because, related or not, he would rather employ them on merit and would not mind lending money to them. In other words, he was willing to shift to a 'long-term morality' of kinship, but his motive was not 'moral' as Bloch (1973) has described the concept, nor was it because of the longevity of the relationship that the two sides felt obliged to deal with each other in the future, as Carrier (2018) described. In Cemal Bey's moral framework, although as an employer he wanted to keep his skilled employees, he was faced with the fact that those who had started their own businesses no longer wanted to by loyal to him, devoting long hours of work to him for low pay. From the point of view of their moral framework, like those I described in Chapter 5, they preferred to become independent of wage-work and hence broke their ties with Cemal Bey.

The Hopes and Failures of Family Members in Çor-Mak

The longer term morality of kinship applies only to family members and close relatives who are regarded as loyal and trustworthy in the long run and have a greater willingness to accept imbalances in reciprocity. In Çor-Mak, as is the case in many other medium or even large companies, family members and close relatives are placed in management positions or are trained to take such positions (see Figure 4). The exception in this case would be the least skilled worker, Özcan, who, as the son-in-law of Cemal Bey, has to provide for his daughter and therefore cannot be dismissed. By briefly presenting the life and work stories of three of these people, I shall show that the long-term morality of kinship has high costs and/or benefits for both parties and also that it has its limits.

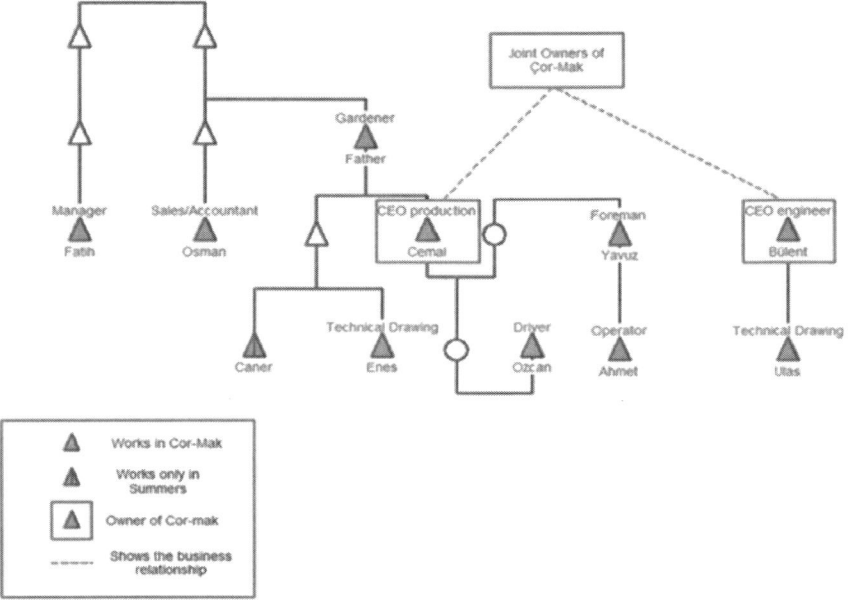

Figure 4. Kinship Diagram of Çor-Mak.

Fatih. He is 33 years old, married with two children, and is Cemal Bey's second cousin. Fatih started working at Çor-Mak at around the age of thirteen, after dropping out of school. In his own words, 'For nineteen years, all with patience. With patience. I never disobeyed them. I was never lazy. I did everything they asked me to...and I believe I did more than they expected'. Despite his failure to complete formal education, Fatih learned all the computer programs, including the 3D drawing techniques and Bülent Bey's advanced engineering calculations, alongside the manual skills he had mastered on the shop-floor. For the last four years he has been working as the company's manager, acting on behalf of Cemal Bey and Bülent Bey; however, he is not fully independent but is obliged to consult them. His work comes before everything else, and he expects the same dedication and ambition from others. At the same time, he has a father-son like relationship with Cemal Bey, who helped him with his father's funeral, at his wedding and in his problems with his wife. He has bought Fatih a flat, a *bağevi*[118] next to his, furniture for his new flat, a new laptop Fatih chose himself and an iPhone. Fatih has been paying for the flat in instalments from his salary,

---

[118] A second leisure house that many provincial middle-class people own. It is usually located on the way to villages in the woods and has a garden.

but he does not know how much the *bağevi* cost because Cemal Bey would not tell him. Since Fatih became the manager, he requires Enes, Osman and Ulaş to work on some Saturdays[119], which he decides arbitrarily. None of them know before Friday at noon if they will have to work or not the next day.

Enes. He is 23 years old and married, and is actually a classificatory nephew of Cemal Bey. He studied technical drawing at a provincial university for two years. Since his adolescence he has been working in Çor-Mak after school and in the summers. He has been trained by Cemal Bey, Yavuz and Fatih in every step of machine production. He has also been taught to obey, keep silent and nod to the powerful male figures that surround him. Enes's memories of his early years of employment as an apprentice in Çor-Mak were always a bit bitter, especially when he talked about Yavuz, who had disciplined him and other apprentices in cruel and abusive ways. He would describe the factory bells as school bells and the rules as military discipline. Still, he has a great deal of respect for Cemal Bey and Fatih, the kind of respect that is driven partially by fear and partially by envy of their wisdom and knowledge. He wished to become like them, a desire that included having the power they have over others. After Enes returned to Çorum from his undergraduate studies, Cemal Bey decided that he should work in the factory's laser department[120] because there were none of 'them' in that department, meaning workers in the lineage of either Cemal Bey or Bülent Bey. However, Enes made a few mistakes that cost the firm a substantial financial loss, and he had a fight with his uncle Cemal Bey about being disrespectful towards his superior. As a result, he was either fired or left the factory of his own accord, it never being clear to me which. With the encouragement of a friend, he went to İzmir to work in a mining company instead. Separating from his uncle's factory was a bold move, and he took risks in testing whether he would succeed in the 'outside world'. However, in his first quarrel with his supervisor, he became very offended, could not handle being scolded by a stranger and felt lonely in İzmir. So he came back to Çorum with an impulsive decision, searched for a job for a long time and found one, but could not get along with the other employees there either. According to the rumours, it was due to the insistence of his grandfather (Cemal Bey's father) that he was taken back by Çor-Mak. While I was there he made several mistakes in the technical drawing and shipping sections,

---

[119] Saturday is holiday for the manual workers on the shop floor and all others except for these four and Cemal and Bülent Bey. See Chapter 7 for how work hours are negotiated.

[120] Where the steel sheets are moulded based on precise measurements as required by the specific order. This is a one-off procedure, and if it is done wrongly the raw material is wasted, potentially meaning a serious financial loss.

which meant substantial losses for the company. Each time, Cemal Bey became furious, cursed him and threatened to fire him. Enes nevertheless works very hard and in a more dedicated fashion to compensate for his faults. Other than being scared of making mistakes again, he wants to prove himself and be give a permanent position in Çor-Mak. Enes looks up to Fatih and dreams of a position like his. At the same time, he keeps his savings in Cemal Bey's account because he thinks it is safer than banks. Moreover, he says that he doesn't want to lend money to those of his acquaintances who ask for it and who assume that, as the nephew of a rich uncle, he must have enough money to lend them. He says he needs to keep it safe for the interests of his own household, meaning himself and his wife.

Osman. He is in his mid-thirties, married with two small children, and is also Cemal Bey's second cousin, like Fatih. He studied computer programming in a larger city in Turkey. Two years before starting to work at Çor-Mak, he had owned a computer shop for some years that provided internet services. His dream was to start a business and buy a house and a car before he turned thirty. Although he achieved his dream to a certain extent, by 2014 the computer shop was not making even one third of the profit it had in 2006. Computer use changed rapidly, and Osman could not really keep up with developments in the sector by investing in the new systems. He had taken out a bank loan to buy his house and was looking for a way to pay back his debt without taking any more risks and avoid bankruptcy. About that time, Fatih approached him and offered him a position in Çor-Mak that required skills in using certain advanced computer programs, in which Osman had no training. Still, both Fatih and Cemal Bey believed he could manage it. Osman also felt encouraged, as he had a certain familiarity with this role, he explained, partly because he had provided IT services to the company in his earlier years, and also because he had kin and/or village ties to most of the workers. However, he could not manage the position, so he was put in charge of sales and accounts instead. Other non-related employees who had worked there longer and had more experience in sales and accounting were not given any priority in this position. Osman had some experience since he had run his own business before, but he did not know the accounting programs, nor was he familiar with the materials that were purchased for the company. Two years later, and Osman is still struggling with his job. He is frustrated with the fact that he might be causing disappointment to Cemal Bey by not fulfilling the latter's expectations. He says that because he is related both to Fatih and Cemal Bey, they would not lay him off or treat him the way they would treat a failing *el adamı* (a synonym for *yabancı*, outsider). Another problem is his discomfort in taking orders from superiors and not being able to act on his own; even in minor tasks, he has to do what he has been told. He finds it increasingly hard to take orders from family members whom he is not supposed to question.

During my fieldwork, some of the most frequent answers of employers to the question, 'What do you think a good employee should be like?' were that they should treat the job as if it were their own, not ask or negotiate for wages, and follow rules and orders. At the same time, employers expected workers to take responsibility and be creative in problem-solving. Their description heavily implies that the worker should leave his side of the wage relationship open-ended. This kind of demand overlaps with kinship relations because they are primarily defined by mutual obligations and general reciprocity, which White (2000: 132) described as: 'mutual indebtedness mean[ing] social relations are kept open-ended: that is without expectation of closure by a counter gift'. Fatih, in that regard, is an example of a 'good employee' in that he conforms to what is expected of him in an open-ended manner and has been ambitious to develop his abilities further to be useful to the company. In this regard, Fatih's moral framework, which shapes his behaviour, is at odds with those of other men who have declared their autonomy. Instead he embraced other men's authority over him and treated wage-work as his 'own'. In return, he has been rewarded with economic privileges and offered a share of his uncle's and Bülent Bey's authority.

However, we cannot talk about a long-term morality of kinship in the case of Fatih because there are no imbalances in the reciprocity to be tolerated, nor is renumeration delayed. It is rather the mutuality of the business and kinship goals that is manifested reciprocally in the relationship with Cemal Bey. Fatih has willingly merged his identity with the interests of Çor-Mak; his financial indebtedness is interwoven with his emotional indebtedness. Cemal Bey has been a mentor, a 'father', a 'brother' to him for the past nineteen years, that is, more than the half of his life. Conversely, Cemal Bey has invested in his 'nephew' as both as an employee and a probable heir, and he needs Fatih's dedication and skills to run his company, as he has no other successors but Fatih.[121] Fatih is aware of this situation and has a latent expectation of taking over Cemal Bey's position. It might be due to the relatedness of the two that Fatih found himself working in his second cousin's factory from a young age, and the moral content of the relationship might have kept it going, but the merger of the business and kinship goals is a result of a long process of negotiation regarding the content of what each party has offered the other.

---

[121] Cemal Bey has three daughters; two of them are not trained for the job, nor are they interested in it, while the third has studied at university but is pursuing a different career in a metropolitan city.

In the cases of Enes and Osman, on the other hand, long-term kinship morality is what keeps them work at Çor-Mak despite their failures and inefficiencies. It is indeed not the content of the reciprocity but the moral motive, as Bloch (1973) argued, and the obligation created by the endurance of the relationship itself, as Carrier (2018) suggests, in which the morality of kinship is made manifest. For reasons of long-term kinship morality, Enes was able to come back, and Osman was hired to work in sales ahead of other more experienced but non-related workers. With a similar moral framework to Fatih, Enes keeps his relationship to Cemal Bey open-ended by keeping his savings in the latter's account, and he submits himself to the company and to the family as if he is not expecting any counter-gift. Although he seems to be in total submission, he struggles to obey and follow the rules. Nonetheless, for him it is more acceptable to be scolded and cursed at by his uncle than by a stranger, which was precisely what motivated him to return to Çorum from Izmir. At least in this company he can hope to reach a higher standard of living like Fatih and to share in Cemal Bey's authority one day, this being the counter-gift he is actually aiming for. A higher standard of living in which one has a position of authority, which he experienced in İzmir, is less likely to work out if he struggles outside the moral codes of the kin ties he grew up in. After all, in the larger cities there are plenty of other young men with similar or better qualifications. Moreover, although his story is shaped by episodes of oppressive treatment, he maintains a desire to convert his situation into some autonomy for his own household, as revealed by his logic in keeping his savings in his uncle's account.

Enes' case also shows that the long-term morality of kinship can also be discarded if high financial costs or disrespect results from it, as Cemal Bey dismissed Enes once. In both Enes' and Fatih's cases, the merger of family and company interests in individual behaviour is evidence of the paternalistic social organization of this workplace, which allows the kind of arbitrariness in decision-making that is involved, such as the decision whether to work at the weekend or not. This suggests that some features of flexible forms of capitalist accumulation are enabled by familial collectivism (Greenhalgh 1994).

Osman's situation is somewhat different from those of Enes and Fatih. First of all, he did not start working in Çor-Mak as his first employment in his adolescence, but merely took refuge in the firm after his failed career in self-employment as a result of his difficulties in adapting to the changing demands of the market. His deep indebtedness to the banks is due to his ideal of living a 'good life' that is based on ownership, a very common trend in Turkey. All of this led him to work in the 'family' business, which he finds familiar but hard to adapt to. His problems in adapting stem first from the fact that Osman's skills and previous work experience came second to his family relationship in his employers' decision to hire him. Cemal Bey and Fatih thought that Osman would 'manage' the work, whether in technical computer programs or sales, as long as he remained trustworthy and loyal, as is taken for granted in the family context. By hiring a family member, the employer can expect full loyalty and dedication to the job more than from non-family members, even when the latter are relatively more experienced. Recruiting Osman was a traditional solution to a modern problem for the employer/uncle as much as it was for Osman. As a result, both parties have fulfilled their mutual obligations as defined by the social structure and value system, and they seem to have solved their individual problems, which they fell into because of market conditions.

Another reason for the problem of adaptation is that ideas of merit and certain freedoms to follow your own mind are in conflict with the logics whereby this company is run and the social structure in which the whole setting is embedded. Even in simple tasks, employees are told to do things in certain ways by Fatih. This can become overwhelming for someone like Osman (also for any worker, but more so for family workers), who left Çorum to go to university, then came back to run his own business, only ultimately to fail. Osman and Enes can avoid the risks of the outside world, which they find uncomfortable and unpredictable, and can deal with the uncertainties of late-capitalism on the basis that they are not '*el adamı*' (strangers) to a rich uncle. By co-owning the company, Cemal Bey can act in the given social structure in the interests of the best management of his family and his work. However, Osman and Enes, like any other employee, can only do so at the cost of compromising their self-esteem and individuality, struggling to adapt to rules they did not create and fulfilling roles they might not be fit for, waiting patiently while working hard for the day their salaries improve and they gain some authority for themselves and some autonomy for their households.

Coming back to the reservations previously made by scholars about the assumption that paying lower wages and hiring relatives automatically generates greater surplus value, these cases nicely illustrate a few complementary points. The first is that related employees do not constitute a cultural asset that eventually develop into economic gain in the industrial districts (Narotzky 1997, also see Introduction), but rather go through ups and downs and continuously negotiate their positions within the relations of production that are transformed by the global context and their local situations. The second is that relatives are actually a cost to the company in many cases, while at other times they also have the potential to generate greater surplus value by working harder, longer and in a more dedicated and loyal manner in the hope of acquiring more authority and more autonomy one day. These hopes, which fuel their hard work and dedication, are not solely motivated by the 'moral' nature of kinship or of the economic relationships that are featured in these cases, but are a response to the volatility of the labour market that makes it nearly impossible to reach these hopes outside the 'familiar' setting. It is not that they did not try; it is because they tried but failed.

Working with Relatives and Family Members in Ozan Ticaret

Ozan Ticaret is run by Eren Bey, who inherited the business from his father (see their origin story in Chapter 4, Section on 'Çorum Massacre's Impact on Alevi Businessmen') and expanded it together with his wife Yasemin Hanım, who is in charge of the firm's accounts. They own two companies[122], one in Çorum and one in Merzifon (a neighbouring city). In one of them, Eren Bey is partners with his maternal uncle's son (MBS), Metin Bey (see Figure 5). As opposed to the first case above, this company is owned and run by family members alone. Another distinguishing factor is that Ozan Ticaret is in the trades and services sector, as it franchises national and international brands in Çorum and the surrounding villages and provinces. The local managers of the franchise are appointed by the headquarters of the parent multinational or national company and follow its rules and targets. Hence, Eren Bey and Yasemin Hanım can recruit accountants, salesmen\ saleswomen, warehouse workers and drivers, but not managers. Their job is to make sure they provide a timely and precise service to their customers (grocery stores, small markets, kiosks, etc.), meet the given sales targets and collect the money owed to them. The fundamental differences between the manufacturing and service sectors reflect the skills, training, time, work schedule, work rhythm and personal traits required for the jobs in Çor-Mak and Ozan Ticaret respectively. In contrast to the manufacturing sector, where work-force stability, various manual and technical skills, sustainability and planning in the labour process are required, the service sector operates with different dynamics. A degree of stability and sustainability is necessary as in any other job, but what defines a sales job especially is its dynamism, quick decision-making ability, good communicative skills, mobility, being reachable at all times and its ability to persuade retailers that they should stock certain products, even when they already have them, to meet centrally determined monthly targets. Most of these skills are not taught at schools, perhaps except for business and management schools, but not many

---

[122] For purposes of simplification, I deal with both firms as one, since the same people are in charge in both cases.

salesmen have been to these schools anyway. Still, the job requires a certain educated, urbanized outlook and manners, as well as verbal skills, which are also encouraged by the decision-makers at the headquarters of the franchising brands. In such a case, it is less likely that co-villagers who have dropped out of school will be recruited to these positions than in the case of Çor-mak, a trend that was already in decline even for that firm. Salesmen and women in Ozan Ticaret are mainly high-school or university graduates. Other office workers are mainly young, high-school graduate women in the accounts department, recruited by Yasemin Hanım. The rest of the workforce consists of male truck-drivers and-warehouse workers, most of whom had dropped out of primary or middle school, who work under very precarious conditions with low pay. Although the latter category might have been recruited from among co-villagers, this was rarely the case in Ozan Ticaret. These jobs might have been just as unappealing to co-villagers and Eren Bey's distant relatives because they offered no skills training, stability or future prospects, in contrast to the training and the hope of a relatively higher wage that apprenticeships in the manufacturing sector offer. Hence, it is less likely that the co-villagers or distant relatives of service-sector employers expect to be employed in these jobs, which in turn reduces the employer's obligation to recruit them. Could we then conclude that the absence of the obligation makes these relationships less moral? Perhaps, if we look at things from the moral economy perspective; yet I would argue that the moral framework that generates this result is one in which the kinship and market goals of the two sides do not overlap in respect of either economic interests or the moral content of kinship.

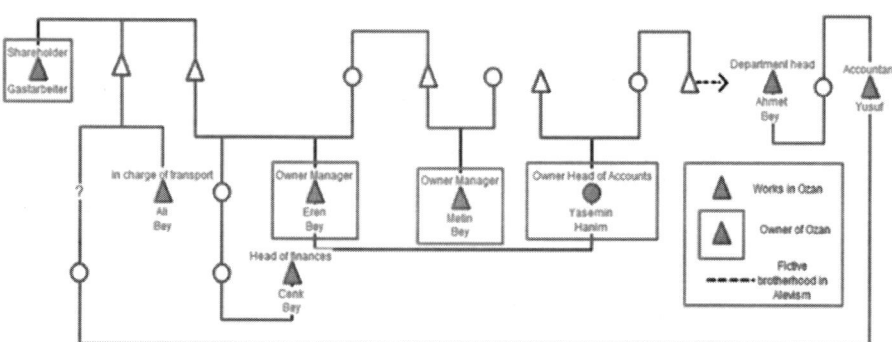

Figure 5. Kinship Diagram of persons working in Ozan Ticaret.

Although Ozan Ticaret was founded and run by family members, hiring relatives was therefore rare, and the discourse of kinship did not circulate among the workers as it did in Çor-mak. Ozan Ticaret' tendency not to hire co-villagers or relatives is also related to the fact that Eren Bey is the second generation of his family to live in Çorum city centre, hence he is not closely connected to his father's place of birth. Despite the relative disadvantages of the sector and Eren Bey's lack of connection with his village of origin, some individuals still use 'relatedness' as a strategy in seeking a job in Ozan Ticaret. For instance, one day the CV of a young girl arrived on Yasemin Hanım's desk. She let me look at it, and what struck me was that at the end she mentioned the name of her village to indicate her connection with Ali Bey (see Figure 5). I asked Yasemin Hanım what she was planning to do with the CV, and she said she would try and find a job for her, but not necessarily in their own company. Previously, we had discussed whether the firm would hire from among the Alevi community in particular and whether they wanted to promote positive discrimination in its favour. Eren Bey was not very keen on that idea, as he does not distinguish between the religious identities of his customers (see Chapter 4). He said that he would not ask which village an applicant came from, which also meant he would not ask whether the applicant were an Alevi or a Sunni.[123]

However, while in principle Eren Bey did not differentiate between workers' religious identities, in practice, as we shall see in the next section, he mainly employed Alevis and Sunnis who had more a secular world-view and lifestyle. Although this recruitment strategy is said to be unintentional, religious rituals and daily routines were rarely observed in this workplace, and the social activities of the workplace community were not particularly designed in accordance with Islamic rules or rituals.[124] For instance, anyone who observed daily prayers occasionally or attended Friday prayers regularly would miss out on lunch or other activities with other salesmen and also disrupt the pace of work. Similarly, anyone who avoided alcohol for Islamic reasons would feel uncomfortable on such social occasions, and topics of daily conversation among more secular-minded individuals might single out a devout Muslim or militant AKP supporter. Hence, even though recruitment in this firm is not exclusionary, the more publicly religious individuals

---

[123] People generally know which nearby village is predominantly Alevi or Sunni and ask which village the person comes from if they are interested in learning if s/he is Alevi or Sunni.

[124] The exception to this was the collective breakfasts and dinners that Eren Bey and/or Yasemin Hanım organized for all their employees on religious feast days. Moreover, they organized collective *iftar* (fast-breaking) meals in the month of Ramadan, even though they did not personally observe this ritual. See Chapter 8 for more on the organization and practice of religious rituals at workplaces.

and/or AKP supporters would soon reveal themselves in a few months. As I myself observed, in some cases their employment was only brief, and they voluntarily left the firm simply because they did not feel they fitted in with the social group.

Despite the fact that the discourse of kinship was absent, some relationships in the firm's workplace were determined by the long-term morality of kinship. For instance, all the brands to which the firm had the franchising rights had their own appointed managers. However, only one of them had an extra person as the head of department, namely Ahmet Bey, who is not related to the family but was a *müsahip* of Yasemin Hanım's father. A *müsahip* is a fictive brother in Alevism, an arrangement whereby two men are responsible for each other, including their livelihoods. Ahmet Bey had years of experience in this sector and was greatly respected, but he was at the same time a very aggressive man who spoke to his workers harshly from time to time in early morning meetings to motivate them to reach the firm's monthly targets. This was always tolerated by Eren Bey and Yasemin Hanım, although they spoke about it behind closed doors, as I observed them having private meetings after one of Ahmet Bey's outbursts. After these meetings, they would say that Ahmet Bey is senior and a brother to them and would ask others to accept that, as they try to calm the employees down. Although Ahmet Bey caused a lot of distress among the salesmen, and sometimes the accountants, the employers tolerated his temper in a manner that would not be tolerated if he were an unrelated employee. Hence, long-term kinship morality again appears as an imbalanced reciprocity that is sustained for moral reasons based on obligation and tradition. Later, Ahmet Bey voluntarily left his job and made a new investment of his own towards his retirement. Everybody else learned about this decision after he had left, so I am not aware whether his departure was due to some conflict, but I rather have the impression that Ahmet Bey wanted to own his own business and be autonomous, free from the authority of other men. As I showed in Chapter 5, this is a common desire for many men who work as wage labourers.

In Ozan Ticaret too, there were cases that did not fit into ideas of long-term kinship morality or the moral economy. Ali Bey was a middle-aged man with two grown-up children who were both university graduates. He spent almost all of his adult life working abroad in construction, making a livelihood for his family and trying to cover his children's education expenses; hence he was very proud of his children. At some point, when Ali Bey felt physically drained from working in construction, he was hired by Eren Bey and put in charge of the company's vehicles. The cars and trucks are one of the major assets of this company, and they need to be taken care of at all times, and their whereabouts need to be monitored. As is the case with other family members who work for this company, such as Yasemin Hanım, Ahmet Bey or Cenk Bey (see Figure 5), Ali Bey too, as a family member, was considered to be more trustworthy than an unrelated employee and was therefore given a managerial position. However, framing these relationships on the basis of long-term kinship morality is unconvincing here because all these family members have the qualifications and the experience to justify their occupying these positions. For instance, Ali Bey meticulously keeps records of all vehicles, follows them with precision and logs every single cent spent on them. Yasemin Hanım has been working at Ozan Ticaret since the day she married Eren Bey and has been trained for her position since then. In the meantime, she obtained her Bachelor's degrees in Economy and International Trade and is still doing her Master's degree in a similar subject. Cenk Bey, a male university graduate in his late thirties, was a high-ranking professional at a local bank before he joined Ozan Ticaret, and was still a partner in other entrepreneurial activities as a side job. Even though these family employees are hired on the basis of the familiarity and trust that are thought to be found in family members, the reason they have enduring positions in the company is because they are competent to fulfil the requirements of the job, as was the case with Fatih in Çor-Mak. Therefore, I argue that long-term employment in the family business is a result of a process of negotiating kinship obligations and business goals that complement each other for the benefit of both the roles and the obligations. Following De Neve (2005: 236), I suggest that 'morality is not an inherent or natural part of kinship relationships, but rather one of its possible qualities that has to be activated over and again by those involved' (ibid.: 236).

Paternalism and Community Identity Beyond Kinship Relations

The moral considerations discussed in the first part of this chapter are not only specific to related employees but are extended to include non-family employees through the everyday practices and rituals of the workplace. These various practices cannot be distinguished by using concepts like strategic, long- and short-term morality. Instead, together they underpin paternalism as the principle of social organization that seem to encompass all workers and to regulate the code of conduct among workers and employers. Paternalism is a loose concept. One who has approached it with reservations is E.P. Thompson (1993: 21). He writes: 'we may call a concentration of economic and cultural authority "paternalism" if we wish', while also setting out his dislike of the concept and similar ones such as 'pre-industrial' or 'traditional'. For him, these concepts have been treated as if they have 'a self-regulating sociological order… as if they were value-free. They also have an eerie timelessness' (ibid.: 19). He points out that 'paternalism' is often used interchangeably with 'patriarchy' but has a softer meaning in comparison to Marx and Engels' (1974) use of 'patriarchal' to define the relationship between masters, journeymen and apprentices in the Middle Ages. With these reservations in mind, there is actually a historically specific use of 'paternalism' that often coincides with the height of the Industrial Revolution towards the end of the eighteenth century and throughout the nineteenth century in England, France and the U.S. This was a time when land enclosures forced peasants to seek livelihoods elsewhere, when the household was separated from the workplace, and when most agricultural workers joined the labour force in the newly emerging factories (Sennett 1992). These immense transformations led to enormous poverty and shattered the material basis of the earlier social structures that are often understood as a symptom of decline throughout Europe. Sennett (ibid.) writes that at the beginning of the nineteenth century in the U.S. there was quite a lot of opposition to the establishment of large-scale factories due to the fear of social decline caused by poverty in the transition from an agricultural-based economy to industry. Hence, American entrepreneurs of the time designed industrial communities that would be compatible with family norms, which included organizing reading and prayer groups, and building dormitories for young women workers to protect their chastity. At first these arrangements did not have the goal of introducing a higher morality or moulding new industrial habits, and they were also considered to be too idealistic and to be too expensive. Rather, by designing workplaces as capable of preserving family traditions, employers thought they could smooth industry's sharp edges.

The emergence of paternalism in England was a parallel process with a concentration and centralization of production in large employers in certain areas and decreasing competition. As operatives and employers acquired more material well-being, they provided more to the workers and to workers related to them, who were often dependent on one employer, and organized social activities for the whole community. Burawoy (1985: 97) describes paternalism in the Lancashire cotton industry around second quarter of the nineteenth century in the following words: 'Although factory owners rarely controlled more than a minority of operative housing, they exercised their influence by constructing a communal leisure life around the factory through the erection of swimming baths, day schools, Sunday schools, canteens, gymnasia, libraries and, above all, churches. There were local sports events, trips to [the] countryside and workers' dinners and the masters' residence. There were public ceremonies and holidays to mark marriage, birth and death in the master's family as well as to celebrate his political victories. In this way employees came to identify with the fortunes and interests of the employer'. Paternalism helped reconstitute the family in the workplace by legitimizing the employers' authority, which itself hinged upon the authority of the father of the family, hence creating the figure of the 'father-boss'. Paternalism was then no longer perceived as an idealistic project but was found to be better for both the employees, who enjoyed the recreational activities, and the employers, who increased their control over their workers. It also became lucrative for the employers, who later started investing in real estate, building company towns and opening retail shops in and around these towns. On the other hand, paternalism metaphorically merges work and family in the employer, who is then in charge of the well-being of the entire worker community while at the same time having authority over them. This means that the authority figure will only stay in charge of the well-being of the workers as long as they serve his interests and remain under his authority (Sennett 1992).

Throughout the nineteenth century, company towns spread along the east coast of the U.S., and residential areas were built alongside factories in Bristol, Birmingham and Leeds in England and on the outskirts of Paris and Lyons in France (ibid.). Unlike the aims of the first attempts, the moral value of providing workers with social services was justified by the employers arguing that the workers were happier, more productive and less liable to strike. In fact, in the absence of state welfare in the nineteenth-century wave of liberalism, paternalism in the company towns was what linked the individual who had been freed from the land and the family to the community. One of the best known examples of industrial paternalism is the case of the Pullman car company (Sennett 1992: 72-86). In Turkey too, the Çanakkale Ceramic Factory that has operated in the town of Çan since 1957 is an example of a decades-long transformation of peasant-workers into worker-peasants under the authority of the father-boss (Güler 2014). Güler (2014), in his historical ethnography, shows that in late capitalism after the 1980s, paternalism retained its strategic importance for the survival of the 'worker-peasants'. I would argue that the previous examples from Çorum described above also provide evidence for the strategic importance of paternalism.

In the following section, I provide a detailed account of how 'boss-fathers' in Çorum feel responsible for their workers based on their own world-views and moral frameworks. Secular and/or religious rituals performed in and outside the workplace play an important role in consolidating a wider work-place community identity, one that extends to non-related workers and sometimes creates fictive kinship. As my ethnographic material shows, the term 'paternalism' refers to the organizational principle that emerged during the dissolution of agriculture and the rise of manufacturing. These data will then be complemented with a detailed analysis of how discipline and authority are practised in the daily lives of the work places in Chapter 7.

I have previously pointed out that employers expect workers to treat the company as if it were their own, not to ask or negotiate for wages, and to follow rules and orders. In this regard, the claim to authority on the part of the employers over the principle of the modern worker-employee contract heavily assumes a villager-*agha* (landowning village patron) relationship. On the other hand, I have come across workers themselves referring to their employers as *agha* several times, in Çor-Mak and Ozan Ticaret and elsewhere. Because of its link with land-owning status, the term *agha* might suggest that what we are examining here is patrimonialism rather than paternalism. However, the authority and status of the bosses cannot be directly transmitted to their heirs without acquiring certain qualities and skills as with patrimonialism, and their authority here is symbolic, unlike with patrimonialism. Nonetheless, workers' use of the term *agha* signals that the village connection of the worker-peasants has not yet become completely distorted and still shapes their vocabulary. More importantly, it highlights their expectation that the employer should take charge of their well-being. The employers, who come from a similar background, embrace this logic, which assigns the *agha*/employer the role of taking responsibility for the worker. Once in a conversation with Cemal Bey and a friend of his who is also a factory owner in the industrial district with a still smaller workshop, I asked the latter if they had similar incentives in his factory. The friend jokingly replied that he is not an *agha* like Cemal Bey because he does not have the same means as he has to be able to take care of the workers. When I then asked what he means by *agha*, he explained using an local idiom: '*efelik vurmaylan, ağalık vermeylen olur*', literally 'forcing makes one *efe*[125], giving makes one *agha*'. The paternalism that is embedded in these metaphors and idioms is shared by both workers and employers, but it offers the latter a useful technique of governance that recalls the distorted patrimonial relationships of the past with nostalgia and creates the boss as a father figure and provider in the workplace, while impeding the workers' proletarianization. Through this mode of governance, the father-employer aims to create a worker community which identifies itself with his interests and lifestyle, has a sense of belonging, and consents to be paid low wages. However, use of this vocabulary and participation in the community do not necessarily imply the workers' consent to the latter in practice.

---

[125] Leader of irregular soldiers or armed outlaws in Ottoman times.

The Çor-Mak Community

I once witnessed a conversation between two employees, Ulaş and Enes, when Enes was saying to Ulaş that the wages in their factory were lower than in other factories. He had asked Fatih why, and Fatih confirmed that in Çor-Mak the wages were lower than elsewhere but also added that the firm provides workers with other benefits and better working conditions, which compensate for their relatively lower wages. Here, I assume, the compensation is not only in material terms but at the level of consent. Fatih explained to Enes that the other factories try to keep their workers by paying them higher wages because they do not provide them with any other benefits. Ulaş, listening to his co-worker, joked in response that Fatih talks as if the wage level was something unimportant or trivial – the lower the better. While his sarcasm reflected the fact that some employees find the practice of compensating low wages with benefits not very convincing, the owners of the factory have their own moral and cultural reasons for how they had designed the labour regime in their factory.

In various conversations, Cemal Bey and Bülent Bey said that they determine the wages and benefits they offer with reference to the structure of the labour force, changing living conditions and workers' expectations. Bülent Bey explained that the workforce they employed initially consisted mainly of young, unmarried men from the nearby villages who used to commute between the village and the factory every day. Back then they could pay even less, but as villagers' agricultural incomes decreased and their workers became more dependent on the market for consumption goods, they changed to more atomized life-styles, separating from their extended families in the village and moving to the city centre with their nuclear families, which created other expenses for them, including rent. Then the factory had to increase their wages accordingly. In his view, it was their responsibility to provide a reasonable wage (which in most cases is a little higher than the minimum wage, depending on seniority), so that the workers are content, can pay their rent or house loans, put food on the table and send their children to school. He admits that he needs the workers as much as the workers need the jobs for the stability of the business; they prefer long-time workers who bond with the factory and the work. The value that shapes his idea of 'the common good' is to serve the stability of the business and the workers at the same time, then both sides are content.

Cemal says: 'When I say "happiness of the workers", I don't necessarily mean we pay them a lot of money'. For him, bonding is also about feeling that one belongs to a community and is being respected. Since he himself had been a factory worker who started his career as an apprentice at a young age and grew up in workshops or on construction sites, he says that he knows what a factory worker expects: 'He comes from a village life or has dropped out of school, couldn't study, then started working ... it was my expectation too, to be in a group where one can feel a sense of belonging. I mean, like I'm a part of this team. If I were in trouble, if there was a problem, I have a team – I am not an individual, but a part of a team. This gives a person tremendous trust, not feeling as an individual, but being a part of a community. This is what people expect. You have to give them the provisions, the incentives, the behaviour that correspond to the satisfaction of this need'. He then continued by giving examples of what kinds of behaviour and provisions create this feeling of belonging: 'When the worker is in trouble, we stand by him. When he has a medical problem, we support him. When he has an accident or needs money, then we stand by him. When these things happen, we show that we will be there'.

It is not only on bad days that they find it important to support their workers but a practice that covers the life-cycle events in workers' lives too: 'Bülent Bey knows the names of at least thirty or even forty of our seventy workers. We keep track of their children, their families, their lives; when someone gives birth, we give them gold[126]; when someone gets married, we help them, we try to give them wedding gifts properly, we support those who are buying a flat'. There are other benefits that were not mentioned in our conversations but which I documented during my fieldwork. Every winter, coal or gas aid was given in cash to all workers; for every religious feast (twice a year) a fair number of shopping vouchers were distributed to staff. During the feast of sacrifice (Eid al-Adha-*Kurban bayramı*), the firm distributes a portion of the meat of the slaughtered animal to everyone, in accordance with Islamic tradition. This ritual was repeated whenever there was a new investment in the factory, like the expansion to a second building in 2015. Moreover, on the first workday at 8 am after every religious holiday before the shift starts, all manual and non-manual workers gather together in the workshop to greet each other one by one, starting with the eldest greeting the youngest. A similar ritual is repeated when a senior worker retires. Not all the rituals of the workplace community are religiously inspired: the employers buy flowers for the non-manual women workers every 8th of March (International Women's Day). Moreover, Fatih organizes birthday celebrations for Bülent Bey and Cemal Bey. Each year, the office workers gather in the meeting room to eat their birthday cake and then take photos. Since their own birthdays are celebrated, Bülent Bey and Cemal Bey allow women workers to celebrate their birthdays in the afternoon break in the

---

[126] 22-carat ornament gold coins registered and produced by the Istanbul Gold Refinery. They are available in quarter (1.75 gr.), half (3.5gr.) and whole (7gr.) sizes. Ornament gold coins are the most popular gift in rites of passage in Turkey.

kitchen. However, other outdoor activities such as going on a picnic with workers' families or competing in an amateur football league with the company team happened only once and did not become a regular company activity. The workers did not want to bring their wives to the picnic because people generally socialize with their relatives and neighbours, and they also found it generally uncomfortable. As this activity did not attract the interest of the majority, it died out.

When the workers were asked, there were several things they were satisfied with about the working conditions. A filling four-course lunch high in protein and carbohydrates was always served in the factory cafeteria; the workers pointed out that this was not common in other factories. New work clothes and equipment were provided twice a year. Even though this is mandated by law, not many employers seem to care about it. Nevertheless, the clothes disintegrate in the second week of use. Moreover, wages were always paid at the end of the month or on the last Friday of the month if the last day of the month coincided with a weekend. Many employers keep it in the account for a few more days to earn interest on the lump sum and pay it on the first Monday after the last day of the previous month. Çor-Mak workers could take the official holidays off depending on the workload, which was also rare in other factories; Saturdays were days off for the manual workers unless there was an emergency, but not always for non-manual family workers. Friday prayers and short breaks for daily prayers were allowed during working hours, provided the workers did not exploit it.

I was told many times that most of these conditions are rarely found in other workplaces, although some of them, such as the timely payment of wages, granting official holidays or providing work clothes regularly are obligatory by law. Employers argue that these practices are designed to cultivate a sense of belonging and to pay respect to the workers, as they see this as their responsibility. Contrary to his engineer partner's rather secular idea of the 'common good', Cemal Bey's attitude is shaped by Islamic moral values and customs, which he believes he shares with the workers, and he projects this on to the factory-community he was aiming to create. In a paternalistic labour regime, workers tend to identify with their employers and their interests and generate a feeling of 'being in the same boat'. This feeling compensates for the relatively low wages and unpaid extra hours of work in the absence of organized labour and in a labour market where in practice many labour regulations are bent in favour of the employer. As a result, once everything is designed with 'responsibility' based on the assumed common 'values', bargaining over wages, extra work hours or daily absences become a personal matter and is certainly not well-received (see Chapter 7). Moreover, those who do not share the general essence that shapes the workplace community, such as praying or fasting, can remain members only if they do not openly make noises about their opposite lifestyles or world views. This is not because Cemal Bey in particular would be bothered, and Bülent Bey himself does not follow an Islamic life-style: the workers' community itself would not take it well (see Chapter 8).

The Ozan Ticaret Community

The only incentive in this company was the bonuses paid to the salesmen when they reached the given targets each month. Apart from this bonus system, everyone was paid more or less the minimum wage, and always on time. Overtime is rare but in any case is never paid; daily and annual periods of leave are easy to negotiate, unlike in the factory discussed above. Compared to the factory, however, the food served at lunch is not as filling, being rather rich in vegetables and healthy, which is appreciated by women workers but not so much by the warehouse workers, who do heavy manual labour every day. There are no material extra benefits, except the gold coins given at weddings, the gold coins and plaques handed out during the annual ceremony, where the workers are rewarded for every five years they spend in the company, and the annual New Year dinner party thrown by Ozan Bey. All salesmen have cars or trucks provided by the company for the job, which they use to travel from home to work every day. The young women accountants are picked up from their homes by Ozan Bey's and Yasemin Hanım's cars every morning and dropped off the same way at the end of the working day. As these are the basic differences between the factory and the working conditions in this company, I focus here on the compensating factors of the low wages, especially for the young women accountants in the absence of benefits. Then I will briefly contrast it with their attitudes towards the warehouse workers.

I discovered this company through an association of business women and asked whether I could become involved in their everyday routines. Through my contacts in the association I met Yasemin Hanım, who was very active in the association's events, where they organized reading groups and cultural trips for women members and prepared projects to encourage women to enter the labour market. Eventually, I learned that Yasemin Hanım adopts a policy of positive discrimination for women in her accounts department. As a woman who married at a very young age and completed her studies after getting married against the will of her own parents, she values mentoring young women to become educated, skilled and independent. Accordingly, she prioritizes recruiting young women, especially those who are supporting their families and children. Most of these women would lack knowledge of the required accounting programs, but she would train them from scratch and teach them to be skilled accountants. That was not the only area she trained them in. During the working day, she would start conversations about how liberated women should be, what kind of men liberated women should be looking for, how to be equal to their husbands in marriage, how to be both a mother and a working woman at the same time, how to raise a child without compromising one's own life, and how to react to the rise of Islamism in Turkey. She would not really lay down her own opinions but on the contrary would listen to all the women, then they would discuss things while doing the accounts by staring at the computer screens. These interventions were always within the limits of being an 'honourable Turkish woman' and did not challenge the institution of marriage itself. Nonetheless, I found them empowering in allowing the young women to speak up, express their views and be challenged politely if she thought necessary. She also helped a few university students in finding a dormitory, an internship or a job, and mentored them on the topics and decisions they needed guidance in. As a result of these conversations and the efforts she puts into training these women to become skilled and independent women, within her perspective of what a middle-class life is, they have formed friendships. Thus they went to dinners, cafes, Turkish baths and on hiking trips, they breakfasted together in the off-hours (everyone paid for themselves), they celebrated their birthdays in their large office, and they socialized outside the workplace as well. She therefore created a sense of community that functioned in and out of the office, based on the sense of responsibility she felt towards other young women, stemming from her values in favour of women's empowerment.

While sharing his wife's views on women's empowerment, Eren Bey contributed to the sense of community from a different angle. A very energetic man, he claimed he could never have succeeded in a repetitive and regular desk job. On the contrary, he liked to plan things and set targets on a daily basis, being very ambitious to reach his goals. He would calculate every single thing and go over every detail of the reports he received from the accountants and salesmen, moving from one room to another relentlessly every day. However, he would always stop working around 6pm to go and do sports. In fact, according to the rumour, he had a special fitness room in his own flat. Eren Bey believed that keeping the body moving and in shape keeps the mind fresh. The connection he made between mind and body recalled a famous saying that is often attributed to Mustafa Kemal Atatürk: '*Sağlam kafa sağlam vücutta bulunur*' (A sound mind is found in a sound body), a reflection of the importance of and mission given to physical training in the early republican era. Some have argued (e.g. Akın 2014) that the politics of sports and physical training at that time represented an attempt to govern the population and individual bodies to create and discipline the Turkish citizen, as well as militarizing the nation. In my opinion, physical training in the early republican era envisaged a new type of individual who can develop his/her bodily skills under the institutions and facilities of the new modern state with a particular target of liberating women. When Eren Bey formulated the relationship between mind and body, he did not necessarily have nationalism in mind. Rather, it was an answer to the question of how to spend his leisure time. This was so deeply entangled with his class position that he can find the time to go to a fitness studio, only a few having been opened recently in Çorum, and moreover could afford to do so.

In the first few days of my encounter in this company, I realized that Eren Bey and a 23-year-old young women accountant, Gülin, had made a bet on the weight she would reach by New Year 2016. This young woman, preconditioned by the standards of beauty based on the male gaze and looking up to Yasemin Hanım's always fit and well-groomed style, was concerned that she was a little chubby and wanted to lose weight. There was a lot of talking about diets, yet doing sport was not discussed. There are physical training classes at school for both genders, and children often play games on the street, but often when a young girl reaches puberty she is no longer allowed to play on the street with boys, nor to join their football teams. While boys might form amateur football or basketball teams and continue being physically active into their adulthood, girls rarely do sports unless their families actively encourage them to do extra-curricular sport activities or join teams, especially in working-class families. Gülin, who is a high-school graduate from a working-class family, never did sports in her life until she was challenged to do so by Eren Bey, who often joked about their hard diets and conveyed to them the merits of doing sport. In the end, he convinced Gülin and other young women accountants that the way to lose weight is to do sport, then they would be healthy at the same time. That winter, the young women accountants, together with Yasemin Hanım, signed up for a sports course in a fitness studio. Losing weight, body shape and the funny things that happened while playing sport were the topics of every morning and evening in the office. They would joke and laugh about it, and eventually I realized that the care and responsibility the male employer projected over his young women workers' bodily discipline and shape has facilitated a sincere brother/sister-like bond of friendship between them, removing the age and gender barriers that normally prevent unrelated women and men from socializing in Turkish provincial social life. In this way, woman employees identify with the workplace by being trained in professional skills and socializing with their employers. While these discussions and social activities are mind-opening and empowering, they also create the illusion sometimes that these young women and their employers belong to the same class. This illusion is shattered when Yasemin Hanım comes to work wearing her newest outfit, when they discuss which of Yasemin Hanım's outfits they would like to have when she decides to give them away, or when she does not invite the women employees to the activities and meetings of the businesswomen's' association.

Yet again, the community feeling was used to compensate for the low wages and long working hours. Nonetheless, unlike the factory workers, these women were not the only breadwinners in their households, and therefore the absence of benefits would concern them less than it would the factory workers. It could also be argued that the empowerment and the skills they acquired from this company would enable them to support themselves and/or their families financially and to find other decent jobs in the future, which is less possible for many other unskilled women. Finally, just as Cemal and Bülent Bey were boss-fathers, these women workers see Eren Bey as an older brother/father and Yasemin Hanım as a sister. Yet, unlike the dynamics of paternalism at Çor-Mak in which Cemal Bey's fatherly care especially is merged with his traditional authority (see Chapter 7), Eren Bey and Yasemin Hanım care for the well-being of their women workers by referring to a different moral framework that prioritizes self-improvement and independence. These dynamics do not provide the benefits expected of a paternalist boss, but nonetheless on one social occasion the six-year-old daughter of one of these women employees referred to Eren Bey as '*patron-dede*' (boss-grandfather), indicating that the kind of relationship they have also has its paternalistic features. In their different parenting style, traditional forms of authority are replaced with a regime of soft power that allows these women to be empowered, speak up and challenge traditional roles.

The male workers, on the other hand, rarely received such special attention in this company. Especially the warehouse workers, who were at the bottom of the social hierarchy in the workplace, had long and arbitrary working hours without extra payment. Whenever there was a miscalculation made by an accountant or the bills collected by the salesmen did not match the products sold that day, they had to go through everything stocked in the warehouse and re-count them; this was repeated at the beginning and end of every week. The warehouse is a huge space with many shelves as high as the ceilings forming narrow corridors; hence counting every single product meant climbing these high shelves, moving heavy boxes from one place to another and keeping all these numbers in one's head while maintaining one's balance. The working conditions were even tougher in warehouses where dairy products and frozen products were kept at cold or even freezing temperatures. Although being 'unskilled' is often used as a justification for low wages, being a warehouse worker is a tiresome job that requires a lot of strength and ability to count and keep track of thousands of items at the same time. Moreover, it is as necessary as and more time-consuming than accounting. Yet the workers are not treated as if it were. In one hour of overtime when the warehouse workers stayed through the evening to do the counting, they ordered take-away food for dinner, to be reimbursed later by the company. However, the next day they heard the finance manager (Cenk Bey, see Figure 5) complaining about the high price of the dinner, which was a simple meatball sandwich in whole bread. Apart from the fact that that is quite a cheap menu, the fact that the manager made a fuss about the price of their dinner really upset the warehouse workers.

On another occasion, one of the franchise companies decided to give a one-off bonus to the warehouse workers. Normally, although they are a part of the process, only the salesmen receive bonuses based on their sale rates. This time the headquarters wanted to make an exception and gave around half of the minimum wage to each warehouse worker as bonus. To celebrate the occasion, a little ceremony was organized in the company cafeteria where the local manager made a speech about how all the workers in this company were a family. At the beginning I thought that this was going to be a cheerful event because the workers would be glad to be receiving a bonus. On the contrary, the men looked sulky and seemed to be annoyed by this event. Later on, when I asked about it, I was told that this one-off bonus is nothing compared to the long extra hours they work every month and that they regarded the ceremony as a joke. These moments of mistreatment and disappointment reveal that the rhetoric of 'being a family' does not serve its purpose when the actual 'care for well-being' component of the family is missing from the equation. These moments also mark an experience of class in that one group feels treated and remunerated differently from the others, an experience that the paternalistic incentives in Çor-Mak aim to avoid.

The absence or weakness of organized labour under regimes of flexible accumulation reinforces workers' dependence on their employers and strips them of their ability to negotiate the terms of their employment. Hence, 'unskilled' workers like the warehouse workers in this case are considered replaceable with any other manual 'unskilled' worker, something that is also a result of the low-skilled labour on the Çorum labour market. Conversely, neither the women accountants nor the factory workers are easily replaceable, since they need to be trained to be competent for the job for at least a year or even more. These cases illustrate the consequences of labour regimes that are shaped by individual responsibility and the employer's value system, such as paternalism. They may partially replace the gap created by the absence of organized labour and regulations, and they do constitute the ideological apparatus of labour control to some extent, but they may also fall short in meeting workers' demands that do not fall within the scope of employers' ideas of responsibility and enhance further dependence and exploitation.

Conclusion

This chapter is the first of three in the third, main part of the book in which I focus the everyday lives of workplaces. In the first part of the chapter, I have concentrated on the 'moral frameworks' that operate behind recruiting, working with and laying off people with different degrees of relatedness to the employers. In the cases of distant relatives and co-villagers, as well as family members, I have tried to show how imbalances in reciprocity can end in discarding the relationship, depending on how threatening the imbalance becomes to the interests of the company. A degree of relatedness can justify hiring someone in the initial stages of a business, but merit and skill are required for the long-term moral aspect to emerge in not-so-close relationships. Even when long-term morality or the moral aspect of an economic relationship is present in kinship, as in the case of Fatih, the content of the reciprocity matters. In Ozan Ticaret too, family employees are hired on the basis of the familiarity and trust which is believed to be found in family members, yet the reason they have enduring positions in the company is because they are competent in fulfilling the requirements of the job. These findings make the arguments of Bloch (1973) and Carrier (2018) that the 'moral' aspect of the relationship is the motive for long-term interaction unconvincing. It is rather the mutuality of the goals and roles that people identify with that make the relationship work in favour of both business and kinship goals. The ethnographic examples given above have also shown that these roles and goals in kinship and business are not stable, but rather are constantly being negotiated and subject to challenge. Hence, morality is not the natural and stable component of kinship relations but is one of its properties that is set into motion by those involved. Imbalances in reciprocity are still more tolerable for those family members whose efficiency is not as useful to the company, and hence these enduring bonds are more 'moral'. This does not mean that they are not disposable or that the imbalance will be tolerated forever. Rather, it means that, given the shortage of skilled workers in Çorum and the volatility of the labour market in the larger cities, both employers and workers are obliged to make the best out of their given circumstances.

In the second part of this chapter, I examined how the roles and obligations in a family or a kin group are stretched to include non-family employees through various incentives, Islamic and non-Islamic workplace rituals, and outdoor activities, creating wider workplace communities through paternalism. While the two cases under scrutiny here depart from each other due to differences in sector, labour force and organization, each employer follows a 'moral framework' in the effort to create workplace communities. Employers' individual priorities over what to provide to their workers other than wages reflect their own value systems and socio-economic backgrounds. While not all workplace activities and rituals are all-inclusive and positively received by all workers, they have the potential to create fictive kinship relations or friendships in the workplace that strengthen the workers' attachment to their work and enable them to identify with their employers' interests, life-styles and world views. In other words, attempts are made to bridge the gap between the class positions of the workers and employers through common customs, life-styles and world views. Paternalism partially replaces the gap created by the absence of organized labour and regulations, and it constitutes the ideological apparatus of labour control to some extent, but it also falls short in meeting workers' demands when these do not fall within the scope of the employer's idea of responsibility and enhance the worker's further dependence and exploitation. Nonetheless, it is employers' world views and values that endow the social life of a workplace with its specific character. As a result, workplace communities are mainly shaped along the lines of existing differences in socio-political belonging in Turkish society more widely and in Çorum in particular. In a certain workplace community, workers who remain silent about their opinions or internalize the workplace rules of conduct are absorbed as members, while workers who choose to stand out by speaking out or not complying with the values that organize the community are pushed out or threatened with this, if not by employers, then by their own co-workers.

Chapter 7
Discipline, Labour Control, Management: Value Realm of Consent and Coercion

Introduction

In the previous chapter, I mentioned E.P. Thompson's (1993) reservations regarding the concept of 'paternalism'. Apart from its treatment as a timeless and self-regulating order, he adds that it 'tells us little about the nature of power and of the State; about forms of property-ownership; about ideology and culture' (ibid.: 21). It provides a depiction from above connoting a 'one-class society', but 'cannot rid itself from the normative implications: it suggests human warmth, in a mutually assenting relationship' (ibid.: 22). If we limited ourselves only to the testimonies of employers without undertaking ethnographic research, one could easily think of Çor-Mak almost as a social institution that is designed to care for workers' needs and expectations based on the shared Islamic values and customs of the employer and his or her workers. However, this would be a normative and incomplete depiction of how ideology, culture and power operate in the social life of a workplace. As Mollona (2009: xvi) argues, 'the factory is a social space and not, following some sociological and managerial theories, merely a technological and productive one'. Hence, the reproduction of relations of production is achieved through the customs and values of the specific locality. While paternalism is the organizing principle of the reproduction of relations of production, the ethnographic evidence in Chapter 6 showed that the incentives, rituals and mentorship provided to the workers also serves as compensation for low wages, flexible working hours and job insecurity in the absence of an organized labour movement. This finding also hints that these practices and rituals are an inherent aspect of the labour control mechanisms operating in workplaces.

In the capitalist mode of production, unlike a feudal one, there are no spatial or temporal distinctions between the use value (commodity), necessary value (wages) or surplus value (profit) being produced in a working day. Although workers work for an entire working day of eight or nine hours, their wages correspond only to the labour time needed to reproduce themselves, the rest of the working day being surplus labour time appropriated as profit by the capitalist. Given this premise, Burawoy (1985: 32) argues that 'the dilemma of the capitalist labour control is to secure the surplus value at the same time keeping it hidden'. Hence, following Burawoy (1985), one could argue that, for instance, Çorum employers' expectations that the workers should treat the job as their own is an attempt to hide the relations of production that emerge in production. Similarly, some of the practices, rituals and social activities elaborated in Chapter 6 are actually 'games' 'obscuring the surplus value' (ibid.). If, on the one hand, paternalistic practices obscure the existence of surplus value and generate consent, on the other hand they also secure the surplus value, but only to a certain extent. In the contract between the 'free' worker and the capitalist, the latter only purchases the capacity to labour. This recalls a classic problem in Marxist theory: 'What are the mechanisms that explain the capacity of capitalists to actually appropriate surplus labour from workers?' (Buroway and Wright 1990: 251). In other words, as Mollona, De Neve and Parry (2009: 105) put it: 'The problem for capital is generally less one of persuading workers to come to work than of persuading them to work when they come'. To be able to turn the capacity to labour into labour, rules, regulations and management mechanisms are put in place to secure surplus value. The consent created by the 'warmth' of a paternalistic employer does not necessarily mean that the coercion necessary to turn the capacity to labour into labour is lacking.

This chapter continues the story from the previous chapter and aims to show the other side of the coin by delving into the ways which employers persuade workers to work for longer hours and lower wages in more effective ways, such as everyday practices and the imposition of time discipline, labour control and management techniques that overlap with the paternalist patterns of worker-employer relations. Relations of production constitute the 'political (production of social relations) and ideological (experience of those social relations) dimension' that is inseparable from the economic (production of things) dimension (Burawoy 1985: 39) in any work context. This chapter analyses the value regime (see Introduction) within which these social relations are produced and experienced by focusing on the everyday life of a medium-size factory. In doing so, I try to open a discussion about the role of gender, age and skill in the spatial and temporal organization of work, and reveal social norms and values that legitimize and substantiate the practices of labour control.

Before concentrating on the everyday life of a workplace, I shall describe the legal framework that regulates labour relations in Turkey. As already discussed in Chapter 2, what is generally called 'neoliberalism' takes place in changes in state policies such as deregulation and privatization, financialization, shifting the tax burden in favour of the elites and dismantling labour unionism (Harvey 2007). The military coup of 12 September 1980, followed by the new constitution of 1982 and the enactments of collective labour laws[127] to regulate the labour regime, provided the 'spatio-temporal fix' needed to implement the new economic plan, including 'de-regulation/re-regulation and de-constitutionalizing the labour law' (Özdemir and Yücesan-Özdemir 2005: 64). Under the military regime, the unions were closed down and labour movements suppressed. Even after the military regime, during the 1980s real wages and the share of wage-labour in the manufacturing sector significantly declined (Köse and Öncü 2000: 83). In parallel with global trends, the Turkish labour market underwent a radical transformation and restructuring, what Harvey (1989: 149-150) calls 'flexible accumulation', which 'appears to imply relatively high levels of "structural" ... unemployment, rapid destruction of skills, modest (if any) gains in the real wages and the roll-back of trade union power'. Unionization rates in Turkey declined from 22.2% in 1988 to 5.7% in 2010 (Çelik 2013: 44), despite 'the significant increase in the rate of wage- and salary-earners in total employment from 39% in 1990 to 64% in 2013' (Çelik 2015: 623). While changes in the collective labour laws encouraged flexible and informal work patterns, the new Labour Act (No. 4857) passed in 2003, in the first year of AKP rule[128], 're-regulate(d) the individual labour law in conformity with the neoliberal conceptualization and imagination of capital-labour relations in which labour is seen as an ordinary commodity calculable in terms of production costs' (Özdemir and Yücesan-Özdemir 2005: 69). Despite the deterioration in both the collective and individual labour laws, the minimum wage, individualized social insurance legislation, unemployment and retirement benefits and minimum living allowances[129], together with family networks and charity-based

---

[127] The amended laws are the Collective Labour Agreement Strike and Lockout Law No. 2822, on 7 May 1983, and Trade Union Law No. 2821, on 5 May 1983.

[128] See Çelik (2015) and Özdemir and Yücesan-Özdemir (2005) for a detailed overview of the labour regime since the 1980s and during the AKP years, as well as further analysis of the New Labour Act passed in 2003.

[129] The minimum wage as of 2018 is 1603TL, equivalent to the starvation threshold calculated as 1615TL based on the calculations of Turk-Is, the largest labour union in Turkey. See https://www.evrensel.net/haber/344166/aclik-siniri-asgari-ucretin-ustunde Social insurance is paid by the state and partially by the employer for all wage labourers. If one is unemployed, one has to pay oneself based on individual income, a recent system called General Health Insurance. There is also the *Asgari Geçim Indirimi* (Minimum Living Allowance), introduced in 2018. This is available for everyone over the age of sixteen who is

philanthropic organizations, ensure the reproduction of labour power at a certain level.

In the light of these developments, Turkey has consolidated its position as specializing in the production and export of labour-intensive intermediate consumption goods within the global division of labour (Köse and Öncü 2000: 84). The emerging Anatolian economies in cities such as Konya, Kayseri, Gaziantep and Çorum has become a destination for investors due to its competitive advantage in labour-intensive industries because of its cheap labour (ibid.). Köse and Öncü (2000) characterize the production processes of these labour-intensive sectors in Anatolia as '*ilkel* (primitive) Taylorist' because their competitive advantage is largely based on saved wages and the employment of unskilled labour in mechanized technologies (ibid.: 87). This makes it inevitable that managements must find ways to *persuade* their workers to cooperate with them, as in the 'hegemonic regimes' described by Buroway (1985: 126). However, the low collective bargaining power of labour, the legal status of flexible work regimes and the partial dependence of workers on their employers due to paternalistic patterns of conduct give rise to *despotic* elements in the labour processes. Hence, I refrain from defining how *hegemonic* or *despotic* a work regime is in a certain context and merely point out aspects of coercion and consent while referring to the phenomena as 'flexible labour regimes', following Ong's terminology (1991). This is firstly due to the significant variations in labour control regimes, not only geographically, but also in size, the nature of the labour supply, production technology and the system of labour regulation (Peck 1996: 35). Secondly, 'labour control ... depend[s] in important ways on the social context in which employment relations are embedded', requiring that we 'consider the social production and reproduction of work forces and the values which unite and divide them' (ibid.: 34). Thirdly, the binary of *despotic/hegemonic* regimes 'discourages more fine-grained analysis of diverse forms of power relations in newly industrializing countries' (Ong 1991: 285). Finally, as I will try to show, the rules and regulations put in place to generate labour effort oscillate between what Burawoy and Wright (1990: 253) call *domination* and *asymmetrical reciprocity*: 'In the case of domination, labour effort is performed because of the continual presence of various kinds of threats by bosses that individuals face if they are caught shirking. In the case of asymmetrical reciprocity, labour effort is based on consent, on the positive agreement by each of the parties concerned over the mutual, if still unequal, benefits of the exertion of

---

legally employed and is worth varying amounts depending on one's marital status and number of children. The lowest allowance for an unmarried worker is 152 TL, rising to 258 TL if married and with five children. 1 Euro equalled 5,01 TL on 23 April 2018.

such effort'. However, they underline that consent in circumstances of asymmetrical reciprocity does not imply that there is no coercion: it only means that the labour effort generated is not a strategic response to threats and surveillance. Rather, the norms that legitimize obedience might be deeply internalized or might be a result of a belief in the fairness of the bosses. In such contexts, coercion and consent coexist.

The chapter starts with a description of one generic workday to give the reader an impression of the atmosphere and organization of time in the labour process. After drawing attention to debates around the topics of industrial discipline and habits, I will analyse in what circumstances and in response to what kind of needs a craftsmanship based on an *ilkel* (primitive) Taylorist sweatshop turned into a medium-size industry based on the rules of time measurement and thrift and later adopted management techniques that are associated with post-Fordism. The remaining sections are dedicated to changes in the social structure of the factory through which this shift has occurred, as well as the *coercive* and *consensual* elements that are expressed in labour processes and are exercised with reference to values such as respect, loyalty, gratitude and deservingness, and *namus* (honour). By doing so, I aim to reveal the locally specific modes of social control in the factory, that is, the value realm of coercion and consent.

A Work Day at Çor-Mak

I wake up at 6:30 am to catch the personnel shuttle that will pick me up a three-minute walk from the square on the main street at 7:10 a.m. While waiting for the shuttle, other factory buses pass by. When mine arrives, I take a seat just behind the driver together with two other women. By then I have learned that only men sit on the back seats and that it is socially inappropriate to move to the back or look up when getting in. One still can say 'good morning' without lifting one's head. There are two other women sitting in the front seat next to Yavuz (see Figure 4 on page 185), the co-owner's brother-in-law who owns the shuttle and therefore rents it to the company as a side job. The women sit where the shuttle receives more light and where they can be seen by Yavuz, who in this case is our guardian. The shuttle mainly picks up office-workers and only from the main roads, making an exception for the tea-lady who lives in a backstreet. Sometimes we stop by a bakery to buy some *poğaça* or *katmer*[130] to eat for breakfast, everyone paying for themselves. There are two other personnel shuttles for manual workers who live in other neighbourhoods. All the shuttles arrive at

---

[130] *Poğaça* is a pastry filled with cheese, potatoes, olives or minced meat. *Katmer* is made up of layers of flat dough with butter in between and fried in a pan.

the factory before 07:45 a.m. and the male workers get ready for work, changing into their work clothes in their dressing rooms next to the shop floor and smoking their last cigarettes. First, however, the manual workers scan their faces and the office workers their cards to keep track of the minutes they spend at work, their absenteeism and the overtime they work.

Then there are us, the women, Elif the receptionist, Sevim the accountant, Hatice, a technical drawer, Sevda the tea lady and me the researcher. Upon arrival we rush upstairs to the kitchen, where Sevda makes the tea, which takes more than fifteen minutes to be brewed, but we still eat some tomatoes, cucumber and cheese with the bread we have brought from home or the pastries we have bought and drink half-brewed tea in a hurry. After only a few sips of tea, we hear the bell ring at exactly 8 a.m., so the women go to their desks in a stampede. The manual workers start up the cutting, welding and moulding equipment and operate the CNC machines, counting, assembling and dyeing machine parts with the same exactitude as the bell rings. A few seconds after the bell rings, one can hear the unsynchronized rhythms of welding and hammering and actually watch the shop floor from the kitchen window. Therefore I stand up and look hesitantly out of the window, hoping the men don't think I am controlling them. I can see that the different work stations are divided from one another either by shelves neatly piled with work equipment, machine parts that are waiting to be processed or yellow strips on the ground indicating the walking direction. Later on, I will see inside the shop floor that there are charts on a billboard about the past and recent Kazien[131] procedure, forms on which to enter the starting and finishing times of certain tasks and the names of those responsible, and lists of absenteeism. The window I am looking through is identical with the one Cemal Bey has in his office on the same floor. The windows from the employer's office upstairs literally look down on to the shop floor – a very common surveillance technique, as I will discover later. Although many employers have a curtain over these windows that they almost never move, the windows are symbolically there. Today, in their place, are surveillance cameras.

The employers, Bülent Bey and his son and Cemal Bey, usually arrive at work at 08:30 and have a general meeting at 08:45 over a Turkish coffee. Generally, factories have a fifteen-minute tea break at around 10 a.m.. That break is important because manual workers especially do not usually have breakfast or tea before starting work, so they look forward to the break before noon to finally wake up after the first hours of work. However, in this factory the tea break was cancelled a few years ago, so now they work

---

[131] According to the lean production vocabulary, Kaizen means 'betterment'.

uninterruptedly from 08:00 to 12:15. The reason for the cancellation was that on several occasions the workers were caught talking to the garbage collectors who were passing by and did not go back to work after the bell rang. As a result, the manager, Fatih, became angry after catching them still smoking and chatting at the pergola in the backyard and cancelled the pre-noon break just like that. This meant he added fifteen minutes to the daily work hours. Although the workers wanted their break again, they never told Fatih.

However, the office workers can order tea, Nescafé or Turkish coffee, mineral water, chilled *ayran*[132] or fruit soda from the kitchen at any time of day: '*Hadi bi çay söyleyek!*' ('Let's order a tea!' in local dialect) or '*E hadi sana bi kahve ısmarlayalım!*' ('Let's order you coffee!') After the first round of tea service early in the morning, generally at around 10 am, they call Sevda *abla*[133] from the extension and order these beverages on the phone for themselves, for each other or for guests (or for me if I am there). *Ismarla-* means to order or buy for someone, so that person is your guest. This use of the word gives the impression that treating someone as a guest detaches oneself from the work context for a while. Sevda *abla* arrives with the orders: she likes going up and down, and the workers joke with her on the phone, and also when she brings the orders. It feels to me that ordering a beverage is a game, one the younger workers especially have fun playing: 'Yes, this place is quite strict, but the most fun thing we have here is ordering tea on the phone, with that no one meddles', is what Ulaş told me once. So we usually played the game for maybe five to ten minutes until the manager Fatih called out, or better shouted one of the young men's names to remind him of some task that is not really necessary at that moment but that Fatih used as a way to bring the game to an end. We would then all go back to a deathly silence, and I would disappear slowly with a somewhat guilty feeling for having exploited these moments to chat with the workers and because my presence encouraged them to order even more tea.

Around 11:30 everybody starts counting down the minutes to lunch. At exactly 12 noon, the women workers start walking to the dining hall. We eat before the men in the factory, so we are not present in the dining hall when their break starts at 12:15. One can use a rear door from the offices on to the shop floor, pass through it and enter the dining hall, or take the external door and walk around the building from the outside. Unless it is a very rainy or snowy day, we take the external door to go for lunch because women are not allowed to pass through the shop floor, through the men. For

---

[132] Salted yoghurt drink.

[133] *Abla* means elder sister, but it is also used to refer to unrelated woman with whom the age gap is not that wide or who has a relatively higher social status.

lunch there is almost always a soup, at least three days a week a stew with meat and rice or pasta, and *cacık*[134], salad, fruit or dessert. Restaurant dishes, like *döner*, are also served. The meal is always very delicious and rich an improvement that was achieved by workers' demands conveyed to Fatih and then to the employers, who hired a cook and ordered meals high in carbohydrates and proteins to be served. We take the food on plates to our trays and sit at the closest table. Usually there is a discussion about current politics. Generally, the AKP voters among the women do not reply to the CHP-voting Alevi women when the latter criticize the government and needle them for being responsible for the troubles the country is in. But the conversation is very short. They eat so fast that I cannot catch up and make sense of the hurry because I think of a lunch break as lasting a whole hour and as time that can be used however we like. That is naïve of me. One of the workers says that she left lunch without finishing the food in the first weeks of her employment here and was hungry all day but then got used to the pace, as I too did eventually. Just before we finish eating, the employers show up the dining hall and greet us saying *Afiyet olsun* (Bon Appetit), and we thank them. They take their food in trays too; nobody serves them in a special way. However, they sit at a table that is farthest away from the serving station, in a corner next to the window. We leave the hall in a hurry at almost 12:15 because that is when the lunch bell rings for the male workers.

Now it is time for tea again. If the weather is fine, we sit together at the pergola, that is, in the front garden that is visible from all the offices. We still check whether the employers are back or not, and while we have our tea and listen to music some women smoke, hiding their cigarettes mainly from the employers. If the weather is cold, then we sit in an office, but the women will not go out for a smoke, even though they really want to, as they are really worried that the manager or the bosses can see them. On some days, they smoke in the parking area on the way from the dining hall to the office, where one can hide between a parked car and the sunshade placed over it. Sometimes they say they quit smoking for a while because they want to keep a low profile, and sometimes they just light a cigarette, again hiding. They explain that Cemal Bey hired them under the condition that they quit smoking, a condition he only expressed verbally. He knows they are smoking for sure, but acts as if he doesn't know, while the women cannot risk confronting and disappointing him. What they avoid is the shame they would have to go through if he commented on their smoking, like one would feel towards a father when he catches you smoking when you're a teenager.

---

[134] A cold soup made out of water, yoghurt, cucumber, garlic and dried mint.

In the end, both parties avoid the situation, and only once did he make a comment to one woman: 'Smoking doesn't suit you at all!' The woman did not respond directly, and only complained later to other women, asking 'What's it to him!' In the meantime, at the pergola behind the dining hall, the male workers are enjoying their tea and cigarettes. Mainly older and more senior workers sit at the pergola, while the others, those who are younger or new to the factory, gather elsewhere or disperse into the backyard in twos or threes, especially the youngest ones, who also hide when smoking. Some do their noon prayers in the *mescid* (prayer room), which has been refurnished with new carpets and had a new heater put in at the request of the workers and on Fatih's own initiative, while others sit in the dining hall. I join those sitting at the pergola every day, first hesitantly introducing myself, then on the following days ask permission to sit and talk. On later days they start greeting me, and we chat about various topics.[135]

We go back to work when the bell rings at 13:15 until the fifteen-minute tea break at 15:45. In the afternoons, and actually all day long, Fatih the manager is around, giving instructions to the technical draftsmen, checking the production going on at different work stations, meeting clients, ordering tea and coffee for them, going back and forth from the employers' offices to the shop floor, talking to the workers and on the phone to others, chasing up orders and shipping, and repeating these activities all day. In the last few years Fatih has become more involved and the bosses have stood back a little, only controlling things from a distance and keeping up with the finances and their clients. Workers say Cemal Bey used to come to the shop floor more often to check things but has done so less in the recent years, only turning up when there is a problem. And whenever he walks into an office everyone has to behave: stop chatting, and look as if you are concentrating and interested in nothing but work. On the days he is on a business trip and doesn't show up everyone is more relaxed, as they admit to being afraid of him. For example, Enes hides his earphones while listening to some music and doing his drawings on the PC program, and when I ask him why, he looks at me and says, 'You have been long enough here to know why'. On the other hand, Bülent Bey's presence does not create such fear and anxiety

---

[135] Later I hear that a worker had asked the receptionist: 'Who is this girl walking around men with no shame?' She tries to explain that because my up-bringing is different, I don't feel shame at being around men. Months later the same worker tells me that I should come back next summer to go to a picnic with his family. To begin with Cemal Bey does not like me spending time with his workers either. He says he thought I was only interested in the technical stuff, but later I persuade him that the story of how a workplace functions is incomplete without the workers' own accounts. I add that he would understand this because he himself was a worker once. He does. I may also have been allowed to act in this way because nobody complained about my presence and I was careful not to disturb anyone.

in the workers; he too is very much respected, but gives a friendlier impression. For example, when he listens to music or talks loudly on the phone in his office, he apologizes to the receptionist, who can hear him from her desk, if he has bothered her. He is not at all involved in personnel matters, therefore the workers say he is 'the best boss ever', most likely because he is not bossing people around himself but has others to do that for him.[136] Some afternoons Cemal Bey's father comes to the factory; he likes to take care of the garden in the front yard. Towards the end of spring, he plants roses and trims the grass. He is old and slow, so I help him. Around the same hours, Cemal Bey's son-in-law Özcan drops by with his pick-up truck, delivers the equipment orders to the warehouse, and loads the machines or machine parts that need to be delivered elsewhere. He talks to Osman and then to Fatih, and then they order tea for each other. Then he talks to Enes and Ulaş about the recent *halal* scent (perfume without alcohol) he bought, a new smart phone somebody else has, his conviction that Ulaş should get married soon or some donations he is collecting for religious causes. He is never present in the proper work hours, but always talks about religious matters in a way that is not appreciated by the others. I sometimes feel he represents an irregularity in this context.[137]

In the afternoon, there is one more round of ordering things that Sevda *abla* brings down for the technical draftsmen and accountants. When there is finally a break, this time the smokers in the office, Osman, Ulaş and sometimes Enes, sneak outside to where the surplus machine parts are kept. Others stay in the office. I think this is only possible because, if Ulaş (the co-owner's son) dares to sneak out, so can the others, otherwise it would have been quite unlikely. I take the opportunity as well and join them most of the time; we come back before the break ends. By 5 pm, everybody is already tired. Around that time Cemal Bey's friend and Bülent Bey's brother usually show up; they order beverages too, make jokes about ordering things for me too, and play billiards upstairs in a room next to the kitchen. Then they go into their office and shut the door to talk about business, debts, loans, workers, etc., at which point I leave them to their privacy again.

Around 6 pm, everybody is counting the minutes to go home. When we hear the bell at 18:30, I expect the workers to be ready to go with their coats on and bags over their shoulders. However, nobody seems to be moving as fast as they did to the lunch and tea breaks. Office workers are finalizing their work on their computers and then turning them off, putting their coats on, getting their bags, scanning their cards and finally gathering

---

[136] In Chapter 6, I analysed in depth how this division of labour came about.

[137] His non-presence is discussed briefly along with the account of kinship morality in Chapter 6.

either inside or outside the entrance. The earliest we get into the shuttle bus is 18:45. I ask why we are moving so slowly, and an office worker replies that we shouldn't act too enthusiastically about leaving work, but instead should linger a little after the bell, so the bosses and the manager don't think we want to get away as quickly as possible, otherwise it might even be a reason for being fired, because the bosses might be offended at what they might regard as a disrespectful act. Sometimes it takes even longer, as we wait for others to lock the outer doors and offices, sneak off somewhere to smoke or chat, or for the manager to tell us we can now get into the shuttle. There are times when Fatih deliberately makes us wait more than necessary just to make the point that he is in power and that we have to obey him. At those times, he has an annoying hidden smile on his face, when he says: '*Hadi binin!*' (Now you go!). Some workers murmur: '*Şerefsiz!*' (someone without honour, a scumbag!) We reach home at the latest at a quarter past seven.

The working week ends on Friday for manual workers and many of the office workers except for the close family members working here (a topic discussed in Chapter 6). Not so long ago, everyone would also work on Saturdays until 4 pm, thus exceeding the legal 45-hour working week, but Fatih negotiated with the managers for that to be reduced to 1 pm, and then eventually he argued that it should be cancelled because between 8 am and 1 pm, together with the lunch break, the day ends before the workers can even concentrate, which is unproductive. He offered to add half an hour to each normal working day, which would therefore be extended from 18:00 to 18:30. The bosses agreed, but I don't know whether this was ever put to the workers. On my way back home, I calculate in my head the result of this negotiation; five days multiplied by 30 minutes make 150 minutes, plus the 15 minutes lost from the morning breaks every day, making 225 minutes, equivalent to 3 hours 45 minutes: almost equivalent to the Saturday work time from 8am to 1pm minus the fifteen-minute tea break. Then I stop and realize that in terms of the time spent at work nothing has changed, only been reallocated, though it was presented as a successful negotiation on Fatih's part for the benefit of the workers.

Time in an Industrial Context: Imposition, Discipline, Shirking, Making-Out

In his seminal essay 'Time, Work-Discipline and Industrial Capitalism', E.P. Thompson (1967) argues that the transition to industrial capitalism is marked by a shift in the apprehension of time from orientation to a task to time-discipline, a shift that 'entailed a severe restructuring of working habits –

new disciplines, new incentives, and a new human nature' (ibid.: 57). Even though the change in the apprehension of time is to a degree 'a symptom of a new Puritan discipline and bourgeois exactitude', (ibid.: 56) Thompson mainly questions how far this change affected labour discipline and the worker's inward notation of time (ibid.: 57). Throughout the essay he reveals the rule of the 'time-sheet, the time-keeper, the informers and the fines' (ibid.: 82) over industrial work and shows how 'factory workers were taught by their masters the importance of time... [and] had learned their lesson, that time is money, only too well' (ibid.: 86).

Thompson traces the shift in time apprehension back to the spread of clocks at the end of the eighteenth century, when owning watches and clocks ceased to be luxury and became a convenience. As he argues, '[i]ndeed, a general diffusion of clocks and watches is occurring (as one would expect) at the exact moment when the industrial revolution demanded a greater synchronization of labour' (ibid.: 69). Nonetheless seventeenth-century manufacturing was still conducted on a domestic or small-workshop scale in a task-oriented manner, accompanied by the irregularity of labour patterns (ibid.: 71) and irregular cycles of the working day and week (ibid.: 72) 'within the larger irregularity of the working year, punctuated by its traditional holiday and fairs' (ibid.: 76). However, the transition is not only about the shift in technique but also about the time-thrift needed to increase the employer's profit. Hence, the workers' irregular work habits were to be prevented through the imposition of time-discipline.

Thompson observes that the workers initially resisted the imposition of the new industrial time; in the following generations, however, they fought 'not against the time but about it' (ibid.: 85), learning their employers' rules and fighting within them. As we return back to the initial question of how far the workers internalized this radical social structuring and these working habits, Thompson replies, 'this discipline was indeed internalized'. As in all varieties of industrial societies, a clear demarcation between life and work has been established, marked by time-thrift (ibid.: 93). However, the transition from peasant society to industrial capitalist society, Thompson finally argues, is not the unavoidable result of technological change but a far-reaching conflict that is 'one of exploitation and of resistance to exploitation' (ibid.: 93-94).

Thompson's work has been widely discussed by labour historians and anthropologists of labour. Relevant to the purposes of this chapter are criticisms of his time-imposition argument. For example, Smith (1986: 166) criticized Thompson's thesis for seeing the imposition of time-discipline as 'a universal element of conflict'. In fact, his research showed that Tokugawa peasants already had a morally rooted and communally regulated apprehension of time even before the Industrial Revolution, and that time-discipline in the Japanese factory was not imposed unilaterally but jointly created by workers and management. Parry's ethnography (1999: 122) in the Bhilai steel factory in India also challenges Thompson's thesis by showing that shirking is an important element of work life at BSP: 'chatting, drinking tea and going for a stroll' after not very intensive work is possible, and 'managerial surveillance is minimally constraining'. As opposed to Parry, Burawoy's (2009) 'Thirty Years of Making Out' treats factory discipline and work organization as 'externally imposed', though his case study showed that the workers had created 'the art of making-out' as a way of manipulating the externally imposed stages of the work process. As a result, Burawoy (ibid.: 162) says that 'the specific organization of work structures and direct confrontation between management and worker is by no means its most common form'. With the help of the concepts introduced and discussed in this discussion around industrial discipline, habits and consent, I will try to demonstrate the transition that Çor-Mak went through.

The Demise of the Foreman and the Timely-Paid Wage as a Mechanism of Consent

As my description of a working day at this factory should indicate, time is strictly measured by means of the face and card scanners, the charts on billboards, and imposed by bells, camera surveillance, verbal warnings, shaming and scolding. In the effort to generate labour, technological time measurement and surveillance mechanisms are enmeshed with constant threats of being fired from the bosses, a form of domination (Burawoy and Wright 1990). The time-discipline and Taylorist techniques imposed on workers at Çor-Mak cannot be compared to the examples of assembly line production in multinational corporations in Liton Electronics Limited described by Lee (2009), Japanese factories in Malaysia by Ong (1991) or the automobile industry in northwest Turkey by Yücesan-Özdemir (2000) due to their size, the kinds of product they produce with advanced technologies and their multinational character. Nor it is comparable with the Measured Day Work system in the StitchCo hosiery and knitting factory described by Westwood (1984), nor even with the large textile factories in Çorum, where the times needed for each task are measured by chronometers. Nonetheless, the case of Çor-Mak tells us a lot about the circumstances in which and in response to what kinds of needs the rules of time-measurement and thrift and a management technique were adopted, as well as the qualities of the value regime that make oscillation between coercion and consent possible. Here I will argue that the transition was not at all about the change in technology in this case because assembling machines parts is still done as a matter of task-orientation, but about changing 'working habits – new disciplines, new incentives, and a new human nature' (Thompson 1967: 57). In one of our long conversations, Cemal Bey explained the transition on their charts, which show the company's turnover per worker/square meter over the last twenty years.[138] As I showed in Chapter 4, Çor-Mak's expansion was forced by market demand. Accordingly, it hired more workers and rented additional work space, but increasing spending and turnover did not bring an equivalent profit. Cemal Bey's narrative resembles Thompson's, even in his choice of words, so I leave it to him to explain:

> The business was expanding. You need to respond to this expansion, this has to happen under control. This has to be done in *discipline and order*. Do we do it like that? Yes. According to what? We do it with our experience; so, we rent another shop floor, hire three more workers, place the good personnel where they are more useful, take that [machines, benches, personnel] from here, put these there, I help some, you help others, so we were expanding and managing it *gropingly with the eye of a craftsman*. [...] In 2003, we formed our dyeing, sanding and metal-cutting units to bring some order to our jobs. At first we did it, we separated units, like here should be the shipping department, and we bought machines again. We started a new order, but it took less than two years for things to get even worse than before. We had more orders, more men, and not enough space. Our inventories got out of hand because of our *messy, unfettered, irregular style of working*. We start by saying 'Oh crap, what are we going to do?', then we come up with some solutions and advances, think that we are benefiting from them, but then we realize we did more harm than good. This time, within this mess, disagreements started among the personnel over the organization of work, so we started trying to reconcile them, so in short that got out of hand too. In 2007, we admitted it is not going to work like this; once we settle things we make good money but a bit *paldır küldür vurmayla kırmayla* (helter-skelter, like a bull at a gate). We don't know what we have in our inventory, how much of it *we wasted, how much we lost or profited, we cannot keep it under control because we don't have the measurement methods*. [...] And it is not only about arranging your finances and changing the organization of work; there are tasks that are done based on *habits, the ones that everyone is accustomed to*, starting from the boss to the worker.

---

[138] I explain the work they do in Chapter 4. Briefly, they produce packaging systems for wheat-based products such as flour or pasta, rice, bulghur wheat, etc.

> Lean production *involves breaking the resistance of people, distancing them from their habits and gaining new ones.* It is difficult to make people give up their habits, to *shift from one regime to another* [...] What I mean is that, as much as one can outgrow oneself from the apprentice-master period, one can start talking about Kayseri, Konya[139], Çorum. Otherwise the worker is not an industrial worker. That worker leaves you after three months to help his father in the fields. Our worker is also not that worker anymore' [italics are my emphasis unless used to denote an original Turkish word].

After moving to the industrial zone in 2009, they consulted a management expert and later started working together with a consultancy firm to adopt lean production within a state-funded project. Lean production, or more generally Japanese management techniques, require adopting a new mindset regarding the organization of work and social relations in the factory. Kaplinsky (1995: 59-60) neatly summarizes the basic premises of Japanese management techniques as such:

> [T]he emphasis was placed on rapid response and only making to customer orders. This enabled the plant to work with low inventories, but required a different approach to machine layout – these were now grouped together in "production cells" or "mini-factories." But the transition to flexibility also required new quality procedures (since there were no inventories to buffer production in case anything went wrong), that the workers be trained in a variety of skills and perform a number of tasks (hence achieving quick machine changeover) and that relationships with suppliers be restructured. Among other things this reduced the number of indirect workers and required significant changes in social relations, with flexible work teams substituting for individualized tasks and a much flatter organizational hierarchy.

Accordingly, Çor-Mak also decreased its inventories, saved space and created working stations ('production cells') for each unit, grouping and reshuffling them to be able to shorten the distance between the units among which machines are transported to go through different procedures, which shortened the time needed in the labour process to make a certain product. The yellow strips I saw on the ground, the shelves and lined-up machine parts dividing the different cells, were indications of these changes, so-called Kaizen procedures that were displayed on the billboards on the shop floor. Previously, they only kept records of turnover, labour costs and the orders

---

[139] Other Anatolian cities that have witnessed similar changes in the past decades.

they received. To be able to implement the new technique, they started calculating the necessary labour-time for every task and its cost. Only doing so did implementing the Kaizen procedures prove effective such that, with the new arrangements for the use of space and time, they have saved over 20% in terms of real profit over the last eight years, every year.[140]

Reducing inventories also implies producing only in response to customers' orders, which requires workers to be trained in a variety of skills so as to be able to respond to quick machine changeovers, as Kaplinsky points out. Therefore, Çor-Mak workers are also provided with short-time certified training programs that are often outsourced so they can learn to perform different tasks when necessary. However, changing machinery or equipment also means stripping the foremen or masters of their traditional authority and control over the workers and indeed changing the whole social structure of the shop floor. The foreman is often the middleman between the employer and the workers, and is in charge of disciplining, inspecting and training the latter while at the same time taking charge of the distribution of rewards, like bonuses, overtime, allocating vacations and promotion. Generally he is a senior man who has gone through the same training as his master and over the years has attained a position of authority in which he can train, shape, rule and control the younger apprentices. There were several foremen in each basic unit of six in Çor-Mak. At the time of my presence there, only Yavuz was left of those who would have remembered the transition; others had either been retired or had left to start their own businesses. Yavuz was tremendously offended by the changes made on the shop floor, as his seniority no longer ensured him the respect and authority he felt he was entitled to. He felt as if he had lost his role, his well-earned social position and even his masculinity. Even worse for him was having to take orders from younger workers and office workers, especially from the technical draftswoman, Hatice. Initially the foremen resisted these changes, which resulted in verbal quarrels a few times and once almost a fist fight on the shop floor between themselves and Cemal Bey.

The manual workers still have a hierarchy of their own based on seniority or skills that reflect their wages. There are still foremen in charge of specific units, and they are most likely to be close acquaintances or family members of Cemal Bey, but they do not have as much authority and control over the workers as a foreman had before the transition. Nonetheless, they are better paid and have idle time during working hours. As one of them put it: 'My job is easy, I don't get tired that much, and I watch people work'.

---

[140] This figure changes according to the different Kaizen procedures that are applied to each cell, but is still around 20%. There are more detailed figures indicating how much time-thrift and profit was achieved in the documents I was shown, but I prefer not to disclose them.

The manual workers who are not seniors but in their late thirties would say that not much has changed for them, only that they now receive orders from someone else. But once, when the topic of 'discipline' came up in a conversation with one such worker sitting at the pergola in a lunch break, I had a different impression. The worker was complaining about a previous employer for not paying their low wages on time[141] and praising Çor-Mak instead: 'There is discipline here, unlike other *düzensiz* (disorganized/irregular) places where someone shirks and others work. The manager ensures the discipline here [that everyone works]'. By using the word 'discipline', he was initially referring to the non-discriminatory practice of making workers work, the domination that generates the labour effort. But 'discipline' also meant the timely payment of wages to him. When one considers the interdependence between labour and capital, the higher profits earned after implementation of management techniques involving time-thrift and savings mean that the employers are now able to pay wages on time, 'unlike other disorganized places'. Thus, threats and surveillance are considered in terms of the fair treatment of all workers, since it also means the timely payment of wages. I have encountered similar views from women workers too: 'If you go to another place, it will again be the same as here, but at least here they pay wages on time'. Despite their working under conditions of domination, the idea that no other factory pays wages on time creates the conditions for asymmetrical reciprocity, as both parties are considered to benefit mutually, though not equally, from the exertion of labour effort.

The Rise of the Manager, Employer's Time, Respect and Displays of Loyalty

As I described in the last section, Çor-Mak has witnessed the demise of the foreman, whose training function has been replaced with outsourced training certificates, his disciplining with bells and face scanners, and his control over the workers with surveillance cameras. But most importantly, the foreman's authority and control has been shifted on to the manager. For more than five years now, Fatih, who ensures discipline here, as the previous worker phrased it, has been in charge of negotiating workers' demands with employers, determining their wages, granting daily and annual leave, making workers cooperate in decisions regarding the labour process and ensuring order, which includes punishing workers when the factory's time rules are violated. Although a Japanese management technique has been 'externally

---

[141] Irregular payments are common in Çorum.

imposed' on this factory in a remote Anatolian city, the ways in which the social regulation of labour is experienced are very much locally specific, as Peck (1996) has argued, and they are woven into the prevailing power structures that reveal themselves as certain values. The manager's decisions and the worker's responses to them are shaped in accordance with values such as respect, shame, deservingness, gratitude and loyalty, which constitute the value regime of social control within which coercion and consent oscillate. These values were invisible to an outsider, as they were to myself at the beginning of my research. When E.P. Thompson was trying to understand the behaviour of working people in the eighteenth century, he found it necessary to '"de-code" this behaviour and its symbolic modes of expression and to disclose invisible rules' (Thompson 1991: 11). Following Peck and Thompson's suggestions, I will try to de-code the locally specific symbolic expressions and disclose the invisible rules while keeping in mind Ong's (1991) argument that these also identify diverse layers of power relations.

To illustrate my argument, I use an analogy between an 'assault' recently committed against the clock tower in Çorum and the ways which violations of time-discipline and invisible rules are perceived at Çor-Mak.

One of the symbols of Çorum is its clock tower[142], built in 1894 as a gift from Hasan Pasha, the right-hand man of Sultan Abdülhamit II and a marshal in the army originally from Çorum, at the request of Çorum notables (Sabuncuoğlu 2015: 86-87). The spread of these clock towers soon signified the arrival of a shift to a new apprehension of time as a part of the Empire's integration into the global capitalist economy, the replacement of daily prayers with the tick-tock of the clock to track time, and the modernization efforts of the late nineteenth century. Since then, Çorum clock tower has marked the centre of the city as a symbol of its modernization and connection to the capital. Last but not least, the tower represents the loyalty and respect one should pay towards one's roots and hometown, as Hasan Pasha showed by donating the tower.

While I was thinking about the issues of different apprehensions of time and the meanings and values attached to them, a post[143] in a local newspaper appeared on my Facebook newsfeed. Apparently, some people

---

[142] It is a 27.5-meter-tall, minaret-like tower fitted with clocks of a great size on all four of its sides, and indicating the time in both Arabic and Latin numerals. Just below the tower's dome are four windows to increase the reach of the hourly gong, replacing the role of the echo of daily prayers from the mosques to tell the time based on sunrise and sunset. The building of the tower also overlaps with Abdülhamit II's order to build clock towers across the Empire to celebrate the 25th anniversary of his reign in 1901.

[143] Mebet (2018), retrieved from http://www.corumhakimiyet.net/guncel/tarihe-saygisizlik-h437.html.

had had a bit of late-night fun in Çorum and had left three beer bottles at the entrance to the clock tower; the article reported that the incident had caused anger among some people. Accordingly, an eye-witness of the scene in the morning the next day remarked on his inability to contemplate this disrespectful demonstration against their city's symbol, which represents historical values that are '*ecdat*[144] *yadigarı*' (reminiscent of ancestry), which he regretted and condemned (Mebet 2018). In fact, although the clock tower is a historical monument, it is not an Islamic one such that it can be insulted by alcohol being consumed next to it or around it. Nevertheless, people's perceptions of the tower, which was initially built in the name of modernization and to effect a shift to the secular division of the day are associated with their Ottoman ancestry, and hence with Islam, which makes the tower sacred in their perception and makes consuming alcohol near it 'disrespectful'.

Similarly, as I demonstrated in my description of a work day, when the rule of time is violated at the factory it is perceived as an act of disrespect, and the person who is responsible is immediately warned, provoking shame and sometimes anger in him or her. When we gathered in the afternoons in front of the reception desk to chat a little because the office workers were tired or wanted to stretch their legs a bit, or during the *ısmarlama* (ordering drinks) game if it led to chatting and shirking, the workers are immediately warned by their names being called out. Also, being caught chatting or surfing on social media when Cemal Bey walks into the office and realizes a worker is using the firm's time for other purposes is also disrespectful. It is even worse when Cenmal Bey gives a worker a verbal warning, not calling the worker out but giving a face-to-face warning, which people try to avoid as much as they can. The employer's rule is experienced irrefutable, and loyalty always has to be ensured. The worker I mentioned above was complaining about his previous employer, but when I asked him what else bothered him, he avoided speaking further and merely said: '*İnsan yemek yediği kaba ş'aapmaz*' (One does not shit into the bowl one eats from). This shows that loyalty is not only given to the time rules but also perceived as owing to the provider, the one who feeds you, who 'has an effort in your becoming', the literal translation of the Turkish expression '*üzerinde emeği var*'. This example shows that, even though workers sometimes show anger and frustration at the threats and surveillance they are subject to, the norm of respecting one's roots and one's provider, which

---

[144] *Ecdat*, along with *soy* and *ata* are three different words in Turkish that have close meanings to ancestry. However, the selection of the word *ecdat* here refers to the Ottoman ancestry in specific, a vocabulary that has gone popular among Islamist or pro-government circles who support the neo-Ottomanist and jihadist agenda of the government.

justified workers' obedience, is strongly internalized and turns coercion into asymmetrical reciprocity. The analogy with the alleged disrespect shown towards the clock tower shows how deeply the norm of respect is internalized. Hasan Pasha's gift to his hometown is a display of loyalty to his roots, showing that, although he later became high-ranking official, he did not forget his home town's role in his own 'becoming'.

However, there were also situations which do not involve violating the time-discipline and the norm of respect but still are treated as such. Thus, just as the secular clock tower was treated as an Islamic monument to justify the anger against it being shown disrespect, sometimes the meaning of the time-discipline was twisted by means of the invisible rules that were attached to it, and were again perceived as disrespectful. Workers react at these moments with displays of their loyalty. For example, listening to music with an earphone is not a violation of the time-discipline, and it might even be motivating when doing technical drawing, but Enes chooses to hide it and acts as if he is focused only on his work and nothing else in order to avoid being given a warning. Similarly, one can argue that being ready to go home after work hours is not a violation, but it is perceived as one, so the fact that workers do not want to seem too willing to leave work even after the bell has rung is another display of their loyalty. However, workers' loyalty will be tested by delaying letting them go at the end of the working day just to teach them whose time it is and who is in charge. Obviously, time spent at work belongs to the employer-cum-provider. Workers' displays of loyalty at these moments of everyday despotism are strategic responses to avoid direct confrontation and the possibility of being fired. Unlike other moments in which coercion is found to be legitimate based on ideas of fairness, mutuality and respect, coercive measures regarding private matters or those that fall outside working hours are not considered legitimate. Occasionally, workers murmur some swear words in a tone not many can hear. Yet it would be an exaggeration to see these moments as 'hidden transcripts' (Scott 1990) of resistance on the part of the subordinate group.

Throughout the months I spent in a factory as a witness to everyday despotism, I became excited when I heard that Fatih had asked the technical drawing team to come up with suggestions for a new seating arrangement in the offices. Since the new management system also encourages workers' participation in decision-making, I thought Fatih was trying a new approach. In the current seating arrangement, from the main entrance to the left one emerges from a short corridor to reach an open space where the technical draftsmen and women are seated. There were four workers at the time, whose four desks were placed facing each other in pairs, leaving a space in the middle of the room. On the left side of this space, a door opened to the office of Fatih and Ulaş, who sat at two desks that faced each other, with their backs to the opposing walls. The purpose of the re-arrangement was to create a space for Ulaş to join the technical draftsmen so he could adapt more easily and work with them. In the following days, Enes drew up a new seating arrangement and showed it to me with great enthusiasm; he had included Ulaş in the office, put some shelves on the walls that he thought would be useful, and introduced some new desks with new designs, all facing each other. He said that he would show it to Fatih and ask his opinion. That week passed, and when we came back from the weekend we saw that the arrangement was already in place, apparently having been done at the weekend. In the new arrangement, Fatih got his own office. When I spoke to the receptionist, she mentioned sarcastically that he had been looking for a painting to hang on his office wall all last week. On the other hand, all the other desks were lined up next to each other against the wall, with all the workers sitting facing the wall and all the PC screens facing the open space behind them. Later on, I spoke to Cemal Bey; he said that if they are made to face the wall, they will concentrate better. Fatih agreed with him and added that they introduced this new system for Ulaş, as if he had no benefit out of the situation. Finally, when I spoke to Enes asking what happened to his suggestion or whether they had discussed it, he repeatedly said that he wanted this arrangement too and also thought it was better that way, as although he hadn't been the one who was excited about giving an opinion of his own, his thoughts about it would at least be taken into account. If I hadn't seen him so enthusiastic only a few days earlier I might have been convinced, but somehow the situation seemed as if Enes's suggestion had been declined or maybe not even discussed. However, he preferred to act as if he had not had an opinion in the first place (or as if his opinion did not matter) and as if he had completely agreed with his superior, the authority figure, from the start. Not only was my prediction that this might have been an attempt to include workers in the decision-making process proved wrong, I was able to witness another display of loyalty. This time the worker completely changed his mind in order to side with the authority figure, thus showing that they never had opposing opinions in the first place, and strategically it amounted to obtaining consent to further surveillance being introduced at the workplace. Another reason for this strategy lies in Enes's interest in securing his position in Çor-Mak and acquiring positions of greater authority, as illustrated in Chapter 6.

The internet content the workers accessed was already made available to Fatih on a daily basis through a software program. With the new seating arrangement, he can also visually track social media, YouTube or other non-work-related activities of the workers on their PC screens while the latter are 'concentrating better' on their work, facing the wall and knowing that they are being surveilled. Workers already knew that there were cameras around, and Fatih checked their screens once in a while, but the new arrangement made it impossible to hide. What made the situation even more *despotic* is the fact that these workers never really spent that much time online anyway as far as I could observe during the time I spent there. Hence, the new arrangement also suggests there is a degree of mistrust by the employers towards the workers. By itself this mistrust is the reason for workers being pressed to reassure their employers of their loyalty in the first place, as well as being an indicator of the employers' awareness that their methods of persuading workers to work longer hours for lower wages are not so persuasive as to guarantee the creation of surplus value.

The most unexpected display of loyalty, in fact a seemingly crystal-clear demonstration of the hegemonic regime in the factory, came from the manual workers. During this particular lunch break I was having tea with them as usual in the backyard. Some were coming back from the noon prayer; one worker among them told me that they had held a *mevlit*[145] for their bosses that day. I was puzzled because it was not the day of *Mevlid-i Nebi*, nor had there been a death, birth or marriage as far as I was aware that day. I therefore asked what the occasion was. This was interpreted as demonstrating my ignorance about religion, so they laughed at me as I tried to explain that *mevlit* is organized in situations that change the course of a person's life, like death, birth, marriage or circumcision. They were not convinced, but I insisted on learning what exactly the content of their *mevlit* was. Finally, the worker said that they basically prayed for their bosses, which made me think of other prayers in which one prays for a better future, a better income and a better life from *Allah*. Then I asked if they had prayed that their bosses make better profits and that their businesses go well in the future. The worker said it was not for their future that they prayed but for the bosses' past deeds, because so far they have done well out of them, and the

---

[145] *Mevlit* means 'time of birth' and is a ceremony organized to commemorate the birthday of the Prophet Mohammed in the Islamic world. In a more general sense, it can also be organized to celebrate the birthdays of close members of the Prophet's family and the saints. In Turkey, the holy night celebrated as the Prophet's birthday is called '*Mevlid-i Nebi*', *Mevlit* is also the name of a collection of poems about the birth and life of the Prophet. One of the most common collections read in *mevlit*s in Turkey was composed by Süleyman Çelebi at the beginning of the fifteenth century. Beyond being specific to the Prophet's birthday, many Muslims organize *mevlit* readings in their daily lives as a ritual at life-cycle events, such as death, birth, circumcision and marriage (Atay 2004: 59). Tapper and Tapper (1987: 64) write that *mevlit* can be publicly or privately organized or televised, and they describe it as 'a compartmentalized religious activity that none the less allows for complex, varied statements of social identity'.

workers have been provided by them. When I asked why they did not pray for their future but for the past, the worker said that they knew only what they had done so far and didn't know what they will do in the future, so they prayed to what they already knew out of gratitude. Another worker then added: 'One would of course pray for an employer who would let his workers pray at work'. Before the end of the conversation we heard the bell ring, and everybody went back to work, leaving me to return to the office, still puzzled.

I thought maybe they were trying to convey a message to their employers through me, but this was months after I had started going there regularly, and we had at least come to an understanding that I wasn't spying on them. Even if they had the slightest doubt about this, still the fact was whether it was *mevlit* or a simple prayer they had prayed on behalf of their employers out of gratitude. At first, I regarded the act of praying for one's employer as a demonstration of pure consent, in fact an indicator of the hegemony that has been achieved at this factory. As explained in the previous chapter, building a workplace community based on similar religious and/or customary habits and values allows contexts to flourish in which the workers pray for their exploitation and their timely-paid wages, as well as the incentives and freedom of Sunni religious practice. Durak (2011), who investigated the role of religiosity in worker-employee relations in Konya, explains similar situations with reference to the notion of 'cultural hegemony': that is, the workers' and employers' religiosity subsumes them, just like the blurring of the conflict between labour and capital in the same universe, of which both parties are aware but both act as if they are not. Durak describes such moments as I described above as 'theatrical', which suits the present case as well, as I will explain in the next section. In other moments, however, when they learned that their pay rise would not be as much as they expected or when they received warnings for shirking, their reactions were not at all grateful but angry. Moreover, their emphasis on the conditionality of their gratitude led me to question my first impression that this was a hegemonic regime based on consent. The worker emphasized that they were not praying for the future of their employers but only for what they had provided their workers with so far, suggesting that if the future does not turn out to be as gratifying, then they would also not be consenting. On this point, Burawoy and Wright (1990: 255) write that: 'the linkage between consent and conflict implies that consent within asymmetrical reciprocity is always conditional, subject to contestation, renegotiation, transformation'. Hence, I believe the *mevlit* ritual mentioned above should be evaluated as an aspect of asymmetrical reciprocity rather than hegemony – we cannot talk about full consent when it is conditional.

Wages, Leave and Holidays: Ambiguity and Deservingness

Every year towards the end of December, everyone grows excited about the increase in pay they will be granted. Almost every day, they speculate about it. Although Fatih himself warns people when they gather next to the receptionist's desk, still Elif wants to get an impression of what her rise will be, so she asks about it, and we stand there with Fatih and expect him to give us a hint of the percentage or maybe some hope. It is Fatih who will decide on everyone's new salary, or at least so he says. He says that when the bosses decide about his salary he won't question it, but they won't question his decisions on the workers' salaries either. Throughout the year, whenever somebody makes a mistake in production, shipping, book-keeping or anything else one can think of, Fatih reminds people directly or indirectly that this will reflect their pay next year. Workers also talk about it in their breaks. Because I have been asking them about their incomes, reproduction and working conditions about this time of the year, they ask me back, 'So how much raise do you get a year?' Not knowing much about German labour law, I tell them the annual raise is 7 percent.[146] When they hear 7 percent, they become angry to the point that one worker says, '*Onun ağzına sıçarım!*' (I'll kick the crap out of him!). Then, they explain that if one is getting the minimum wage (see Footnote 129), even a 10 percent raise would make around 150 TL, which is nothing compared to what one would get who is paid let's say 2500 TL. Some laughed about it to release their anger, while others who have already reached seniority and have better pay seem more relaxed. Later on, as the end of the month approaches, again we gather next to the receptionist's desk, where Fatih says: 'I have decided the best for everyone, but I won't say it until I know mine'. Elif and I insist, so an approximation of 10 percent comes out of his mouth. But the location is critical in the sense that what we are talking about there, at the receptionist's desk, can easily be heard from the offices inside. Fatih is not speaking in a low voice, as if he wants others to hear. Later the same day, Elif received a phone call from the foreman, Yavuz, asking if it were she who had spread the word that the raise will be 10 percent. She got away with it by blaming me, but also said that Fatih had been talking at the top of his voice, so anyone could have heard. Apparently, when the rumour spread there was disquiet among the workers.

However, once workers learn about their pay increases when they have to sign next to their names on a list at the end of every month at the

---

[146] I learned later that the annual pay increase in Germany was around 3 percent and that it depends on many factors, such as the union involved, the type of contract, the company budget, etc. but I did not change the original dialogue when writing it.

human resources office, there is no way one can object or negotiate it again. In fact, they do not have a chance to negotiate it beforehand either. I asked several times what happens when they do so, and was told that if you want to do that you have to go to Cemal Bey, who will say 'Take it or leave it', This kind of confrontation with him, impossible as it is, also means that you have to leave the firm after taking that risk. However, throughout my time there I was not able to figure out on what basis the wages were decided, other than that Fatih knows what is best for everyone.

This ambiguity also exists when one asks for daily or annual leave. As the new management technique the firm has adopted is based on the labour-time and thrift, it requires consistency from workers to show up at work on a more regular basis and to take fewer casual periods of leave. Hence, I was told by the employers right at the beginning of my research that one of the main achievements of lean production has been to reduce absenteeism. As it is no longer the foreman who grants daily and annual leave but the manager, the latter has an irregular manner of distributing them. If the manager allows a woman worker to pick up her child on the last day of school, on which there is generally a ceremony that parents are expected to be present at, he hesitates to grant her another casual leave. If the request is because of the health of a close family member then he has mercy, but if he finds it somehow irrelevant or too frequent then he will refuse it. Nonetheless there is ambiguity involved, and workers try to prioritize the days they need the most as a strategy. When it comes to annual leave, many basically do not take it because the causal periods of leave are subtracted from ones' annual right to leave. However, if someone has some days left, s/he makes a request to Fatih, who then lets the worker know later when he can use it. Moreover, in general it is not allowed to take Fridays off to have a long weekend; individual treatment is strongly discouraged. Either everyone has a long weekend or no one does. As some official holidays, religious or not, fall on a Thursday or a Tuesday, workers hope that work on the Friday or Monday will be cancelled so that they can have a long weekend. Sometimes this is allowed, but when it is rejected Fatih justifies it by saying '*Haketselerdi*' (They should have deserved it), as if the decline of the request was the result of a failure for which the workers should be punished. What is *despotic* about this practice is that it is not announced until the last minute, as a result of which the workers cannot make plans, even if they actually have the long weekend, and may have to cancel bookings at the last minute if not.

Keeping workers in suspense and not allowing them to know on what basis they will get a pay rise, casual leave or a long weekend does not really work as a motivation for work, nor to promote identification with the workplace. The workers are well aware of their inability to negotiate over their wages or their casual and annual leave. Not being in charge of their free time and not having the power to navigate their daily lives unless they can convince their manager they should create some disquiet such that deep down the workers become angry and resentful, and feel trapped and disappointed. While the practice of disciplining and monitoring workers during working hours was considered fair treatment, as the previous sections have shown, the ambiguity over holidays and the conditions governing pay increases creates the opposite effect. Following Thompson (1967), one can argue that the workers internalize the idea that time at work belongs to the employer, so the conflict does not arise from the imposition of time-discipline but from exploitation. The only way workers can express or resist this is by using a few swear words once in a while, talking behind the manager's back and scheming to come up with a reasonable excuse. In this context, the act of 'praying for the bosses' was 'theatrical', or at least was led by some of the workers who are better paid and in relatively powerful positions based on their seniority, skills or kin ties.

The Gendered Segregation of Spaces, *Namus* and the Sexual Contract

As described in detail in the vignette of my own working day, there were also some unspoken but visible rules that applied only to women workers. These were the prohibition on public smoking, and not sharing public spaces with men in their breaks, in the dining hall or in the personnel shuttle. This is why women workers sat in separate seats in the shuttle, did not pass through the shop floor even in winter, squeezed their lunch into almost ten minutes in what should be an hour-long break, smoked secretly and spent their breaks at a pergola in the front garden or in their offices. These rules segregated the spaces in a gendered way and provided for the social regulation of women in the workplace. Ong (2011: 292-5), who has reviewed the contexts of the industrializing of Asia and Mexico at length, suggests that increasing female employment in industry was regarded as invasion of male public spaces by the Other, leading to employers regulating female activities 'along clearly marked gender lines, defining what is appropriate and what is not'.

Researchers who have investigated the reasons behind low female employment rates in Turkey point out that social norms about the proper behaviour and place of women in society play a restraining role here, among other reasons (Kadam and Toksöz 2004). Social norms about the proper behaviour and place of women in this context are rooted in the notion of the woman's *namus* or honour. This is explained using a Turkish idiom: '*Eline, beline, diline sahip çıkmak*' meaning 'One has to control her hand, her waist and her tongue'. Although this idiom is primarily relevant for men, it is generally used to denote a woman's duty to not lay hands on others' property (the hand), avoid sexual behaviour (the waist) and moderate her encounters with men other than her husband and the language she uses (tongue). A woman's *namus* belongs to her father, husband or brother such that, if the woman behaves in ways that violate 'proper' conduct, then the father's or husband's *namus* is tainted, and the woman should be ashamed of it. That is why the male worker asked the female receptionist how I was freely walking around men without shame (see Footnote 135) because from his perspective, by doing so I was tainting my father's *namus*, for which I should feel shame. In the same logic, when employers hire women as either manual or office workers, they felt the need to create a workplace where the woman's *namus* is not under threat and where her husband or father will not be worried. The gendered segregation of space is designed not only to protect women's *namus*, but also to draw a boundary between female and male workers in the same workplace so that they know the woman's *namus* is under their employers' protection. There is also a traditional aspect here in that, when women and young people smoke in front of their fathers, this is considered a disrespectful act of rebellion. In this context, however, a woman smoking is specifically perceived as violating the gendered boundaries drawn by the employer. Even if the employer did not have such personal convictions about women smoking, since there are only five women workers in Çor-Mak among seventy men, he probably thinks he cannot control what other men think about it anyway. The organization of space would probably differ if the number of women and men employed in the factory were more equal or if this was a women-majority sector.

In their sociological study of a textile mill in Çorum employing largely women under conditions of what they call 'consensual control', Beşpınar, Topal, and Kalaycıoğlu (2014) also encountered gendered spatial segregation at the workplace. They argue that employers' concern for 'so-called conservative cultural values' (ibid.: 229) preserves women's reputations and family structures, thus serving as a consent mechanism. They also underline the fact that a conservative culture is specific to this locality, namely Çorum. Although I agree that preserving women's reputations is a consent mechanism, I would refrain framing the context as 'a conservative culture specific to this locality'. The honour and shame paradigm is not specific to Çorum, nor to other provinces in Turkey, but is in fact a widespread patriarchal power structure that goes beyond 'a specific locality'. Following Pateman (1988), I would rather frame what is going on here as a form of patriarchal discipline that is required for women's subordination to men in a capitalist context of employment relations and is different from the discipline through which some men are subordinated to other men (ibid.: 142). This is because men enter into an employment contract as 'workers', but when women enter into an employment contract they are incorporated not primarily as 'workers' but as 'women'. This is due to the fact that 'the sexual contract is an integral part of civil society and the employment contract; sexual domination structures the workplace as well as the conjugal home' (ibid.). In my own fieldwork site, the 'sexual contract' is expressed through the vocabulary of *namus*.

Conclusion

This chapter has focused on the labour control mechanisms that have been put in place at Çor-Mak. While paternalistic provisioning can obscure surplus value, it is insufficient to ensure it. This chapter has illustrated the rules, regulations and management mechanisms that serve to secure the surplus. First, I presented the legal framework that introduced the flexible labour regime under circumstances of far-reaching state restructuring and the deregulation of both individual and collective labour laws. I then provided a narrative of a regular working day at the factory before expanding on the changes it went through at different stages of the imposition of time-discipline and thrift, and the lean production techniques that were subsequently introduced. By doing so, I showed that, although this model may be externally imposed, notions like industrial discipline, the industrial worker, industrial habits and thrift have been integrated into the local employer's vocabulary and practice in managing a business. I have also demonstrated the locally specific ways and values through which these management techniques are implemented. The changes to the factory regime led to changes in the social structure of the factory, which at first met resistance but later re-configured the power relations between the manager and the workers, senior and young workers, skilled and unskilled workers, women and men.

The ways in which the rules, regulations and management techniques are understood, enacted and received revealed areas of consent and coercion. Rather than classify the labour regime as hegemonic or despotic, I have identified the rules, regulations and management techniques that were perceived to be either coercive or consensual and tried to understand the relationship between them. Consent and coercion were both expressed symbolically through the values that unite and/or divide workers from employers, namely respect, loyalty, deservingness and gratitude. I have also adopted Burawoy and Wright's (1990) notion of asymmetrical reciprocity in which labour effort is based on consent that is to the mutual benefit of both parties, yet that does not imply there is no coercion. Accordingly, some coercive measures can be perceived as mutually beneficial when the norms that legitimize obedience are deeply internalized or when there is a belief in the bosses' fairness. Moreover, unlike what the notion of hegemony would imply, with asymmetrical reciprocity the consent is conditional.

The ethnographic findings of this chapter show that the rules and regulations that are put in place to promote labour effort oscillate between domination and asymmetrical reciprocity. As I have repeatedly pointed out, the working conditions that have been achieved in the workplace and that are conveyed through the manager to the employers concern the quality of the lunches, the freedom to observe Sunni religious practice and the space and time provided for it, and allowing the *ordering* game and reallocation of work time to other days so that Saturdays are free, which in reality did not reduce the total weekly working hours, which are already above the legal limit. These low-cost improvements are made to *persuade* workers to work for longer hours and more efficiently. They also secure the *surplus value* and constitute the realm of *consent*. Although threats and surveillance are widespread, the workers find the discipline necessary as long as these conditions are met and their wages are paid on time; hence their belief in the fairness of the bosses is strong. Moreover, the values of respect and loyalty that are very much internalized and that promote labour effort are non-strategic responses on the part of the workers. However, some of the surveillance and disciplining reflects the fact that the employers and the manager distrust the workers, compelling the latter to be prepared to display their loyalty constantly. These incidents are rather strategic, and consent is based on the fear of being fired or otherwise falling from favour, yet expressed in the silent murmuring of one's anger. Displays of loyalty and gratitude can also be non-strategic expressions of consent, as in the prayers said for the bosses. Even at this theatrical moment, the workers implied that their consent was conditional.

Another management strategy at this company was to leave the workers in uncertainty over their pay increases and holidays, with constant reminders that they should deserve them. Although the workers considered the daily threats to ensure discipline during working hours fair, they did not feel the same about the control over their free time and the rhetoric of being 'deserving'. These moments created anger and resentment, yet this was not expressed openly. The wages, periods of leave and actual time of work could not be negotiated, discussed or even brought up by any worker to either the manager or the employers. These are high-cost demands that would directly lead to conflict and were therefore avoided through strict *coersive* measures and the threat of being laid off. Avoiding these conflict-ridden areas, which are essential to labour relations, are only possible through the state restructuring of individual labour laws and by depoliticizing the collective labour laws, which demarcate the framework of the relations described in this chapter.

Chapter 8
Religious Arrangements of Work Hours as an Exception to Time-Discipline

Introduction

This chapter scrutinizes on how work time is arranged for certain religious rituals and how these arrangements affect pious and non-pious Alevi and Sunni workers. Having witnessed visible and invisible strict time regulations and how workers are taught that time belongs to the employers, observing the irregularities was rather surprising. It was very rare for the workday routine to be interrupted. Even on days when the whole country was going through political turmoil in the aftermath of the several ISIS attacks that occurred that year or because of the attempted military coup of 15 July 2016, people occasionally followed the news on social media at work and maybe took slightly longer breaks to discuss such situations, but their workday routine was not interrupted. As I showed in Chapter 6, some religious and non-religious rituals and activities were organized at the work places, and I showed in Chapter 7 that religious rituals performed in the work place can especially be a source of gratitude to employers and constitute an important pillar of consent to generate labour effort. As these findings show, contrary to Thompson's (1967) thesis as elaborated in Chapter 7, acquiring industrial habits and imposing time-discipline do not necessarily mean that traditional habits and rituals are completely abandoned. In fact, they play a facilitating rather than a hindering role in workers' adaptation to the factory regime.

Historians of labour who have engaged critically with Thompson's work have shown that in the U.S., for instance, migrant workers carried their pre-industrial traditions and customs over into the modern factory system and that these habits played a crucial role as a resource for purposes of adaptation (Gutman 1988). Moreover, although the apprehension of time changed drastically, traditions often have their own timings at odds with time-discipline. Some scholars have suggested that multiple time-reckoning systems have continued to operate simultaneously in industrial capitalism and accordingly propose to study the multiplicity of these time-reckoning systems and their degrees of imposition at the levels of the sector, community and enterprise (Whipp 1987). Following these scholars' inspiration, in this chapter I will focus on daily prayers, Friday prayers and Ramadan fasting to argue that a religious apprehension of time exists simultaneously with time-discipline to a certain extent. I will also describe how the different value systems of pious and non-pious Sunni and Alevi employers shape the organization of and participation in these rituals. Thus, I will also try to show how these arrangements impact differently on workers and employers who have different relations to religion and Sunni Islam. Before delving into ethnographic detail, the chapter will first discuss the significance of prayers in Islam and the context in which the establishment of the working day in the late nineteenth century took place.

Significance of Daily Prayers and Collective Friday Prayers

Prayers[147] are central to all belief systems, especially to Islam, it being one of the ritual obligations of a Muslim.[148] Prayers (*salāt* in Arabic, *namaz* in Turkish) should be offered five times a day, every day. The times of the prayers are determined according to the earth's movement around the sun. All five prayers are *farz* (obligatory commands). Each prayer has a different number of sections (*rekat*), some of which are considered to be *farz*, while the other sections are *Sunna* (non-obligatory, though advised by the Prophet). Before starting a prayer, one has to purify one's heart of bad thoughts and intentions and clean one's body from ear to toe. The ritual of cleansing the body is called *abdest*, for which almost all mosques have water fountains with seats around or in front of them outside the mosque for men to make their ablutions. Not all prayers have to be performed in a mosque, except for Friday prayers (which replace the midday prayer), prayers at religious feasts and exceptions such as the *Teravih*[149] prayer. All five prayers are announced from the mosques with an *ezan* (call to prayer) that consists

---

[147] The English word 'prayer' is used to denote both '*dua*' and '*namaz*' in Turkish, however the two words are quite different. *Namaz* is the daily ritual that is explained here, one has to move his\her body in a certain way,and recite the specific suras in a certain pre-determined order for each *namaz*. *Dua* is a prayer in the literal sense, it could be the verses and suras in Quran that one recites in Arabic during the performance of *Namaz* or any other time when one wants to pray. At the same time, *dua* could also mean a one-sided dialogue with a superior force in any language one can do anytime and anywhere on whatever topic one wants. The topic handled in this chapter is *namaz* ritual and the word 'prayer' is used to denote this ritual, not any prayer.

[148] For explanations of the Islamic concepts in this part, see Chapter 3.

[149] One of the longest prayers offered after breaking the fast in the Ramadan month. Women are not required to go the mosque for Friday prayers and religious feast prayers, and they mostly do not. But women participate in great numbers in groups for the *Teravih* prayer.

of the main themes of *namaz*: 'the affirmation of God's magnificence and singularity, and the truth of the revelation received by Muhammad' (Henkel 2005: 494). The prayer ritual is a highly structured and formalized performance[150] that allows the practitioner to become detached from his or her social context and engage with the foundational concepts of Islamic belief (ibid.), 'purposefully molding ... intentions, emotions, and desires in accord with orthodox standards of Islamic piety' (Mahmood 2001: 828). Henkel (2005) observed that his interlocutors in Istanbul found that prayer strengthens their beliefs, while Mahmood (2001) draws attention to how practising women in Cairo continuously and consciously submit themselves to a moral-ethical framework through the practice of the prayer.

The Friday prayer has a special significance because the first Friday is considered a holy day and the second a day of communal prayer. It responds to the order that: 'O you who believe! When the call is made for prayer on Congregation Day, hasten to the remembrance of God, and drop all business. That is better for you, if you only knew'[151] (Sura 62, Verse 9). The prayer of congregations (*cemaat*) is given great importance in the history of Islam. According to one tradition underlined in the *Encyclopedia of Islam*, it is believed that '[t]he prayer which a man performs in congregation is worth twenty-five of his prayers in his home or in the market-place' (Monnot 2017 [1955]). The logic behind the worth of prayers is also prevalent at the local level. '*Kıl beşi, kurtar başı*' is a saying I was told by one of my respondents in Çorum; it underlines the value of *namaz* in general that, on judgement day, when everyone will be held accountable for their good deeds and sins, if one has prayed five times, one can be saved.[152] When a man regularly attends Friday prayers, he becomes a part of a congregation (*cemaat*) of the mosque where people socialize weekly and talk about personal, religious and worldly problems. Showing up for Friday prayers is quite important. For example, I recently learned that nowadays the congregation does not take

---

[150] For the choreography of the prayer ritual, see Henkel (2005: 495-496). What Henkel describes and is elaborated on here is based mainly on the Sunni and more specifically the Hanefi tradition.

[151] English translation retrieved from http://www.clearquran.com/062.html. In the Turkish translation of Elmalı, Friday is stated instead of Congregation Day.

[152] In one of my interviews with a male employer in his forties at a small workshop, I was trying to strike up a conversation about which religious practices he himself performs and what they mean to him. Instead of talking about his practices, he kept telling me about the religious orders that we all must follow because we will be asked on the judgement day: for example, *namaz* will appear in a concrete form, face us and say 'If you have been with me before now I will stand by you too'. Then he talked about how one's sins will be subtracted from one's good deeds on that day, which will determine whether one will end up in heaven or hell in the afterlife (see Chapter 3, Section 4.2 'Fundamentals of Islam').

kindly to men who don't show up three times in a row. It is also important to note that when men stand side by side in rows to submit themselves to God and praise him, they all become servants (*kul*) of God, regardless of their socio-economic and cultural differences. This has the effect of making inequalities disappear, at least for that time being. In populist politics in Turkey one frequently sees television news about political elites who show up in different mosques every week and join with the congregation, mainly in historical mosques.

Establishment of the Duration of a Work Day and Official Holidays

As I have already explained above, prayers are central to Islamic belief. A Muslim can prefer to perform just some of these practices or none at all for various reasons (see Chapter 3). On the other hand, if one prefers to say one's prayers as instructed, it can be difficult to say all of them flawlessly if one is employed or self-employed in any sector in an urban context because of the daily work rhythms, and for obvious reasons it is even more difficult in workplaces ruled by time-discipline. Before time-discipline became so prevalent, throughout the centuries of Ottoman rule there was no law regulating working hours or holidays. As in any pre-industrial context, the idea of leisure time had not developed, nor had work and life been separated.

It was only towards the end of the nineteenth century that *Mecelle-i Ahkam-ı Adliye*[153] entered into force, one of its articles stating that the work day runs from sunrise to sunset and that people should behave according to custom (İleri 2009: 88). Which custom was followed depended on which religion the employer belonged to: if the employer was a Christian, then Sundays were a holiday, if a Muslim then Friday. However, since there was no law restricting working hours, the average working day lasted twelve to fourteen hours, seven days a week, and holidays were to be decided arbitrarily. Within the same timeframe, only in the state factories were Fridays officially holidays. Nonetheless, during the wave of workers' strikes from 1870 to 1918, among other demands, which were mainly centred around wages, were having paid weekends and not working on Sundays (Karakışla 1998: 194).

Finally, right after the establishment of the republic, Friday was declared to be an official (though unpaid) holiday at the İzmir Economy Conference in 1923, this measure being legalized in 1924. Then, in 1935, the

---

[153] The first civil code to be issued in the Ottoman Empire. It is based on the Hanefi legal tradition and excludes family law. It was drawn up between 1869 and 1876 by a commission headed by Ahmet Cevdet Pasha.

official (and still unpaid) holiday was changed from Friday to Sunday starting on Saturday at 1 pm. The main reason for this change was to avoid economic losses and synchronize Turkey with western capitalist markets. It can also be interpreted as a response to workers' demands for a weekend holiday. In the same manner, the 1935 law restricted the working day to nine hours. Another reason for changing the official holiday from Friday to Sunday was the republic's secularization policies. For a long time, at least in state offices, schools and universities, going to Friday prayers and saying daily prayers more generally was quite unpopular, though later, after the transition to a multi-party system in 1945, these practices gained more and more in popularity. Having a pair of plastic sleepers that men use when washing their feet during their ablutions underneath or next to their desks or carrying a *seccade*[154] under one's armpit were ways of making a political statement against the secular arrangements of the public space. Today, many medium or large workplaces, state offices, schools and universities have several *mescit*s[155] and several nearby mosques in their neighbourhoods. It is certainly more practical and politically legitimate for one person to conform freely to Sunni practice nowadays, and also more popular than before. Despite these changes, however, it would be too straightforward to assume that the number of people who regularly say daily prayers or go to the mosque has increased as exponentially as the number of *mescit*s and mosques everywhere in Turkey. In fact, since 2018 there has been a public discussion in Turkey over whether the young are distancing themselves from religious duties and leaning towards deism and atheism instead.

Namaz in the Workplace

According to a survey of 'Religious Life in Turkey', conducted by the Directorate of Religious Affairs in 2014, 42.5% of the whole population, 34.8% of men, 49.2% of women and 29.4% of the employed always say the daily prayers. Among the different low-impact factors involved, one is women's low employment rates (27.1% in 2014, based on the Turkish Statistical Institute's data), as there is a roughly 15% difference between men and women always saying their prayers, and around the same percentage difference from the employed people's rate in comparison to the whole population. For the latter, the daily rhythm of work is itself a major factor. Nevertheless, employment is almost as central to people's lives as prayers are to religious belief, and this seems to create a controversy

---

[154] A small carpet one lays on the floor as a prayer mat.
[155] A standard room where the floor is covered with carpet, especially for people to do their prayers.

between the two spheres with which both workers and employers deal their own ways.

My experience and observations of Çorum show that whether the daily prayers are said, and if so their frequency and the role they play in the worker-employer relationship, depends first on the size of the workplace and second on the community the employer belongs to. As explained in the Introduction, industry in Çorum is dispersed into three main areas. In the lower industry, there are mainly car-repair shops that seem very disorganized and dilapidated from the outside and where the work is mainly piecework and task-oriented, carried out by at most five workers. In these small work places, one can find the time to say the daily prayers if that does not get in the way of the work that needs to be done, whether a tyre change or a motor check. The upper industry, on the other hand, is composed of small-size manufacturing workshops with up to fifteen workers on average. As with the lower industry, the rule of thumb is not to let daily prayers get in the way of your work. Lastly, in the organized industry zone, the factories seem quite modern and follows rather a time-discipline type of regime. In most of them, as now in many state buildings and schools, there would be a *mescit* at every workplace, if not for the workers or even the employers themselves, then for any customers who might ask for it. However, in many sectors it is rare to spare time for the daily prayers, while even going to toilet too many times would upset the managers and employers, and the permitted breaks are already very short. Being occupied with one's work and even seeming to do it during working hours is imperative. During working hours, the work routine and the tasks to be completed are the priority. As the Directorate of Religious Affair's survey (2014) revealed, already one third of the men (because in the industry it is mainly men who work there) have the habit of saying the daily prayers. I would argue that this would be the case even less in the private sector and in the younger age groups, assuming we could access the segmented data of private and public sectors and different age groups.

The frequency of the practice of praying at the workplace can also depend on which community the employer belongs to. Very simply, the different communities can be defined as consisting of pious or non-pious Alevis or Sunnis. In all three settings described above, but especially in the lower and upper industry, the workers follow the custom of the employer: that is, if the employer is a pious Sunni who prays regularly or shares cultural habits with the workers, then the worker who wants to say the daily prayers has a legitimate ground for doing so himself as well. In Çor-Mak, whose history and structure I have extensively written about in Chapter 4, together with the relations of family and non-family workers and employers in Chapter 6, the manager, Fatih, is a second cousin of the co-owner, Cemal Bey. Both started as apprentices when they were teenagers and basically grew up on the shop floor, and both are pious Muslims with similar cultural habits. In Çor-Mak, around one third of the workers say the afternoon prayer, as that coincides with the tea break at 15:30, and even fewer say the other two prayers, one in the morning and other at midday. There is a *mescid* and a separate place to do one's ablution. Fatih's explanation for the arrangement is as follows:

> For example, here, we have three times of prayers. If the boss wants, he has the right to ask everyone not to do the *sunna* (non-obligatory) parts. Our bosses let us be. ... But to *farz* (obligatory)! He cannot say anything about *farz*! But he can say 'Fellas, you are taking away from my work time, that is why I don't want you to do the *sunna* parts!' That is his right. And no one can object to that. But to *farz*! He too cannot object to that. Everyone can do their *farz*.

As we understand matters from Fatih's point of view, he and Cemal Bey agree that nobody can object to workers performing the *farz* parts of a daily prayer and affirm that God's law is above the boss's rule. This lays the basis for regular religious practice at the workplace, each performance of which punctuates the working day for at least ten minutes.

If the employer were a non-pious Sunni or an Alevi, he would not openly tell the workers not to spare time for prayer, but then the basis for agreement would be different. Bülent Bey, the other co-owner of Çor-Mak who is a non-pious Sunni and who has no interest in religious topics and practices, explains his position as follows:

> Bülent Bey: In the office, there are people you cannot find when you look for them. Where is he? Went to do his prayers.
> Ceren: On Fridays, you mean?
> Bülent Bey: No, this happens during the day, it can be at midday or in the afternoon. They cannot do it on the shop floor, but if this becomes the order of things, it would start on the shop floor too. But how do you stand against this? Then comes freedom of religion, things like one wanting to do the prayers. Then avoiding this becomes a severe problem, we don't make an issue out of it. I am sure there are places where such problems occur.

It is hard to believe that Bülent Bey, who is always there during working hours, is unaware that some of his workers on the shop floor are doing their daily prayers, but as he also half-heartedly admits, for the sake of freedom of Sunni religious practice he overlooks the fact, so the workers do not turn it into a serious demand. Whether on Cemal Bey's or Bülent Bey's terms, overlooking the loss of time caused by the practice of Sunni religious rituals is not always feasible and is very open to abuse. In all cases, no matter how religious the employer is, disappearing from the workplace very regularly would attract a lot of attention for the managers and one's fellow workers, would be considered wasting time and shirking, and therefore would not be tolerated. In fact, not even pious employers themselves, such as Cemal Bey or his manager Fatih, always find the time because there are workers to be organized and monitored, calls to be made, tasks to be completed and so on. It might also be the case that the more pious prefer to do something else, instead of saying the daily prayers. For example, Cemal Bey likes to play billiards with his guests and his partner Bülent Bey in the afternoons in the saloon across from his office. Towards the final months of my fieldwork, after Ramadan in summer, Fatih himself was complaining that the workers had become too relaxed and undisciplined, so to exert their authority over the workers, he told me that the bosses had banned the practice of saying the daily prayers. While the final decision was made by both Cemal Bey and Bülent Bey, we understand that Fatih's point of view that the bosses can never object to *farz* prayers is an over-dramatization of the situation. I cannot predict whether the ban will last, but it is very likely that Fatih will bring the issue up again, as he values the *farz* prayers so much. Nonetheless, a regular practice that requires discipline and dedication in its own logic of time but which conflicts with the daily work rhythm can inevitably tail off in the ordinary flow of work life, especially in the private sector.

While it is still manageable to have a few workers saying the daily prayers in the manufacturing sector, where the workers and the employer share a common understanding of religious practice, this mainly occurs in the smaller work places, the issue being treated differently in the service sector. In the OzanTicaret marketing company, besides the office personnel who do the accounting, the workers were either salesmen, deliverers or warehouse keepers. The salesmen and the deliverers were regularly on the road driving and visiting customers, taking orders or delivering goods, whereas the warehouse-keepers were moving heavy packages around the warehouse and filling the new lorries with them. They were always in a hurry, racing against time because all the orders are taken and the deliveries made on a daily basis. In this daily work rhythm, it was not possible for them to do anything else, let alone say the daily prayers. While in this company the owner Eren Bey and his wife and the co-owner Yasemin Hanım were all Alevis who do not practice the Sunni rituals, the Sunnis working in Ozan Ticaret did not say the prayers either.

It is important to bear in mind that saying the daily prayers is not a direct indicator of one's religiosity. According to the Directorate of Religious Affairs' survey (2014), 19.6% of the whole population, 20.4% of men, 13.6% of women and 21.5% of the employed never say the daily prayers, and 8.8 of the whole population, 11% of men, 6.6% of women and 11.9 % of the employed, rarely say them. It could also be the case that these people are not religious at all, have not developed the habit of praying, or think that the belief in one's heart and one's intention are more important than the practice itself. Sema Hanım, a believing Sunni in her mid-fifties originally from Denizli who has lived in Çorum all of her adult life and is now the co-owner of a building audit company, explained the latter situation by means of a tale (*masal*) told her by her grandmother:

> A man converts to Islam in the first years of the religion, but he doesn't know how to do the religious service. He wanted to do *namaz* in his own way. He didn't know how or who would do it. Then he put a stick on the ground and read some *dua*s jumping over the stick from one side to the other. One guy passing by says, 'What are you doing? Are you crazy?' He says that he is doing *namaz*. The guy replies, 'Is this the proper way to do it! You don't even know how to do it; what kind of Muslim are you?' Then they died, both went to the other side and stood side by side during the interrogation. The one who had been jumping over the stick had all his *namaz* accepted, but the other did not. The guy asks 'Why? I did all my *namaz* in the proper way, but he was jumping over a stick'. Then the angel replied to him, saying, 'But when you were doing your *namaz*, you were always wondering what others would do, whereas he thought of that stick as *namaz* with all his heart and jumped over it. What matters is not the form of the *namaz* but the intention of the person'. When you were brought up with this kind of teaching, you become a person like me.

Friday Prayers

On the issue of daily prayers, in the tug-of-war between religious time and work time, it seems that work time tended to win. However, one cannot argue the same for Friday prayers. As I stressed at the beginning of this chapter, Friday has a greater symbolic value for both worldly affairs and the afterlife. Bülent Bey previously alluded to the fact that it would create a serious demand if the saying of prayers in the workplace were banned. Asking workers not to go to the Friday prayers would create an even stronger reaction. I never encountered employers with such expectations of their workers in the small and medium-size workplaces I visited, despite the fact that the majority of these employers (who were included in the survey) did not go to Friday prayers themselves (see Table 2). In the cross-tabulation I derived from the survey results, of a sample of thirty employers, eleven of the nineteen Sunni employers and none of the Alevi employers attend religious services once a week or more than once a week.[156] On the other hand, if we had segmented data for going to Friday prayers based on class or income, we might have a slightly different picture.

Table 2. How often employers of different beliefs attend religious services

		Do you attend religious services? And if yes, how often?							
		practically never	once a year	only on special holy days	once a month	once a week	more than once a week	no answer	total
If you belong to a religious belief, please specify:	belief is not specified	1	0	0	0	0	0	1	2
	Alevi	3	4	1	0	0	0	1	9
	Sunni	2	0	5	1	6	5	0	19
Total (n)		6	4	6	1	6	5	2	30

Bülent Bey, after returning to Turkey at the beginning of the 1990s after his training in engineering in Germany, remembers going to the industrial zone in Ankara one Friday lunchtime. He says groups of workers were coming out in force towards him, so at first he thought there was a strike going on, and then he realized that the workers were going to Friday prayers. His eyes were wide open as he remarked that we wouldn't have gone like that in my youth. I had a similar experience when passing through the upper industry, which you enter from a gate with most of the workplaces on the left-hand side of the road and the mosque on the right-hand side. Many men were heading from left to right in crowds. While passing through them, I didn't even realize at first that they were the workers of the upper industry and was puzzled for a moment. Cemal Bey, who is maybe ten years younger than his partner, also told me that when he was an apprentice and later a master working in the construction of flour factories all over Turkey in the early

---

[156] I consider 'once a week' denotes attendance at Friday prayers; if 'more than once a week' is marked, then it also includes Friday prayers. Two of the thirty employers in my sample were women.

1980s, it was not very usual for his elderly superiors to go to Friday prayers. Today things have changed such that the spectacle of workers going to Friday prayers has become the norm, with varying time-arrangements among workplaces.

For Friday prayers, almost everywhere lunch hours are stretched and the absence of those who have gone to the mosque is overlooked. In most places in both the lower and upper industry there is no a fixed lunchtime, and Fridays are more relaxed. Ahmet Bey, who runs a car-repair shop with his sister and occasionally goes to Friday prayers interchangeably with his workers, tells me unapprovingly that sometimes the owners of other shops do not even wear their overalls in the morning and wait until midday for the prayers. He thinks their behaviour has a bad effect on the workers and ruins the overall work discipline. It is, of course, quite different in organized industry. The example I know best is Çor-Mak, where the regular lunch starts at 12:15 and ends at 13:15, but on Fridays for those who go to Friday prayers alone it starts at 11:45 and ends at 13:30. This means that mosque-goers are given a longer break, whereas others keep to the regular schedule. Once the first bell rings at 11:45, Çor-Mak workers first go to the changing rooms, take off their overalls, do their ablutions, wash off the dirt, grease and sweat on their faces and hands, and put clean clothes on. When they come out of the changing room, they look totally different from what they did ten minutes earlier, not least with shining smiles on their faces, chatting and joking with one another while walking towards the bus that will take them to the mosque. Later on, I realized that this was almost the same as how they looked and behaved when finally going back home at the end of their shift. Apart from the belief that Friday prayers are worth much more than a regular prayer in the afterlife, it provides workers with a break from work during which they enjoy being their individual selves, wearing their own clothes, showing off their care of their bodies and being part a collective.

One of the initial aims of my work was to explore the various pre-industrial customs that were being carried on in Turkish industry, the assumption being that the persistence of religious customs causes irregularities in a factory's time-discipline. However, with this observation I argue further that the overwhelming nature of industrial discipline brings out a new layer of meanings that is attached to religious custom, in this case Friday prayers, which provide workers with an opportunity to relax and socialize with their peers and bond with the rest of the Muslim community on what is otherwise a workday. Friday prayers offer a legitimate reason for downing tools.

In the absence of Cemal Bey and Fatih, who have gone to Friday prayers with the others, those who did not go to Friday prayers find the space to slow down their work before their shift starts, even though their lunch hours have not changed. Those left in the office are only Bülent Bey, his son Ulaş and four women workers. While Bülent Bey is in his office, Ulaş goes out for another smoke, the women sometimes accompany him, or they all stay in the office surfing the internet while waiting for the others to return.

On one occasion, when Ulaş, I and two of the women – Elif the secretary and Sevim, one of the accountants, who are both Alevis – were standing outside the entrance watching the workers go to Friday prayers, Sevim made cynical comments about the scene that presented itself to them. She laughed and she asked rhetorically: 'So, they will go and do their *namaz* and come back saved from their sins?' For her, the public show of religiosity and the simple arithmetic of sins and good deeds were hypocritical: having a clear conscience was enough to be a good person or a Muslim. The underlying context of her attitude lies in the disturbance Alevis feel towards the direct link that had been established historically, institutionally and politically (see Chapter 3) between Sunni belief and practice and high morality. This is reflected in everyday life as a burning need to emphasize the fact that Alevis are as moral as Sunnis, despite their not performing orthodox religious practices.

Especially on Fridays, Sunni practice is overwhelmingly visible and predominant, perhaps not in the same way that upset Sevim, but any man who doesn't attend Friday prayers will be asked to go insistently. To avoid this, Bülent Bey says that he does not visit customers on Fridays if he knows they will insist on attending prayers. Normally, Bülent Bey likes to ride his bike in the industrial zone during the lunch breaks, but that is something he cannot do on Fridays. He says that he waits until it is over and then goes out with his bike. When I ask why, he says:

> It is not very important that I don't go [to Friday prayers], but if I make it obvious in public that I'm not going, they would bitterly resent me, they would get angry and hold a grudge against me. They won't say anything if I don't go, but if I do it is like an official flag, they would take offense. There is no need to present myself to them as someone outside this place. Anatolia is not that easy ... Some people know, but there is a difference between knowing and showing. They can't say anything if they know, and they'd tolerate it, but if I make a show of it they wouldn't accept it ... We have these difficulties in our country, but there is not much that can be done about it, as it is our country too.

Bülent Bey comes from one of the known families with roots in Çorum, a respected member of his community. Nonetheless, he has to hide in his office until Friday prayers are over so he can ride his bike in the industrial zone, where the factories are spread over quite a wide area and are connected with one another with fairly broad roads extending beyond walking distance. Although Sevim's cynical comment about the Friday prayers sounded judgmental on her part in a context where even her employer has to hide, as we shall see in the next section on Ramadan arrangements, as a minimum-wage Alevi woman worker she is more vulnerable to the Sunni dominance under which those who prefer not to take part are easily judged and isolated.

So far, I have described how, on Fridays, the religious apprehension of time reflects the arrangement of working hours more significantly than daily prayers and has an impact on others as well. The imposition of time-discipline is reversed to impose a religious time-discipline on this occasion. However, this does not mean the custom being followed changes the work rhythm: in fact it might be the other way, namely that the custom acquires new meanings in the industrial setting and causes new problems for those who do not identify with the Sunni practice of Islam. I will now demonstrate how a month's worth of Fridays creates even more significant irregularities in working hours, together with deeper conflicts.

Slowing Down Work While Fasting: Ramadan Arrangements

In Islam, as in many other belief systems, fasting is regarded as a religious duty. The purpose of fasting is to discipline the body and strengthen the faith. For those who follow the Sunni tradition of fasting during the month of Ramadan, as indicated by the Hijri calendar, all worldly pleasures, such as eating, drinking, smoking and sexual contact, should be avoided from sunrise to sunset. The Alevis, on the other hand, fast for twenty days in the month of Muharrem. This follows the same logic as Sunni fasting, but in addition Alevis do not drink water for the whole twenty days, commemorating the fact that Caliph Ali's son Hüseyin's army was left thirsty for days before being slaughtered by the Ummayyad Caliph Yazid (see Chapter 3). Alevis rarely fast during Ramadan, and there is a significant percentage of Sunnis who do not fast. Nonetheless the majority holding the dominant belief do fast, and the municipality organizes Ramadan celebrations with prayers and social events in the evenings, unlike the month of Muharrem, which is never marked in public life.

During the daytime in Ramadan most places are like a ghost town. Here in Çorum, most restaurants and cafés on the main streets are closed until the evening prayer, except for a few student cafés in the city centre and those few in the Alevi neighbourhood and the upper district where mainly middle-class people live. These cafes are full from breakfast to late at night, especially at lunchtime, when they probably make their best profits of the year. Others, on the other hand, organize evening meals to break the fast, called *iftar*, and so compensate for their losses in daytime and serve Sunnis after the fasting ends.

The special situation in 2016, as for a few previous years, was that the month of Ramadan started on 6th June and ended on 5th July, when the seasonal length of daytime was the longest of the year (from 3-4 am to 8-9 pm) and it was around 38 degrees Celsius all day. Those who don't work but do fast spend most of the hot day at home sleeping and resting, only going to bed after their last meal at 3 am. Those who work the normal workday hours from 8 am to 6 pm are exhausted. One can observe their movements slowing down, and they think and talk more slowly, postpone appointments and only deal with things they find necessary or absolutely important. Those who have the luxury to slow down are mostly the employers, but the workers must slow down as well. Of course, there are some who do not fast. I had the impression that many of those in the upper industry especially did not fast when I went to a restaurant hidden behind a nylon tarp stretched across the outside, where I had lunch with many others during Ramadan.

Ahmet Bey, whom I referred to earlier in this chapter as the owner of a car-repair shop in the upper industry, doesn't fast anymore because the year before he felt dizzy and hurt his head while repairing a car. He complained about his business slowing down because other workplaces and clients fast and people rarely want their cars repaired in a normal daytime. The existence of a religious apprehension of time simultaneously with time discipline is more obvious in Ramadan than with the daily prayers or Friday prayers, and Ramadan seems to make work very difficult. In fact, the religious apprehension of time seems to undermine the urge to make a profit that is crucial to the time-discipline. Exactly for this reason, in Ramadan alternative work arrangements are made based on the apprehension of cultural/religious time. I will illustrate this with examples taken from three firms in different sectors and run by people from different communities in order to show how multiple time reckonings can co-exist.

Changing working hours during Ramadan is not only specific to restaurants and cafés, it is also practised in Çorum's industrial zone. The usual practice in this zone is to shorten the working hours by two or three hours and let the workers go home early. I heard in some workplaces that employers make their workers work two to three hours more in the previous month to compensate for the hours they miss during Ramadan, but this seems rare and might be only a rumour. As the work in these factories is largely physical, the apprehension of religious time seems to involve an ethical stand on the part of the employers, as well as a pragmatic choice.

In the specific example of Çor-Mak, the working hours were shortened and adapted to the hours of fasting. Cemal Bey explains that this was a decision he made with Fatih and other workers when Ramadan coincided with the summer few years ago. The daily working hours from 8 am to 6:30 pm were shifted to 4 am to 12 am for the blue-collar workers and 8 am to 5 pm for the white-collar workers. At the same time, the daily lunch service was cancelled for a month, and the cook and the tea staff were given a month-long paid holiday. The regular one-hour lunch break was shortened to half an hour for the white-collar staff, regardless of their fasting habits. The idea behind this arrangement was to utilize the blue-collar workers' most efficient and productive hours and to have them start work just after the early morning prayer, which follows the early morning meal (*sahur*). This arrangement was adopted because it was felt that working while fasting would be less exhausting and that respecting the workers' customs would play a role in helping them adapt to the modern factory system, as Bülent Bey confirmed (cf. Gutman 1987). When I spoke to most of the workers, they seemed to like this arrangement because they manage to sleep after work until the evening prayer and then get up to eat their first meal (*iftar*). However, there were other workers who complained not about hunger or not being able to smoke, but sleep deprivation. One told me: 'My eyelids start falling down when I see the sun rising around 6', while another, who was an operator, said: 'Well, I cannot sleep in daylight, so I sleep when I start the machine, put my head down and sleep, and if the manager warns me, I say sorry'. I have also heard from other workers that, for example, one of them disappears for almost twenty minutes with the excuse of going to the toilet or the prayer room and sleeps there. Not only the blue-collar workers but also the white-collar workers, including the manager, Fatih, rested in the *mescit* during the noon prayer. One day the accountant, Osman, came back into the office in a rush saying that he fell asleep in the *mescit*, while another day I heard that Hatice, the woman in the technical drawing department, disappeared for almost two hours sleeping in the kitchen. As a result, the lunch break, which is shortened from an hour to half an hour in Ramadan, is prolonged for those who fast.

The reason I underline the words 'for those who fast' is that so much idleness, laziness and passing the time would otherwise never be allowed for anyone in this workplace except for those saying the daily prayers. This was a shock to me since I know the workers check in and out of the workplace every morning and evening with their ID cards, and that being late or absent without notice is fined by deducting the hours from their annual leave, while using mobile phones or chatting with other workers is not allowed in the manufacturing area, nor in the offices (see Chapter 7). However, now all of this not only could be seen but was tolerated. What is not taken into account in this arrangement is the possibility that some blue- or white-collar workers might not be fasting. In that case, the person concerned would follow the religious time arrangement, that is, would work from early morning and not eat for hours without having the religious commitment to follow the practice. I only knew that one of the blue-collar workers declared he did not fast for health reasons, and I can imagine that none of the others would dare to say that he or she is not fasting in conditions where everyone else is fasting and there is no food or water, not even if one does not fast. In Sunni-dominant circles, there is an almost visible pressure that one should fast if one is a Sunni, otherwise people would stare disapprovingly at one without commenting.

The exceptions to this were two Alevi white-collar woman workers, Elif and Sevim, as well as Bülent Bey and his recently graduated son Ulaş, who had just started working in the factory. They were the only people who did not fast openly; nevertheless, no lunch was served to them for a whole month. The reason why Bülent Bey and Ulaş had to endure hunger for a whole month was that Cemal Bey had recruited most of the workers from his village of origin and was also in charge of managing them, thus creating most of the workplace rules (see Chapter 6). Bülent Bey, his son, and Elif and Sevim had to order lunch or just eat some feta cheese, tomato and bread behind a closed kitchen door for a month. Elif also had to fill in for the tea lady, Sevda (who was given paid leave), whenever there was a guest who requested tea. Elif and Sevim had to swallow their words for a while, making eye contact with each other from time to time and pretending they did not feel discriminated against. All of this increased their sense of discomfort and provided them with new justifications for holding on to their cynicism as a way of dealing with their discrimination. As I have suggested already, just as time-discipline is imposed, the religious apprehension of time and the ethics that go with it are also imposed on the non-fasting people in the workplace. This time, not even Bülent Bey could avoid it. The next year, I heard that Cemal Bey ordered the factory cafeteria to be kept open during Ramadan. I am not sure if this was actually at Cemal Bey's orders or whether those who did not fast, apart from those who openly declared they were doing so, actually did have lunch. However, in a later communication of mine with one of the non-fasting Alevis, they said that they had gone to the cafeteria with their heads down, as they felt some kind of shame.

My second example comes from the marketing company, Ozan Ticaret, I have mentioned before. In this workplace, the working hours are quite flexible due to the nature of the work and do not require continuous presence in the office. Furthermore, some of the accountants and warehouse-workers occasionally stay late without overtime, unlike the factory I described above. Nonetheless, in this workplace there is no change to the working hours because this is not possible as it was in the factory. Lunch is served as normal during Ramadan. The only rule they had was not to bring food or drinks from the dining hall upstairs down to the offices downstairs, in order to show respect to those who were fasting and not to tempt their appetites while they were fulfilling their religious duty. In this workplace too, those who fasted were allowed to slow down the work, so some went to the first-aid room for a short nap during working hours. Eren Bey, who did not fast, would joke about those fasting, commenting on their slowness and clumsiness towards the end of the working day, but he and Yasemin Hanım still did not make a big deal out of the practice of taking a brief nap. Only Yasemin Hanım would sometimes suggest: 'If you feel really bad and sleepy while fasting, maybe you shouldn't fast because you can't work like that'. Since this place was a friendlier working environment from the start, with less strict rules, the employers' attitude was also balanced between the two sides. Here too, however, there was a multiple time-reckoning, but without the imposition of a religious apprehension of time.

Finally, we are at a window pane-designing company run by a devout Sunni man, Ahmet Keskin (see Chapter 5 for his origin story), and his young son and daughter. Although the work is quite difficult and requires some physical strength, they did not change or shorten their working hours for Ramadan. However, they cancelled the lunch service for a month and sent the dining hall staff on vacation. In this company, there was no multiple time-reckoning, but religious practice was imposed. This became clearer when Ahmet Keskin's daughter told me that almost half of the company's workers were Alevis. She told me this in order to give me the impression that they hire Alevis too, meaning they do not discriminate on the basis of religious belief. This shows that, even when Alevis are hired in large numbers in workplaces owned by devout Sunnis, their differences are ignored to the point that the dining hall is closed when at least half of the workers are not fasting. Conversely, having half the workers not fasting could also be a reason not to change or shorten their working hours. At least in this case the workplace was not in the industrial zone but in the upper industry, where non-fasting workers can easily find a restaurant open to order lunch for themselves. In the meantime, fasting workers could rest during at lunch time. During my visit, the employer's daughter also made a comment that explains why workplaces close their cafeterias during Ramadan. She said: 'I'm sorry, I don't know if you are fasting, but even if you're not, we cannot serve you tea or anything because we cannot have people drink tea in front of us when we are all fasting'. According to this logic, when some Muslims are doing their religious duty, they do not perceive it as a personal matter and expect others who perhaps cannot or do not want to fast to act according to the fasting rules. This was a striking contrast to Çor-Mak, where the cafeteria was closed because the majority were fasting and they could still at least offer tea or coffee to their guests. Thus, they had a less imposing attitude towards those who did not fast, workers or not.

Conclusion

In this chapter, I have discussed the meanings and significance of several religious customs and provided a brief historical background to the questions of when and as a response to which demands and conditions a workday and weekend were legally established. Subsequently I showed illustrated how religious customs are practiced in workplaces of different sizes (small and medium) in different sectors (car-repairs, marketing, machine production) with different apprehensions of time (task-oriented, time-oriented or a mixture of both) that are run by people from different religious communities (partnership of one devout and one non-religious Sunni, only Alevi and only Sunni). It is my conclusion that the most regular religious customs (daily prayers in this case) are more likely to cease to exist in workplaces first because people practice them less often, and second because its regularity and discipline are almost as demanding as the work discipline itself, hence such practice would create more conflicts. Therefore they do not entirely survive but are also not completely abandoned depending on the employer's life-style (more so in task-oriented contexts).

Friday prayers and Ramadan fasting arrangements, on the other hand, persist mainly because of their collective character and because they disrupt working hours less frequently than the daily prayers. Unlike what Bülent Bey and Cemal Bey say about the past, workers today seem to participate in Friday prayers more often. In that regard, and bearing in mind that it was the demand of Ottoman-era workers to have not Friday but the weekend off as their official holiday, I hesitate to say that going to Friday prayers represents the persistence of a pre-industrial custom that might have been revived in recent decades due to the increasing encouragement and therefore popularity of Islamic practices, and as a response to the overwhelming nature of work based on time-discipline. Of course, we need further historical evidence and statistical figures to argue this solidly, but I suggest that going to Friday prayers is more than a matter of following God's order. It also provides some relief from work, a chance to care for one's self and one's solidarity with the collective. Those who do not follow the practice also use this time to relax during working hours, a matter of relief for all employees. It therefore has an impact on the workers that makes the working day more bearable. Shirking, slowing down the work and creating irregular patterns are possible even within the most strict workplaces, where religious customs tends more to persist.

However, as religious apprehensions of time co-exist with time-discipline (or task-orientation), they can become as much of an imposition as the latter. Tolerance, connivance and public expressions of personal positions on certain issues fall into the domain of the Sunni, who enjoy religious privileges, while others need to hide their differences from Sunnis in order to maintain their positions and status in the workplace or in society in the wider sense. In Çorum, having segregated neighbourhoods of Alevis and Sunnis aids people in having smoother daily experiences because they do not cross each other's boundaries. On the other hand, at a formal workplace where people are fairly mixed, conflicts and disturbances are created that both sides have to deal with in order to keep the business going. While in some cases the effort is two-sided, as we have seen, in other cases people deal with being ignored and discriminated against by remaining silent, not making a public spectacle of themselves, and from time to time relieving the tensions by making cynical jokes about the situation they find themselves in.

Chapter 9
Conclusion

Findings and Arguments of the Research

I started this research to explore the intermingled relationships between religion, morality and the economy in a provincial context in parallel with the aims of the REALEURASIA project under which this study was funded. The task was to investigate the various moral and religious frameworks in which economic behaviour is rooted in different civilizational contexts with the help of the theoretical tool kits offered by the discussion of the Protestant ethic of Max Weber, the notions of the moral economy of E. P. Thompson and James Scott, and the more recent study of family firms by Sylvia Yanagisako. In the context of Turkey, one of the most recent and lively debates of relevance to the core topics of this project was the literature on the so-called 'Anatolian Tigers'. This was therefore the first place I delved into during the initial preparations for my research. This literature offered a good starting point for insights into the formation of Islamic capital, the motivations of Islamic businesspeople and the implications of their economic success in Anatolia. However, as I showed in the Introduction, I found that, except for a few elaborate studies on these matters, this literature failed to grasp the full complexities of local economies, oversimplified the diversity of the actors involved and their histories, and finally exaggerated the impacts of local economies on national economic development and political change. In Chapter 3 I also pointed out that this particular reading and discussion of Turkish political life had been stuck in a dichotomy between centre and periphery, imported from the work of Max Weber by Şerif Mardin in the early 1970s[157] and until recently still accepted as the 'master narrative', as Deniz Kandiyoti (2012) rightly argued. In fact, the centre/periphery framework provided a theoretical background to the 'Anatolian Tigers' literature and was highly problematic. Uncovering a

---

[157] See Toumarkine (2014) for a discussion of how Weber's thought was perceived and circulated in Turkish academia.

puzzle that was somehow blurred by the ideological and political uses to which the Weberian framework had been put, I came to realize that I cannot solve this puzzle using Weber's theses about 'world religions' or the spirit of capitalism because this seemed to be the point at which the literature went wrong by implicating self-Orientalization and extreme exceptionalism. Therefore, my initial motivations drifted away from Weberian interpretations and leaned towards a more materialistic understanding of the particular economic developments that are the focus of this book. Accordingly, I have shifted the focus from the role of Islam and Islamic belief to the role of regional and personal histories and conditions, as well as individual and collective values, in the formation of local industries. My experiences and observations during fieldwork provided the main encouragement for doing this, since none of my respondents specifically talked about their beliefs as having a particular role in the process of formation, rather, as shown in Chapter 4, they told a different story. My personal and scholarly motivation in this book was to convey this different story, one I was told by people in Çorum, and thus give substance to the 'local' people, their histories and aspirations, which are not solely driven by belief but also by numerous other factors that are woven into the complexity of family, livelihood, self-realization, household autonomy and reputation. The role of Islam came into the picture more substantially in sustaining the businesses rather than in forming them.

In line with my motivations, I studied the emergence, expansion and sustaining of small and medium-size firms and the role of values, customs, religion, family and kinship in these long-term material processes in the central Anatolian province of Çorum in Turkey. I focused on the social reproduction of capitalism in Çorum and its relationship with 'value regimes' in small and medium-size companies. Throughout the study, I have used the term 'value' in a two-fold sense: first from a bottom-up perspective, which also considers institutional meanings of worth and what is worthy in a given society; and second as the relational mechanisms that turn labour into value in local and global processes of capital accumulation. Drawing on long-term ethnographic research, I looked at how these two understandings of 'value' are enmeshed in the conjunction of local and global capitalism as they are enacted through manifold agents and patterns in Çorum. Thus, I contribute to the field of economic anthropology, and more specifically to recent discussions about the moral economy and the anthropology of work and labour.

The economic developments that are the focus of this book are conceptualized within a larger theory and discourse on the post-1980 phenomenon of 'regional economies' emerging on the peripheries of the global capitalist system. The drastic changes in the global economy due to the crisis of Fordism have generated intense scholarly interest in understanding the latter by analysing new developments in capitalism and identifying a 'successor to Fordism'. Scholars have attempted to pick a successor to Fordism using various concepts such as 'post-Fordism' or 'flexible accumulation' and have identified new models of the organization of production, such as 'flexible specialization', independently operating 'industrial districts' and 'Japanization', all of which scholars have found in the clusters of small and medium-size firms in these emerging peripheries. These 'models' are considered to be alternatives to the 'Fordist' accumulation regime; they all suggest a radical break from the previous era and emphasize the roles of community, trust, cooperation and culture in producing the efficacy and profitability of these new regional economies. However, some others – including anthropologists – have criticized these 'ready-made' formulas for failing to understand the realities on the ground. I have followed this critical tradition in this work.

Accordingly, I have placed Çorum in the framework of the phenomenon of regional economies for the following reasons. First, the economic developments that occurred in Çorum after the 1980s took place mainly in small and medium-size manufacturing companies clustered in industrial urban districts. They were referred to as 'Çorum's model of development' and were said to be based on a 'culture of partnership' and 'entrepreneurial spirit' within the larger rhetoric of the 'Anatolian Tigers', as well as being seen as one of the new centres of industry and wealth creation. In fact, the models identified in regional studies have also been adapted to some extent in order to achieve economic efficiency and increase profitability. This book has critically engaged with these 'models' by adopting a combination of a political economy and a moral economy approach to understand the emergence and social reproduction of capitalism in the industrializing town of Çorum. Accordingly, in Chapter 4 I questioned the ahistorical typology of the 'Çorum model of development' and the claims of an 'entrepreneurial spirit' or 'culture of partnership' in the public rhetoric by demonstrating how they emerged historically, what made them work in real life and their significance throughout the process. To be able to do this, I traced the social and occupational histories of the contemporary entrepreneurial stratum in Çorum from the beginning of the twentieth century and demonstrated the various methods of capital accumulation, including the dispossession of non-Muslims and the removal of intermediaries, as well as the role of merchant capital and money-lending mechanisms.

In addition, I looked at the role of cooperation and transfers of skills among Çorum people, as well as the fragmentation and self-exploitation of labour, which among the relational mechanisms of capitalist valorization that have longer roots in the social transformation that preceded the 'break' in economic policy in the 1980s. This chapter also drew attention to the importance of understanding industrial districts as part of a developmentalist program launched by the Turkish state with immense tax and labour-cost reductions, as well as cheap land and utility fees. These were often neglected in business people's testimonies and overlooked in the related literature. Contrary to the claim that these districts are independent, I showed how smaller suppliers and subcontractors within and outside these districts are connected with those in the industrial district through reciprocal networks and by participating in surplus creation in Çorum and transfers of skills down the generations. I also argued that the role of Islamic business associations in Çorum's industrial development has been limited and that its business people have not been able to exploit political connections as much as in other provinces. This, I contend, is mainly a result of the Alevi community in Çorum being not fully incorporated into the Sunni Muslim hegemony historically and therefore still having economic and political power that challenges the rule of majoritarian political (i.e. Sunni) Islam and obstructs the demands made on it by the central government.

Chapter 5 was designed to bring out the moral frameworks that were rooted in business peoples' economic decision-making. It looked at the business stratum in Çorum by focusing on their motivations and aspirations and their changing relationship to 'work' over the course of their lives, with many starting out as labourers and later becoming employers. The chapter mainly questioned the idea of 'neoliberal subjectivity' that is generally attributed to entrepreneurs in the 21st century by juxtaposing the survey results with ethnographic data on their perspectives on the meaning of work. My data showed how some have adopted the 'neoliberal' discourse, blending it into locally embedded understandings of personhood, which is very much associated with the process of self-realization through work and enterprise. In addition, I showed that 'work' is not felt to be an end in itself, as argued by Weber in his thesis of the Protestant work ethic; rather, it is valued as a means to provide for the family and educate the children from the firm's profits. Hence, succession to the firm by the next generation was not the primary expectation of business owners. The patriarchal desire to 'father' both a firm and a family as parallel pursuits was not evident here when it came to handing the firm on to the next generation, but it did manifest itself in how business owners identify their own personhood with their family names and enterprises. These businessmen often gave their motives for starting their enterprises as ambition and resentment as a result of how they, as manual workers, saw themselves in relation to their fellow men. Their stories were also marked by a narrative of suffering and a desire to close the perceived gap between themselves and other men. In cases of the loss of a father or a betrayal by brothers, businessmen expressed sentiments of envy, anger and ambition, which played the role of forces of production in establishing both a new family and a company. However, these incidents can also lead to the estrangement of brothers, downsizing and despair, which can cause, if not the demise of the firm and the family, at least the loss of its reputation. Indeed, reputation stood out as the central notion in businessmen's lives because it connects the enterprise, the family name, the businessman himself and his honour. Untainted reputations depend on years cultivating trust among business partners, in accordance with the emic understanding of the 'work ethic', and they must be sustained as such.

The combination of the political economy and moral economy approaches enabled me to take the historical and relational processes of capital accumulation and class-making into account, which led me to question the radical breaks in both the historical trajectory of the local industry and the personal 'becoming' stories of Çorum's business people. Moreover, this approach helped me incorporate the role of local cultural values into the economic decision-making processes that shape the making and sustaining of businesses and that are shaped dialectically by the influence of the global trajectory of capitalism. Apart from the focus on the emergence of small and medium-size capital in Çorum and the processes of class-making, attention was paid to the organization of production and the role of the community, cooperation and trust, mutual expectations and obligations, and autonomy in work-places in the third part of this work. I showed that the prevalence of these ideas is not the *result* of the adoption of post-Fordist models; rather, they are *pre-existing* modes of conduct that enabled capital accumulation. Among the pre-existing modes of conduct are primordial ties to places of origin, kin ties and family relations, as well as paternalism, all of which I deal with in Chapter 6.

In Chapter 6, I discussed the morality and politics behind recruiting, promoting and laying off co-villagers, kin and family members in work-places. As I showed using cases of distant relatives and co-villagers as well as family members, imbalances in reciprocity can end by discarding the relationship depending on how threatening the imbalance becomes to the interests of the company. A degree of relatedness can be a hiring strategy in the initial stages of a business, but merit and skill are required if the long-term moral aspect is to emerge in less close relationships. Even when long-term morality or a moral aspect of an economic relationship is present in kinship, the content of the reciprocity matters. It is rather the mutuality of the goals and roles people identify with that makes the relationship work in favour of both business and kinship goals. The ethnographic examples in this work have also shown that these roles and goals in relation to kinship and business are not stable, but rather are constantly negotiated and open to challenge. Hence, morality is not the natural and stable component of kin ties, but one of its properties, which is set into motion by those involved. Imbalances in reciprocity are still more tolerable for those family members who are not as efficient for the company's purposes, and hence these enduring bonds are more 'moral'. This does not mean that they are not disposable or that the imbalance will be tolerated forever. The research showed that family employees negotiate debt-management strategies, extra benefits and promotions in return for loyalty and self-dedication. These negotiations not only implied deference and loyalty on the part of family employees, they also increased their chances of having a managerial position and inheritance, ensuring the security of their households' livelihoods and facilitating their own individual and household autonomy.

This chapter also showed how roles and obligations in a family or kin group are stretched paternalistically to include non-family employees through various incentives, Islamic and non-Islamic workplace rituals, and outdoor activities. These practices aim to cultivate workplace communities built around shared values and to compensate for low wages, flexible working hours and job insecurity in the absence of an organized labour movement. This did not mean that all the members of these work-place communities participated in or conformed to the shared values expected of them by their employers. Still, the data showed that both Sunni and Alevi employers saw themselves as responsible for their workers, but how they fulfilled this responsibility depended on their personal perceptions of what is valuable in life and what constitutes the common good. In this chapter in particular, situating people with different levels of relatedness to employers and to decision-making processes and their actions and decisions within a moral economy perspective helped to overcome preconceived differences, thus displaying the common moral obligations and expectations that transcend Sunni/Alevi or pious Muslim/secular dichotomies.

While paternalistic provisioning can help workers identify with the work-places and their employers, as well as compensate for low wages, Chapter 7 looks more deeply into the ways in which employers secure surplus value through the rules, regulations and management techniques of the work-place. This chapter shows that, although time-discipline and thrift are externally imposed, notions like industrial discipline, industrial worker, industrial habits and thrift have become integrated into the local employer's vocabulary and practice of managing a business. I also showed the locally specific ways and values in which these management techniques are implemented. The changes in the factory regime have led to changes in the social structure of the factory, which were first met with resistance but later re-established power relations between management and workers, senior and young workers, skilled and unskilled workers, women and men. The ways rules, regulations and management techniques were understood, enacted and received revealed the areas of consent and coercion. Rather than classifying the labour regime as hegemonic or despotic, I have identified the rules, regulations and management techniques that were perceived as coercive or consensual respectively and tried to understand the relationship between them. Both consent and coercion were symbolically expressed through the values that unite and/or divide the workers from their employers, namely respect, loyalty, deservingness and gratitude.

The ethnographic findings of Chapter 7 showed that the rules and regulations that were put in place to generate labour effort oscillate between domination and asymmetrical reciprocity. The working conditions that have been achieved in the workplace and conveyed to the employers through the manager concern the quality of the lunch, freedom of Sunni religious practice and the space/time provided for it and allow the beverage *ordering* game and the reallocation of work time to other days so that Saturdays remain free. In reality, however, this did not reduce the total working hours for the week, which in this factory are already above the legal limit. The purpose of these low-cost improvements is to *persuade* the workers to work longer hours more efficiently, and they also secure the *surplus value* and constitute the realm of *consent*. Although threats and surveillance are widespread, workers consider the discipline necessary as long as these conditions occur and their wages are paid on time; hence the belief in the bosses' fairness is strong. Moreover, the values of respect and loyalty that generated labour effort as a non-strategic response from the workers have largely been internalized. However, some of the surveillance and disciplining involved reflects the distrust of employers and the manager of the workers, thus forcing the latter to display their loyalty constantly. These incidents are rather strategic, and consent is based on the fear of being fired or falling from favour, though expressed as a silent murmuring of anger. Displays of loyalty and gratitude can also be non-strategic expressions of consent, as was the case for the prayer that some workers organized for their bosses. Even at this theatrical moment, the workers implied that their consent was conditional.

Another management strategy at this company was leaving workers in uncertainty about pay increases and holidays and constantly reminding them that they should deserve them. Although workers found daily threats to maintain discipline during working hours fair, they did not think the same about the way their free time was controlled or the rhetoric of 'deserving'. These moments created anger and resentment, which, however, was also not expressed openly. The wages, periods of leave and actual time off work could not be negotiated, discussed or even brought up by any worker with either the manager or the employer. These are high-cost improvements that would directly lead to conflict and are therefore avoided by means of strict *despotic* measures and the threat of being laid off. Avoiding these conflict-ridden areas, which are essential to labour relations, is only possible within the ambit of the state restructuring of individual labour laws and the depoliticizing of the collective labour laws, which demarcates the framework of the relations described in this chapter.

Chapter 8 built on the previous chapter further by offering an anthropological interpretation of the discussions on the imposition of industrial time in the literature on labour history. It looked at the exceptions to time-discipline in the organization of the daily life of work-places. It showed how the strict rules and measures described in the previous chapter were breached in the performance of religious practices and rituals during working hours in Çorum. I focused on these religious practices, namely daily prayers, Friday prayers and Ramadan fasting. I demonstrated the multiplicity of time-reckoning systems and the degree to which they are imposed at different social levels, such as the sector, the community and the individual enterprise. The aim was to develop an understanding of how the different value systems of pious and non-pious Sunni and Alevi interact, collide or conflict in the workplace. I argued that the religious apprehension of time coexists with time-discipline.

Throughout the book, I have embraced a Polanyian understanding of the economy as an instituted process within which human social interests are an inseparable part of economic pursuits. This approach is generally referred to as 'embeddedness' in the wider anthropological and sociological literature. It entails an assumption that the adoption of market rules 'disembeds' the economy from the social relationships they were formerly linked to. However, my ethnography shows the contrary, and therefore my argument follows instead Gudeman's description of the dialectics of community and market in which economies and human economic behaviour in the community or in the market are not described as opposed endeavours but rather as shifting roles between being an 'individual' and a 'person-in-community'. My discussion in Chapters 6, 7 and 8 not only described the social roles that Çorum business owners are expected to fulfil and themselves expect to fulfil as part of their mutual interaction; it also revealed how business owners' economic interests can go against the social expectations of the community and undermine the expected mutuality, as revealed in the ways in which they appropriate materials, labour and discourse. The ethnography addressed precisely these kinds of tensions that arise throughout the lives of business people in the ways they build their identity as 'business people' by means of their obligations and expectations in respect of kinship and place of origin, as well as among family members employed in workplaces.

These discussions regarding the social context of market practices and their mutually dependent realms are captured in recent anthropological discussions of the notion of 'moral economy'. While the original formulations of this term by Thompson and Scott looked specifically at the dynamics of mobilization and the resistance of the subaltern, recent anthropological studies have extended the concept to cover also the morals of different segments of society and applied it to understanding the inner workings of flexible capitalism. I have followed the reformulations of the concept 'moral economy' by economic anthropologists, who are interested in using it to reveal the different moral frameworks that people personally participate in and collectively hold, as well as the silent compliance of those who do not share these frameworks. This understanding also encouraged exploration of those entanglements of market and non-market relations that enable particular modes of capital accumulation. I thus used the concept of 'value regimes' to refer to these realms of entanglements in which market and non-market relations, individual and community interests, are moulded in ways that create and sustain the core inequalities that are intrinsic to capitalism. Overall, I observed how the everyday dynamics of the domain of market relations, such as self-interest, competition, commodification and exploitation, as well as those in the non-market domain, such as obligations, norms, dependencies and social values, are entangled in inseparable ways. This is the realm of the 'moral economy', or as I call it, 'value regimes'.

Further Implications of the Findings and Arguments

Apart from the contributions I make based on concrete ethnographic findings and observations, I believe that this research also fills in some major gaps in the anthropology of Turkey and indirectly offers contributions to wider political and sociological discussions that correspond to larger global issues. With regard to the anthropology of Turkey[158], the most popular fields in the past couple of decades have been political anthropology and the anthropology of religion (see Chapter 3). However, other than the seminal

---

[158] See Birkalan-Gedik (2011) for a detailed account of the history of anthropology in Turkey.

monographs of Hann (1990), Bellér-Hann and Hann (2000), White (2004), Nichols and Sugur (1996) and Piart (2018), economic anthropology in Turkey remains an almost untouched field. My research follows their lead with the hope of initiating further anthropological discussion regarding the inner workings of the country's economy. Another important gap that this research fills is the lack of work-place ethnographies in Turkey, despite the increasing interest in labour studies in recent decades. Few researchers have conducted work-place ethnographies such as those of Kalaycıoğlu (1995), who unfortunately never published her PhD thesis; Yücesan-Özdemir (2003), who spent three months doing participant observation in an automobile factory; Birelma (2014), who conducted ethnography not exactly within the work-place but outside it, focusing on workers' movements; and Dinler (2016), who followed waste pickers in Ankara in the warehouses where they both live and work. Hopefully, the kind of work-place ethnography presented in Part 3 of this book will encourage more researchers to join me in the conversation with observations from within as contributions to the literature on the anthropology of labour.

Another point worth making here concerns the concept of 'province', or *taşra* in Turkish. Due to the massive rural to urban migration Turkey experienced in the 1950s, masses of rural migrants in metropolitan cities have become actors in rapid social change (Schiffauer 1987; Stirling 1993; White 2010). Not surprisingly, most of the scholarly attention has been channelled into the settlers' impacts on trends in urbanization, economic growth, identity formation and social and political change. On the other hand, those who did not join the wave of internal migration but remained in their home towns in the provinces have not received much scholarly attention. At the same time, the interest in villages as a unit of social change had also faded away by the 1970s. Although anthropologists did not completely abandon the villages and towns, as exemplified by Tapper and Tapper's work (1987) on religion and secularism, Delaney's (1991) on gender cosmology, or Yalçın-Heckmann's (2002) on ethnicity, tribes and kinship, to name just a few, the complexity and diversity captured by the urban transformation of the 1990s naturally enchanted the social scientists. The cultural turn in the social sciences in the aftermath of the 1980s also contributed to identity issues and movements relating to gender, ethnicity and religion, which established a stronghold in social scientific inquiry, focused on urban contexts. On the other hand, in the popular imagery, the word 'provincial' has always signified a unified and undifferentiated mass of people who are assumed to be poor, backward and corrupt (Zeybek 2012). Any places outside metropolitan cities were considered *taşra*, dull and gloomy places from which everybody wanted to run away, remembered in nostalgia and only visited in the summer. This is also reflected in how the people of a *taşra* would perceive themselves and their worth, as I showed in the Introduction to this work. However, this imagery has slowly been challenged over the last couple of decades. Some of these provinces have increased their economic power relatively speaking due to their articulation with global production chains since the late 1980s. They have also gained political power as the coalition of right-wing, conservative political parties and currents in the 1990s under the politically Islamist AKP found the majority of its electoral base in central Anatolia. In recent decades, Anatolia has created its own metropolitan cities, like Konya, Kayseri and Gaziantep, leaving the rest to retain the stigma of being identified on the whole as *taşra*.

Çorum is one of those *taşra* places, and this study is mainly about those who were not part of the internal wave of migration, were therefore 'left behind' and constitute the majority of Turkish population. I contend that the people I have studied in this work reflect some of the core characteristics of the majority in Turkey and can therefore shed light on their ambitions, desires and values about livelihoods and social mobility. I believe that shifting the gaze from the 'subaltern' as the research object, in accordance with the general trend, to the 'majority' on the peripheries of capitalism has the potential to bring out the nuances among a group that is essentialized as a unified and undifferentiated mass and to give them the agency to place them beyond being merely the geographical satellites of metropolitan cities. This is not to deny that economic possibilities on the peripheries (as anywhere else) are conditioned by their connections and the flow of money, people and things to larger centres, by their local histories, social structures, geographical features, central planning and investments. On the contrary, I took these conditions as data with which to contextualize and historicize the specific locality and its people and then narrowed my focus to other constraints, such as the dependencies of class and kinship that establish the conditions for the chances and challenges of livelihoods and social mobility for people living in Çorum. These dependencies overlap with changing global labour market conditions and are a reflection of late capitalist transformations in the locality in that they shape, limit or widen people's desires and ambitions. With this three-fold mechanism as its background, this work revealed the power structures that Çorum people navigate in making a liveable life for themselves. Last but not the least, this study fills a gap in the social sciences literature on Turkey by offering a different perspective to the task of understanding the complexities of a place that is often referred as *taşra* from the viewpoint of Istanbul.

Finally, one of the merits of this study is that it has revealed a number of sentiments held by Çorum business people and workers which I believe are common to sentiments invoked by right-wing populist movements, which are well-received by their supporters in Turkey, as elsewhere. For example, the narratives of suffering, betrayal and resentment of businessmen who started from scratch, illustrated in Chapter 5, resonated greatly with the hegemonic political rhetoric of the AKP, which they suffered throughout the early republican period through religious oppression and the denial of economic benefits and which have now come back to give people what was originally theirs with specific reference to being the real heirs of the Ottoman Empire. In fact, some of the narratives in Chapter 5 were those of militant AKP supporters who play an active role in local party politics. Their voices also echoed a degree of self-assertiveness with a specific emphasis on the first-person pronoun 'I', representing their companies' achievements as their own personal achievements. This also resonated with AKP rhetoric that had been prevalent since the time of its right-wing predecessor, the Democrat Party, which was just as much opposed to the previous static and oppressive state bureaucracy, namely that their government puts things into practice. This particular motto had long been in circulation as a political slogan: '*herkes konuşur, AK parti yapar*' (everybody talks, the AKP acts). Interestingly enough, in a recent study based on media analysis of discursive strategies used by the AKP, Tokdoğan (2018) shows how victimhood, resentment, nostalgia and narcissism had been moulded into a new '*yerli ve milli*' (local and national) identity through the specific mobilization of a 'politics of sentiments' in a formulation of neo-Ottomanism. These very strong sentiments, which I heard from businessmen and also from workers from time to time, made me feel like a 'stranger in my own land', as if there were walls between myself and some people in Çorum, an analogy I borrow from Hochschild (2018), who, as a progressive U.S. citizen, went out of her own comfort zone to study right-wing supporters in the U.S. Her study also revealed similar rightist sentiments of victimhood, resentment, rage and the dislike of state intervention. Similarly, in his very recently published study based on years of sociological research in rural America, Wuthnow (2019) addresses the vast political divide in his country that is framed by similar sentiments of belonging to 'those who have been left behind'. Anthropologists have also drawn attention to the resurgence of right-wing populism (Hann 2019), which they have made a central topic of their scientific enquiry (Kalb and Halmai 2011). All in all, studying the majority in the periphery has become a centre of attention due to the changing political climate in both the Global South and the Global North. This research started with very different research questions and concerns, but in the end the findings I gathered together offer an insight into what makes people vote for the right. This was also revealed in Chapters 6 and 7, in respect of the kinship systems, the ideas of loyalty and deference to one's roots, the silent bargain on gaining power to secure one's own autonomy by fully surrendering to those who hold that power, and the paternalism that persists against the increasingly liberating options that neoliberal capitalism supposedly offers. Of course, as I have repeatedly argued, these options are not preferred because of the restrictions the same system imposes and makes people more dependent than ever. I suggest that more research on sentiments in comparison to different contexts has the potential for theorizing about right-wing populism or populism in general and for pioneering a politically engaged anthropology from the reverse perspective.

Gaps and Suggestions for Further Research

Much more could be argued with the benefit of further research. One of the areas I suggest is missing is the focus on the household. Although I meant to include them as well at the start of my research, the findings on households remained partial and have not been fully incorporated into this work. I am also aware that, as a study of the 'reproduction of capitalism', this work could be criticized from a feminist perspective on the basis that the households have been left out. My discussion of the 'reproduction of capitalism' remains an investigation at the ideological level, but further research should fill the gap I have left in this research.

Another important area that I omitted on purpose is the full perspective of the workers. This research is specifically designed to understand small and medium-scale employers. Therefore whatever I have written in this book either mainly reflects their perspective or positions them in relation to their workers, based on my observations in their work-places. I have nonetheless done my best to incorporate the workers' perspectives, despite the central focus being the employers. That would have constituted another piece of research that would have further complemented the findings of this research. The employers I wrote about are also predominantly male, and the stories I have presented are mainly men's stories. This was not a choice I made myself, but was due to the fact that the metal industry specifically and, except for a few sectors such as textiles, food-processing and some office jobs, the labour force in general was mainly male. As a result, this book also lacks women's voices. Here too I have tried to incorporate both women workers and employers in the writing process as much as I could. I believe the data I gathered could be rewritten so as to put the women's stories at the centre, just as for the workers. However, just as interesting would be to interpret the data as a study of heteronormative masculinity. Many of the stories presented in this book are about men's desires and ambitions, their ideas about work and family, what they see themselves as responsible for in relation to their families and communities, what a good life is, and all in all what a 'man' is supposed to be like. A further reading through the lens of masculinity with additional observations and findings would provide an enriching perspective.

What I found very interesting throughout the processes of researching and writing this book are the histories of factories that had been built in the early years of the republic and the period of import substitution up until 1990s, as well as the stories of those involved in the process. I was fascinated by the functions they have served as schools, recreational centres and living spaces in which people from all walks of life somehow participated and from which they gained something. Further research could examine the archives of these institutions and address the oral histories of those who had been associated with them. I grew up in the 1990s at a time when all these factories had been closed down during a period of privatization and were attacked for being a burden on the state. However, as I delved more into the topic, I discovered that there is a lot more to them that needs to be recalled to public attention. It would also be interesting to compare and contrast today's factory regimes to those of an earlier era.

Bibliography

Açıkel, F. 2006. Entegratif Toplum ve Muarızları: 'Merkez-Çevre' Paradigması Üzerine Eleştirel Notlar (Integrative Society and its Discontents: Critical Notes on 'Center-Periphery' Paradigm). *Toplum ve Bilim* 105: 30–69.
Adas, E. 2003. *Profit and the Prophet: Culture and Politics of Islamic Entrepreneurs in Turkey*. Ph.D. dissertation, University of Illinois at Urbana-Champaign.
Akça, İ. 2014. Hegemonic Projects in Post-1980 Turkey and the Changing Forms of Authoritarianism. In A. Bekmen, İ. Akça, and B. Alp Özden (eds.), *Turkey Reframed: Constituting Neoliberal Hegemony*, pp. 13–46. London: Pluto.
Akça, İ, A. Bekmen, and B. A. Özden. 2014. Introduction. In A. Bekmen, İ. Akça, and B. A. Özden (eds.), *Turkey Reframed: Constituting Neoliberal Hegemony*, pp. 1–9. London: Pluto.
Akçam, T. 2004. *From Empire to Republic: Turkish Nationalism and the Armenian Genocide*. London: Zed Books.
——. 2013. *The Young Turks' Crime against Humanity: The Armenian Genocide and Ethnic Cleansing in the Ottoman Empire*. Princeton NJ: Princeton University Press.
Akgöz, G. 2012. *Many Voices of a Turkish State Factory: Working at Bakırköy Cloth Factory, 1932-50*. Ph.D. dissertation, University of Amsterdam.
Akın, G. G., A. F. Aysan, and L. Yıldıran. 2008. *Transformation of the Turkish Financial Sector in the Aftermath of the 2001 Crisis*. Available online, https://mpra.ub.uni-muenchen.de/17803/, accessed 9 November 2019.
Akın, Y. 2014. *Gürbüz ve Yavuz Evlatlar: Erken Cumhuriyet'te Beden Terbiyesi ve Spor* (Strong and Brave Children: Body Training and Sports in Early Republic). İstanbul: İletişim.
Akşin, S. 2007. *Turkey, from Empire to Revolutionary Republic: The Emergence of the Turkish Nation from 1789 to Present*. New York: NYU Press.
Aktüre, S. 1986. 19. ve 20. Yüzyıl Başında Çorum (Çorum in 19th and early 20th Century). In M. Ercan, and İ. Yiğit (eds.), *5. Hitit Festivali Komitesi Çorum Tarihi* (5. Hitit Festival Committee Çorum History), pp. 121–66. Çorum: Çorum Belediyesi.
Alexander, C. 2000. The Factory: Fabricating the State. *Journal of Material Culture* 5 (2): 177–195.

——. 2002. *Personal States: Making Connections Between People and Bureaucracy in Turkey*. New York and Oxford: Oxford University Press.
Amin, A. 1989. Flexible Specialization and Small Firms in Italy: Myths and Realities. *Antipode* 21 (1): 13–34.
——. 1994. Post-Fordism: Models, Fantasies and Phantoms of Transition. In A. Amin (ed.), *Post-Fordism: A Reader*, pp. 1–7. Oxford: Blackwell.
Appleby, J., L. Hunt, and M. Jacob. 2011. *Telling the Truth about History*. New York: W.W. Norton & Company.
Atay, T. 2004. *Din Hayattan Çıkar: Antropolojik Denemeler (Religion roots in Life: Anthropological Essays)*. İstanbul: İletişim Yayınları.
Avcıoğlu, D. 1975. *Türkiye'nin Düzeni (İkinci Kitap). The Order of Turkey. (Second Book)*. İstanbul: Tekin Yayınevi.
Ayata, S. 1990. Aile İşletmesinin Krizi: Serbest Piyasa Ortamında Buldan Dokuma Sanayi (The Crisis of Family Business: Buldan Weaving Industry under Free Market Conditions). *Toplum ve Bilim* (48–49): 163–185.
Aydın, S. 2001. Cumhuriyet'in İdeolojik Şekillenmesinde Antropolojinin Rolü: Irkçı paradigmanın yükselişi ve düşüşü (Role of Anthropology in the Ideological Shaping of the Republic: the rise and fall of racist Paradigm). In A. İnsel (ed.), *Modern Türkiye'de Siyasi Düşünce: Kemalizm* (Political Thought in Modern Turkey: Kemalism), pp. 344–369. İstanbul: İletişim Yayınları.
Azak, U. 2012. Secularists as the Saviors of Islam: Rearticulation of Secularism and the Freedom of Conscience in Turkey (1950). In B. Turam (ed.), *Secular State and Religious Society: Two forces in play in Turkey*, pp. 59–78. New York: Palgrave Macmillan.
Balkan, N., E. Balkan, and A. Öncü (eds.). 2015. *The Neoliberal Landscape and the Rise of Islamist Capital in Turkey*. New York and London: Berghahn.
Bayar, Y. 2012. The Dynamic Nature of Educational Policies and Turkish Nation Building: Where Does Religion Fit in? In B. Turam (ed.), *Secular State and Religious Society: Two Forces in Play in Turkey*, pp. 19–38. New York: Palgrave Macmillan.
Bayırbağ, M. K. 2007. *Local Entrepreneurialism, State Re-scaling and Scalar Strategies of Representation: The Case of the City of Gaziantep, Turkey*. Ph.D. dissertation, Carleton University.
Becattini, G. 1990. The Marshallian Industrial District as a Socio-Economic Notion. In F. Pyke, G. Becattini, and W. Sengenberger (eds.), *Industrial Districts and Inter-Firm Co-Operation in Italy*, pp. 37–51. Geneva: International Institute for Labour Studies.

Bedirhanoğlu, P., and G. Yalman. 2009. Neoliberal Küreselleşme Sürecinde Türkiye'de 'Yerel' Sermaye: Gaziantep, Denizli ve Eskişehir'den İzlenimler ('Local' Capital in Turkey during Neoliberal Globalization: Impressions from Gaziantep, Denizli and Eskişehir). *Praksis* (19): 241–266.

Bellér-Hann, I., and C. Hann. 2000. *Turkish Region: State, Market & Social Identities on the East Black Sea Coast*. Oxford: James Currey.

———. 2003. *İki Buçuk Yaprak Çay: Doğu Karadeniz'de Devlet, Piyasa, Kimlik* (Two and a Half Leaves of Tea: State, Market and Identity in Eastern Black Sea). İstanbul: İletişim Yayınları.

Berkes, N. 2002. *Türkiye'de Çağdaşlaşma* (Modernization in Turkey). Istanbul: Yapı Kredi Yayınları.

Beşpınar, F. U., Ç. Topal, and S. Kalaycıoğlu. 2014. Consensual Control Through the Articulation of Technology and Local Culture: Evidence from a Textile Factory in Turkey. *New Technology, Work and Employment* 29 (3): 224–236.

Birelma, A. 2014. *Ekmek ve Haysiyet Mücadelesi: Günümüz Türkiye'sinde Üç İşçi Hareketinin Etnografisi* (Struggle for Bread and Honour: Ethnography of Three Labour Movements in Contemporary Turkey). Istanbul: İletişim Yayınları.

———. 2019. Working-Class Entrepreneurialism: Perceptions, Aspirations, and Experiences of Petty Entrepreneurship among Male Manual Workers in Turkey. *New Perspectives on Turkey* 61: 45–70.

Birkalan-Gedik, H. 2011. Anthropological Writings on Urban Turkey: A Historical Overview. *Urban Anthropology and Studies of Cultural Systems and World Economic Development* 40 (1/2): 1–66.

Blim, M. 1990. *Made in Italy: Small-Scale Industrialization and its Consequences*. Pennsylvania: Penn State Press.

Bloch, M. 1971. The Moral and Tactical Meaning of Kinship Terms. *Man*: 79–87.

———. 1973. The Long Term and the Short Term: The Economic and Political Significance of the Morality of Kinship. In J. Goody (ed.), *The Character of Kinship*, pp. 75–87. Cambridge: Cambridge University Press.

Bondár, M. 2018. Prehistoric Innovations: Wheels and Wheeled Vehicles. *Acta Archaeologica Academiae Scientiarum Hungaricae* 69 (2): 271.

Boratav, K. 2006. *Türkiye İktisat Tarihi 1908-2005* (Economic History of Turkey 1908-2005). Ankara: İmge Kitapevi.

Bourdieu, P., and L. Wacquant. 2001. Neoliberal Newspeak: Notes on the New Planetary Vulgate. *Radical Philosophy* 105 (Jan): 1–6.

Bozdoğan, S., and R. Kasaba. 1997. Introduction. In S. Bozdogan, and R. Kasaba, *Rethinking Modernity and National Identity in Turkey*, pp. 3–14. Seattle: University of Washington Press.

Brenner, N., J. Peck, and N. Theodore. 2010. Variegated Neoliberalization: Geographies, Modalities, Pathways. *Global Networks* 10 (2): 182–222.

Buğra, A. 1994. *State and Business in Modern Turkey: A Comparative Study*. New York: SUNY Press.

———. 2014. *New Capitalism in Turkey: The Relationship Between Politics, Religion and Business*. Cheltenham: Edward Elgar Publishing.

Buğra, A., and O. Savaşkan. 2010. Yerel Sanayi ve Bugünün Türkiyesi'nde İş Dünyası (Local Industry and Business in Contemporary Turkey). *Toplum ve Bilim* 118: 92–123.

Burawoy, M. 1982. *Manufacturing Consent: Changes in the Labor Process Under Monopoly Capitalism*. Chicago and London: The University of Chicago Press.

———. 1985. *The Politics of Production Factory Regimes under Capitalism and Socialism*. London: Verso Books.

———. 2009. Thirty Years of Making Out. In M. Mollona, G. de Neve, and J. Parry (eds.), *Industrial Work and Life: An Anthropological Reader*, pp. 145–166. Oxford: Berg.

Burawoy, M., and E. O. Wright. 1990. Coercion and Consent in Contested Exchange. *Politics & Society 18* (2): 251–266.

Çağaptay, S. 2006. *Islam, Secularism and Nationalism in Modern Turkey: Who is a Turk?* London: Routledge.

Cahen, C. 1970. *Le Probleme du Shi'isme dans l'Asie Mineure Turque Preottomane*. Colloque de l'Université de Strasbourg, 6–7 May 1968.

Çam, S. 2002. Neo-Liberalism and Labour Within the Context of an 'Emerging Market' Economy – Turkey. *Capital & Class* 26 (2): 89–114.

Capello, C. 2015. Family, Social Capital and Internal Migration in Italy: The Case of the People of Tramonti. *Human Affairs* 25 (1): 40–57.

Carrier, James G. 2015. The Concept of Class. In James G. Carrier, and D. Kalb (eds.), *Anthropologies of Class Power, Practice and Inequality*, pp. 28–40. Cambridge: Cambridge University Press.

———. 2018. Moral Economy: What's in a Name? *Anthropological Theory* 18 (1): 18–35.

Çelik, A. 2013. Trade Unions and Deunionization During Ten Years of AKP Rule. *Perspective-Political Analysis and Commentary from Turkey* 3 (2013): 44–48.

———. 2015. Turkey's New Labour Regime Under the Justice and Development Party in the First Decade of the Twenty-First Century: Authoritarian Flexibilization. *Middle Eastern Studies* 51 (4): 618–635.
Cengiz, K. 2013. *'Yav İşte Fabrikalaşak' Anadolu Sermayesinin Oluşumu: Kayseri-Hacılar Örneği* ('Let's Build an Industry' Formation of Anatolian Capital: The Case of Kayseri-Hacılar). Istanbul: İletişim Yayınları.
Cindoğlu, D., and G. Zencirci. 2008. The Headscarf in Turkey in the Public and State Spheres. *Middle Eastern Studies* 44 (5): 791–806.
Çoban, A. 2000. Çorum'un Nüfus Coğrafyası Özellikleri (The Features of Geography of Population in Çorum). *Marmara Coğrafya Dergisi* 33: 410–438. Available online, https://dergipark.org.tr/tr/download/article-file/286999, accessed 10 March 2021.
Collier, S. J., and A. Ong. 2005. Global Assemblages, Anthropological Problems. In A. Ong, and S. Collier (eds.), *Global Assemblages: Technology, Politics, and Ethics as Anthropological Problems*, pp. 3–21. Oxford: Blackwell.
Cooper, F. 1992. Colonizing Time: Work Rhythms and Labor Conflict in Colonial Mombasa. In N. Dirks (ed.), *Colonialism and Culture,* pp. 209–245. Ann Arbor: University of Michigan Press.
Copeaux, E. 2000. *Tarih Ders Kitaplarında (1931-1993): Türk Tarih Tezinden Türk İslam Sentezine* (History is in School Books [1931-1993]: From Turkish History Thesis to Turkish Islam Synthesis). İstanbul: Tarih Vakfı Yurt Yayınları.
Davison, A. 2003 Turkey, a 'Secular' State? The challenge of Description. *The South Atlantic Quarterly* 102 (2): 333–350.
de Lima, A. P. 2000. Is Blood Thicker than Economic Interest in Familial Enterprises. In P. Schweitzer, *Dividends of Kinship: Meaning and Uses of Social Relatedness*, pp. 153–178. London Routledge.
de Neve, G. 2005. *The Everyday Politics of Labour: Working Lives in India's Informal Economy.* Delhi: Social Science Press.
De Sardan, J.P.O. 1999. A Moral Economy of Corruption in Africa? *The Journal of Modern African Studies* 37 (1): 25–52.
Delaney, C. 1991. *The Seed and the Soil: Gender and Cosmology in Turkish Village Society.* Berkeley: University of California Press.
Demir, Ö., M. Acar, and M. Toprak. 2004. Anatolian Tigers or Islamic Capital: Prospects and Challenges. *Middle Eastern Studies* 40 (6): 166–188.
Demiralp, S. 2009. The Rise of Islamic Capital and the Decline of Islamic Radicalism in Turkey. *Comparative Politics* 41 (3): 315–335.

Demiröz, D., and A. Öncü. 2005. Türkiye'de Piyasa Toplumunun Oluşumunda Hegemonyanın Rolü: Bir Gerçeklik Projesi olarak Beyaz Türklük (Role of Hegemony in the Formation of Market Society in Turkey: White Turkishness as a Project of Authenticity). In A. Öncü, and O. Tekelioğlu (eds.), *Şerif Mardin'e Armağan* (A Gift to Şerif Mardin), pp. 171–199. İstanbul: İletişim Yayınları.

Demirpolat, A. 2002. *The Rise of Islamic Economic Ethic, Rationality and Capitalism in Modern Turkey: The Case of Konya.* Ph.D. dissertation, Middle Eastern Technical University.

Dinler, D. Ş. 2003. Türkiye'de Güçlü Devlet Geleneği Tezinin Eleştirisi. *Praksis* 9: 17–54.

──. 2016. *A Multi-Sited Analysis of Rules and Regulations in the Recycling Market from Ankara to London.* Ph.D. dissertation, SOAS University of London.

Diyanet İşleri Başkanlığı. 2014. *Türkiye'de Dini Hayat Araştırması* (Research on Religious Life in Turkey). Ankara: Diyanet İşleri Başkanlığı.

──. 2019. *Türkiye'deki Dinî-Sosyal Teşekküller, Geleneksel Dinî-Kültürel Oluşumlar ve Yeni Dinî Akımlar* (Socio-Religious Institutions, Religio-cultural Formations and New Religious Trends in Turkey). Available online, https://mk0medyascopetblqooo.kinstacdn.com/wp-content/uploads/2019/05/diyanet-rapor-1-1.pdf, accessed 20 March 2021.

Doğan, A. 2007. *Eğreti Kamusallık: Kayseri Örneğinde Islamcı Belediyecilik* (Makeshift Public: Islamist Local Governance in the Case of Kayseri). Istanbul: İletişim.

Dreßler, M. 2013. *Writing Religion: The Making of Turkish Alevi Islam.* Oxford: Oxford University Press.

──. 2019. Religionization and Secularity. In *Companion of the Study of Secularity*, edited by HCAS 'Multiple Secularities: Beyond the West Beyond Modernities'. Available online, https://www.multiple-secularities.de/media/css_dressler_religionization.pdf, accessed 12 November 2019.

Dubetsky, A. 1976. Kinship, Primordial Ties, and Factory Organization in Turkey: An Anthropological View. *International Journal of Middle East Studies* 7 (3): 433–451.

Dunn, E. C. 2004. *Privatizing Poland: Baby Food, Big Business, and the Remaking of Labor.* Ithaca NY: Cornell University Press.

Durak, Y. 2011. *Emeğin Tevekkülü: Konya'da İşçi-İşveren İlişkileri ve Dindarlık* (Resignation of Labour: Worker and employer Relations and Religiosity in Konya). Istanbul: İletişim.

Düzgün, E. 2012. Class, State and Property: Modernity and Capitalism in Turkey. *European Journal of Sociology/Archives Européennes de Sociologie* 53 (2): 119–148.
Edelman, M. 2005. Bringing the Moral Economy Back in to the Study of 21st-Century Transnational Peasant Movements. *American Anthropologist* 107 (3): 331–345.
Eraydın, A. 1999. Sanayinin Anadolu'ya Yaygınlaşması ve Son Dönemde Gelişen Yeni Sanayi Odakları (The Spreading of Industry in Anatolia and Recently Emerging Centres of Industry). In O. Baydar (ed.), *75 Yılda Çarklardan Chip'lere* (From Cogwheels to Chips in 75 Years), pp. 257–277. Istanbul: Tarih Vakfı Yurt Yayınları.
Ertan, M. 2017. *Aleviliğin Politikleşme Süreci: Kimlik Siyasetinin Kısıtlılıkları ve İmkânları* (The Process of the Politicization of Alevism: Opportunities and Constraints of Identity Politics). Istanbul: İletişim Yayınları.
———. 2019. The Latent Politicization of Alevism: The Affiliation between Alevis and Leftist Politics (1960–1980). *Middle Eastern Studies* 55 (6): 932–944.
ESI (European Stability Initiative). 2005. Islamic Calvinists Change and Conservatism in Central Anatolia. *Insight Turkey*: 59–88.
Faroqi, S. 1986. Fatih Döneminden Evliya Çelebi Seyahatine Kadar Çorum (Çorum from the Era of Fatih the Conqueror to Evliya Çelebi's Travels). In M. Ercan, and İ. Yiğit (eds.), *5. Hitit Festivali Komitesi Çorum Tarihi* (5. Hitit Festival Committee Çorum History), pp. 79–120. Çorum: Çorum Belediyesi.
Fassin, D. 2009. Les économies morales revisitées (Revisiting Moral Economy). *Annales. Histoire, Sciences Sociales* 64 (6): 1237–1266.
———. 2014. The Ethical Turn in Anthropology: Promises and Uncertainties. *HAU: Journal of Ethnographic Theory* 4 (1): 429–435.
Fassin, D., and S. Lézé. 2014. *Moral Anthropology: A Critical Reader*. London: Routledge.
Ferguson, J. 2010. The Uses of Neoliberalism. *Antipode* 41 (s1): 166–184.
Filiztekin, A., and İ. Tunalı. 1999. Anatolian Tigers: Are They for Real? *New Perspectives on Turkey* 20: 77–106.
Fine, B., and A. Saad-Filho. 2004. *Marx's Capital*. London: Pluto.
Fischer, M. M. J. 1982. Islam and the Revolt of the Petit Bourgeoisie. *Daedalus 111* (1): 101–125.
Gilsenan, M. 2000. *Recognizing Islam: Religion and Society in the Modern Middle East*. London: IB Tauris.
Göle, N. 1996. *The Forbidden Modern: Civilization and Veiling*. Ann Arbor: University of Michigan Press.

―――. 1997. Secularism and Islamism in Turkey: The Making of Elites and Counter-Elites. *The Middle East Journal* 51 (1): 46–58.
Gölpınarlı, A. 1969. *100 Soruda Türkiye'de Mezhepler ve Tarikatler* (Religious Denominations and Brotherhoods in Turkey in 100 Questions). İstanbul: Gerçek Yayınevi.
Gözel Durmaz, O. 2015. The Distribution of the Armenian Abandoned Properties in an Ottoman Locality: Kayseri (1915–18). *Middle Eastern Studies* 51 (5): 838–853.
Graeber, D. 2001. *Toward an Anthropological Theory of Value: The False Coin of Our Own Dreams*. New York: Palgrave.
Greenhalgh, S. 1994. De-Orientalizing the Chinese Family Firm. *American Ethnologist* 21 (4): 746–775.
Gudeman, S. 2009. Necessity or Contingency: Mutuality and Market. In C. Hann, and K. Hart (eds.), *Market and Society: The Great Transformation Today*, pp. 17–37. Cambridge: Cambridge University Press.
Gülalp, H. 2003. Whatever Happened to Secularization? The multiple Islams in Turkey. *The South Atlantic Quarterly* 102 (2): 381–395.
Güler, H. 2014. *Patron Baba ve İşçileri: İşçi Sınıfı, Köylülük ve Paternalizm* (The Boss-Father and his Workers: Working Class, Peasantry and Paternalism). İstanbul: İletişim Yayınları.
Güler-Müftüoğlu, B. 2000. *İstanbul-Gedikpaşa'da Ayakkabı Üretiminin Değişen Yapısı ve Farklılaşan İşgücü* (Changing Structure of Shoe Production and Proliferation of Labour Force in Istanbul-Gedikpaşa). *Toplum ve Bilim* 86: 118–138.
Güneş-Ayata, A. 1994. Roots and Trends of Clientelism in Turkey. In L. Roniger, and A. Güneş-Ayata, *Democracy, Clientelism and Civil Society*, pp. 51–63. Boulder: Rienner Publishing.
Gürbey, S. 2012. Islam, Nation-State and Military: A Discussion of Secularism in Turkey. In B. Turam (ed.), *Secular State and Religious Society: Two Forces in Play in Turkey*, pp. 39–57. New York: Palgrave Macmillan.
Gutman, H. G. 1973. Work, Culture, and Society in Industrializing America, 1815-1919. *The American Historical Review* 78 (3): 531–588.
Güven, B., and E. Kaygın. 2013. *Çorum Swot Analizi* (Swot Analysis of Çorum). İstanbul: Veritas Akademi.
Hall, S., and M. Jacques (eds.). 1989. *New Times: The Changing Face of Politics in the 1990s.* London: Lawrence and Wishart.
Hann, C. 1990. *Tea and the Domestication of the Turkish State*. Huntingdon: Eothen Press.

——. 2006. *'Not the Horse We Wanted!': Postsocialism, Neoliberalism, and Eurasia*. Münster: LIT Verlag.
——. 2010. Moral Economy. In K. Hart, J.-L. Laville, and A. D. Cattani (eds.), *The Human Economy: A Citizen's Guide*, pp. 187–198. Cambridge: Polity Press.
——. 2018. Moral(ity and) Economy: Work, Workfare, and Fairness in Provincial Hungary. *European Journal of Sociology/Archives Européennes de Sociologie* 59 (2): 225–254.
——. 2019. Anthropology and Populism. *Anthropology Today* 35 (1): 1–2.
Hareven, T. K. 1993. *Family Time & Industrial Time: The Relationship between the Family and Work in a New England Industrial Community*. Boston: University Press of America.
Harris, O. 2007. What Makes People Work? In R. Astuti, J. P. Parry, and C. Stafford, *Questions of Anthropology*, pp. 137–165. Oxford: Berg.
Hart, K. 2013. *And Then We Work for God: Rural Sunni Islam in Western Turkey*. Stanford: Stanford University Press.
Hart, K., and C. Hann. 2009. Introduction: Learning from Polanyi 1. In K. Hart, and C. Hann (eds.), *Market and Society: The Great Transformation Today*, pp. 1–16. Cambridge: Cambridge University Press.
Harvey, D. 1989. *The Condition of Postmodernity*. Oxford: Blackwell.
——. 2005. *A Brief History of Neoliberalism*. New York and Oxford: Oxford University Press.
Haynes, D. 1999. Just Like a Family? Recalling the Relations of Production in the Textile Industries of Surat and Bhiwandi, 1940-60. *Contributions to Indian Sociology* 33 (1–2): 141–169.
Henkel, H. 2005. Between Belief and Unbelief Lies the Performance of Salāt': Meaning and Efficacy of a Muslim Ritual. *Journal of the Royal Anthropological Institute* 11 (3): 487–507.
Hirst, P., and J. Zeitlin. 1991. Flexible Specialization Versus Post-Fordism: Theory, Evidence and Policy Implications. *Economy and Society* 20 (1): 5–57.
Hochschild, A. R. 2018. *Strangers in Their Own Land: Anger and Mourning on the American Right*. New York: The New Press.
Hoşgör, E. 2011. Islamic Capital/Anatolian Tigers: Past and Present. *Middle Eastern Studies* 47 (2): 343–360.
İleri, Ü. 2009. *Türkiye'de Toplumsal Değişimin Çalışma İlişkileri Üzerindeki Etkileri* (Impact of Social Change on Employment Relations in Turkey) TÜHİS. Available online, https://www.tuhis.org.tr/resim/files/yay%C4%B1n_62.pdf, accessed 10 October 2017.

İnsel, A. 2003. The AKP and Normalizing Democracy in Turkey. *The South Atlantic Quarterly* 102 (2): 293–308.
İzmen, Ü. 2012. *Bölgesel Kalkınmada Yerel Dinamikler Çorum Modeli ve 2023 Senaryoları* (Local Dynamics in Regional Development, Çorum Model and 2023 Scenarios). Istanbul: Türkonfed.
Jessop, B. 1990. Regulation Theories in Retrospect and Prospect. *Economy and Society* 19 (2): 153–216.
Kadam, F., and G. Toksöz. 2004. Gender Based Discrimination at Work in Turkey: A Cross-Sectoral Overview. *Ankara Üniversitesi SBF Dergisi* 59 (4): 151–172.
Kalaycıoğlu, S. 1995. *Formation of a Working Class? A Study of Factory workers in Bolu, Turkey.* Ph.D. dissertation, University of Kent at Canterbury.
Kalb, D. 1997. *Expanding Class: Power and Everyday Politics in Industrial Communities, the Netherlands, 1850-1950.* Durham: Duke University Press.
———. 2012. Thinking About Neoliberalism as if the Crisis Was Actually Happening. *Social Anthropology* 20 (3): 318–330.
———. 2014. Elias Talks to Hayek (And Learns from Marx and Foucault): Reflections on Neoliberalism, Postsocialism and Personhood. In N. Makovicky (ed.), *Neoliberalism, Personhood and Postsocialism: Enterprising Selves in Changing Economies*, pp. 187–202. Farnham: Ashgate.
———. 2017. Regimes of Value and Worthlessness: How Two Subaltern Stories Speak. In S. Narotzky, and V. Goddard (eds.), *Work and Livelihoods: History, Ethnography and Models in Times of Crisis*, pp. 123–136. New York: Routledge.
Kalb, D., and G. Halmai. 2011. *Headlines of Nation, Subtexts of Class: Working Class Populism and the Return of the Repressed in Neoliberal Europe.* New York and London: Berghahn Books.
Kalkınma Bakanlığı (Ministry of Development). 2011. *İllerin ve Bölgelerin Sosyo-Ekonomik Gelişmişlik Sıralaması* (Socio-Economic Development Ranking of Cities and Regions). Available online, https://www.sbb.gov.tr/wp-content/uploads/2018/11/Illerin_ve-Bolgelerin_Sosyo-Ekonomik_ Gelismislik_Siralamasi_ArastirmasiSEGE-2011%E2%80%8B.pdf, accessed 2 March 2021.
Kandiyoti, D. 2002. Introduction: Reading the Fragments. In D. Kandiyoti, and A. Saktanber, *Fragments of Culture: The Everyday of Modern Turkey*, pp. 1–24. London and New York: IB Tauris.

——. 2012. The Travails of the Secular: Puzzle and Paradox in Turkey. *Economy and Society* 41 (4): 513–531.
Kaplan, Y. 2002. İslam'ın Özne olarak Yeniden Tarih Sahnesine Çıkışı ve İslam'ı Protestanlaştırma Projesi (Islam's Re-appearance on the Stage of History as a Subject and the Project to Protestanization of Islam). *Umran* 96: 26–36.
Kaplinsky, R. 1995. Technique and System: The Spread of Japanese Management Techniques to Developing Countries. *World Development* 23 (1): 57–71.
Karadağ, R. 2010. Neoliberal Restructuring in Turkey: From State to Oligarchic Capitalism. *MPIFG Discussion Paper* 10 (7): 1–32.
——. 2013. Where Does Turkey's New Capitalism Come From? Comment on Eren Düzgün LIII, 2 (2012). *European Journal of Sociology/ Archives Européennes de Sociologie* 54 (1): 147–152.
Karakışla, Y. S. 1998. Osmanlı İmparatorluğu'nda 1908 Grevleri (1908 Labour Strikes in Ottoman Empire). *Toplum ve Bilim* 78: 187–208.
Karaömerlioğlu, A. 1998. Bir Tepeden Reform Denemesi: Çiftçiyi Topraklandırma Kanununun Hikâyesi (An Attempt of a Reform from Above: The Story of the Law on Providing Land for Farmers *Birikim* (107): 31–47.
——. 2006. *Orada Bir Köy Var Uzakta: Erken Cumhuriyet Döneminde Köycü Söylem* (There is a Village Afar: Peasantist Discourse in Early Republican Era). İstanbul: İletişim Yayınları.
Kasaba, R. 1997. Kemalist Certainties and Modern Ambiguities. In S. Bozdogan, and R. Kasaba (eds.), *Rethinking Modernity and National Identity in Turkey*, pp. 15–36. Seattle: University of Washington Press.
Kehl-Bodrogi, K. 1992. *Kızılbaş/ Aleviler* (Kızılbash/ Alevis). Istanbul: Ayrıntı Yayınları.
Kepenek, Y., and N. Yentürk. 1994. *Türkiye Ekonomisi* (The Economy of Turkey). Istanbul: Remzi Kitabevi.
Keyder, Ç. 1987. *State and Class in Turkey*. Verso Books: London.
——. 1989. *Türkiye'de Devlet ve Sınıflar* (State and Class in Turkey). İstanbul: İletişim Yayınları.
Keyman, F., and B. Koyuncu Lorasdağı. 2010. *Kentler: Anadolu'nun Dönüşümü* (Cities: The Transformation of Anatolia). İstanbul: Doğan Kitap.
Khalaf, S., and E. Shwayri. 1966. Family Firms and Industrial Development: The Lebanese Case. *Economic Development and Cultural Change* 15 (1): 59–69.

Kipnis, A. 2008. Audit Cultures: Neoliberal Governmentality, Socialist Legacy, or Technologies of Governing? *American Ethnologist* 35 (2): 275–289.

Kıray, M. 1984. *Ereğli-Ağır Sanayiden Önce bir Sahil Kasabası* (Ereğli - A Pre-industrial Coastal Town). İstanbul: Iletişim Yayınları.

Kıray, M., and J. Hinderink. 1970. *Social Stratification as an Obstacle to Development: A Study of Four Turkish Villages*. New York: Praeger Publishers.

Kofti, D. 2016. Moral Economy of Flexible Production: Fabricating Precarity Between the Conveyor Belt and the Household. *Anthropological Theory* 16 (4): 433–453.

Köker, L. 1990. *Modernleşme, Kemalizm ve Demokrasi* (Modernization, Kemalism and Democracy). Istanbul: Iletişim Yayınları.

Konda. 2010. *Konda Barometresi Toplumsal Kutuplaşma* (Konda Barometer Social Polarization). Available online, https://konda.com.tr/wp-content/uploads/2017/03/KONDA_1004_TOPLUMSAL_KUTUPL ASMA.pdf, accessed 5 July 2018.

Köse, A. H., and A. Öncü. 2000. İşgücü Piyasaları ve Uluslararası İşbölümünde Uzmanlaşmanın Mekansal Boyutları: 1980 Sonrası Dönemde Türkiye İmalat Sanayii (Labour Markets and Spatial Aspects of Specialization in Global Division of Labour: Manufacture Industry in Turkey in post-1980s). *Toplum ve Bilim* 86 (2): 72–90.

Kösebalaban, H. 2007. The Rise of Anatolian Cities and the Failure of the Modernization Paradigm. *Critique: Critical Middle Eastern Studies* 16 (3): 229–240.

Kuran, T. 1996. The Discontents of Islamic Economic Morality. *The American Economic Review* 86 (2): 438–442.

Kuru, A. 2007. Passive and Assertive Secularism: Historical Conditions, Ideological Struggles, and State Policies toward Religion. *World Politics* 59 (4): 568–594.

Kuru, A., and A. Stepan (eds.). 2012. *Democracy, Islam, and Secularism in Turkey*. New York: Columbia University Press.

Lash, S., and J. Urry. 1987. *The End of Organized Capitalism*. Madison: University of Wisconsin Press.

Lee, C. K. 2009. Localistic Despotism. In G. de Neve, M. Mollona, and J. Parry (eds.), *Industrial Work and Life: An Anthropological Reader*, pp. 239–56. London: Berg.

Lerner, D. 1958. *The Passing of Traditional Society: Modernizing the Middle East*. New York: Free Press.

Lewis, B. 1961. *The Emergence of Modern Turkey.* Oxford: Oxford University Press.

Lindisfarne, N. 2002. *Elhamdülillah Laikiz: Cinsiyet, İslâm ve Türk Cumhuriyetçiliği* (Thank God We are Secular: Gender, Islam and Turkish Republicanism). İstanbul: İletişim Yayınları.

Lipietz, A. 1986. Behind the Crisis: The Exhaustion of a Regime of Accumulation. A 'Regulation School' Perspective on Some French Empirical Works. *Review of Radical Political Economics* 18 (1–2): 13–32.

Lord, C. 2018. *Religious Politics in Turkey: From the Birth of the Republic to the AKP.* Cambridge: Cambridge University Press.

Lovering, J. 1990. Fordism's Unknown Successor: A Comment on Scott's Theory of Flexible Accumulation and the Re-Emergence of Regional Economies. *International Journal of Urban and Regional Research* 14 (1): 159–174.

——. 1999. Theory Led by Policy: The Inadequacies of the 'New Regionalism' (Illustrated from the Case of Wales). *International Journal of Urban and Regional Research* 23 (2): 379–395.

MacLeod, G. 2001. New Regionalism Reconsidered: Globalization and the Remaking of Political Economic Space. *International Journal of Urban and Regional Research* 25 (4): 804–829.

Madi-Şişman, Ö. 2017. *Muslims, Money, and Democracy in Turkey: Reluctant Capitalists.* New York: Springer.

Magnarella, P. J., O. Türkdoğan, N. Abu Zahra, W. Eberhard, N. Erdentuğ, B. Güvenç, and I. Yasa. 1976. The Development of Turkish Social Anthropology [and Comments and Reply]. *Current Anthropology* 17 (2): 263–274.

Mahmood, S. 2001. Rehearsed Spontaneity and the Conventionality of Ritual: Disciplines of Şalat. *American Ethnologist* 28 (4): 827–853.

Makovicky, N. 2014a. Introduction: Me, Inc.? Untangling Neoliberalism, Personhood, and Postsocialism. In N. Makovicky (ed.), *Neoliberalism, Personhood, and Postsocialism: Enterprising Selves in Changing Economies*, pp. 15–30. Farnham: Ashgate.

——. (ed.). 2014b. *Neoliberalism, Personhood, and Postsocialism: Enterprising Selves in Changing Economies.* Farnham: Ashgate.

Marcus, G., and P. D. Hall. 1992. *Lives in Trust: The Fortunes of Dynastic Families in Late Twentieth-Century America.* Boulder: Westview Press.

Mardin, Ş. 1973. Centre-Periphery Relations: A Key to Turkish Politics? *Daedalus* 102 (1): 169–190.

———. 1980. Turkey: The Transformation of an Economic Code. In E. Özbudun, and A. Ulusan (eds.), *The Political Economy of Income Distribution in Turkey*, pp. 23–53. New York and London: Holmes and Meier Publishers.

———. 1997. Projects as a Methodology: Some Thoughts on Modern Turkish Social Science. In S. Bozdoğan, and R. Kasaba (eds.), *Rethinking Modernity and National Identity in Turkey*, pp. 64–80. Seattle: University of Washington Press.

Martin, E. 2009. *Bipolar Expeditions: Mania and Depression in American Culture*. Princeton: Princeton University Press.

Marx, K. 1978. *Capital Vol I*. London: Penguin.

Marx, K., and F. Engels. 1974. *The German Ideology*. Edited by C. J. Arthur. London: Lawrence & Wishart.

Massicard, E. 2007. *Alevi Hareketinin Siyasallaşması* (Politicization of Alevi Movement). İstanbul: İletişim Yayınları.

Mebet, R. 2018. Tarihe Saygısızlık! (Desecration of History). *Çorum Hakimiyet*. Available online, http://www.corumhakimiyet.net/guncel/tarihe-saygisizlik-h437.html, accessed 12 April 2018.

Meeker, M. 2002. *A Nation of Empire: The Ottoman Legacy of Turkish Modernity*. Berkeley: University of California Press.

Melikoff, I. 1994. *Uyur İdik Uyardılar Alevîlik-Bektaşîlik Araştırmaları* (They Warned us in our Sleep: Research on Alevism-Bektashsim). İstanbul: Cem Yayınevi.

Mikuš, M. 2016. The Justice of Neoliberalism: Moral Ideology and Redistributive Politics of Public Sector Retrenchment in Serbia . *Social Anthropology* 24 (2): 211–227.

Miller, P., and N. Rose. 2008. *Governing the Present: Administering Economic, Social and Personal Life*. Cambridge: Polity Press.

Mintz, S. W. 1986. *Sweetness and Power: The Place of Sugar in Modern History*. London: Penguin Books.

Mittermaier, A. 2013. Trading with God: Islam, Calculation, Excess. In J. Boddy, and M. Lambek (eds.), *A Companion to the Anthropology of Religion*, pp. 274–293. West Sussex: John Wiley & Sons.

Mollona, M., G. De Neve, and J. Parry (eds.). 2009. *Industrial Work and Life: An Anthropological Reader*. Oxford and New York: Berg.

Mollona, M. 2009. General Introduction. In G. De Neve, M. Mollona, and J. P. Parry (eds.), *Industrial Work and Life: An Anthropological Reader*, pp. vi-xxviii. Oxford and New York: Berg.

Monnot, G. 1995. Salāt. In P. Bearman, Th. Bianquis, C. E. Bosworth, E. van Donzel, and W. P. Heinrichs (eds.), *Encyclopedia of Islam*, Vol. 8, pp. 925–934. Leiden: Brill.

Narotzky, S. 1997. *New Directions in Economic Anthropology*. London: Pluto Press.
──. 2009. Regulation and Production in a Globalized World: What Ethnography Brings to Comparison. *Ethnology* 48 (3): 175–193.
──. 2015. The Payoff of Love and the Traffic of Favours. In J. Kjaerulff, (ed.), *Flexible Capitalism: Exchange and Ambiguity at Work*, pp. 173–206. Oxford: Berghahn Books.
Narotzky, S., and G. A. Smith. 2006. *Immediate Struggles: People, Power, and Place in Rural Spain*. Berkeley: University of California Press.
Narotzky, S., and N. Besnier. 2014. Crisis, Value, and Hope: Rethinking the Economy: An Introduction to Supplement 9. *Current Anthropology* 55 (S9): S4–S16.
Navaro-Yashin, Y. 2002. *Faces of the State: Secularism and Public Life in Turkey*. Princeton: Princeton University Press.
Nichols, T., and N. Sugur. 1996. Small Employers in Turkey: The OSTIM Estate at Ankara. *Middle Eastern Studies* 32 (2): 230–252.
Ocak, A. Y. 1996. *Türkiye'de Tarihin Saptırılması Sürecinde: Türk Sufiliğine Bakışlar* (In the Process of Distortion of History in Turkey: A Look into Turkish Sufism). İstanbul: İletişim Yayınları.
Önal, N. E. 2012. Osmanlı İmparatorluğu'ndan Cumhuriyet'e Geçişte Büyük Toprak Sahiplerinin Sınıfsal Rolü ve Dönüşümü (The Role and Transformation of Big Landlords in the Transition from Ottoman Empire to Republic). *Middle East Technical University Studies in Development* 39 (1): 137–169.
Öncü, A. 1999. Istanbulites and Others: The Cultural Cosmology of Being Middle Class in the Era of Globalism. In Ç. Keyder (ed.), *Istanbul: Between the Global and the Local*, pp. 161–172. Lanham: Rowman & Littlefield.
Ong, A. 1991. The Gender and Labor Politics of Postmodernity. *Annual Review of Anthropology* 20 (1): 279–309.
──. 2006. *Neoliberalism as Exception: Mutations in Citizenship and Sovereignty*. Durham: Duke University Press.
Öniş, Z. 2012. The Triumph of Conservative Globalism: The Political Economy of the AKP Era. *Turkish Studies* 13 (2): 135–152.
Orta Karadeniz Kalkınma Ajansı (OKA). 2015. *Çorum Sosyal Analiz Raporu* (Çorum Social Analysis Report). Available online, https://www.oka.org.tr/assets/upload/dosyalar/corum-sosyal-analiz-raporu.pdf, accessed 12 March 2021.
Ortaylı, İ. 2006. *İmparatorluğun En Uzun Yüzyılı* (Longest Century of the Empire). Istanbul: Alkım Yayınevi.

Ozan, E. D. 2011. *Gülme Sırası Bizde, 12 Eylül'e Giderken Sermaye Sınıfı* (It is our Turn to Laugh, Capitalist Class on the path to September 12). İstanbul: Metis.

Özcan, G. B. 1995a. *Small Firms and Local Economic Development: Entrepreneurship in Southern Europe and Turkey*. Aldershot: Avebury.

——. 1995b. Small Business Networks and Local Ties in Turkey. *Entrepreneurship & Regional Development* 7 (3): 265–284.

Özdemir, A. M., and G. Yücesan-Özdemir. 2005. Social Regulation Under Neo-Liberalism: New Forms of Labour Contract and Labour Flexibility in Turkey. *SEER-South East Europe Review for Labour and Social Affairs* 3: 63–78.

Özdemir, Ş. 2004. MÜSİAD ve Hak-İş'i Birlikte Anlamak: Sınıflı Bir İslami Ekonomi mi? (Understanding MÜSİAD and Hak-İş Together: Class-based Islamic Economy?). In T. Bora, and M. Gültekingil (eds.), *Modern Türkiye'de Siyasi Düşünce İslamcılık* (Political Thought in Modern Turkey: Islamism), pp.837–69. İstanbul: İletişim.

Özden, B. A., İ. Akça, and A. Bekmen. 2017. Antinomies of Authoritarian Neoliberalism in Turkey: The Justice and Development Party Era. In C. B. Tansel (ed.), *States of Discipline: Authoritarian Neoliberalism and the Contested Reproduction of Capitalist Order*, pp. 189–210. London: Rowman & Littlefield International.

Özkazanç, A. 1996. Türkiye'de Yeni Sağ (The New Right in Turkey). In *Cumhuriyet Dönemi Türkiye Ansiklopedisi 15* (Encyclopaedia of Republican Turkey 15), pp. 1218–1224. İstanbul: İletişim Yayınları.

Özoral, B. 2014. Economic Engagement of Religious Ethics in the Global Economy: The Raising of Islamic Capital in an Anatolian City, Kayseri as a New Economic Power. *Economics World* 2 (2): 79–91.

Özuğurlu, M. 2008. *Anadolu'da Küresel Fabrikanın Doğuşu: Yeni İşçilik Örüntülerinin Sosyolojisi* (The Birth of the Global Factory in Anatolia: The Sociology of New Patterns of Labouring). Istanbul: Kalkedon Yayınları.

Özyürek, E. 2006. *Nostalgia for the Modern: State Secularism and Everyday Politics in Turkey*. Durham: Duke University Press.

——. 2012. Christian and Turkish: Secularist Fears of a Converted Nation. In B. Turam (ed.), *Secular State and Religious Society: Two Forces in Play*, pp. 95–119. New York: Palgrave Macmillan.

Paldam, M. 2003. Economic Freedom and the Success of the Asian Tigers: An Essay on Controversy. *European Journal of Political Economy* 19 (3): 453–477.

Palomera, J., and T. Vetta. 2016. Moral Economy: Rethinking a Radical Concept. *Anthropological Theory* 16 (4): 413–432.

Pamuk, Ş. 2007. Economic Change in Twentieth Century Turkey: Is the Glass More than Half Full? In R. Kasaba (ed.), *The Cambridge History of Turkey*, pp. 266–300. Cambridge: Cambridge University Press.

Pamuk, Ş. 2008a. 150. Yılında Baltalimanı Ticaret Anlaşması (Baltalimanı Treaty in its 150th Anniversary). In A. Berkaty (ed.), *Seçme Eserleri II: Osmanlıdan Cumhuriyete Küreselleşme, İktisat Politikaları ve Büyüme* (Selected Works II: Globalization, Economy Politics and Growth from Ottoman Empire to the Republic), pp. 29–37. Istanbul: Türkiye İş Bankası Kültür Yayınları.

—. 2008b. Bağımlılık ve Büyüme: Küreselleşme Çağında Osmanlı Ekonomisi (1820-1914) (Dependency and Growth: Ottoman Economy in the Age of Globalization [1820-1914]). In A. Berkaty (ed.), *Seçme Eserleri II: Osmanlıdan Cumhuriyete Küreselleşme, İktisat Politikaları ve* Büyüme (Selected Works II: Globalization, Economy Politics and Growth from Ottoman Empire to the Republic), pp. 3–37. Istanbul: Türkiye İş Bankası Kültür Yayınları.

—. 2008c. İkinci Dünya Savaşı Yıllarında İaşe Politikası ve Köylülük (Politics of Provisioning during the Second World War and Peasantry). In *Seçme Eserleri II: Osmanlıdan Cumhuriyete Küreselleşme, İktisat Politikaları ve Büyüme* (Selected Works II: Globalization, Economy Politics and Growth from Ottoman Empire to the Republic). Istanbul: Türkiye İş Bankası Kültür Yayınları.

—. 2008d. Globalization, Industrialization and Changing Politics in Turkey. *New Perspectives on Turkey* 38: 267–273.

Pamuk, Ş., and Ç. Keyder. 2008. 1945 Çiftçiyi Topraklandırma Kanunu Üzerine Tezler (Thesis on the 1945 Law on Providing Land for Farmers). In A. Berktay (ed.), *Seçme Eserleri II: Osmanlıdan Cumhuriyete Küreselleşme, İktisat Politikaları ve Büyüme* (Selected Works II: Globalization, Economy Politics and Growth from Ottoman Empire to the Republic), pp. 199–213. Istanbul: Türkiye İş Bankası Kültür Yayınları.

Parla, A. 2019. *Precarious Hope: Migration and the Limits of Belonging in Turkey*. Stanford: Stanford University Press.

Parry, J. P. 1999. Lords of Labour: Working and Shirking in Bhilai. *Contributions to Indian Sociology* 33 (1–2): 107–140.

Pateman, C. 1988. *The Sexual Contract*. Stanford: Stanford University Press.

Peck, J. 1996. *Work-Place: The Social Regulation of Labor Markets*. New York: Guilford Press.

Piart, L. 2018. *Making Things Fit, Making Ends Meet: Small Entrepreneurs in Istanbul's Garment Industry*. Ph.D. dissertation, Vienna/ Paris: Universität Wien/ École des Hautes Études en Sciences Sociales.

Piore, M., and C. Sabel. 1984. *The Second Industrial Divide: Possibilities for Prosperity*. Vol. 19. New York: Basic Books.

Polanyi, K. 2001 [1944]. *The Great Transformation: The Political and Economic Origins of Our Time*. Boston: Beacon Press.

Polatel, M. 2009. *Turkish State Formation and the Distribution of the Armenian Abandoned Properties from the Ottoman Empire to the Republic of Turkey (1915-1930)*. Ph.D. dissertation, Koç University.

Rodinson, M. 1973. *Islam and Capitalism*. New York: Pantheon Books.

Sabuncuoğlu, M. İ. 2015. *Çorum Tarihine ait Derlemelerim I, II, III & Maarif Hayatımız* (My Essays on Çorum History I, II, III & our Educational Background). Çorum: Çorum Belediyesi.

Saktanber, A., and G. Çorbacıoğlu. 2008. Veiling and Headscarf-Skepticism in Turkey. *Social Politics: International Studies in Gender, State & Society* 15 (4): 514–538.

Şar, E. 2019. Laiklik and Nation-Building: How State–Religion–Society Relations Changed in Turkey under the Justice and Development Party. In R. Ö. Dönmez, and A. Yaman (eds.), *Nation-Building and Turkish Modernization: Islam, Islamism and Nationalism in Turkey*, pp. 111–145. London: Lexington Books.

Schiffauer, W. 1987. *Die Bauern von Subay* (The Farmers of Subay). Stuttgart: Klett-Cotta.

Scott, A. J., and M. Storper. 2005. *Pathways to Industrialization and Regional Development*. London: Routledge.

Scott, A. J. 1988. Flexible Production Systems and Regional Development: The Rise of New Industrial Spaces in North America and Western Europe. *International Journal of Urban and Regional Research* 12 (2): 171–186.

Scott, J. C. 1977. *The Moral Economy of the Peasant: Rebellion and Subsistence in Southeast Asia*. New Haven and London: Yale University Press.

—. 1990. *Domination and the Arts of Resistance: Hidden Transcripts*. New Haven: Yale University Press.

Şen, M. 2010. Transformation of Turkish Islamism and the Rise of the Justice and Development Party. *Turkish Studies* 11 (1): 59–84.

Sennett, R. 1992. *Otorite* (Authority). Istanbul: Ayrıntı Yayınları.

Shankland, D. 1999. *Islam and Society in Turkey*. Huntingdon: Eothen Press.

—. 2003. *The Alevis in Turkey: The Emergence of a Secular Islamic Tradition*. London and New York: Routledge.

Smart, J., and A. Smart. 1993. Obligation and Control: Employment of Kin in Capitalist Labour Management in China. *Critique of Anthropology* 13 (1): 7–31.
Smith, G. 1991. Writing for Real: Capitalist Constructions and Constructions of Capitalism. *Critique of Anthropology* 11 (3): 213–232.
Smith, T. 1986. Peasant Time and Factory Time in Japan. *Past & Present* (111): 165–197.
Somer, M. 2013. Is Turkish Secularism Antireligious, Reformist, Separationist, Integrationist, or Simply Undemocratic? *Journal of Church and State* 55 (3): 585–597.
Sönmez, M. 1987. *Kırk Haramiler Türkiye'de Holdingler* (The Forty Thieves Holdings in Turkey). Istanbul: Gözlem Yayıncılık.
———. 2010. *AKP-IMF ve Cemaat Kapitalizmi* (AKP-IMF and Gülen Community Capitalism). *Cumhuriyet* 19 March 2010 (online publication).
———. 2013. 2000'ler Türkiye'sinde AKP, Hâkim Sınıflar ve İç Çelişkileri (AKP, Dominant Classes and their Internal Conflicts in Turkey in 2000s). In İ. U. B. Duru (ed.), *AKP Kitabı Bir Dönüşümün Bilançosu* (The AKP Book Balance Sheet of a Transformation), pp. 179–191. Ankara: Phoenix.
Stirling, P. 1965. *Turkish Village*. London: Weidenfeld & Nicolson.
———. 1993. Introduction. In P. Stirling (ed.), *Culture and Economy: Changes in Turkish Villages*, pp. 1–16. Huntingdon: Eothen Press.
Storper, M. 1995. The Resurgence of Regional Economies, Ten Years Later: The Region as a Nexus of Untraded Interdependencies. *European Urban and Regional Studies* 2 (3): 191–221.
Tanyılmaz, K. 2015. The Deep Fracture in the Big Bourgeoisie of Turkey. In N. Balkan, E. Balkan, and A. Öncü (eds.), *The Neoliberal Capital and the Rise of Islamist Capital in Turkey*, pp. 89–117. New York and London: Berghahn Books.
Tapper, N., and R. Tapper. 1987. 'Thank God We're Secular!' Aspects of Fundamentalism in a Turkish Town. In L. Caplan (ed.), *Studies in Religious Fundamentalism*, pp. 51–78. Albany: State University of New York Press.
Tapper, R. (ed.). 1994. *Islam in Modern Turkey: Religion, Politics, and Literature in a Secular State*. New York: Palgrave Macmillan.
Taşkın, Y. 2008. AKP's Move to 'Conquer' the Centre-Right: Its Prospects and Possible Impacts on the Democratization Process. *Turkish Studies* 9 (1): 53–72.
Tekeli, İ. 1986a. 1923-1950 döneminde Çorum'daki Gelişmeler (Developments in Çorum between 1923-1950). In C. Beledivesi

(ed.), *5. Hitit Festivali Komitesi Çorum Tarihi* (5. Hitit Festival Committee Çorum History), pp. 197–232. Çorum: Çorum Belediyesi.

———. 1986b. 1950-1980 döneminde Kentin Faaliyetlerindeki Gelişmeler (Developments in the Activities of the City between 1950-1980). In C. Beledivesi (ed.), *5. Hitit Festivali Komitesi Çorum Tarihi* (5. Hitit Festival Committee Çorum History), pp. 235–284. Çorum: Çorum Belediyesi.

Terpe, S. 2018. Working with Max Weber's 'Spheres of Life': An Actor-centred Approach. *Journal of Classical Sociology* 20 (1): 22–42.

Tezel, Y. S. 1994. *Cumhuriyet Dönemi İktisat Tarihi (1923-1950)* (Republican Era Economic History (1923-1950). Istanbul: Tarih Vakfı Yurt Yayınları.

Thompson, E. P. 1966. *The Making of the English Working Class*. New York: Vintage Books.

———. 1967. Time, Work-Discipline, and Industrial Capitalism. *Past & Present* (38): 56–97.

———. 1971. The Moral Economy of the English Crowd in the Eighteenth Century. *Past & Present* (50): 76–136.

———. 1991. *Customs in Common*. London: Penguin Books.

Tickell, A., and J. A. Peck. 1992. Accumulation, Regulation and the Geographies of Post-Fordism: Missing Links in Regulationist Research. *Progress in Human Geography* 16 (2): 190–218.

Tokdoğan, N. 2018. *Yeni Osmanlıcılık: Hınç, nostalji, narsisizm* (New Ottomanism: Envy, Nostalgia, Narcissism). Istanbul: İletişim.

Toprak, B. 2005. Secularism and Islam: The Building of Modern Turkey. *Macalester International* 15 (9): 27–43.

Toprak, Z. 2012. *Darwin'den Dersim'e Cumhuriyet ve Antropoloji* (The Republic and Anthropology from Darwin to Dersim). Istanbul: Doğan Kitap.

Toumarkine, A. 2014. The Introduction of Max Weber's Thought and Its Uses in Turkey National Stakes and Foreign Actors. In M. Kaiser, and H. Rosenbach (eds.), *Max Weber in der Welt: Rezeption und Wirkung*, pp. 33–46. Tübingen: Mohr Siebeck.

Tuğal, C. 2004. Islamic Political Identity in Turkey. *Political Science Quarterly* 119 (2): 360–361.

———. 2009. *Passive Revolution: Absorbing the Islamic Challenge to Capitalism*. Redwood City: Stanford University Press.

Turam, B. 2012. Secular State and Pious Muslims: Neither Eternal Rivals nor Allies for Life. In B. Turam (ed.), *Secular State and Religious Society: Two Forces in Play in Turkey*, pp. 1–18. New York: Palgrave Macmillan.

TurkSTAT. 2013. *Çorum Seçilmiş Göstergeler* (Çorum Selected Indicators). Available online, https://docplayer.biz.tr/7839296-Secilmis-gostergelerle-corum-2013-turkiye-istatistik-kurumu.html, accessed 10 March 2015.

———. 2016. *Küçük ve Orta Büyüklükteki Girişim İstatistikleri* (Statistics of Small and Medium Size Entrepreneurialism). Available online, http://dipmo.net/wp-content/uploads/K%C3%BC%C3%A7%C3%BCk-ve-Orta-B%C3%BCy%C3%BCkl%C3%BCkteki-Giri%C5%9Fim-%C4%B0statistikleri.pdf, accessed 10 November 2019.

Türkün-Erendil, A. 2000. Mit ve Gerçeklik Olarak Denizli-Üretim ve İşgücünün Değişen Yapısı: Eleştirel Kuram Açısından bir Değerlendirme (Denizli as a Myth and Reality Changing Structure of Labour Force: An Analysis from the Lenses of Critical Theory). *Toplum ve Bilim* 86: 91–117.

Turner, B. 2013. Islam, Capitalism and the Weber Thesis. In B. S. Turner, and K. M. Nasir (eds.), *The Sociology of Islam: Collected Essays of Bryan S. Turner*, pp. 23–36. London: Routledge.

Uçar, M. 2009. *Nerelisin, Kimlerdensin?: Mezhep, Cemaat ve Yurttaşlık arasında Çorum.* (Where are you from, Whom you Belong to?: Çorum between Religious Denomination, Community and Citizenship). Ankara: Dipnot.

Ünlü, B. 2018. *Türklük Sözleşmesi Oluşumu, İşleyişi ve Krizi* (The Turkishness Contract: Its Formation, Functioning, and Crisis). Ankara: Dipnot.

Üngor, U., and M. Polatel. 2011. *Confiscation and Destruction: The Young Turk Seizure of Armenian Property.* London: Continuum International Publishing.

Uygur, S., L. J. Spence, R. Simpson, and F. Karakaş. 2017. Work Ethic, Religion and Moral Energy: The Case of Turkish SME Owner-Managers. *The International Journal of Human Resource Management* 28 (8): 1212–1235.

Uzel, Ü. 2013. *Korumasız Başkan-2* (The Unshielded President-2*).* Çorum: Papirüs Matbaacılık.

Wacquant, L. 2012. Three Steps to a Historical Anthropology of Actually Existing Neoliberalism. *Caderno CRH* 25 (66): 505–518.

Weber, M. 1978. *Economy and Society: An Outline of Interpretative Sociology.* Edited by Guenther Roth and Claus Wittich. Berkeley: University of California Press.

———. 1992. The Religions of Civilization and Their Attitude to the World. In S. Whimster (ed.), *The Essential Weber*, pp. 81–110. London: Routledge.

——. 2001a. *The Protestant Ethic and the Spirit of Capitalism*. New York and London: Routledge.
——. 2001b. Weber's First Reply to Rachfahl. In D. Chalcraft, and A. Harrington (eds.), *The Protestant Ethic Debate*, pp. 61–86. Liverpool: Liverpool University Press.
Westwood, S. 1984. *All Day, Every Day*. London: Pluto.
Whipp, R. 1987. A Time to Every Purpose: An Essay on Time and Work. In P. Joyce (ed.), *The Historical Meanings of Work*, pp. 210–36. Cambridge: Cambridge University Press.
White, J. 2000. Kinship, Reciprocity and the World Market. In P. P. Schweitzer (ed.), *Dividends of Kinship: Meanings and Uses of Social Relatedness*, pp. 124–50. London: Routledge.
——. 2004. *Money Makes Us Relatives: Women's Labor in Urban Turkey*. London: Routledge.
——. 2010. Tin Town to Fanatics: Turkey's Rural to Urban Migration from 1923 to the Present. In C. Kerslake, K. Öktem, and P. Robins (eds.), *Turkey's Engagement with Modernity: Conflict and Change in the Twentieth Century*, pp. 425–442. Basingstoke: Palgrave Macmillan.
——. 2011. *Islamist Mobilization in Turkey: A Study in Vernacular Politics*. Seattle: University of Washington Press.
——. 2012. *Muslim Nationalism and the New Turks*. Princeton: Princeton University Press.
Wolf, E. 2010. *Europe and the People Without History*. Berkeley: University of California Press.
Wuthnow, R. 2019. *The Left Behind: Decline and Rage in Small-Town America*. Princeton: Princeton University Press.
Yalçın-Heckmann, L. 2002. *Kürtlerde Aşiret ve Akrabalık İlişkileri* (Kinship and Tribal Relations among the Kurds). Istanbul: Iletişim Yayınları.
Yalman, G. 2002a. The Turkish State and Bourgeoisie in Historical Perspective: a Relativist Paradigm or a Panoply of Hegemonic Strategies? In N. Balkan, and S. Savran (eds.), *The Politics of Permanent Crisis: Class, Ideology and State in Turkey*, pp. 21–54. New York: Nova Science Publishers.
——. 2002b. Tarihsel Bir Perspektiften Türkiye'de Devlet ve Burjuvazi: Rölativist bir Paradigma mı Hegemonya Stratejisi mi? (State and Bourgeoisie in Turkey from a Historical Perspective: A relativist paradigm or a strategy of hegemony?). *Praksis* 5: 7–23.
Yanagisako, S. J. 2002. *Producing Culture and Capital: Family Firms in Italy*. Princeton: Princeton University Press.
Yankaya, D. 2014. *Yeni İslâmî Burjuvazi: Türk Modeli* (New Islamic Bourgeoisie: Turkish Model). Istanbul: İletişim.

Yavuz, H., and A. E. Öztürk. 2019. Turkish Secularism and Islam under the Reign of Erdoğan. *Southeast European and Black Sea Studies* 19 (1): 1–9.
Yavuz, H. 2000. Cleansing Islam from the Public Sphere. *Journal of International Affairs* 54 (1): 21–42.
———. 2003. *Islamic Political Identity in Turkey*. New York: Oxford University Press.
———. 2006. Introduction: The Role of the New Bourgeoisie in the Transformation of the Turkish Islamic Movement. In H. Yavuz (ed.), *The Emergence of a New Turkey: Democracy and the AK Party*, pp. 1–22. Salt Lake City: The University of Utah Press.
Yeşilbağ, M. 2015. Changing Hegemonic Strategies of Business in Turkey Before and After the Neoliberal Turn: From Defence to Counter-Attack. *Enterprise & Society* 17 (1): 116–150.
Yılmaz, M. 2004. Çorum İlinde Endüstrinin Tarihsel Gelişimi (Historical Development of Industry in Çorum). *Coğrafi Bilimler Dergisi* 2 (1): 57–71.
Yücesan-Özdemir, G. 2000. Başkaldırı, Onay ya da Boyun Eğme? Hegemonik Fabrika Rejiminde Mavi Yakalı İşçilerin Hikâyesi (Rebellion, Consent or Compliance? Story of Blue-collar Workers in a Hegemonic Factory Regime). *Toplum ve Bilim* 86: 241–259.
———. 2003. Hidden Forms of Resistance Among Turkish Workers: Hegemonic Incorporation or Building Blocks for Working Class Struggle? *Capital & Class* 27 (3): 31–59.
Zeybek, S. O. 2012. 'Fraudulent' Citizens of a Small Town: Occidentalism in Turkey. *Antipode* 44 (4): 1551–1568.
Zürcher, E. J. 1993. *Turkey: A Modern History*. London and New York: IB Tauris.

Index

accumulation; export oriented 59, 61; flexible 10, 11, 28, 206, 211, 261; primitive 45-6, 109, 124; regime(s) of 8, 10, 12, 13, 21, 57, 261

Alevi(s); Alevism 6n, 72, 90-1, 95-6, 128, 194; identity 37, 98

ambition 9, 110, 151, 159, 161, 164, 170, 185, 263, 269, 271, *see also azim*; *hırs*

Anatolian; bourgeoisie 57; businessmen 15; capital 14, 16, 17, 43, 58, 116, 137; entrepreneurs 15-6; industrialists 58; Tigers 2, 9, 10, 14-20, 24, 37, 68, 71, 101-2, 125, 259, 261

Armenian; massacre/ genocide 107; properties 107-9

assimilation 87, 97, 106n, 129

autonomy 24, 46, 89, 140, 162-5, 178, 188-9, 260, 263, 264, 271

azim [positively connoted ambition] 164-5

Bloch, M. 177-8, 184, 189, 207

bourgeoisie; creation of Muslim Turkish (national) 15, 43, 45-6, 48, 58-9, 68, 92, 102; Istanbul and north-western 15, 17, 45, 57, 113, 114, 118, 137; local 21, 49, 139, 157

brother(s); and betrayal 159, 170, 263; and envy 170, 263

business owners; and honour 163-5, 170, 263; and personhood 38, 139-40, 144, 151-4, 157, 165, 169-70, 262; and responsibility 1, 38, 141, 188, 198-9, 201, 203-4, 206-8, 264; aspirations of 37-8, 260, 262; children of 148-50, 159, 162-3, 166, 168-9, 262; co-villagers of 33, 38, 118, 178, 180-1, 192-3, 207, 263; kin and family members of 25, 27, 38, 178-9, 181, 184, 188, 191, 193, 195, 207, 219, 224, 263-4, 267; motivations of 9. 37-8, 177, 259, 262; non-family members of 38, 179, 190, 195, 207, 244, 264; origin stories of 139, 151, 154; relationship to work 21, 37, 194, 244, 262; sentiments of 263

capital; accumulation 9, 22, 25, 28-9, 37, 45, 65, 69, 102, 103, 179, 260-1, 263, 267; investment 118, 122; merchant capital 23-4, 37, 261

Carrier, J. 21, 28, 177-9, 184, 189, 207

centre versus periphery 16, 71, 81-2, 91, 259

community; Alevi 193, 262; and identity 24, 86, 175, 195, 197; Gülen 101, 129-30; religious 15, 102; workplace 175, 193, 200, 202, 208, 231

credit(s); preferential credit 53-4, 59, 62-4, 113-5, 118, 133, 160

culture; of living together 127-9, 132; of partnership 9, 24, 37, 101-3, 112, 124, 127-9, 134, 136-8, 261

çekememezlik [public envy] 161, 163-5, 170

Çorum (city); exceptionalism 5, 7; industry 2, 5, 7, 33, 34, 104, 107, 111, 114, 119-20, 122, 125, 133, 138, 150, 164, 166, 244, 261, 263; labour market 206-7, 269; massacre (*see also* Alevi[s]) 117, 128, 131, 191; miracle 7, 8, 124; model of development 9, 24, 101-2, 124, 261; supply chain 119-20, 137, 179

despotism; despotic 25, 72, 212, 228, 230, 233, 236, 265-6
discipline; and timely payment of wages 225; and upbringing 159, 162
discrimination 51, 117, 131, 193, 202, 254
Diyanet 56, 76, 87, 89, 90-1

economic liberalization 79
enterprise; as a brand 161, 165-6; genealogy of 166, 168
etatism 48-50

fathers/ men; authority of 155, 189, 194, 197, 224; desire of 150, 262; father-boss 197, 205; inheritance from 159, *see also* paternalism
Fethullah Gülen/ FETÖ/ Gülen community 15, 16, 101, 102, 128, 129, 133, 136, 165
flexible specialization 10, 11, 23, 124, 176, 261
forces of production 154, 158-9, 161, 170, 263
Ford; crisis of 10, 22, 261; franchise 114; (Post)Fordism 10-2, 22, 213, 261; truck 107-8, 114
foreman 120, 137, 152, 161, 183, 221, 224, 233

grudge [*hınç*] 117, 164, 250
Gudeman, S. 26, 178, 266

Hann, C. 25-8, 83, 87, 89, 268, 270
hegemony; cultural 25, 231; in relations of production 25, 231; neoliberal 43, 61-2; Sunni Muslim 262
hırs [negatively connoted ambition] 159-65

iftar 134, 193, 252-3
incentives; at the workplace 62, 102, 111, 133, 179, 198, 200, 209, 220, 231, *see also* paternalism; Özal 113, 115-6, 121, 126
industry; and imitation 113, 120, 143; automobile 221, 268; chemical 48; flour 1, 104, 112, 114-6, 122-3; machine 119, 123, 186, 256; manufacturing 135, 138; Marshallian industrial district 12; mining 48-9, 53, 61, 186; tile 1, 33, 166; tile and brick 113, 116, 124
Islam; and national identity 37, 71-2, 77n, 82-3, 87-8, 91-2, 129, 270; fundamentals of 37, 83, 241n
Islamic; and non-Islamic workplace rituals 38, 208, 264; bourgeoisie 17, 55, 137; brotherhoods/ sects [*tarikat*s] 15, 17, 63, 90, 91; business association(s) 37, 262; Calvinists 15-7; capital 63, 137, 259; (Muslim) community 84-6, 249; (work) ethic 15, 18, 67, 68; life style 202; secular/ binary (distinction) 63, 71, 93-4; Turkish-Islamic synthesis 92
Islamist; modernization 30; movement 64, 65, 98; political Islamist 16, 56, 68, 98

Kalb, D. 3, 7, 8, 21, 29, 143-4, 148, 156, 270
kinship; discourses of 176-8, 193; fictive 177, 197, 208; morality of 177-9, 184, 188-9, 191-2, 194-5, 207, 263; politics of 177, 263; relatedness 38, 176, 178, 180, 188, 193, 207, 263-4; tactical meaning of 177-8, 181, 183

labour control 25, 38, 207-8, 210, 212
laiklik 37, 48n, 71, 75n, 79, 82-3, 87, 105, 134, *see also* secular, Turkish secularism
loyalty; to one's roots 4, 7, 183, 228; to the AKP 136; to the employer 176, 190, 213, 227, 230, 264; to the state 77, 108

Mardin, Ş. 71, 80, 81, 260
masculinity 163, 224, 271-2
mevlit 230-1
military coup(s) 6, 36, 43, 59, 76n, 129n, 135, 211, 239
moral economy 9, 21-2, 25, 27-9, 34, 179, 263, 267, *see also* value(s), regimes (of)

Narotzky, S. 12, 24-5, 29, 144
narratives of; personhood 139, 140, 144, 152, 154; success 110; worth(lessness) 3, 5
neoliberalism; neoliberal subjectivity 37, 143, 262; neoliberalization 60, 72
non-Muslims 24, 37, 45-7, 51, 73-4, 87, 105, 261

paternalism; and *agha*(s) 104n, 189; and authority 195, 197; history of 295-7
Polanyi, K. 26-7, 266
prayer [*dua/ namaz*]; Friday prayer 134, 193, 241, 247-50, 252, 256, 266
Protestant ethic thesis of Max Weber 15, 67, 259, 262, *see also* Islamic, Calvinists

reciprocity; asymmetrical 38, 212-3, 225, 228, 231, 236-7, 265; general 188
religious time 251, 254
reputation 150, 160-1, 170, 235, 260, 263

secular; entrepreneurs/ employers/ business people 14n, 15; life-style 31, 193; religio-secularization 87; ritual 197; secular versus Muslim binary 11, 20, 37, 58, 63, 71, 94, 212, 259, 264, *see* Islamic, secular/ binary (distinction); Turkish secularism 71, 75n, 76, 79, 82, 87
sexual contract 234, 236
skill; lack of 4; teaching/training 192, 203, 223-4; transfer of 24, 37, 112, 120, 137, 143, 167, 262; unskilled 24, 38, 110, 205-6, 212, 236, 265
social mobility 147, 154, 269
social reproduction 21, 28, 260-1
suffering 50, 95n, 154-5, 157-8, 161-3, 170, 263, 270

Thompson, E. P. 21, 25, 27-8, 195, 209, 219-22, 226, 234, 239, 259, 267
trade unions 58, 211n
transfer of; skills 24, 37, 112, 120, 137, 143, 167, 262, *see* skill; technology and know-how 111-2
Turkish flag 136
Turkish nationalism 48, 75, 87, 97, 107, 168

value(s); Islamic 31, 209; non-religious 36; of work/ hard work 88, 148, 154, *see also* suffering; regimes (of) 8, 25, 29, 142, 260, 267, *see also* moral economy; religious 36, 88; traditional 19 women's; honour and shame 234-6; reputation 235

women; and smoking 216-7; in industry 151, 154-7, 159, 180, 192, 196, 200, 202, 204-5, 213-6, 225, 234, 250, 271

workers'; coercion 38, 151, 154, 210, 212-3, 221, 226, 228, 236, 265; consent 179, 198; control, *see* labour control; deservingness 38, 213, 226, 236, 265; displays of loyalty 228, 237, *see also* loyalty, to the employer; domination 10, 38, 59, 78, 79, 177, 212, 221, 225, 236-7, 265; exploitation 23-5, 118n, 123, 151, 207-8, 220, 231, 234, 267; 'good employee' 188; gratitude 38, 213, 226, 231, 236-7, 239, 265; promotion 38, 46-7, 180, 224, 264; recruitment 180, 182-3, 193; respect 38, 159-60, 186, 194, 199, 201, 218, 224, 226, 228, 236-7, 253, 255, 265; surveillance 213-4, 221, 225, 227, 229, 237, 265; working hours 126, 201, 205, 224, 234, 237, 245, 251-3, 255, 265-6

working-class entrepreneurship 147

Halle Studies in the Anthropology of Eurasia

1 Hann, Chris, and the "Property Relations" Group, 2003: *The Postsocialist Agrarian Question. Property Relations and the Rural Condition.*

2 Grandits, Hannes, and Patrick Heady (eds.), 2004: *Distinct Inheritances. Property, Family and Community in a Changing Europe.*

3 Torsello, David, 2004: *Trust, Property and Social Change in a Southern Slovakian Village.*

4 Pine, Frances, Deema Kaneff, and Haldis Haukanes (eds.), 2004: *Memory, Politics and Religion. The Past Meets the Present in Europe.*

5 Habeck, Joachim Otto, 2005: *What it Means to be a Herdsman. The Practice and Image of Reindeer Husbandry among the Komi of Northern Russia.*

6 Stammler, Florian, 2009: *Reindeer Nomads Meet the Market. Culture, Property and Globalisation at the 'End of the Land'* (2 editions).

7 Ventsel, Aimar, 2006: *Reindeer,* Rodina *and Reciprocity. Kinship and Property Relations in a Siberian Village.*

8 Hann, Chris, Mihály Sárkány, and Peter Skalník (eds.), 2005: *Studying Peoples in the People's Democracies. Socialist Era Anthropology in East-Central Europe.*

9 Leutloff-Grandits, Caroline, 2006: *Claiming Ownership in Postwar Croatia. The Dynamics of Property Relations and Ethnic Conflict in the Knin Region.*

10 Hann, Chris, 2006: *"Not the Horse We Wanted!" Postsocialism, Neoliberalism, and Eurasia.*

11 Hann, Chris, and the "Civil Religion" Group, 2006: *The Postsocialist Religious Question. Faith and Power in Central Asia and East-Central Europe.*

12 Heintz, Monica, 2006: *"Be European, Recycle Yourself!" The Changing Work Ethic in Romania.*

13 Grant, Bruce, and Lale Yalçın-Heckmann (eds.), 2007: *Caucasus Paradigms. Anthropologies, Histories and the Making of a World Area.*

14 Buzalka, Juraj, 2007: *Nation and Religion. The Politics of Commemoration in South-East Poland.*

15 Naumescu, Vlad, 2007: *Modes of Religiosity in Eastern Christianity. Religious Processes and Social Change in Ukraine.*

16 Mahieu, Stéphanie, and Vlad Naumescu (eds.), 2008: *Churches Inbetween. Greek Catholic Churches in Postsocialist Europe.*

17 Mihăilescu, Vintilă, Ilia Iliev, and Slobodan Naumović (eds.), 2008: *Studying Peoples in the People's Democracies II. Socialist Era Anthropology in South-East Europe.*

18 Kehl-Bodrogi, Krisztina, 2008: *"Religion is not so strong here". Muslim Religious Life in Khorezm after Socialism.*

19 Light, Nathan, 2008: *Intimate Heritage. Creating Uyghur Muqam Song in Xinjiang.*

20 Schröder, Ingo W., and Asta Vonderau (eds.), 2008: *Changing Economies and Changing Identities in Postsocialist Eastern Europe.*

21 Fosztó, László, 2009: *Ritual Revitalisation after Socialism. Community, Personhood, and Conversion among Roma in a Transylvanian Village.*

22 Hilgers, Irene, 2009: *Why Do Uzbeks have to be Muslims? Exploring religiosity in the Ferghana Valley.*

23 Trevisani, Tommaso, 2010: *Land and Power in Khorezm. Farmers, Communities, and the State in Uzbekistan's Decollectivisation.*

24 Yalçın-Heckmann, Lale, 2010: *The Return of Private Property. Rural Life after the Agrarian Reform in the Republic of Azerbaijan.*

25 Mühlfried, Florian, and Sergey Sokolovskiy (eds.), 2011. *Exploring the Edge of Empire. Soviet Era Anthropology in the Caucasus and Central Asia.*

26 Cash, Jennifer R., 2011: *Villages on Stage. Folklore and Nationalism in the Republic of Moldova.*

27 Köllner, Tobias, 2012: *Practising Without Belonging? Entrepreneurship, Morality, and Religion in Contemporary Russia.*

28 Bethmann, Carla, 2013: *"Clean, Friendly, Profitable?" Tourism and the Tourism Industry in Varna, Bulgaria.*

29 Bošković, Aleksandar, and Chris Hann (eds.), 2013: *The Anthropological Field on the Margins of Europe, 1945-1991.*

30 Holzlehner, Tobias, 2014: *Shadow Networks. Border Economies, Informal Markets and Organised Crime in the Russian Far East.*

31 Bellér-Hann, Ildikó, 2015: *Negotiating Identities. Work, Religion, Gender, and the Mobilisation of Tradition among the Uyghur in the 1990s.*

32 Oelschlaegel, Anett C., 2016: *Plural World Interpretations. The Case of the South-Siberian Tyvans.*

33 Obendiek, Helena, 2016: *"Changing Fate". Education, Poverty and Family Support in Contemporary Chinese Society.*

34 Sha, Heila, 2017: *Care and Ageing in North-West China.*

35 Tocheva, Detelina, 2017: *Intimate Divisions. Street-Level Orthodoxy in Post-Soviet Russia.*

36 Sárközi, Ildikó Gyöngyvér, 2018: *From the Mists of Martyrdom. Sibe Ancestors and Heroes on the Altar of Chinese Nation Building.*

37 Cheung Ah Li, Leah, 2019: *Where the Past meets the Future. The Politics of Heritage in Xi'an.*

38 Wang, Ruijing, 2019: *Kinship, Cosmology and Support. Toward a Holistic Approach of Childcare in the Akha Community of South-Western China.*

HALLE STUDIES IN THE ANTHROPOLOGY OF EURASIA

39 Coşkun, Mustafa, 2020: *Improvising the Voice of the Ancestors. Heritage and Identity in Central Asia.*

40 Roth, Sascha, 2020: *Politics of Representation. Housing, Family, and State in Baku.*

41 Pranaitytė, Lina, 2020: *The Coffin in the Attic. Gifts, Debts and the Catholic Church in Rural Lithuania.*

42 Bellér-Hann, Ildikó, and Chris Hann, 2020: *The Great Dispossession. Uyghurs between Civilizations.*

43 Hornig, Laura, 2020: *On Money and* Mettā. *Economy and Morality in Urban Buddhist Myanmar.*

44 Berta, Anne-Erita, 2021: *Small is Good. Business and Morality among Danish Shopkeepers.*

45 Tereshina, Daria, 2021: *Managing Firms and Families. Work and Values in a Russian City.*